Critical Essays on
JONATHAN SWIFT

CRITICAL ESSAYS
ON
BRITISH LITERATURE

Zack Bowen, General Editor
University of Miami

Critical Essays on

JONATHAN SWIFT

edited by

FRANK PALMERI

G. K. Hall & Co. / New York
Maxwell Macmillan Canada / Toronto
Maxwell Macmillan International / New York Oxford Singapore Sydney

G. K. Hall & Company
Macmillan Publishing Company
866 Third Avenue
New York, New York 10022

Maxwell Macmillan Canada, Inc.
1200 Eglinton Avenue East
Suite 200
Don Mills, Ontario M3C 3N1

Library of Congress Cataloging-in-Publication Data

Critical essays on Jonathan Swift / edited by Frank Palmeri.
    p.   cm. — (Critical essays on British literature)
    Includes bibliographical references and index.
    ISBN 0-7838-0003-7 (alk. paper)
    1. Swift, Jonathan, 1667–1745—Criticism and interpretation.
  I. Palmeri, Frank. II. Series.
  PR3727.C76   1993
  828'.509—dc20   92-42993
                                         CIP

The paper used in this publication meets the minimum requirements of American National Standard for Information Sciences—Permanence of Paper for Printed Library Materials. ANSI Z3948-1984.∞™

10   9   8   7   6   5   4   3   2   1

Printed in the United States of America

Contents

♦

General Editor's Note

◆

The Critical Essays on British Literature series provides a variety of approaches to both classical and contemporary writers of Britain and Ireland. The formats of the volumes in the series vary with the thematic designs of individual editors and with the amount and nature of existing reviews and criticism, augmented by original essays by recognized authorities. It is hoped that each volume will develop a new overall perspective on its particular subject.

Palmeri's introduction sets forth the innovative theory he established in *Satire in Narrative*, that Swift's writing is essentially dialogic, with signed, publicly acknowledged works expressing an official, politically conservative point of view and with another body of satiric parodies, not formally acknowledged, expressing radically subversive perspectives. Further, Palmeri sees these two conflicting voices as often implying self-parody, the parodies being "inverted opposites" of official discourse, including Swift's own.

Palmeri's selection of essays, all from the eighties, includes only those never before reprinted or never printed in earlier collections. Three, by Melvyn New, Frank Stringfellow, and Everett Zimmerman, were written especially for this volume. The selections are divided into five sections: Swift's life and attitudes toward writing; *Gulliver's Travels*; *A Tale of a Tub* and eighteenth-century literature; Swift's poetry; and Swift's nonfictional prose.

ZACK BOWEN

University of Miami

Publisher's Note

♦

Producing a volume that contains both newly commissioned and reprinted material presents the publisher with the challenge of balancing the desire to achieve stylistic consistency with the need to preserve the integrity of works first published elsewhere. In the Critical Essays series, essays commissioned especially for a particular volume are edited to be consistent with G. K. Hall's house style; reprinted essays appear in the style in which they were first published, with only typographical errors corrected. Consequently, shifts in style from one essay to another are the result of our efforts to be faithful to each text as it was originally published.

Acknowledgments

♦

For helpful advice and guidance in the preparation of this collection, I am grateful to Zack Bowen, Hermione de Almeida, George Gilpin, and Patrick McCarthy. My thanks to Melvyn New, Everett Zimmerman, and Frank Stringfellow for graciously agreeing to write new essays for this volume. I would also like to thank Ellen Pollak, Ronald Paulson, and Arthur Scouten for special help that facilitated the inclusion of their work here. Mihoko Suzuki's uncounted contributions in the preparation of this volume were stellar.

FRANK PALMERI

Introduction: The Divided Swift

◆

Frank Palmeri

Within a few decades after *Gulliver's Travels* was published, an increasing belief in the benevolence and inherent goodness of human nature led to a widespread turn of feeling against Swift, largely because of his fiercely satiric—and, it was felt, misanthropic—fourth book. Almost always conflating the author and his protagonist, this line of criticism has accused Swift of libeling humankind. Thus, Edward Young in 1759, William Thackeray in 1851, and John Middleton Murry in 1955 all condemned both Swift and the fourth book as being monstrous, filthy, and blasphemous. Some early commentators, such as Thomas Sheridan in 1784 and William Hazlitt in 1818, considered the dominant object of Swift's satire to be hypocrisy and thus defended Swift against the charge of unhealthy misanthropy. Still, between the mid-eighteenth and the mid-twentieth centuries, the greatest number of remarks about Swift not only identified him with the Gulliver of the "Voyage to the Houyhnhnms" but also condemned both author and work as reprehensible, even mad.

Leslie Stephen introduced a more dispassionate tone late in the last century, arguing that Swift exhibited a unique character and intelligence by seeing through all the fashionable philosophies of his day. However, modern scholarship on Swift begins after the First World War, with Theodore Wedel's "On the Philosophical Background of *Gulliver's Travels*" (1926) and W. A. Eddy's *Gulliver's Travels: A Critical Study* (1923).[1] Wedel maintains that we might read *Gulliver's Travels* with more understanding if we recognized the change in the prevailing view of human nature, which was described above—a change from the traditional, skeptical view of human nature as weak and imperfect to the more optimistic view that denied the existence of original sin and asserted the possibility of human perfectibility. Eddy finds precedents for *Gulliver's Travels* in accounts of imaginary voyages written by Lucian, Rabelais, and Cyrano de Bergerac, and thus he draws attention to the work's whimsical imagination and ironic assertions of veracity rather than its tragic misanthropy.

From the twenties through the fifties, criticism attempted to understand Swift's works by placing them in the context of one or another kind of history—political, intellectual, or ecclesiastical. The most influential attempt to specify the political meanings of *Gulliver's Travels* has been Charles Firth's "The Political Significance of *Gulliver's Travels*" (1919), which draws most of the significant parallels between political figures and fictional characters, especially in the first voyage where the satire is most topical. Some of Firth's identifications have been challenged,[2] but the disagreements that remain concern only relatively unimportant matters. The more difficult task of providing an account of Swift's political beliefs throughout his life, based on analysis of both his fictional and nonfictional writings and their relation to contemporary events and issues, had to wait until the appearance of two books in the eighties: F. P. Lock's *Swift's Tory Politics* (1983) and J. A. Downie's *Jonathan Swift: Political Writer* (1984). Downie views Swift as consistently liberal in the political positions he adopts; Lock sees a continuing conflict between such a libertarian strain and a reactionary, authoritarian pull in Swift's thought and character.

The study of Swift's writings in relation to intellectual history has produced two very striking arguments. In 1937, Marjorie Nicolson and Nora Mohler demonstrated that all but two of the projects undertaken by the academicians of Lagado exactly reproduce experiments performed by members of the Royal Society and recorded in its *Philosophical Transactions*; they thus showed that Swift's satire in the third book is not a wildly exaggerated result of a personal animus against scientific research but an almost unaltered transcription of experiments actually performed by early scientists.[3] In a similar vein, in 1959 R. S. Crane has pointed out that in the fourth book Swift neatly inverted some fundamental assumptions of early textbooks of logic, which defined man as *animal rationale* and which contrasted and juxtaposed man most frequently with the horse as an example of *animal irrationale*.[4] His article helps account for the frequent shock produced by the encounter with Houyhnhnms and Yahoos, whose natures bewilderingly overturn established and cherished ideas of ourselves. Although less striking in its implications, Louis Landa's essay on Swift's economic ideas and their relation to mercantilism constitutes another important result of the historical method.[5] Landa also places Swift's ecclesiastical activities in historical context in *Swift and the Church of Ireland* (1954). A few years earlier, J. C. Beckett analyzed Swift's ideas about the proper relation between church and state and asserted the consistency of his High Church positions throughout his career.[6] Other studies that have placed Swift in varying contexts of intellectual history include Kathleen Williams's *Jonathan Swift and the Age of Compromise* (1958) and Phillip Harth's *Swift and Anglican Rationalism* (1961).

However, by the mid-fifties, the dominant method in studies of Swift had shifted from historical and biographical to rhetorical and formal. This change of approach figures clearly in the work of a single prominent critic. In *The Mind and Art of Jonathan Swift* (1936), Ricardo Quintana considers Swift as a representative thinker in an age of rationalism; in *Swift: An Introduction* (1954), however, he turns away from assertions of historical exemplarity to provide close readings of individual texts consistent with the formalist canons of the New Criticism. The former work explicates the thought of the writer; the latter investigates the ironies produced by his formal strategies. *Swift's Rhetorical Art* (1953) by Martin Price is the earliest book to introduce this focus into studies of Swift's works; it traces the common rhetorical patterns linking apparently unrelated passages and episodes throughout Swift's writings. William Ewald, in *The Masks of Jonathan Swift* (1953), concentrates his attention on the different authors implied by many of Swift's works; he analyzes more than a dozen authorial personae, half of whom function as objects of Swift's satiric parody.

Much of the formalist criticism of Swift naturally investigates the structures of satire and analyzes Swift's practice because it constitutes the preeminently successful use of satiric forms in English. Thus John Bullitt discusses Swift's works in *Jonathan Swift and the Anatomy of Satire* (1953) in order to illuminate the comic satire of false logic, including the conversion of metaphorical into literal meanings. In *The Power of Satire* (1961), Robert C. Elliott argues that Swift's use of Gulliver exemplifies the pattern of the satirist satirized. Edward Rosenheim, in *Swift and the Satirist's Art* (1963), uses Swift's parody of particular authors in his works to demonstrate his understanding of satire as an attack on a specific historical object. Ronald Paulson shows the coincidence between kinds of satire and political orientations; thus, he devotes a chapter each to Whig satire and Swift's Tory satire in *The Fictions of Satire* (1968). In pursuing his own approach to satire in *Satiric Inheritance: Rabelais to Sterne* (1979), Michael Seidel analyzes Swift's narratives as examples of the satiric debasement and diminution of epic lines of descent.

The fifties also saw the first sustained analyses of *A Tale of a Tub*, after F. R. Leavis's famous attack on Swift's irony in the *Tale* for being nihilistic.[7] Not only do the books of Price, Ewald, and Rosenheim contain chapters on the *Tale*, but a number of books have been devoted entirely to its explication. Mariam Starkman focuses on the abuses of learning in the digressive sections. Paulson analyzes the Gnostic nature of the hack author's misrecognitions. In a monograph-length article, John Traugott shows that the parodic aims with which Swift begins the *Tale* repeatedly lead to the indirect expression of his more searching and more subversive impulses. John Clark analyzes in the *Tale* a consistent pattern of the author's rhetoric rising only in order to fall into bathetic illustrations that the perfect modern possesses neither past nor memory. Frederik Smith argues strikingly for extensive parallels between the language used by the fictional mad author of the *Tale* and the use of language by modern victims of schizophrenia. Finally, Everett Zimmerman places both the *Tale* and *Gulliver's Travels* in relation to Michel Foucault's formulation of eighteenth-century paradigms of thought.[8]

Writers in the nineteenth century commonly expressed the view that Swift too was mad, like the *Tale*-teller, Gulliver, or the modest proposer; that belief has been discredited.[9] Still, studies of Swift from a psychoanalytic perspective have used the writings largely as evidence of the author's obsessions and neuroses. Thus, for example, Evelyn Hardy's *The Conjured Spirit* (1949) and Phyllis Greenacre's *Swift and Carroll* (1955) consider biographical and textual evidence equally in pursuing the analysis of Swift's personality. The most illuminating psychoanalytic approach to Swift, however, considers him not as an object of observation but as a thinker whose insights anticipated those of Freud. In *Life Against Death* (1959), Norman Brown finds significant expressions in Swift's writings of such major psychoanalytic theses as the cultural significance of anal eroticism, the upward displacements of sublimation, and the universality of neuroses in civilization. Claude Rawson pursues a psychological analysis that sees at the core of Swift's writings a concern with a universal and incurable restlessness of human nature.[10] Irvin Ehrenpreis takes a moderate psychoanalytic approach in his essential biography, *Swift: The Man, His Works, and the Age* (1962, 1967, and 1983), arguing, for example, for the importance of understanding ambivalences in the author's personality rather than analyzing narrative personae in the manner of Ewald, Paulson, or Elliott.[11]

Since the harvest of writings on Swift and satire in the fifties and sixties, one of the most notable developments has been the extraordinary surge of works on Swift's poetry in the late seventies and early eighties. It is perhaps understandable that there should be some turning away from the preceding close and productive focus on the prose works. In addition, many of the poems—not only those sometimes considered scatological but also *Cadenus and Vanessa*, Stella's birthday poems, and others—hold a particular interest because of their focus on women, who figure only peripherally in the narratives and prose. The poems seem to call for feminist analyses, while the prose works may be fairly intractable to such an approach. The five years after 1978 saw the publication of five books and two collections of essays on Swift's poetry.[12]

Partly because so much work on the poetry has appeared and been reprinted in the last 15 years, and also because some of the essays in other sections discuss Swift's poems as well, it has not been necessary to include a large selection of essays on the poetry here. In fact, I have chosen as a matter of policy not to include here any essays that have been previously reprinted or that were originally printed in other collections, because they are readily available elsewhere.[13] This book instead gathers together some of the best previously uncollected work of the eighties on the satiric narratives, the poetry, and the nonfictional prose, drawing largely on journals that may not be easily accessible in many libraries.[14]

The attention to Swift's poetry has made direct comparisons with Pope's poems unavoidable, and such comparative scrutiny has led to a new and sharper recognition of the contrasts and even antagonisms between the literary productions and individual perspectives of Swift and Pope. Four of the essays included here illustrate how the recent work on Swift's poetry has revised the yoking of Pope and Swift that passed unexamined in much previous criticism. The five volumes of *Miscellanies* have been taken ever since their publication as definitive indexes of the affinity and friendship between Swift and Pope. But Arthur Scouten shows that by the time the third volume was published in 1732, Swift had good reasons to believe that Pope had been using his role as collaborative editor to maintain his own poetic preeminence at Swift's expense—for example, by disregarding Swift's desire to include some of his best poetry and by excising large sections from poems he did include. Scouten also notes that on a number of occasions Swift satirically parodied Pope's poetry, suggesting criticism of both Pope's poetic theory and his practice.

The other essays contrast Pope to Swift not on such matters as form of publication but on Pope's use of traditional hierarchies; Swift employs more leveling and unconventional examples of poetic diction and subject. Ellen Pollak argues that Swift's poetry is defetishizing: that is, it stands in marked contrast with the usual practice—which is also Pope's—of idealizing women in order to objectify and control them; in Swift, however, "the moment of discursive mastery over woman never comes."[15] Margaret Doody draws the same contrast as part of a related argument about Swift, which shows that many female poets saw in Swift's poetry a model of unpretentious poetry concerning the private, domestic world, rather than the public and exclusively male world of heroic poetry. They also found precedent in the indecent poems for acknowledging mundane unromantic facts about the bodily products of women, as opposed to the depersonalizing idealizations of conventional poetry by others, among them Pope. For Carole Fabricant, the contrast applies in the realm of landscape as well as gender. She argues that Swift's insistent depiction of actual landscapes in his poetry, including their unattractive and unpleasant contents, such as dung, stands as a demystifying opposite of the idealizing tendencies of poets such as Pope or Thomson.

If the essays on Swift's poems exemplify one trend in recent criticism, the essays on *A Tale of a Tub* illustrate another, by investigating the strong though mostly submerged relations between the *Tale* and works written later in the century. Because of its peculiarly indeterminate mixture of genres, the *Tale* reveals close connections with works in various genres, including the novel, narrative satire, and history. Everett Zimmerman draws a perhaps unexpected connection between the *Tale* and *Clarissa*, arguing that the attempt in Richardson's novel to create a monument in print out of occasional and fragmentary materials such as letters corresponds to the project of the modern author of Swift's *Tale*. The *Tale* thus may satirically parody the modern assumptions behind the novel before the novel had taken recognizable shape.[16] My own essay also suggests that in the *Tale* Swift parodied cultural authorities in the first stage of the early modern paradigm, and that Gibbon in *The Decline and Fall of the Roman Empire* parodied such authorities at a later stage. Melvyn New extends the affinities between the *Tale* and *Tristram Shandy* to demonstrate an emptiness between opposite extremes in both these works, a void at the center of the vision of each writer. Ronald Paulson observes a similar emptiness in the *Verses on the Death of Dr. Swift* as well as in the *Tale*: in both works, the monuments to cultural authority as well as the poetic monument to the self are not only ruined but also empty of contents.

The essays on *Gulliver's Travels* do not converge on a shared perspective but instead illustrate the results of a variety of approaches to that text. Michael Seidel diagnoses in *Gulliver* not an absent center but more and more extreme travels away from the center, an increasing eccentricity that illustrates the tendency of satiric narrative to be paradoxically but consistently degenerative. Eric Rothstein finds the third book to be organized around varieties of history—human, natural, and divine—but in each case, the normative taxonomy is inverted, the history debased, the implications radically skeptical. Frank Stringfellow's essay suggests a psychoanalytic understanding of the two levels of ironic discourse as an officially authorized position or voice and a voice or point of view that protests or rebels against such authority; it thus offers a model for combining the psychoanalytic and the rhetorical approaches to Swift's satires. Laura Brown's essay uses a materialist approach to show that although Swift's representation of women in *Gulliver* may be misogynistic, it also helps advance Swift's critique both of the growing commercial economy and also, perhaps more importantly, of the colonialism that such an economy both feeds and feeds on.

The focus of these last two essays on the opposed impulses in Swift's writings continues in the essays on Swift's nonfictional prose. F. P. Lock concludes from his examination of Swift's writings on politics that Swift combined liberal opposition to concentrated and unreasonable political authority with an authoritarian personality that asserted the claims of established authority as a bulwark against anarchy and immorality. Ann Cline Kelly finds in the "Proposal for Correcting the English Tongue" not only the direct arguments for such an authoritative institution but also an atypical vagueness and abstraction implying that Swift himself did not wholly endorse his own idea. Similarly, Terry Castle argues that Swift offers the example of a writer who himself distrusts and fears writing.

This collection of essays thus exemplifies the critical attention that has been paid in the last generation to Swift's divided nature, which George Orwell captured when he characterized Swift as a "Tory anarchist."[17] Some critical commentary has emphasized one side of Swift—the anarchic opponent of a knavish establishment—but often at the expense of the other—the undeniably reactionary opponent of mad innovation. It has been more common to consider the reactionary as the authoritative Swift and to appeal for textual authority not to the ambiguous, satirically parodic works but to less ironic works such as letters and sermons. Such documents have been taken to give more direct access to Swift's beliefs, and these beliefs then offer a standard or point of reference with which the critic can try to bring the more ambiguous satires to agree.[18]

I would suggest an alternative to this procedure that does not merely invert and replicate it by discounting one of the opposing tendencies. Distinguishing between Swift's acknowledged and his pseudonymous works,[19] I would agree that the signed or publicly acknowledged works, such as the "Sentiments of a Church of England Man," the "Project for the Advancement of Religion," and the "Proposal for Correcting the English Tongue," express an official, hierarchical, and conservative point of view. They maintain a single perspective, asserting the authority of an established order; they are extremely monological. In contrast, the writings that are pseudonymous or remain unacknowledged use parodic impersonations to express conflicting perspectives: one through the voice of a supposed author, the teller of the *Tale*, the arguer against abolishing Christianity, Gulliver, or the modest proposer; the other through the point of view from which such voices are parodied.[20] The self-parodic pseudonymous works are thus strongly dialogical.[21]

The contradictions within Swift's writings might indicate not only conflicts between parts of Swift but, perhaps more significantly, contrasts between kinds of discourse and the understandings they express—one centralizing, authoritarian, and monological, another centrifugal, skeptical, and dialogical. Instead of giving greater weight to the writings that express an official perspective on the world in a single voice, one could argue that the parodic satires embody both an eccentric, unauthorized perspective and, by their very nature, the perspective of a traditional, established world from which that unauthorized view is parodied. The parodic satires then would be understood not so much as the inverted opposite of the official discourse but as more capacious expressions of thought and feeling than the single-voiced, more nearly single-dimensional works.

Swift's writings do not, of course, divide neatly into two sets, one consisting of pseudonymous dialogical writings and the other of signed monological ones; to begin with, almost all his works were published anonymously. A whole spectrum of kinds of authorship stretches between *A Tale of a Tub* at one extreme and the "Project for the Advancement of Religion" at the other. In the middle ground, one can distinguish between anonymous works published in defense of an established order, such as the *Examiner* essays, and pseudonymous works such as the *Drapier's Letters* that attack a governmental order. At the extreme, even Swift's most monological works convey doubts about the perspective they embrace through self-contradictions and strategic silences, as Ann Cline Kelly demonstrates regarding the strongly official "Proposal for Correcting the English Tongue."

It has sometimes been said that Swift's satires resist deconstructive approaches because they are always already self-deconstructive. In fact, the more monological, official, and public works of Swift are prime objects for a deconstructive tracing of their internal, suppressed fault lines. However, the pseudonymous dialogical works, having dissolved their formal unity through parody, do exemplify the satiric clash between opposed orders and perspectives that, by leaving such oppositions unresolved, can clear a space for new paradigms of thought.[22]

Notes

1. Emile Pons's study of Swift's early years should also be mentioned, *Swift: Les années de jeunesse et "le conte du tonneau"* (Strasbourg: Librairie Istra, 1925). Although Pons's work has been superseded in many of its details and conclusions, it made a valuable contribution by directing attention to Swift's life and authorship before he became known publicly.

2. For example, Arthur Case, "Personal and Political Satire in *Gulliver's Travels*," in *Four Essays on "Gulliver's Travels"* (Princeton N.J.: Princeton University Press, 1945).

3. Majorie Nicolson and Nora Mohler, "The Scientific Background of Swift's Voyage to Laputa," *Annals of Science* 1, 2 (1937): 299–334, 405–30.

4. R. S. Crane, "The Houyhnhnms, the Yahoos, and the History of Ideas," in *Reason and the Imagination: Studies in the History of Ideas, 1600–1800*, ed. J. A. Mazzeo (New York: Columbia University Press, 1962), 231–53.

5. Louis Landa, "Swift's Economic Views and Mercantilism," *ELH* 10 (1943): 310–35.

6. J. C. Beckett, "Swift as an Ecclesiastical Statesman," in *Essays in British and Irish History in Honour of James Eadie Todd*, ed. H. A. Cronne, T. W. Moody, and D. B. Quinn (London: Muller, 1949).

7. F. R. Leavis, "The Irony of Swift," *Scrutiny* 2 (1934): 364–78. This article provoked a thoughtful response by William Frost, "The Irony of Swift and Gibbon: A Reply to F. R. Leavis," *Essays in Criticism* 17 (1967): 41–47.

8. Mariam Starkman, *Swift's Satire on Learning in "A Tale of a Tub"* (Princeton N.J.: Princeton University Press, 1950); Ronald Paulson, *Theme and Structure in "A Tale of a Tub"* (New Haven: Yale University Press, 1960); John Traugott, *"A Tale of a Tub,"* in *Focus: Swift*, ed. Claude Rawson (London: Sphere Books, 1971); John Clark, *Form and Frenzy in Swift's "A Tale of a Tub"* (Ithaca, N.Y.: Cornell University Press, 1970); Frederik Smith, *Language and Reality in Swift's "A Tale of a Tub"* (Columbus: Ohio State University Press, 1979); Everett Zimmerman, *Swift's Narrative Satires: Author and Authority* (Ithaca, N.Y: Cornell University Press, 1983).

9. Most authoritatively by Walter Russell Brain, in "The Illness of Dean Swift," *Irish Journal of Medical Science* 6 (1952): 337–45.

10. See Claude Rawson, "The Character of Swift's Satire: Reflections on Swift, Johnson, and Human Restlessness," in *The Character of Swift's Satire: A Revised Focus*, ed. Claude Rawson (Newark: University of Delaware Press, 1983), 21–82.

11. Ehrenpreis makes his argument most explicitly in "Personae," in *Literary Meanings and Augustan Values* (Charlottesville: University of Virginia Press, 1974); Elliott articulates his position in *The Literary Persona* (Chicago: University of Chicago Press, 1982).

12.   The books are: Nora Jaffe, *The Poet Swift* (Hanover, N.H.: University Presses of New England, 1977); John Fischer, *On Swift's Poetry* (Gainesville: University of Florida Presses, 1978); Peter Schakel, *The Poetry of Jonathan Swift* (Madison: University of Wisconsin Press, 1978); A. B. England, *Order and Energy in the Poetry of Swift* (Lewisburg, Pa.: Bucknell University Press, 1980); and Louise Barnett, *Swift's Poetic Worlds* (Newark: University of Delaware Press, 1981). The collections of essays are: *Contemporary Studies of Swift's Poetry*, ed. John Fischer, Donald Mell, and David Vieth (Newark: University of Delaware Press, 1981); and *Essential Articles for the Study of Swift's Poetry*, ed. David Vieth (Hamden, Conn.: Archon Books, 1984). There is also "A Symposium on Women in Swift's Poems," in *Papers on Literature and Language* 14 (1978): 115–51. The forerunners of the recent work on Swift's poetry are Herbert Davis, "Swift's View of Poetry," in *Jonathan Swift: Essays on His Satire and Other Studies* (New York: Oxford University Press, 1964), and Maurice Johnson, *The Sin of Wit* (Syracuse, N.Y.: Syracuse University Press, 1950).

13.   Previous collections of essays on Jonathan Swift include: Ernest Tuveson, ed., *Swift: A Collection of Critical Essays* (Englewood Cliffs, N.J.: Prentice-Hall, 1964); Brian Vickers, ed., *The World of Jonathan Swift: Essays for the Tercentenary* (Cambridge: Harvard University Press, 1968); Kathleen Williams, ed., *Swift: The Critical Heritage* (New York: Barnes & Noble, 1970); A. N. Jeffares, ed., *Swift: Modern Judgments* (London: Macmillan, 1970); Denis Donoghue, ed., *Jonathan Swift: A Critical Anthology* (Harmondsworth: Penguin, 1971); Claude Rawson, ed., *Focus: Swift* (London: Sphere Books, 1971), revised and reissued as *The Character of Swift's Satire: A Revised Focus* (Newark: University of Delaware Press, 1983); Clive Probyn, ed., *The Art of Jonathan Swift* (New York: Barnes & Noble, 1978); Harold Bloom, ed., *Jonathan Swift: Modern Critical Views* (New York: Chelsea House, 1986); and Frederik Smith, ed., *The Genres of "Gulliver's Travels"* (Newark: University of Delaware Press, 1990).

14.   The essays by Melvyn New, Everett Zimmerman, and Frank Stringfellow are printed here for the first time.

15.   See p. 220 in this collection.

16.   Paulson, in *Theme and Structure*, and Clark, in *Form and Frenzy*, stress that the *Tale* both attacks and exemplifies modernity. For readings of *Gulliver's Travels* in relation to some modern novels, see W. B. Carnochan, *Lemuel Gulliver's Mirror for Man* (Berkeley: University of California Press, 1968), and Claude Rawson, *Gulliver and the Gentle Reader: Studies in Swift and Our Time* (London: Routledge & Kegan Paul, 1973). J. Paul Hunter has argued recently that the *Tale* is a parody of emerging novelistic techniques and presumptions, in *"Gulliver's Travels* and the Novel," in *The Genres of "Gulliver's Travels,"* 69–72.

17.   George Orwell, "Politics *v.* Literature: An Examination of *Gulliver's Travels*," in *Jonathan Swift: A Critical Anthology*, ed. Denis Donoghue, 354. See also Edward Said, "Swift's Tory Anarchy," *Eighteenth-Century Studies* 3 (1969): 48–57. Other recent works that pay attention to the divisions in Swift include: Peter Steele, *Jonathan Swift: Preacher and Jester* (Oxford: Clarendon Press, 1978); and Patrick Reilly, *Jonathan Swift: The Brave Desponder* (Carbondale: Southern Illinois University Press, 1982).

18.   Some critics have argued that Swift saw more deeply into the insatiability of human nature in his satiric than in his official works. Such readings show an interest in the chaotic or violent energies that Swift's works express, but they also explicate sympathetically Swift's disapproval of such energies.

19.   Irvin Ehrenpreis noted that Swift's works can be divided between those that were signed or effectually acknowledged and those whose authorship remained fundamentally anonymous or pseudonymous, in *Swift: The Man, His Works, and the Age* (Cambridge: Harvard University Press, 1967), 2:276–77, 294, 335. Ehrenpreis characterized the Swift of the acknowledged writings as an establishment preacher and the author of the anonymous works as a comic rebel with a satiric genius.

20.   Frederik N. Smith has argued that paying attention specifically to the voices in

Swift's satiric works might offer a way around the well-worn arguments about whether they make use of personae. See "Vexing Voices: The Telling of Gulliver's Story," *Papers on Language and Literature* 21, 4 (1985): 383–98.

21. In formulating this argument, I make use of the categories of discourse elaborated by Mikhail Bakhtin. See especially the essays collected in *The Dialogic Imagination* (Austin: University of Texas Press, 1984).

22. I develop this theory of narrative satire in *Satire in Narrative: Petronius, Swift, Gibbon, Melville, and Pynchon* (Austin: University of Texas Press, 1990). In the case of Swift, I would contend that the poetry is also predominantly parodic, informal, and dialogical, as opposed to formal verse satire, which is almost all monological and reactionary.

LIFE AND WRITINGS

◆

Swift among the Women

Margaret Anne Doody

A certain view of Swift has been powerfully represented in Middleton
Murry's shocked denunciation:

> Nevertheless, it is not his direct obsession with ordure which is the chief cause
> of the nausea he arouses. It is the strange and disquieting combination of his
> horror at the fact of human evacuation with a peculiar physical loathing of
> women. It is an unpleasant subject; but it cannot be burked by any honest
> critic of Swift. The conventional excuses made for him are ridiculous. . . .
> Lust is natural and wholesome compared to the feeling Swift arouses.

According to this view, Swift is not only obsessed and perverted but professedly inimical to womankind. His "animus against women became more
and more disproportioned, vituperative, and shrill."[1] The mad Irishman's
wandering dirty thoughts betray the chiefest of misogynists. Swift detests
the female and the feminine.

  Murry's Freud-tinged view is only an elaboration of what has been said
by some others before him. Lord Orrery, for instance, in his *Remarks on the
Life and Writing of Swift* judged Swift lacking in appropriate sexual feelings:

> If we consider SWIFT's behaviour, so far only as it relates to women, we shall
> find, that he looked upon them rather as busts, than as whole figures. In his
> panegyrical descriptions, he has seldom descended lower than the center of
> their hearts: or if ever he has designed a compleat statue, it has been generally
> cast in a dirty, or in a disagreeable mould: as if the statuary had not conceived,
> or had not experienced, that justness of proportion, that delicacy of limb, and
> those pleasing, and graceful attitudes which have constituted the sex to be the
> most beautiful part of the creation.

Swift's "The Lady's Dressing Room" merely discovers his inexcusable "want
of delicacy and decorum"; the author "too frequently forgets . . . politeness
and tenderness of manners."[2]

  If Swift is guilty of inexcusable misogyny, of shrill animus against

From *The Yearbook of English Studies* 18 (1988): 68–82. Reprinted with the permission of the Modern
Humanities Research Association.

women, then surely women readers in particular ought to have taken notice—
and umbrage. Surely, then, women writers of the eighteenth century must
have mocked Swift, or expressed horror of him, or shunned him. Indeed, we
can find some examples of female censure of Swift. Sarah Green, in her
conduct-book *Mental Improvement for a Young Lady; on her Entrance into the
World; Addressed to a Favourite Niece* (London, 1793), quite simply advises
that "Favourite Niece" to shun all of Swift's writings save his Sermons; the
other works are "vulgar, indelicate, and satiric." Nobody could say this is
not true. But the improving aunt also disapproves of Pope: "He was, as you
will find, for I recommend his works to your perusal, no friend to our sex;
as such I cannot esteem the man, though I admire the poet" (95–96). Swift's
"vulgar" works may be dismissed from the presence of refined young ladies,
but it is Pope who is specifically the misogynist.

Lady Mary Wortley Montagu (1689–1762) had waxed caustic against
Swift, and Pope, upon reading Lord Orrery's *Remarks*: "D[ean] S[wift] (by
his Lordship's own account) was so intoxicated with the love of Flattery, he
sought it amongst the lowest class of people, and the silliest of Women, and
was never so well pleas'd with any Companions as those that worship'd
him while he insulted them." Swifts letters show him "vain, triffling [*sic*],
ungratefull." Lady Mary dismisses Pope and Swift together: "These two
superior Beings were entitl'd by their Birth and hereditary Fortune to be
only a couple of Link Boys."[3] This is the Lady Mary of 1754, still recalling
the resentments of her old estrangement from Pope, and from Swift. She
turns for defensive consolation, in a rather pitiful snobbery, to the rights of
"Birth"; these genius-enemies were "low." Her more general charges against
Swift are the not uncommon ones of ingratitude and religious infidelity. But
Lady Mary does not rank Swift as a misogynist; on the contrary, her Swift is
meanly fond (like Richardson in certain hostile representations) of the company of women, who ought to be beneath the notice of a man of genius.
This notion Lady Mary has taken from Orrery, who elaborates with fascinated
hostility on Swift's friendships with women: "You see the command which
SWIFT had over all his females; and you would have smiled to have found
his house a constant seraglio of very virtuous women, who attended him
from morning till night, with an obedience, an awe, and an assiduity, that
are seldom paid to the richest, or the most powerful lovers; no, not even to
the Grand Seignior himself." There is something very like envy in Orrery's
tone, even as he sharpens his ridicule; he blames the publication of "many
pieces, which ought never to have been delivered to the press" upon these
foolishly-trusted women: "He communicated every composition as soon as
finished, to his female senate" (*Remarks*, 83).

In her commonplace book Lady Mary picked up and elaborated Orrery's
metaphor, noting "Dr S[wift] in the midst of his Women, like a master
E[unuch] in a seraglio."[4] Swift in his "constant seraglio" becomes a master
Eunuch, or a tamed caponized Macheath with his doxies about him. Lady

Mary raises an interesting problem. Was Swift too fond of women, of women's manners and women's company? The question is first raised by Orrery, who seems blissfully unaware of certain contradictions in his portrait of a Swift unable to appreciate the female as real men do, and yet able to attract the devoted service and admiration of all those women. Lady Mary's language plays with the feminine. If Swift was "vain" and "triffling" and fond of flattery, why, these are well-known feminine vices. Was Swift (again like a certain picture of Richardson) too womanly a man?

Indeed, for every female voice raised against Swift there are several to speak for him. Laetitia Pilkington (1712–50), once one of Swift's "virtuous seraglio" (she was still "virtuous" at that point) addressed a poetic epistle to Swift, praising him as the equal of the "God-like Men of Old." This "Patriot, Bard and Sage" is a subject for Irish pride; Ireland "in that Name / Shall rival *Greece* and *Rome* in Fame."[5] According to her own account, Laetitia Pilkington was serving an immediate interest in writing this set of verses, for she hoped through them to gain admission to the presence of the famous Dean. Flattery operated successfully. But Pilkington also had national as well as personal interests to serve. Praise of Swift was praise of the national literary identity. Mary Davys (1674–1732) in her autobiographical novel *The Merry Wanderer* (1725) self-consciously defends both herself and Ireland through an allusion to Swift: "To tell the Reader I was born in *Ireland*, is to bespeak a general Dislike to all I write, and he will, likely, be surprised, if every Paragraph does not end with a Bull; but a Potato's a fine light Root, and makes the Eater brisk and alert. . . . And I am going to say a bold word in defence of my own Country; the very brightest Genius in the King's Dominion drew his first Breath in that Nation: and so much for the Honour of *Ireland*."[6] The Irish have been supposed the butts of wit, not wits, but Swift has changed all that. The "very brightest Genius" raises downtrodden Ireland, as Pilkington also asserts: "As the *Irish* are the eternal Ridicule of the *English* for their Ignorance, I am proud *Hibernia* had the Happiness of producing this brilliant Wit, to redeem the Credit of the Country; and to convince the World, a Man may draw his first Breath there, and yet be learned, wise, generous, religious, witty, social and polite" (*Memoirs*, I:67). Swift redeems a group at apparent disadvantage; he proves the potential excellence of those traditionally judged by (imposed and alien) authority to be dull and inferior. Such a liberation has an interesting suggestiveness for women, another group whose writings may "bespeak Dislike" upon identification of the author, another group eternally ridiculed "for their Ignorance" by those who constitute themselves as superior. It is not surprising that a number of Irish women writers were attracted into Swift's orbit.

The women who achieved acquaintance with Swift discovered not only the celebrated author but also an oddly domestic individual. Laetitia Pilkington recollects Swift entertaining her in performing a hospitable household task:

The bottle and glasses being taken away, the Dean set about making the Coffee; but the Fire scorching his Hand, he called to me to reach him his Glove, and changing the Coffee-pot to his Left-hand, held out the Right one, ordered me to put the Glove on it, which accordingly I did; when taking up part of his Gown to fan himself with, and acting the character of a prudish Lady, he said, "Well, I do not know what to think; Women may be honest that do such Things, but, for my Part, I never could bear to touch any Man's Flesh—except my Husband's, whom, perhaps, says he, she wished at the Devil." (*Memoirs* I:58–59)

In a little riff of sudden mimicry, Swift satirically adopts the role of the absurdly prudish woman, at the same time reminding everyone present of "Man's Flesh," and delivering this impromptu travesty-role in the midst of performing a rite which might be considered feminine. Teasingly conscious of the interplay of gender roles, the Swift of this anecdote can remind us of the female persona in some of his poems, in, for instance, "The Humble Petition of Frances Harris" (1700), or "Mary the Cook-Maid's Letter to Dr. Sheridan" (1718), or "A Panegyrick on the Dean in the Person of a Lady in the North" (1730). In this last Swift imagines himself celebrated by a pleased hostess not only as a master of conversation and a fount of knowledge but also as a help around the place: "You merit new Employments daily; / Our Thatcher, Ditcher, Gard'ner, Baily" (l.155). This Swift successfully takes a hand at churning the butter for breakfast by shaking a bottle of cream:

> Now, enter as the Dairy Hand-maid:
> Such charming Butter never Man made.
> Let others with Fanatick Face,
> Talk of their *Milk* for *Babes of Grace*;
> From *Tubs* their snuffling Nonsense utter:
> Thy *Milk* shall make us *Tubs* of Butter.
> The Bishop with his *Foot* may burn it;
> But, with his *Hand*, the Dean can churn it.
> How are the Servants overjoy'd
> To see thy Deanship thus employ'd!
> Instead of poring on a Book,
> Providing Butter for the Cook.
>
> (l.167)[7]

The masculine calling of preaching, orating (from "*Tubs*"), has been displaced by the feminine calling, as "the Dairy Hand-maid" hopes to make "Tubs of Butter," although in humble reality the three hours' tossing yields only "an Ounce at least." Yet the Dean thinks himself well paid for long "Jumblings round the Skull" if he squeezes out "four Lines in Rhime." Butter-making and verse-making are equated. This employable worthy in his round of humble tasks completes his contribution by designing two structures which might vie with the proudest architecture; these models of the "Art of Building" are two outhouses, with separate offices for male and female. From food (breakfast butter) Swift moves to the privy, but not without reminding us that the various needs of a household's routine have their place in a not unpleasing round of daily activities. This poet of domestic life, however ostentatiously and carefully he may separate the sexes' privies, is seldom content to remain on his side of the gender line. He prefers mercurial ease (and easement) to the pomposity of generic masculine grandeur. It is this Swift that Laetitia Pilkington encountered making coffee.

Swift's kind of teasing evoked a recognition of physical realities ("Man's Flesh"), including his own reality and idiosyncrasies. Pilkington makes her own private teasing observation: "I could not help smiling at his odd Gait, for I thought to myself, he had written so much in Praise of Horses, that he was resolved to imitate them as nearly as he could." Swift, guessing her mental lampoon, comments that Mr. Pilkington was "a Fool . . . to marry you, for he could have afforded to keep a Horse for less Money than you cost him, and that, you must confess, would have given him better Exercise and more Pleasure than a Wife," (*Memoirs* I:79–80). This ridicule of wives and marriage is a reminder of the Swift of the satiric poems. But the open teasing is explorative, a challenge to women in the sex war to which they were allowed to respond. The effect of Swift's humour is not to silence the woman but to force her into utterance. According to Pilkington, she composed her satiric poem "The Statues" specifically in order to answer Swift's ridicule: "As the Dean, and after his Example, Mr. P{*ilkingto*}n, were eternally satyrizing and ridiculing the *Female* Sex; I had a very great inclination to be even with them, and expose the Inconstancy of Men" (*Memoirs* I: 91–92). In her poetic tale the fair Queen Lucida must try the constancy of her enraptured bridegroom by visiting her father's under-sea realm for one day. "Twice twenty noble Youths" have already failed the test. The youth swears undying constancy, but of course proves incapable of spending a day on his own without falling for the charms of a nymph. Led to a spacious grotto "Where forty Youths, in Marble, seem'd to mourn, / Each Youth reclining on a fun'ral Urn," the Prince imagines he is about to consummate his new love. But the angry nymph suddenly dashes the fountain's magic water upon him, accusing him of the general male weakness: "Thy changeful Sex in Perfidy delight, / Despise Perfection, and fair Virtue slight." The enticing nymph proves to be the injured Queen, disguised, and the magic water turns the Prince to stone; he joins the marble group as the forty-first monument to male lightness: "A STATUE now, and if reviv'd once more, / Would prove, no doubt, as perjur'd as before."[8]

"The Statues" is an interesting reversal of a constant masculine trope. Women are often presented as Lord Orrery thinks of them, as statues with delicately-shaped limbs and "pleasing and graceful attitudes." Here a woman, both within and without the poem, turns a multitude of men into such cool shapes (elegant, marmoreal, and inanimate) but only as a punishment. The male fault for which the Prince suffers is not specifically Swift's; in fact Pilkington in her *Memoirs* takes care to defend him from the charge of unsuitable gallantries. (Her husband's infidelities were the spur to resentment.) Her satiric poem is a literary riposte to such satires as Swift's "The Progress of Love" (1727), and, as she reconstructs the history and conditions of her writing the poem, Swift's satiric ridicule of "The *Female Sex*" prompted this written reply. One of the first anti-masculinist satires by a woman in an age over-rich in anti-feminist satires by men, this poem is produced in a sense under Swift's aegis. The presence of Swift the satirist encourages the release of female energies in utterance.

Swift's "female senate" was composed largely of writers or would-be writers, a matter which Orrery seems determined to ignore. Swift in fact did encourage a number of his women friends to write. He not only encouraged Mary Barber (1690-1757) but introduced her to the public, as he wrote the "Dedication" to her *Poems on Several Occasions* (London, 1734). When she was in financial difficulties Swift not only gave her aid but ultimately offered her the manuscript of *Polite Conversation* with full rights of publication for her own benefit. Swift is a visible influence upon Barber's literary work, an influence not to be summed up as a mere source of imitation. Mary Barber endeavours to create her own kind of satire. She seizes upon the one kind of authority she certainly has that the world might acknowledge: her maternal authority. This strangely allows her access to the male world and the masculine voice, or at least to the voice of her young son, imagined ventriloquizing her words in a greater theatre of action.

An Apology written for my Son to his Master, who had commanded him to write verses on the Death of the Late Lord—

> I beg your Scholar you'll excuse,
> Who dares no more debase the Muse.
> My Mother says, if e'er she hears
> I write again on worthless Peers,
> Whether they're living Lords, or dead,
> She'll box the Muse from out my head.
>
> (*Poems on Several Occasions*, 50)

Just as Swift takes his clerical position as an opportunity for speaking with prophetic roughness and biting wit rather than for suave moralizing, so Mary Barber takes her position as mother as an opportunity to exercise satiric criticism rather than sweetly maternal sentiments. The poems grow out of the assertiveness of Barber's position as mother, and an almost pugnacious insistence on her real social status as the wife of a Cit. From this apparently low position she can take a high comic line against "worthless Peers." Those who write panegyrics on them deserve to get their ears boxed in a good bourgeois parental manner, and the Muse gives way to the assertive Mother, as schoolmasters and lords are vicariously slapped. Barber presents herself in the guise of the oft-criticized scribbling woman, careless of dress, while at the same time so careful of her children's lives and morals as to give rise to alarm in governing powers. The presentation of the self as a comic and sometimes awkward figure, not simply or smoothly in the right: this is a self-presentation common in the Swift of the *Poems*, and was perhaps learned from him.

With her son as a pretext Barber could write upon Irish topics, noting the unhappy position of young Irishmen who, even if educated, are "Doom'd in Obscurity to dwell" while "Strangers [the English] make the happier Claim."[9] Taking on the man's point of view (or rather, the view of the innocent boy) she is able to promulgate female rational opinion against the abuses and constrictions of the masculine world. One of her poems takes up a subject not elsewhere treated in Augustan verse as a topic of satire: the absurdity of *masculine* wear for male grown-ups. Ridicule of women's dress is a standard satiric topic, but Barber, through voicing her son's distress, makes a criticism ultimately levelled at the whole great male world:

> What is it our Mammas bewitches,
> To plague us little Boys with Breeches?
> To Tyrant *Custom* we must yield,
> While vanquish'd *Reason* flies the Field.
> Our Legs must suffer by Ligation,
> To keep the Blood from Circulation, . . .
> Our wiser Ancestors wore Brogues,
> Before the Surgeons brib'd these Rogues
> With narrow Toes, and Heels like Pegs,
> To help to make us break our Legs.
>
> Then, ere we know to use our Fists,
> Our Mothers closely bind our Wrists;
> And never thinks our Cloaths are neat,
> Till they're so tight we cannot eat.
> And, to increase our other Pains,
> The Hat-band helps to cramp our Brains.
> The Cravat finishes the Work,
> Like Bow-string sent from the Grand Turk.[10]

Male costume is absurd, tyrannous, damaging to the physical being. Men, as well as women, undergo socialization by dress, which in their case too is oppressive: here "Tyrant *Custom*" is associated with English invasion and the suppression of Irish tradition ("Our wiser Ancestors wore Brogues"). One can see how Barber's witty contempt for authority and custom, for public English authority and custom, would appeal to Swift, who wrote of Mary Barber's poems:

> They generally contain something new and useful, tending to the Reproof of some Vice or Folly. . . . She never writes on a Subject with general unconnected Topicks, but always with a Scheme and Method driving to some particular End; wherein many Writers in Verse, and of some Distinction, are so often known to fail. In short, she seemeth to have a true poetical Genius, better cultivated than could well be expected, either from her Sex, or the Scene she hath acted in, as the Wife of a Citizen.[11]

The influence of Swift's own verse style on Mary Barber's poems is evident. His kind of quick colloquial rhymed tetrameter offered her, as it was to offer other women writers, more control with less pretension than would be involved in the pentameter heroic measures. The rhymed pentameter assumes a grand ideal, a public language, and the hope that private and public self may become one. The women could not adapt the private to the public self with anything like equal ease, because women had no public function, no available public persona. They had to start with the private self, and invent a public voice. This manoeuvre is one that many of Swift's poems are engaged in, and his manner of quick, colloquial, impudent rhyme provides a usable model for effective criticism of life. In Mary Barber, an Irishwoman who saw the state of Ireland much as he did, Swift apparently recognized a kindred tough impishness. He acknowledged her right to utter "Reproof of some Vice or Folly."

The private Swift was sometimes hectoring, often teasing, about female behaviour and roles. But he did not demand constant pastel femininity. His disgusted remark on Addison, "let him fair-sex it to the world's end" is peculiarly satisfying.[12] Many Western writers (not satirists only) instinctively (if often unconsciously) reach for images of woman when they wish to symbolize the inadequacies of human intelligence, the uncomfortable demands of the physical, and the eternal obstruction that lies between the heart and the heart's desire. Swift is not one of them. He never attributes to womankind the earthy conspiracy against the (male) grand spiritual aspiration, nor is woman presented as the deranged and fearful underside of consciousness. To a woman reader the fact that "Celia shits" is probably less upsetting or annoying than the Magna Mater business in the *Dunciad*. In Pope's poem femaleness and motherhood are in effect condemned as obscene images of frightening power. But in Swift's satiric world, when things go wrong it is not because women are in control.

In *Cadenus and Vanessa* (1726), that verse compliment at once convoluted and straightforward, cryptic and open, Swift could at least imagine a woman endowed with qualities that womankind is customarily supposed to lack, qualities "For manly Bosoms chiefly fit," such as "Knowledge, Judgment, Wit . . . Justice, Truth and Fortitude." Pallas and Venus combine to produce a lady who outdoes the men so much that they cannot even comprehend her. Men's complaints about women's ignorant shallowness prove empty clichés; shallowness is what they want. Swift's poem implies a sympathy for the intelligent woman who does not fit into the socially-prescribed role, and could not fit into that mould without self-injury and diminution.

The poem itself can be read by women as sympathetic to the hardships of their position, unlike Pope's *The Rape of the Lock or Epistle to a Lady*. So Ellen Pollak has recently read it in a full and lengthy analysis.[13] Certainly, while the "Lady" in Pope's *Epistle* must learn to accept, submit, and obey, Vanessa in Swift's poem is praised for accepting nothing that she does not like. Disdainful of feminine behaviour, she is "silent, out of spight" (l.406), but she is silent only when she chooses to be. She has no notion of charming by submitting. She "condescend[s] to admit" those who please her. She acts according to her own judgment and power, which includes the power of speech. "All humble Worth she strove to raise; / Would not be prais'd, but lov'd to praise" (l.456). When Vanessa realizes she loves Cadenus she openly debates with him, speaks her feelings; she reasons, urges, and argues. The lady is not only a seducer but a seducer with powers of argument, all without censure from the poet.

That Swift is at the same time paying himself as Decanus the most terrific compliment need not be disputed; masculine critics tend to find the affair unsavoury and the poem indelicate. But Swift presents his unhandsome hero in an oddly "feminine" position, as observed and desired object rather than subject; Cadenus's awkward reactions show a masculinity that does not rely on cultural phallic certainty. In any case Swift could compliment himself only by presenting himself as loved by a woman of intelligence, learning, force of character, and full command of language. His Vanessa, like the Mary Barber he praises, speaks forcefully, "with a Scheme and Method driving to some particular End." We do not know the end: "But what Success *Vanessa* met, / Is to the World a Secret yet" (l.818). Ellen Pollak suggests in effect that Swift could find no ending to his poem because his culture, as he knew, allowed for no women save for the well-known types of docile (or shrewish) wives, longing old-maids, and light-minded whores, none of which suited the "Vanessa" of life or fiction. "How," Ellen Pollak asks, "could he pay tribute to a woman within the confines of a language and a logic by whose terms she was either fallen or unloved?" (151). That Swift's portrait of an able and lively woman was distressing in itself is evidenced in Orrery's comments. All Orrery wants us to see in Vanessa is a lightminded foolish female: "Vanity makes terrible devastation in a female breast. It batters down all restraints of modesty . . . VANESSA was excessively vain" (*Remarks*, 70). Orrery wants to say that no such woman as Swift describes could exist.

Lord Orrery in effect tries to shut Vanessa up. In his relations with

women Swift (inside and outside his own poems) never shuts them up.
Women writers were likely to find in him an encouragement to speak. It is
not surprising that a little group of Irish women writers forms part of Swift's
personal circle, particularly if we remember that the condition of Ireland
encouraged men and women who felt alike about political issues to band
together. All the members of Swift's "seraglio" of writing women (Mary
Davys, Laetitia Pilkington, Constantia Grierson, Mary Barber) might be
described as "self-made women." They were middle class, perhaps, but close
to the working class, and most of them worked at something aside from
writing (and housework) at some point in their lives in order to earn a living
or to eke out that of a spouse.[14] Swift's Irish women friends were "low,"
appropriately "low" if we take Lady Mary's view of "Birth"; the offspring of
a man-midwife and the spouse of a haberdasher are fit associates for a being
entitled by Birth and Fortune to no higher status than that of a Link Boy.
Uppity women surrounded an uppity man. They are an unusual group, these
Irish writing women of Swift's circle: energetic, self-reliant, self-conscious,
and witty. They might perhaps be seen as a group of Vanessas, new women
freshly compounded "of Wit and Sense," illustrating Vanessa's maxim
(learned from Cadenus himself) "That common Forms were not design'd /
Directors to a noble Mind" (1.612).

The case for Swift's influence on women writers cannot, however, be
made properly by considering only those women he himself knew. Swift was
an influence on women writers who had never met him. Much of the poetry
written by Englishwomen during the middle and later eighteenth century
exhibits an awareness of Swift and a sense of his importance as a model. This
is evident as soon as one turns to the poetry columns of the *Gentleman's
Magazine*, which in its early years was an important medium for women
writers, as Phyllis J. Guskin has shown.[15] The poetry pages, in which Swift
and Barber appeared, might in some respects be seen as an extension of Swift's
"seraglio." The verse of "Fidelia" of Lincoln, for instance, acknowledges
Swift in brisk tetrameters as the author humorously complains about the
inadequacy of a fifty-pound prize for a poetical essay on "Life, Death, Judgment, Heaven and Hell":

> But 50 pounds!—A sorry sum!
> You'd more need offer half a *plumb*;
> Five weighty subjects well to handle?
> Sir, you forget the price of candle;
> And leather too, when late and soon,
> I shall be pacing o'er my room; . . .
> 'Tis known old *Swift, Dan Pope*, and *Young*,
> Those leaders of the rhiming throng;
> Are better paid for meditations,
> On the most trifling Occasions;

The *Broomstick, Benefit of Fa—ing,*
Or any whim they shew their art in.[16]

Though Swift may be better paid, "Fidelia" proclaims in a later poem
"I love the Dean with the utmost affection; / I'm charm'd with his writings,
I admire his brave spirit," and she bids Sylvanus Urban tell the Dean that
"Fidelia" is quite willing to marry him, and "That *Vanessa*, that favourite of
Vulcan's fair dame / For her dear *Decanus* ne'er felt such a flame." If "good
Mr. Urban" will only speak to Swift in her favour, "Fidelia" can forego the
fifty pounds: "And then for your prizes your poets may shift. / I shall have
all I wish, when I get Doctor *Sw--t*."[17] After this mock-proposal of November
1734 various masculine correspondents express in comic verse their objections
to her offer for Swift: "Strange is Fidelia's passion!—for I swear, /
I thought to match him with my sorrel mare" says one prize epigram on the
subject.[18] The topic became a running joke in the poetry section of the
Gentleman's Magazine in 1735. While pretending to be hurt that the "dear
dean . . . continues mum," "Fidelia" repeats her admiration; though correspondents "call the doctor ugly names," she loves him so unswervingly "That
whoe'er hopes to gain my favour, / Must not speak ill of him however."
Even Swift's satiric verses on women, such as "The Furniture of a Woman's
Mind" (in the *Gentleman's Magazine* for February 1735), show "That while
he chides he pleases too; / A secret, known to very few."[19] The marriage
proposal is a joke, expressing that attraction towards Swift that many women
feel and that men evidently find hard to comprehend in them. "Fidelia,"
too, wants to be a Vanessa, and the successfulness of the true Vanessa of wit
and sense and independence is ultimately equated with success in writing
and publishing. "To get Doctor *Sw—t*" is not to marry the aged deaf dean,
but to become like the poet, to take advantage of his voice.

Swift had distinguished himself in finding an immediate and quite
unheroic voice, a critical grumbling impish voice that emerges not from the
centre of authoritative power but from somewhere on the sidelines. The
tetrameter verse form Swift inherited from Butler, but the bullying public
narrative manner of the Hudibrastic style is modulated into something suited
to the private meditative personality in touch with gritty fact. This personality does not cease to be satiric while relating thoughts to homely experience
and undramatic events, or non-events. Swift's is a good mode for pointing
out uncomfortable truths in a bearable way. In his tetrameter verse, and in
parodic mimicry of other breathless voices (as in "Mrs. Frances Harris's
Petition"), the manner seems to make up its own rules as it goes along. This
effect is often emphasized by the touch-and-go rhymes and sprightly running
of the four-beat verse. It is not Swift's verse form alone but the voice and
manner in general that could attract female writers. Women poets were to
pick up Swift's kind of energy, pungency, and pointedness. They appreciated
the absence of ponderous *gravitas*, the celebration of the unignorable not

dressed up as the noble. They could share his kind of interest in that which is homely, unofficial, and truthful.

Above all, perhaps, the women poets of the mid-century are affected by the gender-related topics of Swift's verses (we can see how "Fidelia" has picked up the sexual teasing in Swift). The conflict between masculine and feminine as Swift presented it might disgust men such as Orrery, who wished their females presented by the poet-statuary as figures of "delicacy of limb" and "pleasing and graceful attitudes." The women writers who respond to Swift are hardier than Orrery, and less interested in the pleasing and graceful. They, like Swift, are moved to question the romanticizing of conventional behaviour. In their works the conflicts between men and women are picked up and developed from a female point of view.

Mary Leapor (1722–46) is another of the women writers both energetic and low born who dared to speak out. Leapor (commonly known as "Molly") gives herself the romantic name of "Mira," but defies the conventions of feminine propriety and beauty, and the pastoral ideal, in her comic pastoral "Mira's Picture" in which she is discussed by two "swains" in the most unflattering terms. Her self-presentation, which picks up the conventions of men looking at a woman and the conventional repudiation of the woman writer as physically ugly, mockingly makes Leapor unbelievably repulsive (dirty, hump-backed, with teeth falling out). Leapor plays with the fascination of female ugliness in such a manner as to free herself from conventional claims of feminine proprieties. Unheroic (or, rather, unheroinic) "Mira" is able to assume a parodic masculine voice, as Swift had adopted and ventriloquized a feminine one.

Freeing herself of conventional expectations, Leapor casts a cool amused eye at the half-truths of a socially-trained sexual sensibility. She picks up Swift's characters, or anti-characters, of Strephon and Chloe and introduces us to her own version of these anti-pastoral persons in two poems. In "The Mistaken Lover" the husband Strephon has fallen out of love with his wife Chloe, and finds fault with her appearance:

> "Your Lips I own are red and thin,
> But there's a Pimple on your Chin:
> Besides your Eyes are gray,—Alack!
> Till now I always thought 'em black."

The reader expects that poor Chloe will be offended and unhappy, and is surprised when she cordially agrees that the marriage is a vexatious mistake. The pair will, she says, channel their energies into the techniques of polite separation:

> "But now, my Dearest, as you see
> In mutual Hatred we agree,

> Methinks 'tis better we retreat,
> Each Party to a distant Seat;
> And tho' we value each the other,
> Just as one Rush regards another:
> Yet let us often send to hear
> If Health attend the absent Dear."

Another of Leapor's mock-pastoral couples appears in *"Strephon* to *Celia.* A modern *Love-Letter"*:

> Now Madam, as the Chat goes round,
> I hear you have ten thousand Pound:
> But that I as a Trifle hold,
> Give me your Person, dem your Gold;
> Yet for your own Sake 'tis secur'd,
> I hope—your Houses too ensur'd,
> I'd have you take a special Care,
> And of false Mortgages beware.[20]

What such women as Molly Leapor evidently heard most clearly in poems like Swift's "The Lady's Dressing Room" was a refreshing challenge to the ideology of courtship, the conventional romanticizing of the female, and other absurdities of male-female relations. Taking up the Swiftian style of verse (though the "modern *Love-Letter*" has echoes of Hudibras to the Widow, as well) Leapor can offer parodic ventriloquizing of the masculine voice and masculine pretentions and pretenses. A feminine word can be put in against marriage as so often constituted. Such a word is put in by Ann Yearsley, for instance, at the end of the century, in her iambic tetrameter narrative "Lucy. A Tale for the Ladies." Lucy suffers from an unhappy middle-class marriage to the dull Cymon. She eventually finds a friend in her husband's friend, a man she can talk to, and she is then accused of adultery. The wretched marriage, however, drags miserably on until Lucy finds release in death:

> She dies! and Cymon's poignant grief
> Is finely wrought in bas-relief.
> To prove he does his wife lament,
> How grand, superb, her monument:
> There weeping angels cut in stone,
> The rose snapt off ere fully blown,
> The empty urn—must surely prove,
> Cymon's deep sorrow, and his love.[21]

Women poets of the period seem inclined to record a suspicion that men want their women static and monumental. The conventional images evoked by Yearsley, the stone angels, rose, and urn are all, like the urn, empty; real living women are despised and neglected, while elaborate stone monuments offer men the double satisfaction of getting rid of the real woman and celebrating their own false idealization. The "bas-relief" is half relief. When the women look, as Swift did, at the Progress of Marriage, they too are apt to find images of meanness, failure, folly, and greed, though they place the blame slightly differently.

If the women writers share Swift's interest in marital failures and courtship absurdities, they also share his sense of strong physicality. Indeed, some of Swift's own imagery of intimate physical domestic unpleasantness may have come to him not from a Latin-based satiric tradition alone but also from some of women's own writings. Everyone who has read Swift's "The Lady's Dressing Room" (that violent irruption into woman's realm) has been struck with its forceful imagery of matter in the wrong place, of contaminating physical proximities:

> Now listen while he next produces.
> The various Combs for various Uses,
> Fill'd up with Dirt so closely fixt,
> No Brush could force a way betwixt. . . .
> But oh! it turn'd poor *Strephon's* Bowels,
> When he beheld and smelt the Towels,
> Begumm'd, bematter'd, and beslim'd
> With Dirt, and Sweat, and Ear-Wax grim'd.
> No Object Strephon's Eye escapes,
> Here Pettycoats in frowzy Heaps; . . .
> The Stockings, why shou'd I expose,
> Stain'd with the Marks of stinking Toes
> (11. 19–52)

Women writers have also occasionally been fascinated with sluttery and produced rich imagery of feminine dirt. Swift's poem should be compared with the fantasia of dirt and disorder created by Margaret Cavendish, Duchess of Newcastle, in her play *The Matrimonial Trouble*, published with her other plays in 1662. In the second scene of *The Matrimonial Trouble* there is a dialogue between Master Thrifty the Steward and Briget Greasy the Cookmaid. Thrifty accuses the incompetent Briget of sending up puddings made of stinking guts and fowls insufficiently drawn. This "Slut" has other nasty habits:

Besides, your sluttery is such, as you will poyson all the House: for in one place I find a piece of butter, and a greasie comb, full of nitty hairs lying by it; and in another place flour and old-worn stockings, the feet being rotted off with sweat; and in a third place, a dish of cold meat cover'd with a foul smock, and your durty shooes [*sic*] (for the most part) stand upon the Dresser-board, where you lay the hot meat; besides, by your carelessness you do waste and spoil so much, as it is unsufferable: for you will fling whole ladlefuls of dripping into the fire, to make the fire blaze underneath the pot.[22]

The maid is actually given a sexual reward for her sloppiness; crying about the Steward's treatment of her she is discovered by her master, and rapidly consoled by being made his mistress. The mix of body dirt, sexuality, and kitchen stuff is very striking. Swift's lady's dressing room is also associated with the kitchen in his illustrative imagery, drawn from cooking "Mutton Cutlets":

> If from adown the hopeful Chops
> The Fat upon a Cinder drops,
> To stinking Smoak it turns the Flame
> Pois'ning the Flesh from whence it came;
> And up exhales a greasy Stench,
> For which you curse the careless Wench
>   (l. 99)

Swift appears to be elaborating on Margaret Cavendish's Briget Greasy, a "careless Wench" indeed, whose spirit seems to pervade Celia's chamber.

Swift seems especially fascinated with kitchen life, its accidents, squalor, and creativity. Although women novelists of the eighteenth century prefer to steer clear of the kitchen (perhaps determined not to cast their heroines into the pudding-making role), the women poets share Swift's fascination with kitchenry. In "Crumble-Hall" Mary Leapor takes us through an old-fashioned stolid manor house, and includes a visit to the kitchen where "The fires blaze; the greasy pavements fry; / And steaming odours from the kettles fly." We return to the kitchen to see overeaten Roger snoring at table and the maid doing the washing up, a redeeming if comic domestic activity seldom described in literature: "The greasy apron round her hips she ties, / And to each plate the scalding clout applies." There is a touch of mock-georgic here, reminiscent of Swift's "A Description of the Morning" (1709): "Now *Moll* had whirl'd her Mop with dext'rous Airs, / Prepared to Scrub the Entry and the Stairs" (l. 117).

Leapor's excursion through Crumble-Hall (an excursion which is a way of entertaining the visitor at this place where little happens) includes a trip to the lumber rooms at the very top of the house:

> These rooms are furnish'd amiably and full;
> Old shoes, and sheep-ticks bred in stacks of wool;
> Grey Dobbin's gears, and drenching-horns enow;
> Wheel-spokes—the irons of a tatter'd plough.[23]

The relaxed description of a visit neither brilliant nor unpleasant, paid to a place unglamorous but characteristic and insistently rich in particulars, is much in Swift's manner. He has written several descriptions of semi-boring or not-utterly-satisfactory visits, as, for instance, his account of the houseparty in Gaulstown given in "The Journal" (1721). The country woman "Shews all her Secrets of House keeping, / For Candles, how she trucks her dripping" (l. 81). The party pass their time in a desultory way, going fishing, playing backgammon. Nothing much happens until the advent of new guests brings changes unpleasant to visitors already in residence:

> This Grand Event half broke our Measures,
> Their Reign began with cruel Seizures;
> The *Dean* must with his Quilt supply,
> The Bed in which these Tyrants lie:
> *Nim* lost his Wig-block, *Dan* his Jordan,
> My Lady says she can't afford one;
> *George* is half scar'd out of his Wits,
> For *Clem* gets all the dainty bits.
>
> (l. 113)

Swift's work is rich in the kind of observed details (not necessarily satiric) that cannot be subsumed in or covered by some pretty literary convention. His minor grumbling, his attention to minute circumstances, create an odd sideways mock-heroic effect in such poems as "The Journal"; masculine grandeur (which belongs to a grand historical world of Events, Seizures, and Tyrants) is turned into mere diurnal physical survival. (Gulliver, too, is of course the hero of unheroic diurnal physical survival, the man who experiences to an extreme degree the importance of quilts, dainty bits, and jordans.) This aspect of Swift shows him as very close not only to women's particular concerns, which he can describe seriously or mockingly (matters of candles and dripping), but to a view of the world that they can share. He acknowledges the vigorous presence of the mundane, the unliterary, which the women writers also wish to do, and must do if they are not to be swallowed up in literary conventions that ignore them and their lives, or turn them into lovely statues.

It seems, above all, the insistent unmarmoreal (or anti-marmoreal) physicality of Swift that attracted (and attracts) female writers. When Swift writes to and about Stella in his poems he writes of her as a physical human being, subject to pain and age. The talents and abilities she manifests are thus real human qualities, with all the credit of being exerted in the circumstances of life's constraints. Stella may be an Angel, or an hospitable entertainer, like the Angel-Inn, but the inn-sign, her face, shows the marks of age and wear: "Now this is Stella's Case, in Fact / An Angel's Face, a little crack't" ("Stella's Birth-Day. 1720–21," l. 15). This celebration of reality seems to have impressed the poet Mary Jones of Oxford (d. 1778), whom Thomas Warton praised as "a very ingenious poetess . . . a most sensible, agreeable, and amiable woman."[24] In a poem (published with Jones's other works in her *Miscellanies in Prose and Verse* [Oxford, 1750]) written to a woman friend who has suffered from the small-pox, Mary Jones borrows Swift's image of the sign, and the name of his lady:

> When skillful traders first set up,
> To draw the people to their shop,
> They strait hang out some gaudy sign,
> Expressive of the goods within. . . .
> So fares it with the Nymph divine;
> For what is Beauty but a Sign? . . .
>   What tho' some envious folks have said,
> That *Stella* now must hide her head,
> That all her stock of beauty's gone,
> And ev'n the very sign took down: . . .
> For if you break a while, we know,
> 'Tis bankrupt like, more rich to grow.
> A fairer sign you'll soon hang up, . . .
> Which all your neighbours shall out-shine,
> And of your Mind remain the Sign.
>   ("After the Small-pox," 79–80)

Although often a Popean in her verse Mary Jones turns to the style of Swift when she wishes to deal with harsh or humorous physical facts, and she frequently does wish to deal with physical facts. Indeed, she deals with the less salubrious matters alluded to in Swift's scatological poems. In "Holt Waters. A Tale. Extracted fom the *Natural* History of *Berkshire*" (93–100) she tells a surprising fabliau. The story has a decorous and polite beginning. "Two nymphs of chaste *Diana's* train, / Both fair, and tolerably vain" set out in a coach one morning with "a brace" of "well-dress'd Beaus." The coach party proceeds, talking "Of Queens and grottos, wars and Kings." Soon Cloe feels uneasy; she wishes for something, and the author comments defensively: "Yet trust me, Prudes, it was no more / Than you or I have wish'd before." Cloe excuses herself from the coach, saying she must pay a quick visit of condolence to a friend whose parrot has just died, and shaking off the gallant offer of "Sir Fopling" to attend her. She speeds off alone, and comes to a little farm, but cannot see what she needs. "What shall she do? Her wants are pressing / And speedily require redressing." Cloe finds the dairy, uninhabited, and there is no further time to consider; the business must be done:

> The cream-pot first she filled with liquor,
> Fit for the thorax of the Vicar.
> Nay *Jove* himself, the skies protector,
> Would call such liquor heav'nly Nectar.

> So in a grot, I've seen enthron'd
> Some river goddess, osier-crown'd,
> Pour all her copious urns around,
> Hence plenteous crops our harvest yield,
> And *Ceres* laughs thro' all the field.
> A pan of milk, unskimm'd its cream,
> Did next receive the bounteous stream . . .
> Back to her company she flies,
> Quite unobserv'd by vulgar eyes.
> The muse indeed behind her stood,
> And heard the noise, and saw the flood.

The Muse, however, does not warn "Goody *Baucis*," who returns unsuspiciously to the dairy; she is surprised at the full containers everywhere, and thinks they indicate magic assistance: "How did she life her hands, and stare! / And cry'd 'What Fairy has been here?' " She immediately puts the magic gift to use:

> Now *Baucis*, who came hot from work,
> Was very dry, her dinner pork, . . .
> She drank, and down the liquor went;
> "A little, and therewith content,
> We learn, says she, from good St. *Paul*:
> And sure Content is all in all!
> Our beer is dead, but no great matter,
> 'Tis better still than *common* water."

Jones's countrywoman is obviously derived from the Ovidian "Goody *Baucis*" of Swift's "Baucis and Philemon" (1709) in which the cottagers are impressed with the miraculously filled jug, "replenished to the Top" (l. 3).

One may object that in Jones's tale the genteel Cloe's secret misdeed is paid for by the unsuspecting lower-class woman who mistakes the lady's piss for flat beer. The emphasis is on the physicality of both women, which they share with us. Cloe's wish is "no more / Than you or I have wish'd before." There are no pastoral nymphs, figures of the body without bodily needs, and the goddess as statue with dry stone urn is replaced by the living function of physical Cloe. Cloe's product is certainly not divine liquor, and she is no goddess who so desperately needs to find such relief. If Swift's Celia shits, Jones's Cloe pisses and pisses. We are reminded of some real "*Natural History.*" In "Holt Waters" (the title seems a pun, as to hold the waters was what Cloe could not do) the female Muse presides knowingly over this female story of needs and liberations.

A still more surprising poem is Mary Jones's "Epistle from Fern-Hill" (133–38). (It is a tribute to the robustness of this Age of Sensibility that both these poems were later included in *Poems by Eminent Ladies*.) Written jokingly about a visit to the author's close friend Charlot Clayton, the "Epistle" is a complaint about the trials of such a visit with an overcomplaisant hostess. The guest feels imprisoned, overstuffed with food, overheated with a scorching fire. "But still in all I do, or say, / This nuisance *Breeding's* in the way." The author works out her dissatisfaction in an elaborate comparison to a particular kind of unease. Consider, she urges, the way the General permits himself to fart in company when disturbed with inward wind:

> He wisely thinks the more 'tis pent
> The more 'twill struggle for a vent:
> So only begs you'll hold your nose,
> And gently lifting up his clothes,
> Away th' imprison'd vapour flies,
> And mounts a zephyr to the skies.

This uncomfortable instance is the basis of a comparison; to our surprise we find it means that the visitor must be as uncomfortable to Charlot as the General's wind is to him. Like the unwelcome intestinal gas, the discontented visitor tumbles things about and proves a disturbance which the hostess is too polite to appear to notice: "Yet, spite of all this rebel rout, / She's too well bred to let me out." The speaker pleads for impolite release:

> O *Charlot*! when alone we sit,
> Laughing at all our own (no) wit,
> You wisely with your Cat at play,
> I reading *Swift*, and spilling tea;
> How would it please my ravish'd ear,
> To hear you from your easy chair,
> With look serene, and brow uncurl'd,
> Cry out, A—for all the world!
> But You, a slave to too much breeding,
> And I, a fool with too much reading,
> Follow the hive, as bees their drone,
> Without one purpose of our own:
> Till tir'd with blund'ring and mistaking,
> We die sad fools of others making.

It is hard to think of any other poetical work in which the poet is self-compared to a fart. The reference to "reading *Swift*" points to influence and analogue. This is meant to be (and to be seen to be) a woman's original poem re-creating the Swiftian manner and subject-matter. In this piece, in a reversal of some of Swift's strictures, males prove unpleasantly physical (the General's fart) whereas the females are too proper, too restricted, too unkind to their physical and emotional desires. The poem is a striking plea for freedom from polite rules and lady-like squeamishness. Manners and reading are turning the women into "fools of others making." In following the proprieties they are acting inappropriately to themselves and to each other. Jones takes the Swiftian physical manner in order to reverse some of Swift's (and others') strictures of decorum, but Swift's manner and precedent allow for the discussion of such realities. The freedom from squeamish lady-like decorum is vividly acted out in a poem by one of the eighteenth century's "Eminent Ladies" that still has the power to surprise and shock us.

It is not only the female verse writers who manifest the influence of Swift. The novelist Frances Burney (1752–1840) read both Pope and Swift in her youth, and on reading Pope's *Letters* in her teens she was moved at Pope's "long friendship with Swift . . . the attachment of such eminent men to one another . . . almost awes me, and at the same time inexpressibly delights me."[25] In 1774, four years before the publication of *Evelina*, in a conversation with her elderly mentor Samuel Crisp and some uneducated ladies, Burney extemporized a mock-project, a book of etiquette:

> I told them I intended to write a *Treatise upon Politeness* for their edification. . . .
> "Will it be like Swift's 'Polite Conversation'?" said Mr. Crisp.
> "I intend to dedicate it to Miss Notable," answered I; "it will contain all the *newest fashioned* regulations. In the first place, you are never again to cough."
> "Not to cough?" exclaimed every one at once; " 'but how are you to help it?' "
> "As to that," answered I, "I am not very clear about it myself, as I own I am guilty sometimes of doing it; but it is as much a mark of ill breeding, as it is to laugh, which is a thing that Lord Chesterfield has stigmatized."
>
> (*Early Diary*, 1: 324–26)

After reprehending "*sneezing*, or *blowing the nose*" as impermissible, but admitting that breathing is "not yet . . . quite exploded," Burney promises to send Crisp, who requires instruction, six copies of this important work. Burney shows her knowledge of Swift in immediately picking up Crisp's reference to *Polite Conversation* and alluding to the young "heroine" of that work, the would-be-smart Miss in Swift's comic gallery of vulgarians. Once again a woman associates Swiftian material with the need to escape repressive rules of breeding, here parodied by being augmented to the point of impossibility. *Evelina* (1778) can be seen as Burney's shrewd "Treatise upon Politeness"; it is also her version of *Polite Conversation*. Burney has an interest akin to Swift's in the clichés of public conversation and behaviour. Swift's characters in *Polite Conversation* speak in the pert clichés and old smart answers which he pretends to present as "the Flowers of Wit, Fancy, Wisdom, Humour, and Politeness."[26] Burney's characters often speak in similar hackneyed remarks, like the smart things and ugly faded compliments uttered by Mr Smith in *Evelina*. The climactic scene of that novel, in which the foppish Mr Lovel, confronted with his parodic counterpart the dressed-up monkey, attacks the beast and then is seized and bitten on the ear, has a Swiftian ring; it is reminiscent of the scene with the Brobdingnagian monkey and of episodes of Yahoo-encounters in *Gulliver's Travels.*[27]

Burney shares with Swift a violent imagination, and like him she makes us see the vulnerable living body beneath foppish disguise or constricting proprieties. Her fantasia upon a theme of a "Treatise upon Politeness" points out the physical need which unheroically resists elaborate systems and refined pretences. For Frances Burney, as for Mary Jones, the Swiftian manner is associated with physical need, and with resistance to the social pressures that are so hard upon women, turning them into "sad fools of others making." It is little wonder that one of the first literary quotations we come upon in Burney's *Cecilia* (1782), that big satiric novel in which, as contemporaries noted, Burney wielded the lash, is that important couplet from *Cadenus and Vanessa*, misquoted slightly as "For common rules were ne'er design'd / Directors of a noble mind."[28] Burney's misquotation shows that she had rather challenge "rules" than mere "Forms," just as she imaginatively challenged through parody "the *newest fashioned* regulations," those inanities that pinch women's lives and impede the exercise of both Sense and Wit.

Frances Burney's friend Hester Lynch Thrale (later Piozzi) was also an admirer of "the admirable Swift." Indeed, she was one of his female imitators. Her latest biographer, William McCarthy, notes that she had more Swift than Johnson in her library, and that in irony "her chosen precursor" was not Pope or Johnson but Swift. McCarthy illustrates the point by quoting from one of Hester Lynch's earlier poems, "Pompey, or a Doggrel Epistle from Pompey in the Shades—to his Master," in which the satire on Descartes is drawn from the Swift of *A Tale of a Tub*, and what McCarthy calls "her bright-eyed octosyllables" from Swift's verse form: for example, "So Brutes he wisely could maintain / Knew neither Pleasure, Fear nor Pain."[29]

A more original use of Swift as precursor and influence can be found in Hester Lynch Thrale's "Three Dialogues on the Death of Hester Lynch Thrale, Written in August 1779." As she explains in her "Preface," "one of Dean Swift's happier Compositions is certainly the little poem on his own Death. My Death would be a slight Event indeed compared with his—it would I think just bear three Dialogues among the people I chiefly live with, and some of them are insignificant enough too."[30] The morbidly witty dramatic scenes in prose fix for Hester Lynch Thrale her own position in the estimation of her friends, and of rivals like Elizabeth Montagu. Swift had offered a valuable precedent in presenting himself, with some depression and self-pity, in an ironic light, offering a realistic appraisal of his own slight importance in the general social scheme of things. One must not console oneself in imagining others' grief or lamentation: "The Dean is dead (*and what is Trumps?*)" ("Verses on the Death of Dr. Swift" [1731], l. 228). So in Mrs Thrale's case her "friends" of the salons are imagined laughingly remembering her odd bearing with Johnson ("Mrs. Thrale . . . had prodigious strong Nerves"), and Mrs Montagu uses the occasion to display her talent in simile: "She had remarkable good Nerves, and yet—carried off suddenly—pounced by Death like a Partridge upon the *Wing*—caught in one of her *Flights* Mr. Pepys" ("First Dialogue," 27).

Swift is *the* model for ironic self-presentation, for the double-edged view of the hard social perceptions forced on the helpless self. His Dean of the poems is both mentally robust and physically and socially vulnerable; if he maintains his independence it is sometimes at a cost of gaucherie, uncertainty, social inadequacy. Swift had dared to choose this unheroic persona, even though male writers could always assume some grandeur, adopting the cloak of literary greatness of the past. Pope, pretending modesty, merely refers himself to Horace; his poetic persona is always strikingly competent, authoritative, and virtuous. Women writers knew they could not make such claims, at least not in such tones. The tropes of grandeur, of Virgilian or Horatian power, of historical importance, were not for them. The poet who had shown how to present the self as unglamorous, under-appreciated (yet not faultless), vulnerable, and often absurd: this was Swift. Of course, Swift's Swift is no mere victim; Swift presents himself as having mundane unheroic qualities, not only in the "Verses on the Death of Dr. Swift," where he admits to envy and peevishness, but in countless other poems where he is a testy interlocutor, or a busybody, or an uneasy guest.

To summarize the view of Swift generally held by women writers of the eighteenth century, one can say that for them he was the exciting poet of limitation. Swift above all other writers dealt with cross-grained realities against the heroic mode. He made no grand claims for human reason, and thus not for the rational, powerful, all-controlling male. He was not in favour of conquests and systems. He paid attention to the physical, and he acknowledged small as well as large distresses. When women writers of his era think of dealing with their domestic world in its hard detail, and often with some ill humour as well as enjoyment, they tend to look to Swift as one of their models. When they think of female physical needs, of the irreducible demands of a body that stubbornly insists on its needs to piss and fart, to cough and sneeze (and to live and die) they think, to their comfort, of Swift. When they want to assert satiric energies against a world that seems inclined to drain them through the operation of politeness and duty, they turn to Swift again.

Middleton Murry would seem to have his horror to himself, or to share it with a select circle, including Lord Orrery. In every century exclamations over Swift's foul-mindedness have been much more common among critics of Murry's sex. If Swift felt "a particular physical loathing of women" it was not reciprocated. Indeed, in *Cadenus and Vanessa* he made the claim that he was loved. "Fidelia" of Lincoln thought him comically lovable; the persona of Swift has its special kind of sexual appeal. That Swift won women's liking is testified to by Orrery, who notes in jealous surprise Swift's power "over all his females." Orrery does not wish to regard the obvious fact: that "not the richest or most powerful lovers, no, not even the Grand Seignior himself" can expect the kind of friendship and affection from women that the man who is truly friendly to women and values them will naturally receive. Swift liked women, and that feeling was reciprocated. The relationship seems so unusual that Orrery has to devalue it and degrade the women into passive inmates of a "seraglio."

Swift's writings did not enclose women in conventions and impossible stylizations. If, in his "panegyrical descriptions" of women, Swift, as Orrery complained, "seldom descended lower than the center of their hearts" the heart is worth acknowledging. Swift was not doing what Orrery thought a poet dealing with women *should* be doing: creating pleasing inanimate objects for men to enjoy, modelling "that delicacy of limb, and those pleasing and graceful attitudes which have constituted the sex to be the most beautiful part of the creation." Orrery's imagery gives away himself and his whole culture: mention of "Woman" brings to mind something between an art gallery and a strip show. Men are frightened of being robbed of the "wholesome lust" that Murry prefers. When Swift deals with the dirty or disagreeable in females, or when his tone is scolding, he is still urging self-respect, and he never imposes the injunctions to docility, obedience, and mental lethargy so commonly repeated to women throughout the century. He never tells woman that her whole aim must be to charm, or that she rules best when she obeys. A "seraglio" was really what he did not want. He wanted Vanessas.

On the subject of Swift, women writers and critics of the twentieth century seem very much in line with those of the eighteenth century. Women praise Swift, even in considering those particular poems which Murry assumes must make him most repellent to women. Felicity A. Nussbaum, in *The Brink of All We Hate: English Satires on Women, 1660–1750* (Lexington, Kentucky, 1984), is inclined to defend the Swift of the "excremental" poems in which she sees Swift as trying "to release men from passion and its attendant madness." The mythology of love and courtship is itself a burden, and Swift can be a liberator: "Swift seeks to destroy the misapprehensions in both sexes which lead to the folly of love." Unlike Juvenal and others, Swift does not present women as responsible for the downfall of civilization; rather, he sees that "woman, like man, is not a rational animal, but only *rationis capax*" (122–23). In Stella he presents "a positive ideal": "The Stella of the poems is not praised primarily as the chaste guardian of moral values but as an able, alert companion who delights her friend because of her humanity. His ideal woman, fat, grey, and ill, is decidedly not a lady from romance" (115).

. . . From the eighteenth century to the twentieth, women have tended to find Swift comic, sympathetic, and admirable; they do see "the Splendour of his Works" and, like "Fidelia," while "charm'd with his writings" they "admire his brave spirit." The works seem more splendid the more they are looked at, and there are elements in them that are peculiarly helpful to women. Orrery was perhaps right to fear that Swift's view of women was a deep threat to the usual male definition and placement of the fair sex. Swift's very human and expressive voice, particularly in his poems, offered a useful and liberating model. Women writers have drawn Swift, and drawn upon him. He is worth arguing with, worth talking to. Moreover, he has provided a constant model and stimulus for women writers who have found themselves, like the Irish clergyman, Jonathan Swift, in a position of subjugation and supposed docility when they would rather speak out and vex the world a little as well as divert it.

Notes

1. John Middleton Murry, *Jonathan Swift: A Critical Biography* (London, 1954), 439, 441.

2. John Boyle, Earl of Orrery, *Remarks on the Life and Writings of Dr. Jonathan Swift . . . In a Series of Letters . . .* third edition (London, 1752), 78, 81.

3. Lady Mary Wortley Montagu, Letter to Lady Bute, 23 June 1754, in *The Complete Letters of Lady Mary Wortley Montagu*, edited by Robert Halsband, 3 vols (Oxford, 1967), 3: 56, 57.

4. See Halsband's second footnote to Montagu's letter of 23 June 1754, quoted above (Letters, 3: 56).

5. *Memoirs of Mrs Laetitia Pilkington . . . Written by Herself. Wherein are occasionally interspersed, All Her Poems; with Anecdotes of several eminent Persons*, 3 vols (Dublin and London, 1749–54; Garland reprint, New York and London, 1975), 1:50–51.

6. Mary Davys, *The Merry Wanderer* (a revision of her novel of 1705, *The fugitive*), in *Works of Mrs. Mary Davys: Consisting of Plays, Novels, Poems and Familiar Letters*, 2 vols (London, 1725), 1:161–62. Siobhàn Kilfeather has suggested that *The fugitive* may have influenced *Gulliver's Travels*: "Beyond the Pale: Sexual Identity and National Identity in Early Irish Fiction," *Critical Matrix* 2 (Fall 1986): 1–31.

7. Poems are quoted from *Swift: Poetical Works*, edited by Herbert Davis (London, New York, and Toronto, 1967). The three-volume edition of Swift's *Poems*, edited by Harold Williams, second edition, 3 vols (Oxford, 1958), has been consulted for dates of first publication.

8. "The Statues: Or, The Trial of Constancy. A Tale. For the Ladies," in *Memoirs*, 1:92–106. This poem was first published in 1739, after Pilkington's break with Swift, but she attributes the writing of it to an earlier period, and definitely links it to her acquaintance with him. See entry under "Pilkington" in *A Dictionary of British and American Women Writers 1660–1800*, edited by Janet Todd (London, 1984), 251.

9. "An Apology for not bringing an Exercise," *Poems on Several Occasions*, 97–98.

10. "Written for my Son, and Spoken by him at his first putting on Breeches," *Poems on Several Occasions*, 13–14.

11. "To the Right Honourable *John*, Earl of Orrery," "Dedication" to Barber's *Poems on Several Occasions*, vi–vii. See also *"Directions to Servants" and Miscellaneous Pieces 1733–1742, The Prose Writings of Jonathan Swift*, edited by Herbert Davis and others, 16 vols (Oxford, 1939–74), 13:74.

12. Letter of February 1712, *Journal to Stella*, edited by Harold Williams, 2 vols (Oxford, 1948), 2:482.

13. *The Poetics of Sexual Myth: Gender and Ideology in the Verse of Swift and Pope* (Chicago and London, 1985). See also pp. 207–27 in this volume.

14. Laetitia Pilkington was the daughter of a Dutch man-midwife, to whom Constantia Grierson was at one point apprenticed to learn midwifery. Grierson, who edited three major Latin authors before her death at age twenty-seven, was the daughter of an illiterate family, though she married a King's printer. Mary Davys, wife of a schoolmaster, was reduced to running a coffee-shop in Cambridge when she was widowed, and the divorced Pilkington was to try to run a book and print shop. Mary Barber was the wife of a clothier.

15. "Sophia's Secret Sisters: Feminism in the *Gentleman's Magazine*," paper delivered at a conference of the Midwest American Society for Eighteenth-Century Studies, October 1986. I am grateful also to Phyllis Guskin for sending me references to poems referring to Swift.

16. "Fidelia," "To the GENTLEMAN who offer'd 50 Pounds . . . ," *Gentleman's Magazine* 4 (September 1734): 508.

17. "Fidelia," "To SYLVANUS URBAN, Gent.," *Gentleman's Magazine* 4 (November 1734): 619.

18. Prize Epigram No. 2, "On FIDELIA's Passion for D--n S---t," *Gentleman's Magazine* 5 (January 1735): 45.

19. "FIDELIA to SYLVANUS URBAN," *Gentleman's Magazine* 5 (March 1735): 159.

20. Mary Leapor, *Poems upon Several Occasions* (London, 1748), 81–90, 105–6.

21. Ann Yearsley, *Poems on Various Subjects* (London, 1787), 129–30.

22. *The Matrimonial Trouble*, in *Playes Written by the Thrice Noble, Illustrious and Excellent Princess, The Lady Marchioness of Newcastle* (London, 1662), 1.2 (p. 424).

23. *Poems by Eminent Ladies*, 2 vols (London, 1755), 2:126–32.

24. See Warton's annotation, quoted by Boswell, to a letter of 1757 from Samuel Johnson to Thomas Warton containing a reference to "Miss Jones." Warton adds that since she was sister to the Chanter of Christ Church Cathedral "Johnson used to call her the *Chantress*. I have heard him often address her in this passage from *Il Penseroso*: 'Thee Chantress, oft the woods among / I woo, etc.' (Boswell, *The Life of Samuel Johnson, L.L.D.*, edited by George Birkbeck Hill, 6 vols [Oxford, 1887], 1:322–23).

25. *The Early Diary of Frances Burney*, edited by Annie Raine Ellis, 2 vols (London, 1907), 1:146.

26. *The Prose Writings of Jonathan Swift*, 4:111.

27. For Burney's monkey episode, see *Evelina, or the History of a Young Lady's Entrance into the World*, edited by Edward A. Bloom (Oxford, 1970), 400–01.

28. *Cecilia, or Memoirs of an Heiress*. 5 vols (London, 1782), 1:20; and see Samuel Hoole, *Aurelia; or The Contest* (London, 1783), 62: "I stood, a favouring muse, at BURNEY's side, / To lash unfeeling Wealth and stubborn Pride."

29. See William McCarthy, *Hester Thrale Piozzi: Portrait of a Literary Woman* (Chapel Hill, North Carolina, 1985), 16. Despite her admiration for Swift, in her retrospective view of the eighteenth century Hester Lynch Piozzi finds fault with him for being too hard on a female ignorance socially caused. Women such as Swift's character who chats on about her candles and dripping have merely been "disposed to keep in the sphere long assigned them." Piozzi does not, however, object to the more notorious poems on women, only remarking that "Swift tries to shock them [women] into cleanliness." See Piozzi, *Retrospection: or, A Review of the Most Striking and Important Events, Characters, Situations, and their Consequences, Which the Last Eighteen Hundred Years Have Presented to the View of Mankind*, 2 vols (London, 1801), 2:352.

30. *Three Dialogues by Hester Lynch Thrale*, edited by M. Zamick (Manchester, 1932), 23.

Jonathan Swift's Progress
from Prose to Poetry

Arthur H. Scouten

To describe the final phase of Jonathan Swift's career as an author, I propose to show that in the years 1729–31, his writings on the plight of Ireland diminished as he displayed a renewed interest in public affairs in England, he became increasingly concerned with his public image and with how posterity would remember him, this concern led to complications in his relationship with Alexander Pope, and he consciously turned to poetry as his chief form of literary expression.

To begin, I want to review the historical and biographical background. Between 1724 and 1726, Dean Swift moved from a victory over Sir Robert Walpole with the Drapier's letters to permanent fame with the publication of *Gulliver's Travels* and a reunion with Alexander Pope and his other friends in a triumphal visit to England. However, as in watching a Greek tragedy, we know that all victories had ended; in the future the Dean would experience only defeat. His negotiations with Walpole failed, and Sir Robert offset the brief display of Irish independence with a procedure by which all future vacancies in the Irish ecclesiastical hierarchy were filled with candidates loyal to Walpole and Archbishop Boulter. The accession of George II in 1727 confirmed Walpole in power. No one was going to help Ireland, though Swift incorrectly expected Queen Caroline to do so, and, in his prejudice, he considered Lady Suffolk to be false also. The culminating personal blow was the death of Esther Johnson, his beloved Stella, in January 1728. Then, as the years passed, an accumulation of grievances, disagreements, and cross-purposes affected his dealings with Pope.

To trace the gradual change from prose to verse, we might begin by considering Swift's writings in chronological order, a simple and revealing process which is seldom used because we lack a chronological ordering of the Swift canon. Sir Harold Williams, in his monumental edition of the poems, Herbert Davis, in the prose works, and the compilers of the bibliography all arranged the works by subject matter or other nonchronological categories. [1]

Reprinted from *The Poetry of Jonathan Swift: Papers Read at a Clark Library Seminar*, 1981, with the permission of the author and of the William Andrews Clark Memorial Library, University of California, Los Angeles.

Davis's one-volume edition of the poems, however, does present them in chronological order.[2]

About September 1725, Swift composed *A Humble Address to Both Houses of Parliament*. This essay contains proposals toward uniting Ireland, urging the Irish Parliament to behave as if it were independent and truly the representative of both the Protestants and the Catholics—an amazing suggestion for that day and age. The tract reflects optimism on Swift's part. J. Middleton Murry's account of this essay is probably the best part of his biography; of the Dean's proposals, he wrote, "the Irish people salute in him the prophet of an independent Ireland."[3]

Reading Swift's correspondence in the following years, we find this optimism replaced not so much by despair but by a variety of conflicting emotions: growing anger, disgust at the Irish, frustration, and irritability. To rely on any one quotation from Swift's letters is dangerous, as some biographers and critics have done in basing their conclusions on Swift's complaint to Bolingbroke, in his letter of 21 March 1730, that he would "die here in a rage, like a poisoned rat in a hole." In the letter which the Dean was answering, Bolingbroke was handing out some pontifical, philosophical generalizations of contempt of the world, saying, "whilst my mind grows daily more independant of the World . . . the Ideas of friendship return oftner" (3:358), at a time when we learn from the *DNB* that he was writing actively for *The Craftsman* and trying to arrange an alliance between Wyndham's Tories and Pulteney's Opposition Whigs. Bolingbroke's pretentiousness elicited Swift's anger and frustration over his own helplessness. Let us look at the entire extract: ". . . and so I would if I could get into a better [world, i.e., England] before I was called into the best, and not die here in a rage, like a poisoned rat in a hole. I wonder you are not ashamed to let me pine away in this kingdom while you are out of power" (3:383). Furthermore, George Sherburn has shown us that in March 1730 the Dean was enjoying an unusually full social life and was busily composing poems.[4]

A diminishing interest in prose after 1729 is easy to demonstrate, and the Dean signed off as an Irish patriot and as a prose writer with his brilliant tract *A Modest Proposal*, advertised on 8 November 1729. Earlier in this year he had composed six other essays but he did not have them printed. At the very end of the year, he wrote two more prose pieces but left them unpublished. In 1730, he made two trial starts toward a reply to Lord Allen, but did not complete them, and published only one pamphlet, *A Vindication of His Excellency Lord Carteret*; in 1731, he wrote two essays and published neither of them. In 1732, some pending legislation in the Irish Parliament on strictly ecclesiastical matters led Swift to write five short pamphlets, all of them printed, and he published three more tracts in 1733. In 1738, *Polite Conversation* was finally printed, but this amusing treatise had been largely composed around 1704, during Swift's stay in England (*Correspondence*, 4:31–32). *Directions to Servants* was at last published in 1745. Swift probably made some additions to it over the years, though its composition had also begun during his earlier years in England. The sum total of this publication record shows that Swift's chief concern was no longer with prose.[5] The explanation given by Bonamy Dobrée for this change is that Swift found "the medium of prose could not carry what he wanted to say."[6]

At the same time, the Dean's output in verse increased substantially. In 1728, he wrote thirteen poems; in 1729, eleven; in 1730, nineteen; and in 1731, thirteen, some of them being of considerable length. Of these, the significant feature is the change: (1) the Dean is now writing on public affairs in England, and (2) the quality has improved, with some of the poems displaying an imaginative power absent from his earlier verse.

Explanations of these changes contain evidence of both a self-conscious, purposeful shift to the medium of verse and a measure of accidental happenings. One example of Swift's new impulse toward verse comes from an episode in 1730, when he repeated a technique peculiar to his own methods of composition. Where Pope revised, rearranged, polished, and altered recalcitrant material, Swift's favorite method was to abandon an unpropitious draft and start all over again with an entirely different approach.[7] In 1707, Swift was disturbed by an attack on the authority and the fundamental doctrines of the Church of England in Matthew Tindal's *Rights of the Christian Church*, a treatise in which Tindal opposed the very idea of a national, state-supported church. There survive two drafts of replies by Swift, both of them turgid and verbose, each extending to about twenty pages in Herbert Davis's edition.[8] The first, *Remarks upon a Book, Intitled, The Rights of the Christian Church*, is an argumentative disputation. The second has the format familiar to those who have read seventeenth-century polemics: first comes a long quotation from Tindal's book, with page number, then a point by point refutation by Swift. However, he did not complete or revise either version, and he wrote Charles Ford that he had laid it aside. Instead, Swift started afresh and composed his famous essay *An Argument against the Abolishing of Christianity*.

Now I want to relate an episode which may at first sound as if I were summarizing a story by James Joyce. In the early spring of 1730, the Dublin City Council was preparing to honor Dean Swift by giving him the Freedom of the City in a gold box; however, Lord Allen objected vehemently and caused a delay. Swift then composed a prose narrative relating what had happened at the meeting of Lord Allen and the aldermen. This piece was followed by a new and different prose essay in which Swift wrote a lengthy vindication of himself, in a sober, serious style, in which he gave an account of all that he had done for Ireland, including an acknowledgment of the authorship of the Drapier's letters. The treatise is entitled *The Substance of What Was Said by the Dean on Receiving His Freedom*. He began by saying "he thought it became him to give some account of himself for above twenty years. . . ."[9] During that time, he said he had been a constant advocate of those who are called the Whigs and that he had saved two hundred families from ruin by lending them money. However, he never printed either of these two pieces. Instead, in April 1730, he composed a cheerfully libelous verse attack on Lord Allen and his ancestors, and instantly published it. In form it was a two-part, 158-line poem called *Traulus*. Thus, Swift had followed much the same procedure used many years earlier in his reply to Tindal. This time, though, instead of writing in prose as in the earlier instance, Swift finally turned to verse as his medium of expression. It so happens that *Traulus* is not a memorable piece, like the brilliant *Argument against the Abolishing of Christianity*, and Swift may have recognized that the poem had little artistic merit, for he deleted it from page proofs of the 1735 Faulkner edition. The fact that it is not a memorable poem does not, however, affect my contention that Swift was consciously shifting from prose to verse, and its very lack of merit may have concealed from Swift scholars that he was engaged in a change of medium.

Even stronger testimony of a self-conscious turn to poetry is the appearance of experiments in the heroic couplet. The entire body of Swift's verse is marked by metrical experiment. He had written a few poems in rhymed, pentameter couplets over the years, but from 1730 to July 1731 he composed five poems in the measure of the heroic couplet, as can be seen from the following table:

Title	Number of Lines	Date
St. Patrick's Well	102	ca. 1729–30
To a Friend	12	May 1730
On Stephen Duck	8	November 1730
To Mr. Gay	162	March 1731
On Mr. Pulteney	44	After 1 July 1731

Two of these are so short that they can be excluded from consideration, and a third has only 44 lines, but *St. Patrick's Well* has 102 and *To Mr. Gay*, 162. The metrical aspects of this longest venture, *To Mr. Gay*, afford a striking contrast to the prosody of Swift's other verse. The rhyming line is carefully end-stopped in most instances. The phrase in the second half of the line is balanced against the opening phrase, as in Pope's poems: "But princely *Douglas*, and his glorious Dame, / Advanc'd thy Fortune, and preserv'd thy Fame" (13–14). Unlike Swift's normal practice, the poem is stocked with poetic diction, with a heavy dependence upon adjectives: "trusty Servant," "shameless Visage, and perfidious Leer," "honest Care," "hasty Zeal," "subtle Knave," "lawful Perquisites"—the poetic diction of Thomson's *Seasons* and Pope's translation of the *Iliad*. The preponderance of adjectives is most unlike

Swift. His many poems are characterized by the absence of adjectives. In some of his other poems written in the same year, I find, on average, one adjective to every five lines. In his best poem, *Verses on the Death of Dr. Swift*, the average is one adjective to about four and a half lines of verse. Note the following passage from that poem:

> Here shift the Scene, to represent
> How those I love, my Death lament.
> Poor POPE will grieve a Month; and GAY
> A Week; and ARBUTHNOTT a Day.
>
> ST. JOHN himself will scarce forbear,
> To bite his Pen, and drop a Tear.
> The rest will give a Shrug and cry,
> I'm sorry; but we all must dye.
> Indifference clad in Wisdom's Guise,
> All Fortitude of Mind supplies:
> For how can stony Bowels melt,
> In those who never Pity felt;
> When *We* are lash'd, *They* kiss the Rod;
> Resigning to the Will of God.
>
> THE FOOLS, my Juniors by a Year,
> Are tortur'd with Suspence and Fear.
> Who wisely thought my Age a Screen,
> When Death approach'd, to stand between:
> The Screen remov'd, their Hearts are trembling,
> They mourn for me without dissembling.
>
> (205–24)

More statistical evidence is needed to make a full generalization, but I think I can say that Swift was sparing in his use of adjectives, in contrast to the usage of other authors. Consequently, the abundance of adjectives and the combination of adjective plus noun characteristic of eighteenth-century poetic diction show that Swift was consciously attempting the elevated style of the heroic couplet, a style then dominant in English poetry under the leadership of Alexander Pope.

However, neither the ambitious effort shown in *To Mr. Gay* nor the other four poems of this group resulted in any artistic merit. All of them were failures. It is only plausible to assume that Swift recognized that they were unsuccessful, and if so we have a clear explanation for his cessation of attempts in the heroic couplet. Nevertheless, the weakness of these verses does not contradict my thesis that the Dean was consciously attempting to write in the high style of Pope and that he was trying to establish himself as a serious poet rather than a witty versifier. I think I have a new point here, as none of the books on Swift's poetry call attention to this sustained effort in the heroic couplet. An author does not compose eighty-one rhymed, pentameter couplets (the 162 lines of *To Mr. Gay*) without knowing what form he is writing in.[10]

As harsh a critic as Swift was, it does seem plausible to assume that he realized he had spent considerable time and taken great pains in writing a number of unsuccessful poems in the measure of the heroic couplet. We may also note that two of the weakest ones—*To Mr. Gay* and *On Mr. Pulteney*—were written in 1731, just before Swift began composing *Verses on the Death of Dr. Swift* later in the same year. If we contemplate the strong possibility of his awareness of failure in the heroic couplet at this time, we might reread lines 47–52 of *Verses* in a new light:

> In Pope, I cannot read a Line,
> But with a Sigh, I wish it mine:
> When he can in one Couplet fix
> More Sense than I can do in Six:
> It gives me such a jealous Fit,
> I cry, Pox take him, and his Wit.

In reading the entire poem for the first time, we interpret these six lines as a witty and ironic compliment to Pope's poetic genius; on a second reading, with an awareness of the recent failures of *To Mr. Gay* and *On Mr. Pulteney* and with a recollection of the warning just six lines earlier that "Self-love, Ambition, Envy, Pride, / Their Empire in our Hearts divide" (41–42), we may find that we should read the passage literally.[11]

Together with evidence for the purposeful direction toward composition in verse, I want to relate an accidental occasion which led Swift not necessarily to poetry but to writing on public affairs in England. The occasion was provided by Swift's friend the Reverend Dr. Patrick Delany. Though Delany was a pluralist, holding three church offices, he lived extravagantly, far beyond his means. Late in 1729, he wrote a poem in which he made a direct, open appeal to Lord Carteret, Lord Lieutenant of Ireland, for ecclesiastical promotion. As we all know, clergymen in the regime of Sir Robert Walpole obtained preferment by staunchly supporting the government line, dancing attendance upon the great, penning toadying dedications, and flattering every nobleman in sight. Nevertheless, an overt request for promotion was bad form, and Sheridan led the young Dublin collegians in ridiculing and denouncing poor Delany. Swift even joined in the fun with a comical piece called *An Epistle upon an Epistle*. Delany was dreadfully upset, and Swift wrote Pope that the young fellows had pestered Delany too harshly. In February 1730, the Dean took goose quill in hand and in his favorite octosyllabic couplets but without his customary raillery, "made an impassioned attack on the whole tribe of politicians" and the entire patronage system in the

British Isles, in a poem generally called *A Libel on Dr. Delany*.[12] It is one of the most vigorous works Swift ever wrote, said Sir Harold Williams, "and only upon second thoughts did the government decide to ignore it." In fact, Swift wrote Pope that Lord Allen had moved for a prosecution. Almost by accident, Swift had turned to writing on public affairs. I might add that in one section of the poem Swift had praised Pope for his political independence, an innocent and accidental stroke which came just at the time when Pope was making friendly gestures toward Walpole and the court. As I will show later in this paper, Pope was offended and excluded the poem from the *Miscellanies* of 1732, whereupon Swift was offended by this omission.[13] Swift himself said that *A Libel on Dr. Delany* was "the best thing I writt as I think."[14]

After this recital of material quite familiar to Swift scholars, I think I have a new point to offer: I want to lay before you for your consideration the suggestion that the strongest single stimulus for Swift to write major works in verse came from Lord Bathurst, an Opposition leader and friend to Pope. On 9 September 1730, he sent Swift a remarkable letter. It is witty, but more important for our purposes here it employs Swift's techniques of raillery through praise-by-blame. He attacks the Dean's writing severely: he can't find any "pretty flowers" or "just antitheses" or any clever puns or "apt quotations out of Latin Authors wch the writers of the last Age amongst us abounded in." "I'll take y^r works to Pieces," says Bathurst, "& show y^u that it is all borrow'd or stoln, have not y^u stoln the sweetness of y^r Numbers [i.e., versification] from Dryden & Waller, have not y^u borrow'd thoughts from Virgil & Horace. . . ." He then complains that the Dean has set "Kingdoms in a Flame" by his pen. On reading Swift's works, he reports that his brain has heated his imagination, "fir'd just as if I was drunk." Then comes his cleverest stroke: "a Pretty thing indeed for one of y^r Gown to value Himself upon, that with sitting still an hour in his study he has often made three Kingdoms drunk at once."[15]

Circumstances in 1730 should have made such sharp badinage strike Swift with special force. Arresting enough, it came from an unexpected quarter, not from Pope or Gay, Swift's wittiest correspondents, from whom in fact Swift was receiving letters couched in far less wit. Instead, the author was a relatively new correspondent, Bathurst, whom we remember today less as a wit in his own right than as a friend and patron of wits. Twenty years before, in London, Swift and the wealthy young Bathurst had clubbed together—both belonged to the Society of "brothers"—but since Queen Anne's death they had had little or no contact beyond a probable visit by Swift in 1726 and possibly another in 1727 (*Correspondence*, 3:136, 221). Their correspondence had begun only seven months earlier, and it did not come about because either man had literary business with the other. They began writing for far more mundane reasons: Swift had left with Gay some funds which were now deposited with Bathurst.[16] In effect, here was Swift's

banker sending him smarter and more elaborate literary compliments than
even Pope or Gay did—compliments in the peculiarly Swiftian strain to
which Swift himself appears to have been most susceptible. In his biography,
Lord Orrery indicates that Swift could be easily flattered, that he was "open
to adulation." In reply, Delany disputes the point as Orrery puts it, and
denies that Swift was vulnerable to gross flattery, but he concedes that the
Dean was susceptible to ironic praise—"*not insensible to delicate praise.*"[17]

Events make clear how strongly the Dean was struck by Bathurst's
flattering raillery, with its implications that Swift must rank with the greatest
poets (and political writers as well). And what a challenge the letter implies:
if a mere Bathurst can invent such clever Swiftian badinage, how much better
should Swift achieve! Normally Swift delayed weeks or even months before
answering some correspondents, but he answered Bathurst's letter immediately, in October. The reply is one of the longest letter he ever wrote. In
tone, Swift's answer seems to waver between doubt and pleasure: pleasure
that Bathurst has written so cleverly and agreeably, doubt that he can
compose an adequate reply and measure up to the character which Bathurst
has given him. Of the two, the doubting element seems the stronger. I can't
recall another passage where Swift is so clearly on the defensive. He writes,
"I swear your Lordship is the first person alive that ever made me lean upon
my Elbow when I was writing to him. . . ." Then, "I have never been so
severely attacked, nor in so tender a point, nor by weapons against which I
am so ill able to defend myself . . ." (3:410). One can of course argue that
Swift was not at all affected by Bathurst's letter and that he was only replying
in kind. However, other evidence can be found in the letter: "I have endorsed
yʳ name & date, and shall leave it to my Executors to be published at the
head of all the libells that have been writ against me, to be printed in five
Volumes in folio after my death" (ibid.). Do we not have here the imaginative
germ of *Verses on the Death of Dr. Swift*, on which the Dean began work
during the following year? Acting upon this notion, let us go back and look
at an earlier sentence in the letter: "I pretend to have been an improver of
Irony . . . but I will surrender up my title to your Lordship" (ibid.). This
is the first draft of lines 55–58 of *Verses*, where the name Arbuthnot will be
substituted for Bathurst.

> ARBUTHNOT is no more my Friend,
> Who dares to Irony pretend;
> Which I was born to introduce,
> Refin'd it first, and shew'd its Use.

Swift's reply was, as I said, in October 1730. A chronological list of
his poems for the following year yields a total of thirteen. The first two are
the ones in heroic couplets mentioned earlier: *To Mr. Gay* and *On Mr.
Pulteney*, four of the so-called scatological pieces—*The Lady's Dressing Room*,

A Beautiful Young Nymph, Strephon and Chloe, and *Cassinus and Peter*—five other poems of varying lengths, and two of his best works: *Verses on the Death of Dr. Swift* and *The Day of Judgement*. The Dean has now completely shifted from being a prose writer to a poet.

After I concluded that Lord Bathurst's letter may have provided the final impetus in turning Swift's mind toward poetry, I naturally turned to the scholarship to ascertain whether I had been anticipated. To the extent that I have examined the secondary literature, I find no one else making this suggestion. Mrs. Nora C. Jaffe does say, "More than his other friends, Lord Bathurst overwhelms Swift with praise of his poetry," but she says no more than this.[18]

Years ago, I concluded from several exchanges on the topic of fame in the correspondence of Swift, Pope, and Bolingbroke that Swift may have purposely turned to poetry toward the end of his career in order to present a "public image" for posterity. Most of us are sensitive to anachronisms, and I hope you will not object to my use of this modern term. For justification, let me read from Pope's letter to Swift of February 1727: "Our Miscellany is now quite printed. I am prodigiously pleas'd with this joint-volume, in which methinks we look like friends, side by side, serious and merry by turns, conversing interchangeably, and walking down hand in hand to posterity. . . ." (3:201). This statement and Pope's known revisions of his letters for publication certainly permit me to use the term "public image."

These exchanges to which I refer occurred in 1725 and again from the summer of 1729 into the winter of 1730. In the earlier period, Pope explained his plans for future poems and said he would write a "Set of Maximes in opposition to all Rochefoucaults Principles" (3:108). In reply, Swift mentions Pope's plans, but calls Rochefoucault his favorite and announces he will read him again (3:118). Later Bolingbroke returns to this topic: "You Poets . . . teach our Self Love to anticipate the applause which we Suppose will be pay'd by posterity to our names, and with idle notions of immortality you turn other heads besides your own" (3:349). Swift replied in October 1729, saying that he thinks about death all the time, but he wants fame in his own lifetime, rather than for posterity, so that people will seek him out, but a desire for fame after death arises from "the Spirit and folly of youth" (3:355). In an exchange with Pope, Swift implies that Pope has visions of epistolary fame, but Pope's invoking of Montaigne's letters is erroneous, for if Montaigne had been writing for fame his letters would not have been written naturally. Pliny's letters, Swift added, were written with a view to publicity, "and I accuse Voiture himself of the same crime, although he be an Author I am fond of" (3:373). In another letter, Bolingbroke stated that we enjoy Cicero's letters more than those of Pliny, Seneca, and Voiture because their letters were written with a view to circulation, whereas Cicero's were not (3:388).

Care must be taken in assessing these various views concerning literary immortality, as Swift may very well have been teasing Pope and Bolingbroke, especially the latter. Nevertheless, Swift had indicated his desire that Pope dedicate a verse epistle to him. Then, all the jockeying that went on for years over the gathering and the publication of Swift's and Pope's letters illustrates the concern both men felt about presenting a public image for posterity. Basically, both men wanted to advertise their partnership and celebrate their friendship with each other, but their ultimate objects differed. The Swift-Pope *Letters* of 1740–41 represents the result of a process which, if Swift had had his way, would have ended in something quite different, a verse epistle by Pope inscribed to Swift. In a word, Swift wanted to be celebrated in the dignity of heroic couplets—by implication a literary as well as a personal tribute from the leading poet of the age—whereas Pope now wished to establish his own credentials not as a great poet but as a good-hearted individual, a warm and loving friend revealed not through polished verse but the self-consciously "artless" vehicle of his prose letters to Swift, full as they are of treacly professions of virtue, friendship, and unworldliness.[19] Pope plays this role in his letter to Swift of 28 November 1729, when he hints at publication of their correspondence: "I smile to think how Curl would be bit, were our Epistles to fall into his hands, and how gloriously they would fall short of every ingenious reader's expectations?" (3:363). Later, Swift began to counter such hints with requests that Pope *orna me*, that is, that Pope inscribe a verse epistle to him.[20] The two men were at cross-purposes because Swift was thinking of a literary public image while Pope thought of his *personal* "public image." Furthermore, if Swift was becoming more interested in his permanent ranking in English literature, he may very well have been thinking in terms of the classical and Renaissance traditions of the status of the received poet and hence planning to compose some "serious" poetry. Pope had already achieved an enviable public image as England's greatest poet, in the full traditional sense of the term. At least in the public eye, Pope was a man who might bear comparison with Waller and Dryden or with Virgil and Horace, to recall the terms of Bathurst's flattery to Swift. Here too was a man so concerned with his public image, and so skilled in fine-tuning it, that we can hardly discuss some of his greatest work, such as the *Epistle to Arbuthnot*, without constantly referring to it. It may be no coincidence that Pope figures more and more heavily in Swift's story after 1726: as Swift's literary agent in London and Swift's literary confidant in their correspondence; as Swift's celebrated friend and partner in the *Miscellanies*, wherein posterity could see the two "conversing interchangeably, and walking down hand in hand"; as Swift's model for his unsuccessful efforts at rhymed pentameters in the heroic style; as the celebrated poet who would dignify his brother Swift by inscribing a verse epistle to him. In tracing the course of the two friends' association, including the cross-purposes which sometimes arose between them in view of Pope's different goals, we can catch glimpses of Swift's new concern with verse and public image.

Before I present my final section of evidence that Swift was purposely shifting from prose to poetry, I need to make a parenthetical statement about trends and vogues in Swift scholarship. For most of the nineteenth century and through the first thirty years of the twentieth century, Swift was generally under attack. Nineteenth-century views on Progress and on man's natural goodness led to abuse and vilification of the Dean. In the academic world as late as thirty years ago, a promising young graduate student who elected to specialize in Swift was treated in a condescending manner. As a result, Swift scholars banded together to resist hostile criticism, and fiercely beat down any publications which insinuated that Swift was not always telling the truth in his letters, that he acted in a brutal way toward some of his friends, that he might have been the offspring of Sir John Temple, or that Esther Johnson might have been the child of Sir William Temple. Irvin Ehrenpreis's refusal to confront such traditions concerning Swift and Stella (in his biography of Swift) documents what I have just been saying. However, the two world wars have sufficiently revived Swift's reputation to a point where I think this role of protective silence is no longer obligatory.

What I am alluding to is that modern specialists in this period have long known that a rift developed in the Swift-Pope amity but have refrained from discussing this situation. The earliest sign of disaffection came from Pope's general conduct in editing the Pope-Swift *Miscellanies*, particularly the volume called "the Last," in which he had inserted very little from his own works, reserving some completed poems for future publication.[21] When it appeared that not enough material had been gathered to fill the volume, Swift wrote Sheridan from Twickenham (where he was visiting Pope) for copies of the various verses to Stella. When the volume appeared, in March 1728, it contained six of the birthday poems to Stella. However, Pope supposedly told Delany that he wished the poems had never been written.[22] Yet upon the news of Stella's death (in January), Pope could have excluded these poems but he did not do so.

Real difficulty seems to have begun with Pope's reception of Swift's *A Libel on Dr. Delany*, in which the Dean had praised Pope for his independence, saying: "Hail! happy *Pope*, whose gen'rous Mind, / Detesting all the Statesmen kind, / Contemning *Courts*, at *Courts* unseen . . ." (71–73). The timing was most unfortunate, for as George Sherburn points out Pope was on better terms with the court than at any other time in his career.[23] In fact, a few months after Swift composed these lines, Pope had indeed visited Walpole. As a consequence, Pope was immediately vulnerable to charges of hypocrisy and duplicity. He protested at once to Fortescue, a supporter of Walpole.[24]

Difficulties raised by Pope's editorial methods and by his embarrassment over *A Libel on Dr. Delany* came to a head with the publication of the final, yet called "the Third" volume of the *Miscellanies* in 1732. To begin with, Pope was looking at the commercially profitable aspects of publication and was negotiating with Lawton Gilliver, whereas Swift preferred to continue with his old publisher, Motte. In this volume, Pope included several prose pieces which Swift had disowned, he inserted only a small amount of his own work, so that three-fourths of the verse was by Swift, yet even so he omitted A *Libel on Dr. Delany*, in spite of Swift's instructions. It is clear that Pope paid little attention to Swift's feelings. The Dean was especially aggrieved by the deletion of the Delany poem, and he dropped strong hints that Dublin publishers might be found who would be willing to print his works. However, when Swift did eventually turn to Faulkner as his choice for publisher, Pope became alarmed and protested.[25] The continuing correspondence between Swift and Pope becomes evasive on details and ambiguous in tone.

Swift was clearly nursing some resentments. On 22 July 1732, he assigned his "rights" in a number of essays and poems to the young clergyman Matthew Pilkington, and instructed him to use William Bowyer as his publisher, with further instructions to print A *Libel on Dr. Delany*, together with some other pieces. Pilkington and Bowyer were too slow, and Motte and Gilliver forestalled the plan by bringing out "the Third" volume of the *Miscellanies*. Sir Harold William's conclusion is that Swift hoped "to checkmate Pope . . . and regain control over the publication of his writings."[26]

Continuing subterfuge in the correspondence and juggling with publishers suggest that Swift came to suspect Pope of maintaining his own literary preeminence at the Dean's expense, of being overly concerned with the financial rewards of publication, and of being envious of the literary fame of other writers. Reliable, external testimony on these points is difficult to find. Laetitia Pilkington does report that Swift became very angry at her accidental discovery of friction between himself and Pope.[27] The accuracy of Mrs. Pilkington's *Memoirs* is sharply disputed by Swift specialists however. When Mrs. Pilkington was imprisoned for debt, she was extricated by Colley Cibber, who aided her financially.[28] She must have been grateful to Cibber, and we know what Cibber's views of Pope were. Nevertheless, there is an ironic passage in a letter from Swift to Pope of 11 August 1729, soon after Gay's financial bonanza from *The Beggar's Opera*, in which Gay's supposed greed for money is contrasted against Pope's disinterest in finance.[29] Since everyone agrees that John Gay was a simpleton in financial matters, Swift's statement suggests an awareness of Pope's concern with temporal gain.

I do not want to get into the labyrinth of the publication history of the Pope-Swift letters. Instead, I am alluding to that publication history only for the purpose of drawing off the information that as early as 1729 Jonathan Swift was aware of Pope's intention to publish these letters, and that this awareness may have led Swift to thinking about his own public image, to thoughts of competing against Pope and possibly of achieving recognition as a poet. Otherwise, I am not interested in pursuing the topic of difficulties arising between Swift and Pope, nor am I making any hint or suggestion that their strong friendship had ended. They were indeed at cross-purposes over the publication of their letters and over the publication history of the *Miscellanies*, 1727–32, but their friendship was not terminated. The best statement I have seen on this matter was made by Archibald C. Elias, who said, "A touch of friction is natural between two brilliant and strong-willed friends."[30]

Having made this disclaimer, I want to resume my presentation of evidence arising from this friction between Swift and Pope as it bears on my topic of the Dean's shift from prose to poetry. Sometime after Mrs. Laetitia Pilkington met and got into the good graces of the Dean, he set her to work at pasting letters from correspondents into a letter book and permitted her to read the letters, whereupon she relates the following story:

> I could not avoid remarking to the Dean, that notwithstanding the Friendship Mr. *Pope* professed for Mr. *Gay*, he could not forbear a great many satirical, or, if I may be allowed to say so, envious Remarks on the Success of the *Beggar's Opera*. The Dean very frankly owned, he did not think Mr. *Pope* was so candid to the Merits of other Writers, as he ought to be. I then ventured to ask the Dean, whether he thought the Lines Mr. *Pope* addresses him with, in the Beginning of the *Dunciad*, were any Compliment to him? *viz.*
>
> > O *thou! whatever Title please thine Ear.*
> > [Dean, Drapier, Bickerstaff, or Gulliver]
> > Dunciad.
>
> "I believe, says he, they were meant as such; but they are very stiff"— "Indeed, Sir, said I, he is so perfectly a Master of harmonious Number, that had his Heart been the least affected with his Subject, he must have writ better"; "How cold, how forced, are his Lines to you, compared with yours to him":
> > **Hail happy* Pope, *whose generous Mind.*
>
> **See *Swift's* Libel on Lord Carteret.[31]

Support for Mrs. Pilkington's anecdote appears in Swift's poem *A Panegyrick on the Dean, in the Person of a Lady in the North* (1730).

> Ye Hawkers all, your Voices lift;
> A Panegyrick on D[ea]n S{wift}.
> And then, to mend the Matter still;
> By Lady *Anne* of *Market-Hill.*
>
> I thus begin. My grateful Muse
> Salutes the D[ea]n in diff'rent Views;
> Dean, Butler, Usher, Jester, Tutor. . . .
> (33–39)

Let us return to Pope's invocation in book 1 of his *Dunciad*: "O thou! whatever title please thine ear, Dean, Drapier, Bickerstaff, or Gulliver!" (1730 ed., 19–20). Swift has certainly written a parody. Nor can we consider it a "throwaway" line in the poem, for line 39 presents the organizing principle of Swift's *A Panegyrick*. The verse paragraphs in this poem are arranged to begin with and to describe first "the Dean," then "the Butler," "the Usher," "the Jester," and "the Tutor." Besides, parody was Jonathan Swift's favorite technique for retaliation; any survey of his writings will show that when he disliked something or thought something ridiculous, he composed a parody of it. Some nuances need to be observed here. I am not saying that Swift disliked Pope or the above couplet from the *Dunciad*. Instead, much of my previous discussion has been intended to show that Swift had been concerned with his public image, and, in this instance, is dissatisfied with Pope's tribute because, as Swift's parody suggests, it is only a compendium of comic characters. I might add that I have searched in vain through Swift scholarship and have not yet found any recognition of this parody, and I am confident that I have never seen anyone connect the parody with Mrs. Pilkington's anecdote. The question now arises whether Swift ever engaged in any other parody of Pope's verse. One other example does come to mind, in Swift's *Directions for a Birth-day Song*:

> A skilfull Critick justly blames
> Hard, tough, cramp, gutt'rall, harsh, stiff
> Names.
> The Sense can ne're be too jejune,
> But smooth your words to fit the tune. . . .
> (209–12)

Is not Swift here parodying lines 364–73 of Pope's *Essay on Criticism?*

Another parody of Pope, in *A Love Song in the Modern Taste*, has been suggested by Maurice Johnson, who writes, "It has not hitherto been noted that these final stanzas resemble lines from Pope, to whom the poem has sometimes been attributed":[32]

> Melancholly smooth *Meander*,
> Swiftly purling in a Round,
> On thy Margin Lovers wander,
> With thy flow'ry Chaplets crown'd.
> (25–28)

What happened when Swift made his shift from prose to verse? The most significant answer is that he was generally successful; in these years he composed a number of poems of high artistic merit: *The Day of Judgement, On Poetry: A Rapsody, Epistle to a Lady, The Legion Club,* and *Verses on the Death of Dr. Swift*, to name the very best ones. His late poems appear to fall into three categories: (1) the so-called scatological verse, (2) autobiographical poems, and (3) satiric verse on public themes. Of these, what is new? The first group is entirely new, his previous poems on the relation of the sexes were either humorous, like *Cadenus and Vanessa*, or didactic, like *Phillis, or, The Progress of Love*. Autobiographical poems were not a new venture, as *The Author upon Himself* and several imitations of Horace were written back in 1713–14; there are just more of them.

He had also written poems on public affairs dating as far back as the odes during his residence at Sir William Temple's and continuing on down through the years. But the new verse in this category is entirely different in tone from both his prose and his poetry of previous years. In his writings before 1729, Swift gives the impression that something can be done; the indignation appears constructive. From the early *Discourse of the Contests and Dissensions* (1701), *The Project for the Advancement of Religion* (1709), *The Conduct of the Allies* (1712), down through *Gulliver's Travels* (1726), and in numerous poems throughout those years, we find practical proposals. But beginning with *A Modest Proposal* (1729) and continuing through the poetry written after that date, we encounter a spectrum of conflicting attitudes markedly different from those of his previous work: cynicism, irritability modulating at times into sheer rage, frustration, the glee of reckless railing, or simple indifference toward the kinds of vaguely altruistic, limited political goals for which he had previously aimed. The word *despair* would not accurately describe these conflicting attitudes. He abandoned constructive political prose in favor of poetry, both the dignified kind and the reckless (politically and scatologically). In *Epistle to a Lady*, he writes: "(Tho' it must be understood, / I would hang them if I cou'd:)" (169–70) and in *On Poetry: A Rapsody*:

> But now go search all Europe round
> Among yᵉ savage Monsters crown'd
> With Vice polluting every Throne
> (I mean all Kings except our own,)
> In vain you make yᵉ strictest View
> To find a King in all yᵉ Crew,
> With whom a Footman out of Place
> Wou'd not conceive a high disgrace
> A burning Shame, a crying Sin
> To take, his mornings Cup of Gin.[33]

Nor can I claim any consistency in the attitudes reflected in the late poems. Instead, we can see a disparity between Swift's desire to upgrade his public image for posterity, building an impressive and respectable literary representation of himself, and what appears to be an equally strong impulse toward the reckless, e.g., *The Legion Club* and the scatological poems. He seems by turns hag-ridden by conflicting impulses, toward immortality on one hand and the gratification of his cynicism and love of shocking people on the other. My conclusions would have been simpler had I omitted such reflections, but I fear that they would have been less accurate without this tangled web.

Finally, what effect did Swift's progress from proseman to poet have on his literary reputation? The immediate result was to enhance it. *Verses on the Death of Dr. Swift* went through eleven editions in 1739, the year it appeared, for example. In my work on the Swift bibliography, I found five pirated editions in later years. Swift was accepted as a poet, and Oliver Goldsmith called *On Poetry: A Rapsody* "one of the best versified poems in our language," high praise in view of the importance attached to meter in those days.[34] The Dean's status as a poet continued until the beginning of the nineteenth century, when it fell off sharply. The last praise from an important source came from Byron, who said that Swift "beats us all hollow, his rhymes are wonderful."[35]

The Dean's standing in the world of literature then reverted to that of a major prose writer. *A Tale of a Tub* and *Gulliver's Travels* were considered classics, even when the ideas and tone were attacked, but Swift was rejected from the company of poets. The situation in the nineteenth century was not one in which he was called a mediocre, or minor, or even a third-rate poet, but one in which he was not accepted as a poet at all. The explanation for this odd treatment arises from the prevailing theories of poetry at the time, clearly expressed by Hippolyte Taine. This literary historian was one of the few scholars who had read *Verses on the Death of Dr. Swift*, though in a bad text. In his analysis of *Verses,* Taine said that he could not consider Swift as a poet because "All poetry exalts the mind, but this [poem] depresses it; instead of concealing reality, it unveils it; instead of creating illusions, it removes them."[36] Here Taine is presenting the doctrine that poetry should be uplifting, a theory which would make a masterpiece out of Edmund Waller's poem *The Girdle.* As we often have difficulty in finding the basic assumptions underlying poetic theory in older periods of literature, Taine's statements are most helpful; I don't see where a clearer definition could be found: poetry must be inspirational and it must create illusions. It is interesting to observe how close F. R. Leavis was to Taine, though writing seventy-one years later, in 1934, when he describes Swift's poetry as "the most remarkable expression of negative feelings and attitudes that literature can offer."[37] In 1946, John Crowe Ransom wrote Maurice Johnson that Swift's poetry "wasn't worth the reading."[38]

More recently, the term *anti-poetic* has come to be applied to Swift's verse. In 1965, E. San Juan characterized Swift's poetic achievement as "the sense of the immediate, the acute responsiveness to concrete actuality, the energetic control exercised over elements of immediate sensory experience so as to organize them into a harmonious structure of meanings."[39] He proceeds to label this achievement as "anti-poetic," and he asserts that Wallace Stevens was the first to define this term, saying that it signified "that truth, that reality to which all of us are forever fleeing."[40]

The rehabilitation of Swift's poetry began, slowly, after the First World War, partly as a result of a harsher estimate of man's condition replacing the cult of Progress, and partly as a reaction against romanticism. Possibly the first modern critic to justify Swift's poetry was an Englishman named Edgell Rickword. I don't think this fact is generally known.[41] A young poet, wounded in the European War, Rickword was a Marxist critic and later editor of the *Left Review*, and also author of a good book on Rimbaud. In 1925, together with several other critics, Rickword founded a literary journal called *The Calendar of Modern Letters*, in which he frequently directed the reader's attention to the achievement of Swift's poetry. In the opening issue, he prefaced his remarks on Swift by saying: "An effect of the triumph of the romantic movement in the last century has been to separate the poet from the subjects which abound in ordinary social life and particularly from those emotions engendered by the clash of personality and the hostility of circumstances."[42] As a result, continues Rickword, poetry has become more and more limited, subjective, and withdrawn, to the point that the ordinary modern reader of literature judges poetry as "sloppy." Against this situation, Swift's verse is an antidote. However, I will not quote further from Rickword's detailed critique, as I wish only to call attention to his primacy in the rediscovery of Swift as a poet.

Much of the revival of Swift's poetry comes from the scholarly edition in 1937 by Sir Harold Williams, who applied himself to the real problems of the text and the canon. A considerable number of obscene poems had become attached to Swift's works, and much scholarly work had to be done to reject these accretions from the canon. An authentic text was needed for some of the poems. The best example concerns *Verses on the Death of Dr. Swift*. One of the reasons why modern readers are presently finding this poem so exciting is that it has not accumulated a patina of interpretative criticism (even though such an overlay is now developing): that is, Coleridge, Arnold, Saintsbury, T. S. Eliot, and even Cleanth Brooks and Robert Penn Warren had never read this poem. What happened was that editors in the nineteenth century and down to 1937 had printed a 545-line amalgam of Swift's poem interspersed with 62 lines from another poem by Swift which had originally been inserted by Pope, dropped to notes by Sir Walter Scott, and then reintroduced into the text by later editors, a hopeless mishmash.[43] Once Sir Harold had provided an authentic text, scholars and critics alike recognized a major poetic work, even though there has yet been no agreement on its meaning, another sign, I suppose, of its poetic merit.[44]

Notes

1. The following editions of Swift's writings have been used and are referred to in the text in abbreviated form: *Correspondence*, ed. Harold Williams, 5 vols. (Oxford: Clarendon Press, 1963–65)—citations are to volume and page; *Poems*, ed. Harold Williams, 2d ed., 3 vols. (Oxford: Clarendon Press, 1958)—citations are to line numbers; Prose Works, ed. Herbert Davis et al., 14 vols. (Oxford: Basil Blackwell, 1939–68); *A Bibliography of the Writings of Jonathan Swift*, comp. H. Teerink, 2d ed., rev. by Arthur H. Scouten (Philadelphia: University of Pennsylvania Press, 1963).

2. *Poetical Works*, ed. Herbert Davis (London: Oxford University Press, 1967).

3. *Jonathan Swift: A Critical Biography* (London: Jonathan Cape, 1954), 383.

4. "Methods in Books about Swift," *Studies in Philology* 35 (1938): 635–56.

5. This paragraph is abstracted from Davis's introd. to vol. 12 of *Prose Works*.

6. *English Literature in the Early Eighteenth Century, 1700–1740* (Oxford: Clarendon Press, 1959), 465.

7. See George Sherburn, "Pope at Work," *Essays on the Eighteenth Century Presented to David Nichol Smith in Honour of His Seventieth Birthday* (Oxford: Clarendon Press, 1945), 49–64.

8. *Prose Works*, 2:65–107.

9. Ibid., 12:146–47.

10. I hasten to add that there is no hint of burlesque in *St. Patrick's Well* or *To Mr. Gay*, always a possibility in Swift's writings.

11. For a full reading of this poem, see Arthur H. Scouten and Robert D. Hume, "Pope and Swift: Text and Interpretation of Swift's Verses on His Death," *Philological Quarterly* 52 (1973): 205–31. I do not agree with Claude Rawson's reading of these six lines in *TLS*, 10 February 1978, 165.

12. *Poems*, 2:474–99, from which my whole account is taken.

13. *Correspondence*, 3:382.

14. Ibid., 4:83.

15. Ibid., 3: 406–8; quotations on 407.

16. Ibid., 3:287, 305, 324, 357, 371–72, 376.

17. John Boyle, Fifth Earl of Cork and Orrery, *Remarks on the Life and Writings of Dr. Jonathan Swift* (London, 1752), 5; Patrick Delany, *Observations upon Lord Orrery's Remarks on the Life and Writings of Dr. Jonathan Swift* (London, 1754), 15.

18. *The Poet Swift* (Hanover, N.H.: University Press of New England, 1977), 58.

19. See James A. Winn, *A Window in the Bosom: The Letters of Alexander Pope* (Hamden, Conn.: Archon Books, 1977).

20. See *Correspondence*, 4:116–17, 335, 471, 476–77, 547.

21. See Harold Williams's introd., *Poems*, 1:xx–xxii.

22. Delany, *Observations*, 103.

23. *The Correspondence of Alexander Pope*, 5 vols. (Oxford: Clarendon Press, 1956), 3:90n.

24. Ibid., 91.

25. Swift, *Correspondence*, 5:257.

26. *Poems*, 1:xxvi–xxviii.

27. *Memoirs of Mrs. Laetitia Pilkington*, vol. 1 (Dublin pr., London repr., 1748), 75–77, 129–33.

28. See Phillip S. Y. Sun, "Swift's Eighteenth-Century Biographers" (Ph.D. diss., Yale University, 1963), 10. I am obliged to Archibald C. Elias, Jr., for this citation.

29. *Correspondence*, 3:340–42.

30. In his "Jonathan Swift and Letter-Writing: The Natural and the Playful in His Personal Correspondence" (Ph.D. diss., Yale University, 1973), p. 178, n. 83.

31. *Memoirs,* 75–76; Mrs. Pilkington means *A Libel on Dr. Delany.*

32. *The Sin of Wit: Jonathan Swift as a Poet* (Syracuse, N.Y,: Syracuse University Press, 1950), 99. Johnson refers to *The Rape of the Lock,* canto 5, lines 65–66: "Thus on Meander's flow'ry margin lies / The expiring swan. . . ."

33. Lines 9–18 of the text in the Orrery papers; see Davis, *Poetical Works*, 584.

34. *The Beauties of English Poesy,* 2 vols. (London, 1767), 1:175.

35. As quoted in Ernest J. Lovell, Jr., ed., *His Very Self and Voice: Collected Conversations of Lord Byron* (New York: Macmillan Co., 1954), 268.

36. *History of English Literature*, trans. N. Van Laun, 2 vols. (New York: William L. Allison, 1895), 2:175–77; quotation on 176. The original French ed. was published in Paris, 1863.

37. F. R. Leavis, "The Irony of Swift," *Scrutiny* 2 (1934): 377.

38. In a letter shown me by Maurice Johnson.

39. E. San Juan, Jr., "The Anti-Poetry of Jonathan Swift," *Philological Quarterly* 44 (1965): 387–96; quotation on 387.

40. As quoted by San Juan, 389, from *The Necessary Angel: Essays on Reality and the Imagination* (New York: Knopf, 1951), 25.

41. See C. H. Sisson's introd. to Jonathan Swift, *Selected Poems* (Manchester: Carcanet New Press, 1977), 14–15.

42. Edgell Rickword, *Essays and Opinions, 1921–1931*, ed., Alan Young (Cheadle, Cheshire: Carcanet New Press, 1974), 170–75, 203, 245–46.

43. See Scouten and Hume, "Pope and Swift," 205–11.

44. I should like to acknowledge my indebtedness to Archibald C. Elias, Jr., for his advice and suggestions during the preparation of this paper.

Why the Houyhnhnms Don't Write:
Swift, Satire and the Fear of the Text

Terry J. Castle

The Houyhnhnms have no system of writing. When Gulliver transcribes Houyhnhnm words into English in his "Master's Presence," the horse is puzzled. "It cost me much trouble to explain to him what I was doing; for the inhabitants have not the least idea of Books or Literature" (Bk. 4, ch. 3, p. 190).[1] This absence is not due, as one might expect, to the fact that the Houyhnhnms are hooved creatures. In Chapter 9, two paragraphs after noting again their lack of "Letters," Gulliver is careful to tell us that the Houyhnhnms can "do all the work which requires Hands" (Bk. 4, ch. 9, p. 221), including the threading of needles. Clearly a point is being made here. As on so many occasions in *Gulliver's Travels*, however, we may feel it is an enigmatic one. Is the Houyhnhnms' lack of writing, as Gulliver's chapter note suggests, part of a "Defectiveness of their Language" (Bk. 4, ch. 9, p. 218)? But Swift has severely undermined our sense of Gulliver's reliability by this point in Book 4: is the satirist really intending to present the absence of script as good? Is it a necessary feature of the Houyhnhnms' ideal community? Grammaphobia, or fear of the written word, is at least potential within the Swiftian text.

The Nambikwara have no system of writing. In *Tristes Tropiques*—a record, like *Gulliver's Travels*, of voyages to strange lands—Lévi-Strauss presents us with a transformation of the scene between Gulliver and his Master. When the Nambikwara chief first sees the anthropologist making field notes, he, too, is puzzled. Unlike the dispassionate Houyhnhnm, however, the chief immediately demands pencil and paper and begins to imitate this act of writing. Subsequently, he uses the scribbles he has made to mystify his fellow tribesmen: he threatens them with his own version of the anthropologist's magic. Lévi-Strauss, because he is a scientist and not a satirist, can make an explicit comment on all of this; he explicates the parable. It reminds us, he says, of the sinister ease with which writing can be alienated from its ostensible signification. Because of its incontrovertible presence as object, its semantic function may be co-opted by a sociological

Reprinted from *Essays in Literature* 7, no. 1 (1980): 31–44. Permission to reprint granted by Western Illinois University.

one. The written artifact, utterly voided of meaning, nevertheless retains an oppressive, disruptive effect on the human community. Writing "had been borrowed as a symbol. . . . It had not been a question of acquiring knowledge, of remembering or understanding, but rather of increasing the authenticity and prestige of one individual—or function—at the expense of others." The Nambikwara fall into the world of writing: with the discovery of the text in its most arbitrary and superstitious form, a kind of tyranny is instituted and natural personal relations are subverted. For the anthropologist, writing is thus always a pernicious addition to culture, precisely because its significatory function is so quickly betrayed by circumstance: "the primary function of written communication is to facilitate slavery."[2] Grammaphobia is more than potential in Lévi-Strauss's text.

The juxtaposition I have made is not an innocent one. Its consequences for Swift may be drawn out by the following digression. Commenting on the Lévi-Strauss anecdote in *Of Grammatology*, the French theorist of writing, Jacques Derrida, isolates in the anthropologist's assumptions a central myth of the written word. Lévi-Strauss's remarks epitomize for him the "classical ideology" of language in Western culture. Briefly, Derrida suggests that "from Plato to Rousseau to Hegel" an arbitrary relation has been enforced between speech and writing. In our mythic formulation, speech is primary and writing is secondary. We impute to speech a natural priority and purity: we identify it as the mode of signification appropriate to "natural man." Writing, by contrast, is traditionally imagined as an imitation of speech, as a belated development, as an unnatural superimposition upon the primal and exquisite purity of oral communication. The ideological separation soon modulates (following upon Plato) into a moral drama, a Fall: if speech preserves a pure relation between Nature and Word, writing interrupts, compromises, corrupts this relation. The medium of writing itself—because of its impoverished material status—breaches Nature and Word and lays open a ground for falsehood. The Text, as Devil, is "the Father of Lies." As such, it makes itself available in turn as an instrument of corrupt individuals. Thus the fantasy persists that writing is "the dangerous supplement," the shoddy, distracting copy of original truth. Writing "takes on the status of a tragic fatality come to prey upon natural innocence."[3]

The operation of this myth of writing in Lévi-Strauss is patent: a pure (oral) society is disrupted by the intervention of writing, a writing, moreover, that points up, pathetically, its own radical shoddiness, its inauthenticity as signifier. I would like to claim that a similar myth may be seen working in Swift. Book 4 of *Gulliver's Travels* is, in one reading, a complex meditation on the problematic nature of writing and the possible corruption implied by the Text. But the theme reappears often in Swift's work. At these moments his obsessive apprehension of the philosophical and sociological dilemmas posed by writing suggests that he is influenced by a mythic structure of the kind Derrida describes. Swift, as we will see, confronts the Fallen Text in a number of works, and this text itself becomes, with varying degrees of explicitness, a satiric subject par excellence.

Swift, like Lévi-Strauss in *Tristes Tropiques*, makes the ideological assumption of a radical break between speech and writing. This point has played no part, really, in classic commentaries on Swift's work—those, for instance, of Ehrenpreis, Harth, Monk, Landa and others.[4] Indeed, Swift criticism has in general tended to leave aside both the question of the satirist's view of his own medium and the problem of the written artifact that his text raise. In a well-known description of the rationalist utopia of Book 4 of *Gulliver's Travels*, Samuel H. Monk itemizes every feature of Houyhnhnm life except the one an anthropologist would be first to notice—that the horses have an exclusively oral culture. The omission here is typical of general inattention to the question of the written word.[5] Even in recent critical discussions that have focused especially on Swift's view of language, however, the mythic split—the fall of speech into writing—has been presupposed but unacknowledged.[6] Commentators on Swift's linguistic satire have tended to confine themselves to remarks of an unspecific kind—for instance, that the abuse of words satirized by Swift is linked to a larger satire of other kinds of abuse: political, religious, and the like. Thus William Koon writes, in an essay on language in *A Tale of a Tub*, that "the *Tale's* corrupt language marks corrupt religion and learning as well as the fallen nature of man." And again, "man's sinful nature reveals itself in words as well as in thoughts and deeds."[7]

However true these remarks, they tend to ignore the special force Swift applies in the *Tale* and elsewhere to a critique of textuality per se. The corrupt words are, in fact, written words. Speech retains all its natural priority in Swift. His fear, his satiric energy, is aroused by the blotted, besmeared copy of speech, by the perverse materiality of the printed page— by an "excremental" vision of the script. The fallen nature of man is revealed most profoundly not in the fact that he speaks (Adam spoke with God in the Garden), but in the fact that he writes. Thus one must particularize the anxious element underlying Swift's work not simply as linguaphobic but as grammaphobic: his is an exemplary examination of the paradoxes that obtain when words thicken, squirm, and breed before our eyes. Let us approach the enigma of the Houyhnhnms' missing script by placing it in a larger context. All of Swift's satiric pieces, to a greater or lesser extent, reflect upon the problematic status of the written word. The mode of reflection varies. Swift's revelation of the fallen nature of writing is primarily philosophic in *A Tale of a Tub*; sociological implications are drawn out in some of the smaller satires; and finally, *Gulliver's Travels* is regulated by an inclusive fiction of the text.

A Tale of a Tub, the most extensive early satire, is, one might claim, Swift's prototypical (and perhaps most complicated) diagnosis of the problem at the heart of the text. A duplicity, or doubleness, informs Swift's revelation: the *Tale* is simultaneously a history and an embodiment of the corruption potential in the scriptory. It is at once an hallucination of Text and an hallucinatory text. This doubleness has, of course, been noted by commentators.[8] Just as the three brothers puzzle over a text, their father's will, in the embedded history in the *Tale*, so Swift's readers must themselves enact a similar problematic process of textual interpretation as they confront the dark mysteries of his framing text—the prefaces, digressions, notes, addenda. We are made the mad interpreters of Swift's text; it invites us to engage in a *folie de texte* and replicate the process which is described anecdotally in the embedded parable of Peter and the rest. More critics than Wotton have fallen into Swift's trap. This formal complementary quality in the work is usually explained in relation to Swift's explicit satiric project noted in the Apology, the twofold exposure of "gross corruptions in Religion and Learning" (243). Interpretation of text is the theme which conjoins Swift's satire of religious abuse in the allegorical portion of the *Tale* with his satire on pedagogic abuse, exemplified in the Modern editor's insane critical apparatus.

The theme of interpretation, however, suggests a deep structure in the Swiftian satire. The problem of meaning, raised everywhere on the surface of the *Tale*, points, it would seem, to an underlying, consistent fantasy of the Text itself. On the most profound level (the level of dream?), Swift's satire is motivated by a vision—potentially fearful—of the written artifact as a radically unstable object. This latent myth of the text conditions both the convoluted satiric strategy of a *Tale* and the passionate intensity with which this strategy is put into effect. But how might one specify the prototypical, anxious Text imagined in the *Tale*? How does the written word reveal itself to Swift—and to us—as a corrupt mode of signification? Swift's underlying critique of writing depends first of all, as I have already intimated by my own digression to the Derridean analysis, upon an intuition of its compromised relation to speech. The model in Swift is, in the most general application, Platonic—the written object is a material rendering of something ideal, the pure world of speech. Writing is a copy of a pre-existing, naturalized realm of discourse; and for the satirist of the text, its very materiality attests to its corruptness; and the copy, in this case, exemplifies a process of degeneration. The solidification of speech into writing is, to use a Derridean concept, a scandal; to use a Swiftian, a scatology.

Swift suggests much of this, of course, in the elaborate bibliographic boondoggle with which the *Tale* begins. We learn in the Apology prefixing the satire that the original version of the Modern's manuscript has been lost, and that the primary text which we read is, after all, that "surreptitious copy," "with many alterations," feared by the "Bookseller" (257) in his own subsequent Preface. This would appear to explain why the present manuscript is a pocked transcript, one disrupted at all points by obscurities, typographical ellipses, holes. Yet, the Apology blithely admits, the author's missing original itself also held "chasms" though indeed, "not so many" (251) as the received text. At this point an absurdity has intervened into Swift's potted history of the text. This last information hints subtly at an epistemological equivalence among all the texts; each is equally impure, even that version which is described, oxymoronically, as the "original copy" (251). Each is impure in regard to the world of spoken discourse, which maintains here an assumed priority. What has been lost in the process of transmission described in the Apology is not an originally pure manuscript (no such thing exists), but truth itself, specifically located in the voice, the words of a human speaker.

The *Tale* fictionalizes this loss most obviously in the mystery attached to the Modern's identity and whereabouts. Again in the Apology, Swift alludes to the rumor—though discounting it—that the author of the manuscript we read is dead. In any case, the Modern cannot be consulted directly regarding the cruxes in his text; the authority of his voice—the voice of authorial intention—is absent. The point here would seem to be that the Text cannot, ultimately, be referred to the spoken discourse it purports to mirror: the point of contact between speech and writing is breached by accident, by history, by that very plunge into materiality that the written word represents. Symbolically, a death, a disappearance, takes place between oral and written modes. In the embedded allegory death literally intervenes between speech and text: the appearance of the disputed will in the world is here functionally dependent upon the death of an authorial *voice*, the father. The will—an archetypal version of Text—is thus compromised, de-natured, separated from truth at its moment of origin. It is a deathly, parasitic artifact; it feeds off an original, living form of discourse, and replaces it in the world. The Text falls into the world precisely as the voice, traumatically, leaves it—its frustrating, marred surface attests to its belated, unnatural, and ultimately dehumanized status.

The gap between speech and text fantasized in the symbolic fictions of a *Tale* is fearful because it occasions, necessarily, the breakdown of meaning. It brings about a hermeneutic catastrophe. The privileged, single meaning is abrogated by that death which mediates between the worlds of discourse and transcription. Because it cannot be referred back to the truth of the voice, the text's signification is unverifiable; its truth is always indeterminate. Once at large in the world, Swift suggests, the paradigmatic manuscript resolves immediately into an independent, free-floating structure of possible meanings—it constitutes its own infinitely expansive ideology. Yet this is the hermeneutic nightmare at the heart of the *Tale*, the source of the satirist's motivating phobia. Separated from the natural constraints of the voice, the text makes itself available for arbitrary, creative interpretation. Confronting, for instance, one of the famous hiatuses in Swift's own manuscript—the "*Hic multa desiderantur*" ("here much is left to be desired"; sec. 9, p. 331)—the reader can only conjecture what might fill the ellipsis. The text has lost its voice in the most radical way possible. Hence, like the three brothers of the allegory who encounter the "*altum silentium*" ("deep silence"; sec. 2, p. 286) of their father's will and fill the void as they wish, we are invited by the Modern's text to turn imaginists, to become creative readers. Noting his desire that "every prince in Christendom" assign to seven scholars the task of writing "seven ample commentaries" on the *Tale*, the Modern asserts that "whatever difference may be found in their several conjectures, they will all, without the least distortion, be manifestly deducible from the text" (sec. 10, p. 341). No reading is disallowed by the pocked and whorish text.

It is worth noting in passing how close are Swift's insights regarding the problematic nature of textuality to certain discoveries formalized in modern linguistics and extended in contemporary structuralist literary theory. By raising questions about the interpretative process and the peculiar epistemological complexities that afflict any reader's relations to a text, Swift's work anticipates the concerns, in particular, of Continental theorists like Barthes and Kristeva. (The parallel refutes the notion, likewise, that it is only modernist texts of the twentieth century that expose the semantic variability of the literary sign.) To cite just one point of convergence: Swift's allusion to the "Anagrammatick Method" of reading employed by Peter when he looks for the word "SHOULDER" (sec. 2, p. 285) in the will suggests that it is possible to read the orthographic marks that make up the text in a non-sequential order. This graphemic way of reading, Swift knows, is not conventional; yet he also suspects, rightly, that there is nothing in the physical nature of the text per se to forbid it. Interpretation of a given text is based on arbitrary reading conventions—ways of arranging, conceptually, its visible marks—and these conventions may conceivably be broached by the innovative reader. Obviously deformed texts, those filled with typographical transpositions, shock us because they remind us precisely that the way we look at the text is arbitrary, and that we might, indeed, modify the process ourselves. Because its actual structure is always indeterminate, Swift seems to say, any text allows convention-free reading; any text might even be said to encourage such madness. The linguist Saussure, whose theory of signs underlies recent structuralist work on literary hermeneutics, made the same discovery in the early part of this century while studying anagrams in *De Rerum Natura*.[9] After positing the presence of anagrams of "Aphrodite" in the opening lines of the Lucretian text, Saussure was forced to admit that he could not prove the anagrams had been intentionally placed there; the appeal to authority, the voice of the author, was impossible. Moreover, the linguist was left with the realization that just as the truth of his anagrammatic interpretation was indeterminate, so all textual exegesis might be equally indeterminate—shaped only by the desire of the interpreter. Writing, because of its hermeneutic instability, easily accommodates its own exploitation. Saussure was so disturbed by the hallucinatory text, the unconstrained text, that he never published his anagrammatic research. Swift attempts to protect himself from the same discovery by enclosing it within the context of satire, of derision. Yet the fantasy of the mercurial text persists.

The critique of writing implied at the deepest level of *A Tale of a Tub* enforces finally in that work a powerful and revealing troping of the text. The manuscript, with its spots and holes and blurs, becomes a demonic and ghastly material presence. It is a monster. Characteristically, Swift figures its monstrosity by way of an imagery of fertility, of breeding. The Text, for the satirist, is womb-like (might we say female?): it gives birth, in a process at once out of control and horrifying, to replicas of itself. The Modern's own text, with its offshoots and appendages, is our primary model of the oppressive text; it invites commentary, it seeks to generate new texts. It afflicts us with its apparatus—what Swift catalogues in another context as the innumerable, useless "Prefaces, Epistles, Advertisements, Introductions, Prolegomenas, Apparatuses, To-the-Readers" (sec. 5, p. 310). But Swift shows everywhere, in explicit comment, the sickening ease with which any text may reproduce itself. Later we learn, for instance, that texts inspire in their readers "scholastic midwifery" and that the readers deliver them "of meanings" which, the Modern notes by the by, "the authors themselves perhaps never conceived." Written words, he continues, are like seed which "will multiply far beyond either the hopes or imagination of the sower" (sec. 10, p. 341). Human agency is thus excluded from the grotesque process of textual multiplication: the "immense bales of paper" (261)—which threaten ultimately to subsume Nature itself—begin to write themselves. The monstrous text Swift imagines is an utterly mindless entity, a mere physical automaton, endlessly replicating. The world is "nauseated" says the satirist in his Apology, "by endless repetitions on every subject" (243).

The grotesque text troped in *A Tale of a Tub* may be redefined in Derridean fashion, summarily, as the guilty text. The text of *A Tale* itself exemplifies guilt: its truth status is compromised by its corrupt physical nature. Yet it is also guilty in the way that it compels us to construct our own guilty texts. It breeds us, its exegetes, as we read. One might argue at this point, however, that Swift may not necessarily mean to identify every version of Text as potentially corrupt. Do not texts remain somewhere which are in some fashion privileged? Can we not separate good texts from bad texts? Certain commonplace assumptions about satire—particularly, that it implicitly recommends to us an unstated, yet realizable mode of behavior— may mislead here. Viewed superficially, the satire on the evil text in *A Tale of a Tub* might indeed seem to predicate by indirection a good text. If the Modern's manuscript is a negative model of written discourse, it must be possible to extrapolate from it a positive model. Yet in the radical world of writing described in Swiftian satire, the innocent text ultimately does not, indeed cannot exist. So extreme is the anxiety surrounding the Text in the *Tale*, one is forced to conclude that the positive model invoked, paradoxically, is no writing at all. This would seem to be the import of Swift's obsessive returning, throughout the work, to the problem of Biblical interpretation. (The traumatic seventeenth-century discovery of the historical corruption of

Biblical texts underlies Swift's work just as profoundly as it does a work like Dryden's *Religio Laici*.) No text is privileged in regard to truth; no text is scriptural. Swift would not have been surprised, one suspects, by the notorious "Wicked Bible" printed in Leipzig in 1631, which—due to a typographical error—gave the Seventh Commandment as "Thou shalt commit adultery."[10] Such gross and shocking aberrations merely confirm once again, on the basic level of typography, the theme of the satire. Given its inescapably material status, every writing is a site for corruption, no matter what authority—natural, divine, or archetypal—we may wishfully invest in it. Because they constitute an earthly text, the Scriptures themselves pathetically and paradoxically make up part of the fallen world of writing. Is Swift's fiction of the text, then, a kind of blasphemy? Swift does not state so baldly that God's text itself is corrupt, but at the same time, the possibility is implicit everywhere in his satire. The text is to be feared, whatever its ostensible provenance.

I have dwelled at considerable length on *A Tale of a Tub* because it isolates powerfully the essential features of Swift's fantasy of the text. Its energy, I have tried to suggest, derives from what one might call an underlying phobic response to writing. That vision or hallucination of a fearful gap between speech and writing compels the satire, gives it an anxious, obsessive force. Turning to Swift's other satiric works, however—even those which might not seem at first glance to share an equal fascination with textuality— one finds, I think, evidence of the same theme, variants and elaborations of the same textual fiction.

How many of Swift's satiric pieces play off notions of the grotesquely physical text, the intrusive text, of that arrogant and monstrous text intimated by the *Tale*. *The Battle of the Books*, of course, depends upon the phantasmagoric troping of the text already seen in the earlier work. Swift's satire here, like Pope's in the *Dunciad*, is marked by a compelling sense of the materiality of the written artifact and of the pressure it exerts upon Nature. At the most reductive level, the satire hints, no book is free from these oppressive or guilty qualities. In the Bookseller's Preface to the Reader, for instance, Swift makes his characteristic schism between author and book, voice and text, and thus solidifies writing—as an *entity*—before our eyes: "I must warn the reader to beware of applying to persons what is here meant only of books in the most literal sense. So, when Virgil is mentioned, we are not to understand the person of a famous poet called by that name, but only certain sheets of paper, bound up in leather, containing in print the works of the said poet, and so of the rest" (357). Yet the Ancient text, once solidified in such a way as an artifact, is ready to breed a secondary text— the Modern text. The Ancient text itself supplies the necessary condition for the Battle: a world of violence is instituted with this primary materialization of the Word. Swift's overt purpose in his piece is to vindicate the works of the Ancients over those of the Moderns, but one may wonder how much this conscious project is complicated, even undermined, by the implicit fantasy of the text. In some sense, Virgil is responsible for Dryden: the primary text initiates the chain of replication. And both primary and secondary texts share the same compromised physical status in the end; both are equally present as sites for corruption. (This equivalence is suggested symbolically, perhaps, in the mystery surrounding the outcome of the Battle.) The Goddess Criticism, part of Swift's fantastical mock-heroic machinery, must be seen, finally, as his inclusive model of the hallucinatory Text. She, an archetypal transmogrification of every text existing in the world, ". . . gathered up her person into an octavo compass; her body grew white and arid, and split into pieces with dryness; the thick turned into pasteboard, and the thin into paper, upon which her parents and children artfully strewed a black juice, or decoction of gall and soot, in form of letters; her head, voice, and spleen, kept their primitive form, and that which before was a cover of skin, did still continue so. In which guise she marched on . . ." (372). Even Virgil's writings, one must conclude, do not escape the universal reduction of text into paper and "black juice." In such a vision we contemplate the central image of Swiftian grammaphobia.

In works such as the *Bickerstaff Papers*, *A Modest Proposal*, the *Complete Collection of Genteel and Ingenious Conversation*, the satire of the text is given an analogous sociological expansion. Swift's vision of the physical corruptness of writing—likewise the condition of its hermeneutic guilt—modulates here into a vision of its social guilt. All the discoveries made about the text in *A Tale of Tub* still apply, but the satirist's emphasis shifts to a consideration of its social effect. The intuitive leap made in these and similar works is easier to observe than to explicate, but one might brief it as follows. Just as writing is itself a dehumanized mode—physical yet mindless, separated at its moment of origin from the truth of the voice—so it works to enforce a larger pattern of dehumanization in society. Writing clogs the world: it mediates negatively between persons, imposes itself as object, as visible obstruction. The text Swift fears is not only materially corrupt, it is hypnotic, fetishistic. As we focus upon the impressive, yet false facade of truth it presents, we lose contact with human reality. While we read we cannot listen—the naturalized relations of the voice, of human connection, are breached. With the distraction of the text, moral chaos is made possible.

Thus, for instance, in the instructive pieces on conversation Swift shows us the text literally intruding upon the world of human relationships. Simon Wagstaff invites his readers to consult his book while entering into conversational situations; his text subsumes the voice directly, mediates the spontaneous oral interchange between persons. He recommends "the following treatise to be carried about as a pocket-companion, by all gentlemen and ladies, when they are going to visit, or dine, or drink tea; or, where they happen to pass the evening without cards. . . . desiring they would read their several parts in their chairs and coaches to prepare themselves for every kind of conversation that can possibly happen."[11] But if the intrusive text is ludicrous and comical here—and likewise in the Bickerstaff pieces—in *A Modest Proposal* it is less so. Swift's greatest short satire models for us that dehumanized script which encourages the dehumanization of the reader: its rhetoric is indeed hypnotic. Swift's irony devastates precisely because it exploits our conventional, even superstitious assumption about texts—that they are authoritative signs. We imbue the text with authority because it is a text: we fall immediately under its sinister mimetic spell. Yet, the satirist warns, absorption in this dehumanized surface enforces our own dehumanization. To accept the premise of *A Modest Proposal*—the utility of cannibalism—is to divest ourselves, of course, of a natural moral sense of things. The satire shocks and liberates because it points up how easily the text distracts us, co-opts us, separates us from human connections. Yet this effect, as I have tried to show, depends upon those assumptions about the written artifact seen elsewhere in Swift. Writing avails itself as an instrument of social evil because its own nature is essentially evil to begin with. Thus the Swiftian critique of Text—primarily framed upon philosophical issues in the early satiric pieces—quickly takes on here a crucial and profound pragmatic force. The epistemological exposé of writing resolves into moral exposé as well.

The themes Swift associates with writing—its fallen aspect, its hermeneutic indeterminacy, and physical and moral degeneracy—all reappear, finally, within the fictional context of *Gulliver's Travels*. One might even be tempted to claim that satire of the written word is an underlying principle of organization in that work. No matter how other perspectives shift from book to book (most notoriously our view of the narrator himself), a critique of the written word seems to remain a constant. It works as a symbolic reference point against which other elements of the satire may be aligned.

Texts exert a different pressure on each of the societies Gulliver visits, inviting the hypothesis that this pressure is a Swiftian index to the nature of each place. In Book 1, for instance, when Swift satirizes the pettiness and pomposity of the Lilliputians he shows us that their society is pre-eminently text oriented. The Lilliputians are compulsive writers: they organize their lives around significant texts—published "Edicts" (such as the one which initiates the Big- and Little-Endian controversy), the "Proclamations" and "Orders of State" of their prince, treaties (which do not hold), and "Articles" of behavior like those presented to Gulliver on his arrival. The Lilliputians tend to formalize all their experience—silly as it is—as text. Yet this process of textualizing is, as elsewhere in Swift, a suspect one. Witness the distortion that creeps in as the Lilliputians set out to describe, in scientific discourse, the contents of Gulliver's pocket. Likewise, Gulliver's plight in Book 1 worsens precisely as texts intervene. The palace fire—the event that initiates Gulliver's fall from favor—starts because of the "carelessness of a Maid of Honour, who fell asleep while she was reading a Romance" (Bk. 1 ch. 5, p. 44). The Englishman's fate is sealed by the "Articles of Impeachment" ordered against him by corrupt Lilliputians. The text, the satirist suggests, disrupts both the physical and social order of things; it is the primary cause of Lilliputian error and the primary tool of their injustice. The Lilliputians are condemned by the intimacy they share with it.

The Brobdingnagians, in proportion to their greater magnanimity as a people, denigrate and restrict the influence of the text. Gulliver notes that they have printing, "But their Libraries are not very large." Similarly, "they avoid nothing more than multiplying unnecessary Words" (Bk. 2, ch. 7, p. 110), and institute—arbitrarily but as best they can—against the process of interpretation itself: "No Law of their Country must exceed in Words the Number of Letters in their Alphabet; which consists only of two and twenty. But indeed, few of them extend even to that Length. They are expressed in the most plain and simple Terms, wherein those people are not Mercurial enough to discover above one Interpretation. And, to write a Comment upon any Law, is a capital Crime" (Bk. 2, ch. 7, p. 110). Gulliver comments that as a result Brobdingnagian learning is very "confined," but the joke is on him. We predicate Swift's satire on his narrator on a pre-existing satire of the text. Thus, when Gulliver's own pettiness is exposed in this book by the Brobdingnagian king, we find the king analogizing England and its inhabitants to a corrupted text: "I observe among you some Lines of an Institution, which in its Original might have been tolerable; but these half-erased, and the rest wholly blurred and blotted by Corruption" (Bk. 2, ch. 6, p. 106). The immediate focus of Swiftian satire shifts, of course, between Books 1 and 2, but its underlying assumption remains the same: the "little odious Vermin," whether Lilliputian or Gulliver himself, has pen in hand.

Again, in Book 3, the satire of the text underlies Swift's satire on the Academy of Projectors. Laputan writing is perhaps the most nightmarish in *Gulliver's Travels*. Among the various ridiculous inventions that Gulliver finds in Laputa, for example, is that implement "for improving speculative Knowledge by practical and mechanical Operations" (Bk. 3, ch. 5, p. 148)—the text-breeding machine. With this device "the most ignorant Person may write Books in Philosophy, Poetry, Politics, Law, Mathematicks and Theology, without the least Assistance from Genius or Study" (Bk. 3, ch. 5, p. 148). The invention generates arbitrary assortments of letters by mechanical rearrangement of bits of wood and paper, on which are written "all the Words of their Language in their several Moods, Tenses, and Declensions, but without any Order." As in *A Tale of a Tub*, writing is figured as a non-intellectual process; it is automatic, mindless replication. "The Pupils at Command took each of them hold of an Iron Handle, whereof there were Forty fixed round the Edges of the Frame; and giving them a sudden Turn, the whole Disposition of the Words was entirely changed. He then commanded Six and Thirty of the Lads to read the several Lines softly as they appeared upon the Frame; and where they found three or four Words together that might make Part of a Sentence, they dictated to the four remaining

Boys who were Scribes" (Bk. 3, ch. 5, p. 148). Already the texts created thus are many; "several Volumes" exist of "broken Sentences," and the inventor of the machine intends more. With the prospect of five hundred such devices in operation, the number of "Rich Materials" still to be produced is incalculable (Bk. 3, ch. 5, p. 150). Swift here discovers, then, an appropriate physical model for meaningless, inhuman and infinitely reproducing writing. The text factory is the central locus for grammaphobia in Book 3, but one might note, too, the satirist's exposure again of the "Anagrammatick Method" (Bk. 3, ch. 6, p. 156) in the section on political projectors, and his dismissal of "Commentary" (Bk. 3, ch. 8, pp. 159–60) and interpretation in the episode in which Gulliver calls back the Ancient writers from the dead. At all points in the Laputan scenes, even more so perhaps than in Lilliput, the reader encounters a world replete with writing, a world controlled by a technology of the text. In both societies, however, writing itself becomes the mark of an intrinsic intellectual and moral degeneracy.

And here we come back, of course, to the horses. As Gulliver has already told us, "their Knowledge is all traditional" (Bk. 4, ch. 9, p. 220). Unlike any other society in *Gulliver's Travels*, the Houyhnhnms have not taken the catastrophic fall into a world of letters. Their complete ignorance of books suggests an improvement even upon the relatively text-free Brobdingnagians.

The situation, however, is not without paradox. The pattern of grammaphobia in *Gulliver's Travels* conditions the appalling problem that confronts the reader in Book 4. Houyhnhnm society is indeed pure to the extent that it is free from textuality. It is a naturalized society. The Houyhnhnms are bound by a community of the voice; they are bound by a language of pure sound, the neigh. This is the sense in which Houyhnhnm society qualifies (as some critics would like to see it[12]) as a Swiftian version of the Platonic utopia. The secondary mode of signification is absent, along with its attendant corruption. No demonic texts here, getting in the way of the spoken discourse.

Swift queers the pleasant resolution of the grammaphobic situation—the escape to a Platonic Utopia—however, by one simple and ludicrous transformation. The residents in Utopia are not human. By virtue of the essential difference between Houyhnhnm and human, the naturalized society is not, and can never be, our own. Gulliver tries to imitate the gait and speech of the horses, but, most significantly, he is never able to stop writing. Already fallen, he cannot emulate the Houyhnhnms in this crucial respect. (Indeed, Swift hints everywhere of Gulliver's inescapable resemblance to the Yahoos—who, with their enthusiastic and decorative shit-smearing seem, anthropologically speaking, on the way to the discovery of a script.[13]) Thus the satirist's examination of textuality takes its most damning turn. The Houyhnhnms model that situation suggested at all points in Swift from *A Tale of a Tub* on as a good—no writing at all. But they are not we. For humankind, Swift suggests, the text is *inevitable*. It is already here. The evil text and human presence constitute an inseparable unit in the world.

This extension of the grammaphobic argument places the reader in an impossible position. Swift leaves us in Book 4 with confirmation of a logical tautology—because we are human, we are open to dehumanization. Indeed, we already possess the necessary tool. He infects us everywhere with the malignancy of the text, and then says there is nothing we can do about it. Attempted return to the innocence of the Houyhnhnm is doomed to be an incomplete gesture. Meanwhile, the Yahoos drop excrement upon us from the trees. They inscribe our very bodies with a text.

Gulliver's Travels ends, then, with a final implosion of the Swiftian fear of the text. It suspends with paradox, with the extra-logical confirmation of grammaphobia. Such anxiety is wholly appropriate to, and might be said to define, Swiftian satire; but on some level it also defines the author himself. In his own career, Swift lived out the identical paradox of the text figured in Book 4.[14] How, after all, can the writer not write? I have deliberately confined myself in this essay to the mythology of writing revealed in Swift's satiric pieces, yet there is, biographically speaking, another side to the issue. The serious works on language reform—the *Proposal for Correcting, Improving, and Ascertaining the English Tongue* and others—suggest that at moments Swift did believe, or attempt to believe, in a resurrected text. The *Proposal*, for instance, argues that it is possible to reestablish a connection between writing and speech. Swift wishes here that the gap might be bridged nostalgically—that we might go back to the purity of speech when we write. The story, perhaps apocryphal, of Swift reading his works aloud to his servant in order to ensure their comprehensibility works mythically—Swift here resurrects his own text by referring it to the human contact of the voice. Obviously, Swift calls attention at times to a hope that his own plain style—free of "Corruptions"—will be a model for a new purified English prose.[15]

Still, one may wonder, rightly I think, what the force of such wishing is compared with the intensity and reductiveness of the vision presented in Swiftian satire. My own inclination, as should be apparent, has been to associate Swift's myth of the text—and the world of satire itself—with unconscious forces, with underlying traumatized modes of perception. Placed next to *A Tale of a Tub* and the rest, the pieces on language reform look suspiciously like a kind of reaction-formation; they respond, it would seem, to a prior, deeply anxious experience of textuality. It appears questionable whether Swift himself ever succeeded in domesticating—in the *Proposal* or elsewhere—that hallucinatory material for which his satires everywhere provide the evidence.

And finally, it is the hallucinatory perception in Swift that remains with us, not his programmatic effort to resurrect the text. If Book 4 of *Gulliver's Travels* shows that we, unlike Houyhnhnms, cannot be free of writing, Swift's satires show what a problematic supplement this is. Swift powerfully isolates for us the radical indeterminacy of the very texts we allow to influence our lives. The critique is not always logical; it is impelled by an energy that may remind us of the anxiety dream. But its force is not undermined thereby. Particularizing Swift's vision of the text in Derridean fashion, as a myth—as I have tried to here—suggests how one might begin to analyze it, but even this leaves its emotional impact unexplained. Swift's greatest works make up together a Tale of a Text; and it is with this compelling text itself that we, readers and writers all, ultimately fall.

Notes

1.   Unless otherwise noted, the texts used for quotation are those in *Gulliver's Travels and Other Writings*, ed. Louis A. Landa (Boston: Houghton Mifflin, 1960).

2.   Claude Lévi-Strauss, *Tristes Tropiques*, trans. John and Doreen Weightman (New York: Simon & Schuster, 1974), 335–36.

3.   Jacques Derrida, *Of Grammatology*, trans. Gayatri Chakravorty Spivak (Baltimore: Johns Hopkins Univ. Press, 1976), 168.

4.   In *Swift and Anglican Rationalism* (Chicago: Univ. of Chicago Press, 1961), for instance, Phillip Harth confines his description of the satire on interpretation in *A Tale of a Tub* to a theological issue—the perverse effect of "zeal" (located in the interpreter) on Scriptural exegesis. Yet the "zealous" exegete, Swift's own marred text suggests, is one who, among other things, exploits material flaws associated with textuality—*lacunae*, ellipses, visible obscurities and cruxes. It is difficult to escape the conclusion that for Swift the difficulty of interpretation derives as much from problematic elements in the object of interpretation itself, the written artifact, as from the deficiencies of interpreters. See in particular Harth, Chapter 2, "Reason and Revelation." Irvin Ehrenpreis's classic essay on Book 4 of *Gulliver's Travels*, "The Meaning of Gulliver's Last Voyage," *Review of English Literature*, 3 (1962), 18–38, while eloquently particularizing the dilemma Swift's reader faces (to emulate the virtuous Houyhnhnm is to deny one's own humanity) likewise leaves out the "grammatological" dimension of this dilemma: it is impossible for Gulliver (and us) to imitate the purity of Houyhnhnm existence because it is impossible to unlearn the use of ciphers, and thus avoid, as they do, implication in a world of textuality.

5.   Samuel H. Monk, "The Pride of Lemuel Gulliver," *Sewanee Review*, 63 (1955), 48–71.

6.   See, for example, Claudia R. Stillman, "The Theme of Language in the Prose Works of Jonthan Swift," Diss. North Carolina 1973; and John R. Clark's *Form and Frenzy in Swift's Tale of a Tub* (Ithaca: Cornell Univ. Press, 1970).

7.   William Koon, "Swift on Language: An Approach to *A Tale of a Tub*," *Style*, 10 (1976), 28–40.

8.   Clark, 178.

9.   For a discussion of Saussure's work on anagrams, see Jonathan Culler, *Saussure* (Glasgow: William Collins, 1976), 106ff. The "Anagrammatick Method" of interpretation recurs in Book 3 of *Gulliver's Travels*, of course, when the Tribnian experts decipher "*Our Brother Tom has just got the Piles*" as "*Resist; a Plot is brought Home, The Tour.*" Arthur E. Case, in *Four Essays on Gulliver's Travels* (Gloucester, Mass.: Princeton Univ. Press, 1958), 91–92, identifies in this passage a satire on the Jacobites, who were alleged to use anagrammatic codes, and Bolingbroke, who went by the alias "M. La Tour" while in France. Swift's political satire here does not exclude his satire on the malleable text; rather, as so often happens in his works, two targets are struck in a single satiric economy.

10.   Freud calls attention to the "Wicked Bible" in *The Psychopathology of Everyday Life* in the section "Mistakes in Reading and Writing."

11.   Text quoted from Jonathan Swift, *Satires and Personal Writings*, ed. William Alfred Eddy (London: Oxford Univ. Press, 1932), 202.

12.   See, in particular, John F. Reichert, "Plato, Swift, and the Houyhnhnms," *Philological Quarterly*, 47 (1968), 179–92.

13.   Frank Brady makes a point of the Yahoos' approach to human behavior—and hence their transformation into satiric targets—in a note in his introduction to the collection *Twentieth-Century Interpretations of Gulliver's Travels* (Englewood Cliffs, N.J.: Prentice-Hall, 1968), 10: "Strictly speaking, the Yahoos are satirized only to the extent they are assimilated to human beings. As Bergson pointed out, animal behavior is never comic."

14.   W. B. Carnochan has suggested in *Lemuel Gulliver's Mirror for Man* (Berkeley: Univ. of Calif. Press, 1968), 92ff., that Swift's satire modulates finally into "self-satire," an illustration of the satirist's own "self-critical ways." A general paradox arises in that the greater "satire on man" always points back to Swift himself. Carnochan writes of Gulliver: "he embodies all Swift's doubts about his motives and his literary vocation." Under this notion of vocation we may place our own topic—the paradoxical implication of the writer himself in the corrupt world of writing.

15.   Text quoted from Jonathan Swift, *A Proposal for Correcting, Improving, and Ascertaining the English Tongue*, ed. R. C. Allston (Menton, England: Scolar, 1969), 8.

GULLIVER'S TRAVELS

◆

Strange Dispositions: Swift's *Gulliver's Travels*

MICHAEL SEIDEL

In the third book of *Gulliver's Travels*, a person of Luggnuggian quality asks Gulliver if he has seen any of "their *Struldbrugs* or *Immortals*" (207).[1] A progressivist by nature, having "been a Sort of Projector in my younger Days" (178), Gulliver is in raptures at the prospect of the immortal Struldbrugs—he is "struck with inexpressible Delight upon hearing this Account" (207). Why? Because the Struldbrugs "being born exempt from that universal Calamity of human Nature, have their Minds free and disingaged, without the Weight and Depression of Spirits caused by the continual Apprehension of Death" (208). Although Gulliver's reflection here does not seem particularly outrageous, it is just such a notion of bodily integrity in time that the satiric design of the *Travels* subverts. Gulliver is goaded by the Luggnuggian gentleman into the next unfortunate error: he is asked to imagine himself a Struldbrug and to speculate on his immortal rewards. An older and wilier heroic wanderer, Odysseus, had a similar opportunity to test immortality on Calypso's island, but he was forced into it almost against his will. The promise of immortality delayed homecoming, and Odysseus, the all too human traveller, desired nothing so much as a return to the temporally measured life. But not so Gulliver.

Gulliver knows little restraint in pursuing the wrong course. He "projects" the life of an immortal into an expansive and ameliorative view of human "being" and assumes that he and his fellow Struldbrugs "would probably prevent that continual Degeneracy of human Nature, so justly complained of in all Ages" (210). What he soon sees, however, proves otherwise. In suspending the temporal limitation of life, the Struldbrugs incorporate the ravages of time into their nature. The best of their lot are the prematurely senile. At fourscore "they are looked on as dead in Law; their Heirs immediately succeed to their Estates, only a small Pittance is reserved for their Support" (212). At this point, Gulliver ought to realize that continuity and biological life are at imperfectible odds, but he will make the same mistake in Houyhnhnmland when he wishes himself a more perfectible being than his body allows. "In its Etymology," we are told,

Reprinted from *Satiric Inheritance: Rabelais to Sterne*, 201–25. Copyright © 1979, Princeton University Press, reprinted by permission.

Houyhnhnm means *"the Perfection of Nature"* (235). It may be that an abstract or artificial notion of the body of man, like that presented in the opening of Hobbes's *Leviathan*, can hold to perfect form,[2] but the natural human body cannot. The Luggnuggians make the Struldbrugs into satiric fictions. As beings, the Struldbrugs's condition is desperate and degenerate.

> At Ninety they lose their Teeth and Hair; they have at that Age no Distinction of Taste, but eat and drink whatever they can get, without Relish or Appetite. The Diseases they were subject to, still continue without encreasing or diminishing. In talking they forget the common Appellation of Things, and the Names of Persons, even of those who are their nearest Friends and Relations. For the same Reason they never can amuse themselves with reading, because their Memory will not serve to carry them from the Beginning of a Sentence to the End; and by this Defect they are deprived of the only Entertainment wereof they might otherwise be capable.
>
> (213)

The Struldbrugs are condemned to decay—they lose their memories and are thus "ancients" made all too "modern." For the suddenly educated Gulliver the Struldbrugs "were the most mortifying Sight I ever beheld; and the Women more horrible than the Men. Besides the usual Deformities in extreme old Age, they acquired an additional Ghastliness in Proportion to their Number of Years, which is not to be described" (214). What is worse, they are exiles at home; they cannot communicate in any but a dead language, "and thus they lye under the Disadvantage of living like Foreigners in their own Country" (213). Although Gulliver had no way of knowing it at the time, the condition of the Struldbrugs would finally reflect his own—that of a permanent exile in his own land. By believing in the perfectibility of the species (any species), Gulliver drives himself crazy. At the end of his *Travels*, if not "despised and hated by all Sorts of People" (213) as are the Struldbrugs, he himself despises and hates all sorts of Yahoos—those satirically degenerate fellow men he describes as "a Lump of Deformity, and Diseases both in Body and Mind, smitten with *Pride*" (296).

The document, *Gulliver's Travels*, is written by a madman whose recollections at the time of writing are anything but tranquil. His voyagings have unsettled and dispossessed him. He begins as the middle son of a middle-class household from a middle shire of England. He ends bereft of his middling or "mediating" status. Like most of Swift's surrogate authors (or expendable selves), Gulliver *is* satiric potential—the record of his progress becomes confused with the disintegration of his recording powers. *A Tale of A Tub* is told by an author inside his own diversionary barrel. *A Modest Proposal* is advanced by a political arithmetician obsessed by number. *Gulliver's Travels* is related as part of a narrative conspiracy to drive a fool mad. Swift begins the adventures by forcing Gulliver out of all human proportion, and Gulliver ends by wishing himself out of his own nature. Gulliver is vexed by his bodily design. Something has snapped. As a traveller who has made proximity to nature's diverse creatures a perfectible ideal, he is spoiled by his proximate status as degenerate Yahoo. In this sense, his repatriation becomes his longest voyage of all, fated to last for the rest of his life. Seeing how extensive imperfection and degeneration are in the world is discomfiting enough for Gulliver, but seeing how his own body shapes his nature as a Yahoo renders him mindless.

In *Gulliver's Travels* degeneration is literally a vision of history—ego history and human history. As has long been recognized, even the means of arrival in each strange land betray a kind of degenerate regress: shipwreck, desertion, piracy, mutiny. The 1735 edition of the *Travels* opens with Gulliver's letter to his cousin Sympson that complains among other things that Yahoo though he is Gulliver is not "so far degenerated" that he need defend his veracity to other Yahoos, especially when the "united Praise of the whole Race would be of less Consequence to me, than the neighing of those two degenerate *Houyhnhnms* I keep in my Stable; because, from these, degenerate as they are, I still improve in some Virtues, without any Mixture of Vice" (8).

Gulliver may be a raving lunatic by this juncture, but even in his earlier, calmer voice he was preoccupied with degeneration. In Lilliput, ancient institutions undergo an increasingly rapid degeneration from the more noble lineaments of the past, and in relaying the laws of the land Gulliver points out that "I would only be understood to mean the original Institutions, and not the most scandalous Corruptions into which these People are fallen by the degenerate Nature of Man" (60). If the Lilliputians can barely afford a further fall in stature, the Brobdingnagian giants appear enormous even as shrunken descendants of a former race. Gulliver discovers a book on the subject of Brobdingnagian morality that holds that the once mighty are now fallen. Its author writes:

> Nature was degenerated in these latter declining Ages of the World, and could now produce only small abortive Births in Comparison of those in ancient Times. He said, it was very reasonable to think, not only that the Species of Men were originally much larger, but also that there must have been Giants in former Ages; which, as it is asserted by History and Tradition, so it hath been confirmed by huge Bones and Sculls casually dug up in several Parts of the Kingdom, far exceeding the common dwindled Race of Man in our Days. He argued, that the very Laws of Nature absolutely required we should have been made in the Beginning, of a Size more large and robust, not so liable to Destruction from every little Accident of a Tile falling from an House, or a Stone cast from the Hand of a Boy, or of being drowned in a little Brook.
>
> (137)

A little earlier, after listening to Gulliver's recitation of European glories, the Brobdingnagian King commented that even among "little" people the course of events seems to run from tolerable to degenerative: "I observe among you some Lines of an Institution, which in its Original might have been tolerable; but these half erased, and the rest wholly blurred and blotted by Corruptions" (132). Both giants and midgets suffer from a nostalgic historiography and a degeneratively contingent inheritance.

The most sustained treatment of degeneration in the *Travels* occurs in the several lands of Book Three. The Voyage to Laputa is the whore (*la puta*) of the narrative—naturally it has many lands. On the flying doomsday island of Laputa, the local inhabitants literally experience a fear of falling. And on the magical island of Glubbdubdrib Gulliver experiences an actual descent or calling of the shades in his odyssey of strange relations. He confronts time and observes "how much the Race of human Kind was degenerate among us, within these Hundred Years past. How the Pox under all its Consequences and Denominations had altered every Lineament of an *English* Countenance; shortened the Size of Bodies, unbraced the Nerves, relaxed the Sinew and Muscles, introduced a sallow Complexion, and rendered the Flesh loose and *rancid*" (201).

These are the same hundred years to which the King of Brobdingnag had reacted earlier when Gulliver performed as progressivist press agent for a land fully deserving of its bad press: "He was perfectly astonished with the historical Account I gave him of our Affairs during the last Century; protesting it was only an Heap of Conspiracies, Rebellions, Murders, Massacres, Revolutions, Banishments; the very worst Effects that Avarice, Faction, Hypocrisy, Perfidiousness, Cruelty, Rage, Madness, Hatred, Envy, Lust, Malice, and Ambition could produce" (132). The King calls Gulliver's European civilization "the most pernicious Race of little odious Vermin that Nature ever suffered to crawl upon the Surface of the Earth" (132). He does so after Gulliver had tried to defend the most noble of his people, the Lords of his native Parliament, as the "Ornament and Bulwark of the Kingdom; worthy Followers of their most renowned Ancestors, whose Honour had been the Reward of their Virtue; from which their Posterity were never once known to degenerate" (128). Swift's irony and Gulliver's gullibility are manifest later when in the seance of Book Three the Roman Senate is called to stand next to Gulliver's native Parliament (Lords and Commons): "I desired that the Senate of *Rome* might appear before me in one large Chamber, and a modern Representative, in Counterview, in another. The first seemed to be an Assembly of Heroes and Demy-Gods; the other a Knot of Pedlars, Pick-pockets, Highwaymen and Bullies" (195–96). And if the political quibblers would have it that Swift means to distinguish between the noble lines in the Lords and the rabble in the Commons, Gulliver traces the decay of the highborn as an impressionable "great Admirer of old illustrious Families." He experiences a kind of perverse pleasure in the distortions of natural lines.

> And I confess it was not without some Pleasure that I found my self able to trace the particular Features, by which certain Families are distinguished up

to their Originals. I could plainly discover from whence one Family derives a long Chin; why a second hath abounded with Knaves for two Generations, and Fools for two more; why a third happened to be crack-brained, and a fourth to be Sharpers. . . . How Cruelty, Falsehood, and Cowardice grew to be Characteristicks by which certain Families are distinguished as much as by their Coat of Arms. Who first brought the Pox into a noble House, which hath lineally descended in scrophulous Tumours to their Posterity. Neither could I wonder at all this, when I saw such an Interruption of Lineages by Pages, Lacqueys, Valets, Coachmen, Gamesters, Fidlers, Players, Captains, and Pick-pockets.

(198–99)

Gulliver's vision in Book Three becomes his opinion in the maddening last voyage when he explains the decayed state of nobility's lines to his Master Houyhnhnm.

That, *Nobility* among us was altogether a different Thing from the Idea he had of it; That, our young *Noblemen* are bred from their Childhood in Idleness and Luxury; that, as soon as Years will permit, they consume their Vigour, and contract odious Diseases among lewd Females; and when their Fortunes are almost ruined, they marry some Woman of mean Birth, disagreeable Person, and unsound Constitution, merely for the sake of Money, whom they hate and despise. That, the Productions of such Marriages are generally scrophulous, rickety or deformed Children; by which Means the Family seldom continues above three Generations, unless the Wife take Care to provide a healthy Father among her Neighbours, or Domesticks, in order to improve and continue the Breed.

(256)

Of course it is possible to argue that when in Book Three all history is called back to testify against its progressive line, Swift simply follows Lucian and Rabelais in parodying the pretense of older values. Swift is as much satiric mimic as a defender of ancients. If in Lilliput he could have his Cyclopean Gulliver protect his eyes, in Glubbdubdrib he can mock the precursor poet Homer as keener of eye than tradition itself allows. It is a Lucianic touch, indeed, that pairs Homer and Aristotle: "*Homer* was the taller and comelier Person of the two, walked very erect for one of his Age, and his Eyes were the most quick and piercing I ever beheld" (197). Satire is revisionary in every sense, and Swift goes to such extremes to support the ancient cause that one is compelled not only to reject the notion of modern progress but to doubt the legitimacy of past enterprise. Perhaps Homer himself anticipated the problem. No one appreciates the glorification of the past in the *Iliad* so much as the old warrior Nestor, and no one is more tediously represented than Nestor in praising the virtues of a more perfect past order, more perfect because it is more forgettable.

When Swift risks what is unlikely to be believed (or what is tedious in the believing) he does so in extravagant ways. In the last book of the *Travels* his perfectionists, his noble classicists, his reasonable traditionalists are a race of horses. They are not subject to disease; they decay gradually but only a few weeks before death, which is a kind of eternal return, a *Lhnuwnh* or a retirement to their first mother (275). The Houyhnhnms' only real sense of degeneration comes from the antithetical Yahoos. But a horse is still a horse, and the inhabitants of Swift's utopia are only tentatively removed from the degenerative potential that rules the narrative.[3] If Swift's amiable quadrupeds are "placed in opposite View to human Corruptions" (258), one clear and clearly satiric reason is that they are not humans by a long shot. On the other hand, Yahoos are the natural end of the satirically conceived human line. Their very beastliness conforms to the larger regressive inheritance of the *Travels*: "in most Herds there was a Sort of ruling *Yahoo*, (as among us there is generally some leading or principal Stag in a Park) who was always more *deformed* in Body, and *mischievous* in Disposition, than any of the rest" (262). The Yahoos possess and are possessed by "their strange Disposition to Nastiness and Dirt" (263), a disposition that no matter how much Gulliver protests otherwise also plagues him from the beginning to the end of his voyages.

Yahoos are all too human. Even the theory of their generation is degenerative. One local opinion conceived of their nature as the residual substance that once composed them: "whether produced by the Heat of the Sun upon corrupted Mud and Slime, or from the Ooze and Froth of the Sea, was never known" (271). Gulliver's Master Houyhnhnm expresses a view that is more in keeping with the general structure of the *Travels*, a view ominously applicable to Gulliver: "that the two *Yahoos* said to be first seen among them, had been driven thither over the Sea; that coming to Land, and being forsaken by their Companions, they retired to the Mountains, and degenerating by Degrees, became in Process of Time, much more savage than those of their own Species in the Country from whence these two Originals came" (272).

For the Houyhnhnms Gulliver is something of a time capsule of Yahoo history; he provides a look backwards. By the same argument, in the last book of the *Travels* the Yahoos are a look forward into the natural descent of man. Gulliver himself frames the issue of satiric inheritance: "And when I began to consider that by copulating with one of the *Yahoo*-Species, I had become a Parent of more; it struck me with the utmost Shame, Confusion, and Horror" (289). He speaks of his own wife and children here as indistinguishable from the Yahoos of Houyhnhnmland. As the returned wanderer, Gulliver is something less than a family man.

Gulliver's experiences in the last book of his *Travels* confirm a process represented satirically throughout. When he first sets eyes on the Yahoo species, he notes that "Upon the whole, I never beheld in all my Travels so disagreeable an Animal, or one against which I naturally conceived so strong an Antipathy" (223–24). The antipathy is obviously not shared by one libidinous eleven-year-old female Yahoo who tries to mount him. Gulliver is mortified: his attacker is not even a red-head, which he might have been able to justify as an Irish-Yahoo appetite: "For now I could no longer deny, that I was a real *Yahoo*, in every Limb and Feature, since the Females had a natural Propensity to me as one of their own Species" (267). When his Master sees him naked but for his shirt, he concludes that Gulliver must "be a perfect *Yahoo*" (237), an observation that admits of several interpretations. The epithet "perfect" is synonymous with the name *Houyhnhnm* in Houyhn-hnmnese. However *Yahoo* in the Houyhnhnm language is everything that *Houyhnhnm* is not. As perfect Yahoo, Gulliver is a living paradox. But back home and in his final madness he can make no such claim; he betrays his status as a perfect Yahoo by prancing and whinnying like a horse.

◆

Hugh Kenner has written an engaging short book called *The Counterfeiters*, which has an apt subtitle, *an Historical Comedy*. Kenner's subtitle suggests a particular vision of literary process tied to a set of preoccupations that began in the later seventeenth century and characterized "the great artists of an astonishing half-century, 1690–1740": "We call them satirists, they called themselves (having no better word) satirists; they were, Swift and Pope, great realists, great modernists. They had responded, we are going to see, to a new definition of man, proper to the new universe of empirical fact, which definition still obtains because we are still in that universe. They transmuted, to the point of destruction, the old ritual genres, tragedy, comedy, epic, which were proper to an older universe."[4]

Counterfeit is revision with a vengeance—a sly vengeance. The "Historical Comedy" of Kenner's subtitle is itself the counterfeiting of literary history, the comic reproduction or imitation that records and debases at the same time. For the satirist the world of empirical fact works as it does for the counterfeiter: "retaining its contours, altering its nature."[5] Satirists see a double potential in all recorded actions,[6] which reflects a measure of generic displacement or duplicity. Gulliver is a travelling man, *homo viator*, but he is also a decentered or counterfeit hero. He shares a remembered generic destiny with sorts as variable as Odysseus and Robinson Crusoe. In parodying the idea of the nationally displaced hero, Swift addresses the epic of his time, the epic of territorial exploration and expansion in unknown continents and seas of the world. The spaces of the *Travels* are suspiciously extreme: the first and last books are set beyond *terra australis incognita* in a satirical underworld of sorts (or at least "down under"); the second adventure occurs near or about the mythical Northwest Passage (the traditional land of fallen giants); and the third adventure is set in the uncharted waters of the oriental Pacific.[7]

The conjunction of epic and travel literature can be traced back to the Greek geographer Strabo, who based a good part of his writings on the presumed accuracy of the Homeric Mediterranean adventures. Of course the counterassumption formed the ironic basis for Lucian's Homeric parody in the *True History*. Those predisposed to skepticism always treat travel literature in as antagonistic a manner as they treat heroic marvels. Thus Voltaire writes of historical methodology in his *Philosophical Dictionary*: "When Herodotus relates what he was told by the barbarians among whom he traveled, he relates nonsense; but most of our travelers do the same."[8] And although Gulliver is hardly one to trust, he voices a similar sentiment after his rescue from Brobdingnag:

> I thought we were already overstocked with Books of Travels: That nothing could now pass which was not extraordinary; wherein I doubted, some Authors less consulted Truth than their own Vanity or Interest, or the Diversion of ignorant Readers. That my Story could contain little besides common Events, without those ornamental Descriptions of strange Plants, Trees, Birds, and other Animals; or the barbarous Customs and Idolatry of savage People, with which most Writers abound. However, I thanked him for his good Opinion, and promised to take the Matter into my Thoughts.
>
> (147)

That Gulliver demurs is both a joke and a commentary upon the state of the art. Swift's friend Frances Hutcheson offers some observations about the status of travel literature in 1726, the same year Swift published the *Travels*.

> A Late Ingenious Author . . . has justly observ'd the Absurdity of the *monstrous Taste*, which has possess'd both the *Readers* and *Writers* of *Travels*. They scarce give us any Account of the *natural Affections, the Familys, Associations, Friendships, Clans*, of the *Indians*; and as rarely do they mention their Abhorrence of *Treachery* among themselves; their *Proneness* to mutual Aid, and to the Defence of their several *States*; their Contempt of Death in defence of their Country, or upon points of *Honour*. "These are but *common-Storys*—No need to travel to the *Indies* for what we see in Europe every Day." The Entertainment therefore in these ingenious Studys consists chiefly in exciting *Horror*, and making Men *Stare*. The ordinary Employment of the Bulk of the *Indians* in support of their Wives and Offspring, or Relations, has nothing of the *Prodigious*. But a *Human Sacrifice*, a Feast upon Enemys Carcases, can raise an Horror and Admiration of the wondrous Barbarity of *Indians*, in Nations no strangers to the *Massacre at Paris*, the *Irish Rebellion*, or the Journals of the *Inquisition*. These they behold with religious Veneration; but the *Indian Sacrifices*, flowing from a like Perversion of *Humanity* by *Superstition*, raise the highest Abhorrence and Amazement. What is most suprizing in these Studys is the wondrous *Credulity* of some Gentlemen, of great Pretensions in other matters to Caution of Assent, for these *marvellous Memoirs* of Monks, Fryars, Sea-Captains, Pyrates; and for the *Historys, Annals, Chronologys*, receiv'd by Oral Tradition, or Hieroglyphicks.[9]

Hutcheson's complaint is one that had received even more eloquent expression in Montaigne's famous essay "Of Cannibals." Swift's Gulliver arrives as a satiric corrective for such complaints. But as is often the case with satire, it exacerbates before it amends. Try as he might to keep his record within the bounds of mundane description, the extravagances of the travel genre force poor Gulliver to the extraordinary. Each voyage begins with a probable destination and ends with an improbable place. Swift's strategy is primarily Lucianic, but he borrows from travels as remote as Sir Thomas More's *Utopia*, Rabelais' later Northwest Passage books, Cyrano de Bergerac's atmospheric travel histories, even Defoe's allegorical lunar journey, *The Consolidator*.[10]

The satiric traveller is an antithetical figure. As he "moves out," he understands less. In serious travel literature, the home order or the normative order is the basis of measured value so that in the voyage out there is both a psychological and intellectual pressure to move back in, to acclimate, familiarize, adjust, and in one way or another come home. As a narrative or strategic promise, homecoming is the final falling into place of travel literature—no voyager, imagined or actual, leaves home with the *intent* of permanent exile. Perhaps this is why the traditional utopia or *no place* is usually so alien and extreme. Utopia is home only for antithetical natures.

An essential strategy in the satiric or parodic travel narrative is the confusion of the "no place" with the "home place." Primitive forms such as the "Antipodes" satire, where the utopian realm is at geographical and cultural odds with the homeland (that is turned upside down), serve as ready examples of the process in outline, and there are antipodal elements in all of the books of *Gulliver's Travels*. But the more complex satiric parodies of travel narrative work with more subtle means of psychological and spatial unsettlement. In Swift's *Travels*, the most unsettled place is the mental territory of the traveller. Gulliver loses the will to go home because his sense of himself as a homebody deteriorates—he prefers geographical displacement. Even at home he seeks the stable rather than the house. Like Achilles, he can talk to horses, but unlike Achilles, he gains no glory from doing so.[11]

At the end of his travels Gulliver is a figure without a ground. All of his life he has shared a characteristic feature of the wanderer, "an insatiable Desire of seeing foreign Countries" (80), but that desire is finally subverted by an antagonism to the place of origin. The original wanderer, Odysseus, is sanctioned in his wanderlust partly because of his great desire to return. Only after he reestablishes himself as a native force do the post-Homeric legends of his further voyages begin, the most famous of which is recorded in Dante's *Inferno*. Significantly, for Dante the centrifugal spirit is a kind of motion sickness, and Ulysses is the tragic version of the perpetually exiled traveller. Hell's exile is perhaps worse than Gulliver's home stable because the denied home is the promised Earthly Paradise.

In the *True History*, Lucian begins his satiric subversion of the homing epic by insisting that his narrator make the same tragic step that Dante was later to record—the step beyond the Pillars of Hercules into unknown waters.

Lucian abandons the depth of epic values for the abnormal range of parodic displacement. Similarly, Swift works to undermine the measure of the home place by making Gulliver increasingly unsure of what normative measure means. In the initial voyages, accident makes him a monster or a *lusus naturae*. Eventually he succeeds in distorting his own lineaments by mad devising. His homing instinct is shapeless because by the end he has no shape that he wants to call his own. Even earlier in his *Travels*, after the Brobdingnagian adventure, he had realized that proportion was a relative thing, but his realization made it no easier for him to contemplate his altered physical status: "I could never endure to look in a Glass after mine Eyes had been accustomed to such prodigious Objects; because the Comparison gave me so despicable a Conceit of my self" (147). When at the end of the *Travels* he returns home to a place where he would rather not be and to a place that would probably prefer not to have him, he again looks in the mirror, this time with a thought to self-accommodation: "to behold my Figure often in a Glass, and thus if possible habituate my self by Time to tolerate the Sight of a human Creature" (295). Satiric travel is schizophrenic, and Gulliver loses formal integrity when his spatial and proportionate insecurity befuddles his home image. After Brobdingnag all England seems Lilliputian to Gulliver (which, by satiric analogy, it was). He notes that until he can readjust, his family "concluded I had lost my Wits" (149). Later, when first introduced to the estate of the Horse of Quality in Houyhnhnmland, Gulliver reaches the same conclusion about himself: "I feared my Brain was disturbed by my Sufferings and Misfortunes" (229). Gulliver has been set up. His final madness is the satiric concentration of displacement in the homeless body and soul of the traveller.

In Lilliput Gulliver's stature gave him the name of mountain and allowed him the role of human arch. To the Blefuscans he was a veritable Leviathan. In Brobdingnag he is thought to be a species of weasel, toad, spider, or unnamed vermin; a piece of clockwork; perhaps even "an Embrio, or abortive Birth" (104). The kitchen clerk's monkey gives him "good Reason to believe that he took me for a young one of his own Species" (122), something Gulliver has occasion to remember when he is later mounted by a female Yahoo in Houyhnhnmland. At the end of his fourth voyage his wife embraces him at home, and Swift's *homo viator* faints dead away. The smell of his faithful Penelope is alien to his "perfected" nose. Earlier Gulliver's wife protested that the kind of voyaging Gulliver subjects himself to makes torture out of readjustment. She wants no more of unsettled behavior: "But my Wife protested I should never go to Sea any more; although my evil Destiny so ordered, that she had not Power to hinder me" (149). For Gulliver's wife, voyaging is the equivalent of alienated affection, and it is a kind of madness constantly to test one's powers of readjustment. In a narrative sense, to send Gulliver out over and over again is to insure that he loses the capacity to return whole.

Satiric travels are something of an overextension, and at the end of his

Travels Gulliver is like the restless author of *A Tale of A Tub*: once maddened by surfaces, his depths become lunatic. The *Tale's* author is no more a homecomer than is Gulliver.

> For in *Writing*, it is as in *Travelling*: If a Man is in haste to be at home, (which I acknowledge to be none of my Case, having never so little Business, as when I am there) if his *Horse* be tired with long Riding, and ill Ways, or be naturally a Jade, I advise him clearly to make the straitest and the commonest Road, be it ever so dirty; But, then surely, we must own such a Man to be a scurvy Companion at best; He *spatters* himself and his Fellow-Travellers at every Step: All their Thoughts, and Wishes, and Conversation turn entirely upon the Subject of their Journey's End; and at every Splash, and Plunge, and Stumble, they heartily wish one another the Devil.
>
> (188)

The author of the *Tale* views the very notion of the centripetal fiction as singleminded: he prefers the range and pace of modernity. But to be in perpetual motion is to see too much of the surface of things, to start by fits and to end by starts. When Gulliver's travels are over, he begins them again by recording them. Here, too, he feels betrayed by the home front. He protests that cuts have been made in his text after its release to an editor. As a writer, just as a traveller, he would have gone on further if he could. In another sense, his writing simply prolongs the record of his madness. Satire's wanderings do not rest upon terra firma. Gulliver begins his voyaging as a ship's surgeon whose mind is something less than surgical. At the end he is captain, and his ship is served by one Dr. Purefoy. Pure faith is satiric gullibility, and the satiric motion appears to be starting all over again. By navigating through the world, Purefoy will certainly lose the purity and the faith his name is heir to.

The displaced hero courts one or another form of madness. Insecure at home, Hamlet makes a fool of himself; sterile in his capacity as a farmer, Don Quixote travels in circles as a lunatic Hidalgo; parasitical by design, Rameau's nephew is frenetic for his supper. Homelessness is maddening. What makes *Gulliver's Travels* even more intriguing in this respect is that, as in Swift's own *Tale of A Tub* or in Dostoevsky's *Notes from Underground* or in Nabokov's *Pale Fire*, the madman is given just enough presence of mind to record the process of his own lunacy.

When Swift added the letter from Gulliver to his cousin Sympson to the 1735 edition of the *Travels*, he further complicated the problem. How can an author be trusted who rants as does Gulliver to his slightly embarrassed cousin and editor? What generates his values? The tone of the letter makes no sense until we have read the entire *Travels*. If we do read the *Travels* through (and thereby understand the prefixed letter), we are forced to conclude that even the earlier voyages are being relayed from the perspective of a madman whose sense of an audience is no more secure than his grasp on his reason. In the 1735 edition, Gulliver not only gives us an inkling of the way his condition can be held against him but of the way Swift holds a crazed Gulliver against the entire genre of travel literature: "If the Censure of *Yahoos* could any Way affect me, I should have great Reason to complain, that some of them are so bold as to think my Book of Travels a meer Fiction out of mine Brain; and have gone so far as to drop Hints, that the *Houyhnhnms* and *Yahoos* have no more Existence than the Inhabitants of *Utopia*" (7–8).

That a madman should take so offended a tone comports with the earlier Swiftian notion from the *Tale of A Tub* that the brain's fancies have the power to leap astride reason. Of course Gulliver could point to ocular proof—the miniature cows from Lilliput or the wasp stings from Brobdingnag. But perhaps these are figments of his imagination as well. Further, he tells the professor at Lagado of his visits to the Kingdom of Tribnia (Britain) called Langden (England), and since he makes no claims to being the only European to have visited these territories, we could conclude that all his travels are but encoded versions of home as experienced by a madman. Lunacy means to be mentally far away no matter where one's body is, a state admittedly reached by Gulliver at the end of his travels. [12] The loss of powers that enables a narrator to discriminate, concentrate, and penetrate becomes part of the degenerative representation of Swift's satiric fiction. Gulliver's status as a truth teller—a man possessed by imagined truths—is a compromised status. Cousin Sympson boasts (presumably by way of relation, since he is sheepish in most regards) that Gulliver "was so distinguished for his Veracity, that it became a Sort of Proverb among his Neighbours at *Redriff* when any one affirmed a Thing, to say, it was as true as if Mr. *Gulliver* had spoke it" (9). Somehow this remark by Sympson registers more loyalty than conviction.

Given free reign at home, the horse-mimicking Gulliver is likely to run away with himself. By his own testimony he worries that his manuscript has been tampered with, he offers corrections, he prepares supplementary texts detailing a more fully documented madness. Apparently the *Travels* as we have them are but the ur-text of a travelling fancy. Gulliver is similar to the author of the *Tale* who has things in store for posterity. In fact, a quick glance at the proposed oeuvre of the *Tale*'s author momentarily raises the prospect that Swift's two lunatics share satiric experiences. Of the promised titles, two read: "*A Description of the Kingdom of* Absurdities" and "*A Voyage into England, by a Person of Quality in* Terra Australis incognita, *translated from the Original*" (2). *Gulliver's Travels* fulfills a part of the *Tale*'s promise: absurdity is figured in satiric ethnocentricity, and a native of Australia might in one sense be a Hottentot but in another is a would-be Houyhnhnm.

◆

Voyages into or out of kingdoms of absurdity are by nature politically tainted. Long before Swift had begun work on the Scriblerian notion of a gullible traveller, his patron, employer, and subject in the first book of the *Travels*, Robert Harley, had participated in a scheme to cast discredit on an unfortunate traveller. In 1705 Harley, having assumed the post of Secretary of Northern Affairs, wished to fill his vacated Speaker's seat in Parliament with a candidate of his own choosing. To do so he had to block the appointment of one William Bromley. A decade before (1692), Bromley, then a young man of twenty-eight, published a personal memoir, *Remarks on the Grand Tour lately perform'd by a Person of Quality*. The remarks revealed the mind of an innocent enough but somewhat foolish admirer of Catholic Europe—a none too healthy bias at any time in England after the Stuarts. By 1705 Bromley's early exuberance had long been forgotten, except by Harley and whatever counterfeiting crew he could muster for the occasion. Harley's men arranged for the republication of Bromley's *Grand Tour*. In its own way, the hoax was ingenious and satirically economical. Its strategy damned the man through the observations of the traveller.

The *Remarks* were reprinted verbatim, but the new edition added a table at the beginning of the volume. Passages from the body of the text were excerpted or briefly described with page numbers referring to the proper context. In isolation the excerpts destroy the serious record of the *Remarks*. We learn in the table how Bromley is barely able to contain his ecstasy when offered the chance to kiss the Pope's feet, and we are informed that Bromley will discuss (as if the matter were in doubt) whether "Crosses and Crucifixes on the Roads in *France* prove it is not *England*." On page 107 of the *Remarks* as previewed, the humble "Author is Compar'd with our Savior, and wants of his Height, a Hand's breath by Measure." For Harley, the political issue is obvious. Bromley was a noted (and at that time respected) High Churchman. Harley's hoax threatens to push him over the Catholic precipice. The hoaxers undermine Brombley's allegiance to his own land by undermining his status as a traveller: rather than controlling the travels he records, he is controlled by them.

I mention this rather slight literary scheme because in a much more sophisticated manner Swift is up to the same thing in *Gulliver's Travels*. Although he has no particular wish to indict any single victim, he does wish to adjust the contours of mock travel to belittle the affairs of his nation. In this sense *Gulliver's Travels* is well-timed. Between 1699 and 1715 Swift's hero is intermittently out of his native land. There is something significant about these dates because they suggest that Swift's scheme of degeneration applies to the processes of history at large. The details of the contemporary allegory, especially in Books One and Three of the narrative, are well enough rehearsed. But the span of the four voyages sets the *Travels* during a time roughly contemporaneous with the major troubles in Europe and England beginning with the Partition Treaties of 1698 and 1699, continuing through the War of Spanish Succession (1701–13), and concluding with the investigation of Swift's friends and patrons, Harley and Bolingbroke, in 1715.

All of Swift's important historical writings concentrate on segments near the beginning and end of the time periods encompassed by Gulliver's voyages. In his *Contests and Dissentions in Athens and Rome* (1701), he paralleled events in classical history to the Partition Treaty Trials. In his *Conduct of the Allies* (1711) and his *History of the Four Last Years of the Queen* (1713), he treated the latter conduct of the Succession Wars and the negotiations prior to the ordeal of his friends and patron ministers. The time span of *Gulliver's Travels* hints at a kind of historical apostasy—the narrative leaves England during a period of history in which Swift thought England had left her senses. Something of the same order might be argued for a narrative such as Defoe's *Robinson Crusoe*. Crusoe's twenty-eight year exile (1659–87) roughly overlaps a period of equally charged political significance, the years of Stuart restoration in England. For a Dissenting hater of the Stuarts like Defoe, these years may just as well have been spent on Crusoe's island near the mouth of the Orinoco. Home itself, after all, was akin to political exile. Exile is a key metaphor for Gulliver as it was for Crusoe. Not only is Gulliver removed from England by navigational fate but in both the first and last books of his adventures he is barred even from the lands to which accident has consigned him. In separate legal proceedings, Gulliver leaves Lilliput because he is thought to be more scheming than he was; fifteen years later he leaves Houyhnhnmland because he was thought to be less capable than he is.

Charges of treason and sentences of exile displace greater national follies. In 1699 Gulliver starts off as an English voyager, and in 1715 he returns as an outcast from an outcast land, a misanthrope, a sick man of Europe.[13] His giant carcass in Lilliput had made him an invading and standing army, a threat, an engulfer, a saving force and a conspiratorial force. From the first book of the *Travels* Swift announces the gigantic folly of modern politics and war and the "littleness" of all efforts for peace. Gulliver is a human Arch of Triumph as the Lilliputians march beneath him. Passing under, they look up at the holes in the mighty man's dirty breeches, a none too subtle reminder that the particular force Gulliver has to deliver comes as much from the seat of his pants as from the might of his arm. As it turns out, he is useless on land and is at best a necessary tactical force at sea.

Swift's attitude toward the land war raging in Europe was similar to that of Harley and Bolingbroke. A continued Marlborough-like commitment in Europe was madness, a madness figured in the composite of the absurd Lilliputian emperor with this Austrian lip, his fashion "between the *Asiatick* and the *European*," his gold helmet "adorned with Jewels, and a Plume on the Crest," and his symbolically drawn sword (30–31). Gulliver's efforts on behalf of this emperor's kingdom result in a conspiracy against his own powers and in a scheme to relieve the Man-Mountain of his eyes. This is either an Oedipal sentence for the land's putative savior or a strange recall of a more gigantic and barbaric Cyclopean fate.

In the second book of the *Travels*, the sweep of political degeneration is greater, even if less localized. In Brobdingnag, Gulliver, the former Lilliputian victim, becomes Gulliver, the European defender. Swift opens the satiric perspective to the hundred years of recklessness that constitutes, in his mind, the period of decline from the Renaissance to the later seventeenth century. For much of his stay in Brobdingnag, Gulliver is a figure of exhaustion, tired out by his trials. The tactician becomes a boasting domestic gladiator; the state hero betrayed by government becomes a freak of nature betrayed by a dwarf. If Gulliver reacts against political hypocrisy in Lilliput, in Brobdingnag he becomes the state hypocrite. When the King attacks England, Gulliver's "Colour came and went several Times, with Indignation to hear our noble Country, the Mistress of Arts and Arms, the Scourge of *France*, the Arbitress of *Europe*, the Seat of Virtue, Piety, Honour and Truth, the Pride and Envy of the World, so contemptuously treated" (107). He follows the advice of Dionysius Halicarnassensis in his "laudable Partiality to my own Country" (133), and learns after many discourses with the giant-king to "hide the Frailties and Deformities of my Political Mother, and place her Virtues and Beauties in the most advantageous Light" (133). Gulliver is the child of England, unaware of most of his "mother's" deformities and hiding those he suspects: he is the child of a deformed mother that has produced, among other things, Gulliver.

Swift probably began composing the *Travels* about the time that Gulliver's voyages theoretically end, and when he continued work at his own pace through the 1720s he adjusted the allegorical scheme of the narrative to the more generally conceived issues of political and cultural degeneration in the Walpole era. In Lilliput Gulliver practices statecraft; in Brobdingnag he defends it; in Laputa he hears of its abuses; in Houyhnhnmland he attacks it. As in all of the narrative movements of the *Travels*, Gulliver's experiences grow worse and worse. And as far as the theme of political degeneration goes, history becomes something of an *end* in itself. But it remains for Pope, who in some measure acted at Swift's suggestion, to take the historical scene of the 1720s even beyond the end and back to chaos in *The Dunciad*.

Notes

1.   Jonathan Swift, *Gulliver's Travels*, ed. Herbert Davis (Oxford, 1965). All subsequent citations will be to this edition.

2.   Hobbes's giant form in the beginning of the *Leviathan* is the kind of mechanical being that Gulliver might have seemed to the Lilliputians, a *homo mechanicus*.

For what is the *Heart*, but a *Spring*; and the *Nerves*, but so many *Strings*; and the *Joynts*, but so many *Wheeles*, giving motion to the whole Body, such as was intended by the Artificer? *Art* goes yet further, imitating that Rationall and most excellent worke of Nature, *Man*. For by Art is created that great LEVIATHAN called a Common-Wealth, or State, (in latine Civitas) which is but an Artificiall Man; though of greater stature and strength than the Naturall, for whose protection and defence it was intended. (*Leviathan*, Introduction)

3.   These matters are explored in greater depth by John Traugott, "A Voyage to Nowhere with Thomas More and Jonathan Swift: *Utopia* and *The Voyage to the Houyhnhnms*," *Sewanee Review* 69 (1961): 534–65; and Robert C. Elliott, "Swift's Utopias," in *The Shape of Utopia: Studies in a Literary Genre* (Chicago, 1970), 50–67.

4.   Hugh Kenner, *The Counterfeiters, an Historical Comedy* (Bloomington, 1968), 13. For a longer and more detailed study of some aspects of the notion of counterfeit and hoax in the early eighteenth century, see Joseph M. Levine, *Dr. Woodward's Shield: History, Science, and Satire in Augustan England* (Berkeley and Los Angeles, 1977).

5.   Kenner, *The Counterfeiters*, 158.

6.   W. Bliss Carnochan makes the same point in his study of Swift's satiric strategies, *Lemuel Gulliver's Mirror for Man* (Berkeley and Los Angeles, 1968): "[satire] manifests ironically the hope of common assurance and the fact of common doubt" (6).

7.   For a review of the geography of the *Travels*, see the second essay, "The Geography and Chronology of *Gulliver's Travels*," in Arthur E. Case's *Four Essays on Gulliver's Travels* (Gloucester, Mass., 1958). *The Memoirs of the Extraordinary Life, Works, and Discoveries of Martinus Scriblerus*, ed. Charles Kerby-Miller (New York, reissued 1966) provided Swift the more fanciful inspiration for the journeys and places of the *Travels*. Chapter Sixteen of the *Memoirs* contains a list of planned voyages for Martinus to the "Remains of the ancient *Pygmaean* Empire," to "the Land of the *Giants*," to the "Kingdom of *Philosophers*, who govern by the *Mathematicks*," to a land in which "he discovers a Vein of Melancholy proceeding almost to a Disgust of his Species" (165). For the opening adventure in Lilliput, Swift may have remembered a bit of lore about another wandering hero, Hercules, who after conquering Antaeus was so exhausted by his efforts that he fell prey to a horde of attacking pigmies. The sleeping Gulliver finds himself in a similar plight.

8.   Voltaire, *Philosophical Dictionary*, trans. Peter Gay (New York, 1962), entry on "Circumcision," 203.

9.   Frances Hutcheson, *An Enquiry concerning Moral Good and Evil* (London, 1726), 203–4.

10.   Swift's pilferings from Defoe's travel works are intriguing. The ship captain for Gulliver's third voyage is named Robinson, which could not but help recall the famous adventurer of a few years before, and the voyage's destination is Tonquin, precisely where Defoe's much earlier traveller from the *Consolidator* had journeyed to begin his lunar flight. From Tonquin Swift arrives at a flying island and parodies certain experiments of the Royal Society, a program that had also occupied Defoe in the *Consolidator*. It may be that Swift decided to repay Defoe in kind, since much of the *Consolidator* (1706) tried to capitalize on the fame and borrow the allegorical machinery of Swift's *A Tale of A Tub* (1704). The circle is made more vicious by the obvious distaste each writer had for the other.

11.   In *The Counterfeiters*, Hugh Kenner tells a different horse story about a classical hero. For Kenner, Gulliver is a "last Odysseus" doing "his poor best to fulfill yet another ancient scripture, one of which doubtless he has never heard: the mysterious tradition preserved by the Pyrrhonist chronicler Sextus Empiricus, that Odysseus at the end of his life was metamorphosed into a horse" (141).

12.   In his essay, "Of Idleness," Montaigne writes: "The soul that has no fixed goal loses itself; for as they say, to be everywhere is to be nowhere." See *The Complete Essays of Montaigne*, trans. Donald M. Frame (Stanford, 1958), 21.

13.   Significantly, the figure from the third book, Lord Munodi, whose name means hater of the world (although he hardly seems so), is also a political exile of sorts: "by a Cabal of Ministers [he] was discharged for Insufficiency" (175). Unlike the Gulliver to be, Munodi has the discretion to keep his opinions pretty much to himself—his name is attitude enough.

Irony and Ideals in *Gulliver's Travels*

FRANK STRINGFELLOW

In *A Rhetoric of Irony*, Wayne Booth developed a plausible and influential distinction between "stable" and "unstable" irony.[1] For Booth, irony is stable when the reader can translate from the surface meaning of an ironic statement back to some hidden, more or less opposed meaning that lends itself to a definite formulation. This is the irony of the rhetorical tradition, as contrasted with the irony of romanticism and beyond, where often no positive statement can be readily inferred from the ironic communication; we know only what is being rejected. Swift, of course, ought to fall well within the rhetorical tradition of stable irony. Individual ironic statements in *Gulliver's Travels* are, as a rule, readily translatable, and we sense throughout the book the existence of passionate beliefs that serve as the standpoint for the various ironic critiques. But when we come to actually define these beliefs, we often experience more difficulty than we expected, primarily because, when we perform the various translations necessary to get back to Swift's actual beliefs, the results of these translations do not always harmonize very well with one another. The supposedly stable ironies often add up to a great deal of instability—an instability that is perhaps best reflected in the long-standing and seemingly irresolvable critical dispute over the meaning of part 4, "A Voyage to the Country of the Houyhnhnms."

It is my contention that the difficulty we have in establishing Swift's beliefs in *Gulliver's Travels*—or rather, his ideals, as I would prefer to say— is inevitable, given the psychological determinants of verbal irony. Despite Freud's assertion that irony "can be understood without any need for bringing in the unconscious,"[2] irony can be shown to have roots deep in the unconscious, and the ironist, in giving way to his penchant for irony, opens up a path by which the unconscious fears, desires, and ambivalences of childhood can achieve at least partial expression. Of these unconscious emotions, one of the most important to emerge in ironic discourse is what Freudians would see as the inevitable human ambivalence toward one's own ideals. This ambivalence lies behind the contradictions and confusions that have led us in so many directions as readers of *Gulliver's Travels*; and indeed, the equally inevitable attempt to resolve this ambivalence is enacted by Gulliver in part 4 of the satire.

This essay was written specifically for this volume and appears here for the first time.

Before turning to the Houyhnhnms, let us first look at a relatively simple and straightforward example of the kind of contradiction that troubles our reading of *Gulliver's Travels*. The King of Brobdingnag, in his long reply to Gulliver's account of manners and morals in England, seems in many respects a mouthpiece for Swift's own considered views; so rational, moderate, and commonsensical are the King's opinions that we naturally assume that they are endorsed by the author, even without external evidence. For example, on the question of religious differences, the King responds to Gulliver as follows:

> He laughed at my odd Kind of Arithmetick (as he was pleased to call it) in reckoning the Numbers of our People by a Computation drawn from the several Sects among us in Religion and Politicks. He said, he knew no Reason, why those who entertain Opinions prejudicial to the Publick should be obliged to change, or should not be obliged to conceal them. And, as it was Tyranny in any Government to require the first, so it was Weakness not to enforce the second: For, a Man may be allowed to keep Poisons in his Closet, but not to vend them about as Cordials.[3]

In the case of this particular passage, we can even find external evidence that the King's opinion represents Swift's conscious beliefs. Thus, in his "Thoughts on Religion," Swift writes:

> Liberty of conscience, properly speaking, is no more than the liberty of possessing our own thoughts and opinions, which every man enjoys without fear of the magistrate: But how far he shall publicly act in pursuance of those opinions, is to be regulated by the laws of the country. Perhaps, in my own thoughts, I prefer a well-instituted commonwealth before a monarchy; and I know several others of the same opinion. Now, if, upon this pretence, I should insist upon liberty of conscience, form conventicles of republicans, and print books, preferring that government, and condemning what is established, the magistrate would, with great justice, hang me and my disciples. It is the same case in religion, although not so avowed, where liberty of conscience, under the present acceptation, equally produces revolutions, or at least convulsions and disturbances in a state.[4]

However, when Swift is being ironical, he seems to contradict the moderate position expressed by the King. In part 1, Gulliver repeats the history of the religious disputes raging for four generations in Lilliput and Blefuscu between the Big-Endians and their opponents. Here is an excerpt from that history:

> It is allowed on all Hands, that the primitive Way of breaking Eggs before we eat them, was upon the larger End: But his present Majesty's Grand-father, while he was a Boy, going to eat an Egg, and breaking it according to the

ancient Practice, happened to cut one of his Fingers. Whereupon the Emperor his Father, published an Edict, commanding all his Subjects, upon great Penalties, to break the smaller End of their Eggs. The People so highly resented this Law, that our Histories tell us, there have been six Rebellions raised on that Account; wherein one Emperor lost his Life, and another his Crown. These civil Commotions were constantly fomented by the Monarchs of *Blefuscu*; and when they were quelled, the Exiles always fled for Refuge to that Empire. It is computed, that eleven Thousand Persons have, at several Times, suffered Death, rather than submit to break their Eggs at the smaller End.

(1:4;33)

This passage shows the typical structure of verbal irony in that the ironist (Swift) assumes the pose of a naïf (Gulliver), who in turn is repeating the words of some authority. (Gulliver is actually reporting the words of Reldresal, the Principal Secretary of Private Affairs in Lilliput.) Also typically, the fact that these words belong to some adult authority is obscured: At some points in the Secretary's discourse we are reminded grammatically that we are hearing indirect speech, but in the sentences quoted here, such reminders are almost totally lacking. Thus, Gulliver appears to adopt the Secretary's words as his own. The words of the adult authority are repeated without alteration and without comment by the innocent Gulliver who does not see the absurdity of the facts and values embedded in these words. At the same time Swift, through exaggeration and antithesis, points out the absurdity of the basic opinion implied by the Secretary's history: that the present state of affairs, though bad, arose for reasons in themselves good and sufficient. The reader understands that Swift cannot share this opinion, and through further interpretation of the exaggerated allegory the reader also applies Swift's dissent to the official account of the rise of Protestantism in England.

At the very least, we have here an instance where Swift's ironic meanings (in the present passage) seem to contradict his direct meanings (as expressed in the above speech by the King of Brobdingnag); in the King's speech, Swift accepts the right of authority to require public observance of religious and political orthodoxy, whereas in Gulliver's speech he questions this right on the grounds of arbitrariness and cruelty. One might, of course, try to explain away this contradiction in various ways. For example, one might argue that, in imagining a dispute over how properly to break an egg, Swift is alluding only to the relatively insignificant theological differences that were often blown way out of proportion—to theological hairsplitting, as it were—and not to the truly important matters that divided Anglicans from Catholics and Dissenters. And indeed, Swift argued vigorously against oversubtlety in doctrinal matters, which he saw as fomenting needless dissensions. But Swift's allegory does not really admit the possibility of other, more important points of dispute; the proper way to break an egg becomes the founding doctrine of the Lilliputian religion, and the origin of its dispute with Blefuscu. However much we would like to avoid accusing Swift of self-contradiction, he seems indeed to be guilty of it—although his irony serves its usual defensive purpose and requires us to do considerable interpretation before filing our brief, and the ironist, of course, can always repudiate our "interpretations."

In his biography of Swift, Irvin Ehrenpreis takes up a similar problem when he tries to explain how Swift, in *Gulliver's Travels*, could seem to support beliefs so much at odds with the tenor of his life and other works. Ehrenpreis proposes the thesis that Swift held a "general, moral outlook" that could conflict with the specific "historical positions" that he took up.[5] Ehrenpreis implies what we are getting in *Gulliver's Travels* are the general principles, even when these conflict with the principles that could be deduced from Swift's own practice; thus, in his satire, Swift implies that religious and political differences are relatively insignificant, whereas in practice he was a vigorous and combative partisan. Swift, Ehrenpreis argues, did not worry about inconsistency; caught up in the excitement of an argument or a topic, he would pursue it wherever it took him, without worrying about any overall system. Indeed, in one important instance, Ehrenpreis even finds inconsistency within *Gulliver's Travels* itself: "Absorbed in the depiction of the moral life, the life of reason, [Swift] represented the Houyhnhnms as dignified or awesome. Absorbed in the historical drama of his narrative, he let them appear limited and fallible."[6]

To his credit, Ehrenpreis does not try to minimize the contradictions he finds, and the explanation for them that he proposes is psychologically quite suggestive. And yet the theory doesn't really explain what most needs explanation: *Why* was Swift excited by arguments that tended to undermine his ordinary beliefs? Why was he borne off in these particular (conflicting) directions? What do the subversive arguments have to do with the ironic discourse in which they are expressed?

In an article focusing especially on the *Tale of a Tub*, Claude Rawson offers an argument that might answer these questions. According to Rawson, Swift realizes, in part through introspection, that sectarianism and free thinking arise not solely out of moral badness but also out of "an innate mental perversity" that is "a psychological feature of the human condition, implicating all men, including ultimately Swift." Swift's solution to this dilemma is a "repudiating mimicry of the subversive intensities of the human mind."[7]

One virtue of Rawson's theory is that it would account for the emergence of subversive opinions in Swift's *ironic* writings, since irony can be seen precisely as a kind of "repudiating mimicry." In addition, the theory would explain why Swift's irony, far from being simply a rhetorical device for presenting his views, seems to arise from the very depths of Swift's psyche: irony becomes a way of exorcising the devils of doubt and rebellion by which

Swift feels himself beset. But there are also problems with Rawson's theory. For one thing, it assumes that Swift remains in control of his own "innate mental perversity," so that any subversive intensities present in his work are there not as themselves but as a "repudiating mimicry." But if Swift is exerting this kind of control, then we should not find in a work like *Gulliver's Travels* the contradictions that we have been talking about. The other possibility, of course, is that Swift is actually indulging his own "innate mental perversity," even if he doesn't realize that he is doing so or thinks that he is repudiating it. It is this latter possibility that I would like to explore here.

Let us put the question differently. Instead of asking why, in his ironic discourse, Swift seems to contradict beliefs that he elsewhere appears to uphold, let us ask whether any other outcome is possible. Could a positive statement of beliefs and ideals ever harmonize with an ironic statement?

From the rhetorical point of view, the answer is assuredly yes. In interpreting an ironic statement, one translates back from the surface meaning, not truly intended by the author, to the covert meaning, which is the one actually intended; and there is no reason why this covert meaning should differ in form or structure from a similar statement that was not originally hidden by an ironic overlay. But from a psychological point of view, we must reach a different conclusion. The psychological key lies in the relationship between the positive and negative aspects of the superego.

In its negative aspect, the superego is viewed by the ego as prohibitive and brutally punishing. It is the implacable instrument of justice that metes out retribution whenever the individual, even in fantasy, transgresses against its laws. The prohibition against incest would be an archetypal instance of the superego's laws, and indeed, this law figures prominently in the plot of *Gulliver's Travels*: It is possible to show that when Gulliver urinates on the fire in the Empress's apartments in part 1, he enacts an incest fantasy, and that his attempt to flee punishment for this deed precipitates a spiraling regression and prevents him from negotiating the oedipal crisis.[8] The "real" punishment (of blindness and death) that Gulliver flees within the context of the novel's fantasy world represents the fantasied punishment with which the superego threatens the ego. But the superego has a more positive aspect as well. The superego also enforces upon the ego the individual's own ideals; it punishes the ego when the latter fails to live up to these ideals. (Psychoanalysts dispute whether these ideals reside in the ego or in the superego. For our purposes the distinction is irrelevant and is, in fact, an example of how easily the two psychic agencies can be overreified.) This aspect of the superego emerges, for example, in Edmund Bergler's theory that the superego requires the ego to exhibit active control and to avoid passive, masochistic behavior and that it threatens the ego with punishment if it violates this ideal.[9] This more "positive" side of the superego also appears in *Gulliver's Travels*, since— again following Bergler's theory—Gulliver's pseudoaggressiveness (for example, against the Lilliputians, whom he never quite challenges despite his self-assurances that he could easily overpower them) can be analyzed as an attempt to deflect such a threat on the part of the superego.[10]

The connection between these two aspects of the superego, the positive and the negative, is intimate, for both result from the child's attempt to take into herself something alien, something derived from the parental authorities who have coerced as well as nurtured her. This alien structure within the psyche is absolutely necessary, at the very least for self-protection, but it also presents its own dangers to the individual: the superego is capable of merciless and sadistic retaliation for the slightest infraction of its standards. The individual's ego must therefore be strong enough to protect itself from the onslaughts of the superego. Individuals protect themselves in various ways, of which a common, but ultimately rather unsatisfactory, one is what psychoanalysts call (following Anna Freud) "identification with the aggressor." In the present context, identification with the aggressor would mean putting away any conscious sense that the prohibitions and ideals enforced by the superego are in any way alien to the ego. But a total identification with the punitive superego is in fact impossible. Such an identification would deny not only the vital libidinal impulses but also any sense the individual has of possessing some irreducible center that is inalienably his. So even the individual who identifies with his punitive superego is bound to demur as well, at least on an unconscious level, and to insist that the superego's demands are in some ways foreign to him—and inappropriate and unjust. This ambivalent and secret, or quasisecret, rebelliousness is the origin of irony. Sometimes the rebelliousness is directed against the rules and prohibitions laid down by parental (societal) authorities and sometimes against the ideals derived from the same authorities. Sometimes the rebelliousness comes out more as an ad hominem attack against the authority figure himself (or his successors), and sometimes it is directed more at the abstract remnants of authority. Often the aggressiveness is conscious and only concealed in a transparent (though, to the ironist, crucial) manner; sometimes it remains unconscious on the part of the ironist. But in whatever form it appears, irony is the sign that the ironist will not totally identify herself with that foreign element in herself made up of the prohibitions and ideals of parental authority. And since *all* prohibitions and ideals are descendants of those derived from the authorities of childhood, ultimately the ironist is actively resisting her own impulse to identify with any ideal or prohibition whatsoever. In other words, at the very moment when a person chooses to express himself ironically, he is exercising the ambivalent rebelliousness that precludes his full acceptance of the superego's authority and of any of its commands—an acceptance that in many respects the ironist may devoutly wish to force upon himself.

Once we conceive of the genesis of irony in this manner, we can no longer hold on to any hard-and-fast distinction between "stable" and "unstable" irony. The infinite, or at least unstoppable, irony of some of the romantics becomes an extreme case of the instability that must inhere in all irony whose roots lie not in the textbook practice of rhetoric but in the fundamental psychic traits of the ironist. The difference in the irony of a book like *Gulliver's Travels* and of a romantic work like Lermontov's *Hero of Our Times* results not so much from differences in the nature of the irony itself as in differences in what surrounds the irony. As we see in the passages just quoted, Swift is likely to "say the same thing" both ironically and unironically—that is, in some relatively direct, overt fashion. The presence of these overt statements then gives us the illusion that a stable ground underlies the irony, a constant set of beliefs and ideals to which the ironic statements ultimately refer. But when, as in the two passages we have been analyzing, we have the chance to compare seemingly equivalent statements, we see that the ironic statement and the nonironic one are not always in sync. In the present case, indeed, we must consider the two statements as repeating, in their relationship to one another, the same ambivalence that we find within the ironic statement itself. The ironist pays obeisance to the very authorities, and their ideals, that he cannot help ridiculing whenever he feels himself sufficiently protected by his evanescent ironic smoke screen.

We can best understand the relationship Swift the ironist takes toward his own ideals by looking at the celebrated "Utopia" he creates in part 4 of *Gulliver's Travels*.[11] In this connection, let me begin by recalling Theodor Reik's brilliant insight that an obsessional idea can take the form of an ironic statement that the obsessive utters over and over to himself, unaware of his own irony.[12] Reik gives the example of a young nobleman who obsessively repeated to himself the thought that servants and members of the lower classes were devils. Intellectually the young man realized that he did not believe this idea to be true, but he still could not free himself from its power over him. In fact, as Reik shows, the idea belonged not to the young man but to his parents. However, this fact was not recognizable because the idea was no longer in the form in which his parents had taught it to their son. The parents had taught, Be a good Christian and love thy neighbor; simultaneously they had taught a second message, Stay away from the servants. The young man had simply combined the two precepts and drawn the logical conclusion from their juxtaposition: If I am not to love servants, then they must not be my fellow human beings; and if they aren't human beings worthy of my love, then they must be devils. The crucial point here is that in mouthing the precepts of authority, the young man transforms them in such a way that exposes both their absurdity and his contempt for them. The transformation follows the ironist's typical maneuver: the ironist exaggerates an idea in such a way that the statement seems self-evidently false and therefore one that not even the speaker himself could credit. The particular exaggeration is also typical of irony—the ironist pushes an idea to its logical extremes (and beyond), putting it in more literal or graphic form than the idea can tolerate without exploding. Essentially, Reik's young patient has revealed his scorn for his parents' ideals by stating these beliefs in an ironic form—a form that indicates that he himself does not accept the beliefs. Yet because his contempt for his parents and for their precepts seems so dangerous to him, it remains unconscious, and he does not understand the true source of his obsessional idea. Indeed, the very fact that he still "believes" the obsessional idea, even though it is patently absurd, shows his inability to free himself from the parental ideals from which it is derived and for which he has such contempt. Though he, like every obsessive-compulsive neurotic, feels that the obsessional idea is something foreign to him—indeed it is, as the descendant of his parents' teaching—it continues to exercise control over him. And we may note in passing that Reik's obsessional patient torments *himself* with this ironic statement of his parents' beliefs; the authorities themselves are not directly attacked. This last result would seem to be directly opposed to the behavior typical of the ironist—except that, as can be seen in the case of Swift, even relatively overt ironic attacks have as well a hidden masochistic purpose.

How, then, does Reik's obsessional patient afford us insight into Swift's depiction of the Houyhnhnms? The ideal represented in Houyhnhnmland—reason ruling over human behavior—is clear enough, and indeed Freudian theory specifically names this ideal as one likely to be resisted by the unconscious.[13] But Swift obscures his resistance to the ideal of reason by denying, through an elaborate double game, that he is making ironic statements about this ideal. Swift's strategy involves a reversal of the usual time sequence involved in irony whenever it is not an absolutely simultaneous event. Normally, that is, the ironist gives us first the straightforward statement (that will turn out to be ambiguously intended) and afterward the additional remark that retroactively subverts the earlier statement. In part 4, however, Swift *begins* by providing the subversive information—that the speakers who will present the ideals of reason later in the book are in fact horses, brute animals whose "opinions" we would naturally dissociate from the author's. But then, by having Gulliver's Houyhnhnm master speak with what seems like excellent common sense (so that we easily identify the Houyhnhnms' opinions as the author's), Swift effectively denies that he is using his horses to speak ironically. And yet Swift's denial is—purposely—fragile. Should we ever receive too striking a reminder, however brief, that a normally irrational creature is offering dicta about reason, then we would be bound to suspect these dicta of being ironic. Swift sets up a situation that would automatically produce ironic statements, and then he delivers in this situation statements that generally strike us as unironic. The result is twofold. On the one hand, by raising and then frustrating expectations of irony, Swift's implicit denial of ironic intent seems all the more deliberate and sincere. On the other hand, the expectations of irony, once raised, must be continuously suppressed, or they will easily gain the upper hand. Thus, the basic strategy

Swift embarks on in part 4 already reveals a potentially ironic treatment of
its ideals—but also involves a firm denial that there will be any such irony.

The suppression of irony in part 4 depends on two things: first, we
must forget the "horseness" of the Houyhnhnms, and second, the Houyhnhnms' beliefs must be kept from ironizing exaggeration. Swift honors
both of these precarious aims throughout much of the last voyage, but he
undercuts them in the final chapters of the book. Here, for example, is a
passage in which Swift, by confronting us with an overly vivid picture of the
Houyhnhnms as *horses*, makes Gulliver's statements about them ironic: "The
Houyhnhnms use the hollow Part between the Pastern and the Hoof of their
Fore-feet, as we do our Hands, and this with greater Dexterity, than I could
at first imagine. I have seen a white Mare of our Family thread a Needle
(which I lent her on Purpose) with that Joynt" (4:9;258). The irony in this
passage depends, as so often, on exaggerating a statement by making it too
literal and too graphic and by taking it to some logical extreme. If Gulliver
had simply told us that the Houyhnhnms used their hooves "with greater
Dexterity, than I could at first imagine," we could have let his statement
pass. When, however, he adds the ludicrously graphic vignette of a horse
threading a needle, we read the quoted phrase as an ironic understatement.
The politely incredulous phrase "than I could at first imagine" then assumes
all its literal force: *no one* could have imagined this feat, precisely because it
is impossible. Swift is here beginning to distance himself from Gulliver's
astonished admiration of the Houyhnhnms; he is taking us back to our initial
expectations about a society of horses, expectations that he has overthrown
in the intervening chapters. This is the ad hominem part of the ironic
devaluation of the ideals presented in part 4.

Immediately after this passage we see Swift begin to state the ideals
themselves in an ironic manner that points to his hidden, and indeed ambivalent, dissent. The two major instances of this irony are telling, since both
reveal the essentially antihuman features of reason. In the first example,
Gulliver explains that the Houyhnhnms' rationality leads them to express
"neither Joy nor Grief" at the death of family and friends (4: 9; 258). Swift
then states this ideal ironically by giving an exaggerated and overly vivid
example. Gulliver's master was expecting a visit from a friend and his family,
but only the wife and children turn up, and very late at that: "She [the
friend's wife] made two Excuses, first for her Husband, who, as she said,
happened that very Morning to *Lhnuwnh*. The Word is strongly expressive
in their Language, but not easily rendered into *English*; it signifies, *to retire
to his first Mother*. Her Excuse for not coming sooner, was, that her Husband
dying late in the Morning, she was a good while consulting her Servants
about a convenient Place where his Body should be laid" (4:9;258–59). As
we see in this example, when Swift wants (perhaps unconsciously) to attack
the very ideal of reason that he has set up, and that derives ultimately from
the strictures of the superego, he first states ironically reason's prohibition

against mourning. This point of attack is intriguingly counter to one's expectations, for certainly we would think the attack on reason would come from another quarter—from the libidinal impulses to which reason (here almost equivalent to the superego) forbids expression. Instead, we have the refusal to mourn. Why? When we read the passage, it seems clear that the underlying psychic identification is with the dead friend who is being mourned by no one, not by wife, nor children, nor friends. The reason for this identification will become clearer if we turn immediately to the second major example of how Swift states ironically the ideals of reason.

The Houyhnhnms finally decide, in one of their general assemblies, that Gulliver's master, in accordance with the dictates of reason, must expel Gulliver from the country. Gulliver describes his reaction on hearing this news from his master:

> I was struck with the utmost Grief and Despair at my Master's Discourse; and being unable to support the Agonies I was under, I fell into a Swoon at his Feet: When I came to myself, he told me, that he concluded I had been dead. (For these People are subject to no such Imbecilities of Nature) I answered, in a faint Voice, that Death would have been too great an Happiness; that although I could not blame the Assembly's *Exhortation*, or the Urgency of his Friends; yet in my weak and corrupt Judgment, I thought it might consist with Reason to have been less rigorous.
>
> (4:10;264)

In this passage we find the culmination of many of the psychic trends that run throughout *Gulliver's Travels*. We particularly notice that Gulliver takes the part of the powerful adults yet again (as he did in Lilliput and especially in Brobdingnag), even when he thereby sides masochistically against himself. He acquiesces in his own punishment. But we also find here that Gulliver murmurs, in what I take to be ironic tones, against the adults' harshness: "yet in my weak and corrupt Judgment, I thought it might consist with Reason to have been less rigorous." One might perhaps want to argue that there is no irony here, and yet the exaggeration, both in Gulliver's self-abasement and in the attenuation of his complaint, is bound to suggest—especially in the context of this work—that irony is present. But whose irony is it? In one traditional approach, we judge Gulliver to be speaking sincerely, while attributing the irony here to Swift the author. Yet we drive too absolute a wedge between author and character when we take this approach. The extent to which Swift identifies with his character Gulliver, and is present in this character, emerges much more clearly when we see that Gulliver himself is being ironic here, though his irony is unconscious. One might expect that any ambivalence in Swift would be split up so that one side would remain with the author and the other be attributed to his character Gulliver, but on the whole Swift cannot really manage such an easy resolution. Instead, Swift's own ambivalence, though somewhat transformed, is reflected in splits within the character of Gulliver. The irony here belongs to the child who knows that, from the point of view of the adults and the laws of reason they espouse, his own thinking is "weak and corrupt." And there is something in the child that truly accepts this judgment of his own wishful thinking. But there is something else in the child that rebels and that believes in his own judgment. Indeed, the child does not simply *resist* the laws of reason that reality itself, as well as adult authority, is forcing on him, but he also succeeds in finding contradictions within these laws. This approach of exposing the absurdities—the self-contradictions—within the very precepts that one is mouthing, lies at the very heart of irony. The child Gulliver rejects the conclusions that are being imposed on him by adult reason; they appear alien to him not only in the catastrophic results they would bring but even by virtue of their belonging not to him, but to the adult world. Yet even his weak rebellion is borrowed from the adults: Is your powerful reason, he asks, not itself inconsistent and therefore unreasonable? "I thought it might consist with Reason to have been less rigorous."

What is so odd about the Gulliver-Swift revolt against the laws of reason is that it seems motivated more by a sense of fear and betrayal than by a desire to free the libidinal drives from the bondage of the antihedonistic superego. Indeed, Gulliver complains against reason not simply because it is separating him from the beloved figures with whom he has identified, but also because it is condemning him to live among those who recall him to his own sexuality and aggressiveness. At some level, however, Gulliver must realize that, through his identification with the Houyhnhnms, he has tried to make an inhuman bargain with the superego and the laws of reason; and that this bargain can only lead to a terrifying downward spiral of self-destruction which can neither be regretted nor mourned by the implacable agency with which he has cast his lot. Gulliver has identified with—internalized—an ideal against which, being human, he is bound to transgress and whose severe and unyielding punishment he is bound to inflict upon himself. And the more he attempts to escape from his fears, uncertainties, and ambivalences by identifying even more completely with the adult ideals of reason (represented by the Houyhnhnms), the more he condemns himself to masochistic punishment. It is easy enough to see why Gulliver and his creator fear, and murmur against, such ideals—and why Gulliver mourns for himself. It is also easy to see why the rebellion is covert, even unconscious: once a person is caught in this masochistic cycle of self-hatred and self-punishment, the ideals enforced by the superego seem to offer the only chance for an escape. Only a more perfect identification with those ideals, such as Gulliver thinks to achieve in Houyhnhnmland, can carry one away from that sexual and aggressive part of oneself that is hated and must be denied. Once this point in the vicious cycle is reached, the character Gulliver naturally falls apart (in a kind of cautionary tale), and Swift the author—as a way of distancing himself from Gulliver's inescapable predicament—shifts his ironic attack, which is now directed not so much against the ideals themselves as against Gulliver's (and his own) identification with these ideals. And yet, even at the end of the work, when horses become horses again and Gulliver's praise of them threatens to contaminate all of part 4 with retroactive irony (an irony that has been threatening, and has been only partly suspended, since the beginning), we still cannot say that the Houyhnhnms' ideal of reason has been definitively rejected—as the work of many "hard-school" critics would remind us.

The case of *Gulliver's Travels* suggests that the ironist, writing in the ironic mode, cannot give unequivocal consent to any ideal. On the other hand, further analysis would show that the reverse is also true: when the ironist repeats the words—the ideals and commands—of authority with the apparent intention of mocking them, the mockery may in fact conceal a measure of acceptance as well. We are used to saying that, in an ironic statement, the ironist can actually intend only one of the two more or less contradictory levels. But perhaps this is psychologically too simplistic; perhaps it is truer to say that both are intended, so that to speak ironically is necessarily to speak with unconscious ambivalence. [14]

Notes

1. Wayne Booth, *A Rhetoric of Irony* (Chicago: University of Chicago Press, 1974). See especially chapters 1, 8, and 9.

2. Sigmund Freud, *Jokes and Their Relation to the Unconscious*, in *The Standard Edition of the Complete Psychological Works of Sigmund Freud*, ed. James Strachey, 24 vols. (London: Hogarth Press, 1966–74), 8:174.

3. *The Prose Works of Jonathan Swift*, ed. Herbert Davis, 14 vols. (Oxford: Basil Blackwell, 1939–68), 11:115 (pt. 2, ch. 6). All further references to *Gulliver's Travels* will be given parenthetically in the text and will cite Davis's edition. For the reader's convenience, the part and chapter will also be noted, and will precede the page reference (to vol. 11). Thus, the present citation would be given as (2:6;115).

4. *Prose Works*, 9:263.

5. Irvin Ehrenpreis, *Swift: The Man, His Works, and the Age* (Cambridge: Harvard University Press, 1962–83), 3:462.

6. Ehrenpreis, 3:459.

7. Claude Rawson, "The Character of Swift's Satire: Reflections on Swift, Johnson, and Human Restlessness," in *The Character of Swift's Satire: A Revised Focus*, ed. Claude Rawson (Newark: University of Delaware Press, 1983), 30, 58.

8. For a psychoanalytic discussion of the urination episode, *see* Sándor Ferenczi, "Gulliver Phantasies," *International Journal of Psycho-Analysis* 9 (1928): 283–300.

9. See, for example, Edmund Bergler, *The Superego: Unconscious Conscience—The Key to the Theory and Therapy of Neurosis* (New York: Grune & Stratton, 1952), 92–94.

10. See Bergler, *Superego*, 41, and his *Laughter and the Sense of Humor* (New York: Intercontinental Medical Book, 1956), 57.

11. The debate over Swift's attitude toward the Houyhnhnms has been so extensive that it has inspired a famous typology, proposed by James L. Clifford in his "Gulliver's Fourth

Voyage: 'Hard' and 'Soft' Schools of Interpretation" (in *Quick Springs of Common Sense: Studies in the Eighteenth Century*, ed. Larry S. Champion [Athens: University of Georgia Press, 1974], 33–49). According to the "hard" interpretations, Swift means for us to be dismayed by "the obvious impossibility of a human being ever approaching an ideal life such as that of the horses"; the ending of part 4 is thus "shocking and tragic." According to "soft" interpretations, this ending is comic, "representing Swift's admission that the position taken by Gulliver in trying to emulate the Houyhnhnms was meant to be funny"; Swift was also "ready to satirize those with extended ideals" (James L. Clifford, "Argument and Understanding: Teaching Through Controversy," *Eighteenth-Century Life* 5, no. 3 [Spring 1979]: 2–3). See also Richard H. Rodino's *Swift Studies, 1965–1980: An Annotated Bibliography* (New York: Garland, 1984), where entries pertaining to this debate are classified as "hard school" or "soft school."

12. Theodor Reik, "Grenzland des Witzes," *Psychoanalytische Bewegung* 4 (1932): 289–322.

13. For example, in the *New Introductory Lectures on Psycho-Analysis*, Freud writes: "From the very beginning, when life takes us under its strict discipline, a resistance stirs within us against the relentlessness and monotony of the laws of thought and against the demands of reality-testing. Reason becomes the enemy which withholds from us so many possibilities of pleasure" (*Standard Edition*, 22:33). See also the discussion in *Jokes and Their Relation to the Unconscious (Standard Edition*, 8:126). Freud, of course, is using "reason" (*Vernunft*) in a slightly narrower sense than Swift does in *Gulliver's Travels*; nevertheless, Freud's point remains relevant to a discussion of the Houyhnhnms.

14. Several points that I have been able only to touch on here, both about irony and about *Gulliver's Travels*, are elaborated more fully in my *The Meaning of Irony: A Psychoanalytic Investigation*, forthcoming. For help with this essay, I would like to thank Tassie Gwilliam, Frank Palmeri, and Mihoko Suzuki.

Gulliver 3; or The Progress of Clio

Eric Rothstein

Although Part 3, or indeed any Part of *Gulliver's Travels*, resists simple all-inclusive arrangement, the plain narrative focus of each Part tempts one to believe that there may be other sorts of focus as well. I should like to propose an explanatory scheme for the *Travels*, including Part 3, which accounts for the intuition that each Part does have a focus and yet which does not coerce or ignore the heterogeneity of elements so typical of prose satire and so plain in Swift's. Briefly, I propose that each of the four Parts embodies a different conventional mode of taxonomy. Parts 1 and 4 offer the clearest examples of what I mean. Part 1 presents the taxonomy of politics: the mode of thought and analysis proper to the study of politics, the discipline of political science, is brought to bear on institutions, actions, and events in Lilliput. Ethical, religious, amorous, commercial, and biological behaviour become issues there, but all become issues to be seen in terms of the disciplinary questions raised by the study of politics. Life in Part 1 is essentially institutional. Part 4, by contrast, treats institutions, according to my hypothesis, within another taxonomy, that of logic, of reason and reasoning. I assume that in characterizing Part 4 this way, I will enjoy the greatest immediate consensus among Swiftians, revisionist or traditional, hard-boiled or soft-boiled. Let me simply note that in the land of the Houyhnhnms "reason" and its operative definition become a subject matter of a different order from the diversity of more overt subject matters, anthropological, political, moral, and so forth, which they govern conceptually. The Houyhnhnms themselves are constructs of the attributes that our systems assign to "reason" and therefore, by logical inference, to the "rational" animal, man. The actual gap between them and us is taxonomic malocclusion.[1]

In the same way, the two middle Parts also have traditional taxonomies behind them. Part 2 treats of man in the natural order, and Part 3 of history. Since elsewhere I have argued at length for this reading of Part 2, I will only summarize it here.[2] A taxonomy based on the natural order, such as in Swift's time was most notably expounded by the writers of physico-theology, celebrated the body and mind of man as wonderfully apt for the place to

Reprinted from *Proceedings of the First Münster Symposium on Jonathan Swift*, 217–31, ed. Hermann J. Real and Heinz J. Vienken, 1985, with the permission of Wilhelm Fink Gmb.H. & Co.

which God had ordained him. Swift changes man by shrinking him, nothing more, and lets us then watch this wondrous creature, the diminished Gulliver, do dubious battle with domestic pets, small birds, and vermin. Aesthetic claims? The enlarged bodies of the Brobdingnagians remind us how few we can make for our pore-pocked, mole-marked, freckled, and malodorous physical selves, whose beauty is the mere result of a limited point of view. And morally, Europeans are also beasts, a "pernicious Race of little odious Vermin."[3] So are most of their slight moral superiors the Brobdingnagians, who exploit and gawk at their little freak Gulliver. They foster malicious dwarfs and frolicsome, lecherous maids of honour in a society with a history of civil wars and a present that includes ragged beggars, murderers who are publicly decapitated, and moralists who raise vain quarrels with nature.

But Swift also goes beyond these human failures, his obvious satiric targets, to challenge the modes, as well as the conclusions of our hierarchy of values. For example, he characterizes Gulliver's ordinary experience in this Part largely through maintenance functions, those connected with safety, health, and reproduction. Animals, including human animals, have these in common. Swift treats them so negatively that the much revered working-out of God's design, the inner logic of typical natural processes, frightens, disgusts, humiliates, and hurts little Gulliver. Another kind of allusion in Part 2, by which Gulliver's antics are referred to shows and exhibitions in early eighteenth-century London, also tests the taxonomy of natural order. As the sociologist Erving Goffman remarks, "the astounding . . . (in the form of human freaks) and stunts are closely associated with circus sideshows, as if a social function of circuses . . . were to clarify for patrons what the ordering and limits of their basic frameworks are."[4] Part 2 overlaps in subject matter with Part 1, for example, in dealing with excretory processes and a royal court, and it overlaps, too, with Part 4, for example, in dealing with the unreasonableness of European society; but, I am arguing, essentially these similarities in subject matter and in attitude are used within the context of different sceptical arguments. They are arguments about politics in Part 1, the order of nature in Part 2, and "reason" and reasoning in Part 4. All these arguments complement each other and converge in Swift's attack on human pride, of course, as does the sceptical argument in Part 3 on the material of history.

Swift's use of taxonomic systems is not at all idiosyncratic. Other eighteenth-century fiction uses a paradigm of structure in which a central character or characters screen and to some extent shape their worlds through applying certain interpretative systems or bodies of questions: the search for happiness in *Rasselas* and the hobbyhorses in *Tristram Shandy* are examples of these a priori interpretative modes. Events test these interpretative systems, correct them as far as they can be, and make the characters wiser. But no system, and no group of systems, turns out to be adequate to the reality the characters confront, although the plots of most of the works of fiction do come to some degree of aesthetic closure. Needless to say, this procedure differs in Swift because Gulliver is not a character like those in novels: he is not consistent, and he does not develop. What is personal in the novels is impersonal in *Gulliver's Travels*, and so the schemes I have mentioned as lying behind the Parts of the *Travels*—politics, the order of nature, history, and logic—are socially respected taxonomies, not versions of an individual cognitive style. At times when Gulliver can be considered a *persona*, a temporary fixing of character, we may find an imitation of a specific cognitive style. In the *Travels*, though, such passages are not ends in themselves but means to serve a consistent allusiveness to schemata that lie outside any given figure in the *Travels* and that are evoked situationally, as the nature of the characters, the irony, the narrative conventions, and the events keep changing. As in the novels of the period, the interpretative schemata keep being tested and found wanting. No norm emerges to replace them, although norms of course are used to criticize them. But because the schemata are public—the taxonomies of politics, the order of nature, history, and logic—Swift can display through their failure the general failure of Europeans to understand their environment and therefore themselves.

My claim that Part 3 alludes to the taxonomy of history draws upon a traditional subdivision of history into the human, the natural, and the divine; as Degory Wheare wrote, "History has been divided both by the Ancients and some of the modern Writers into *Divine*, which treats of God and Divine things, *Natural*, which treats of Naturals and their causes, and *Humane History*, which relates the Actions of Man as living in Society." These are respectively what Bodin calls the areas of faith, knowledge, and prudence; the last of these categories reflects the traditional *exemplary* function of history.[5] I suggest that a plausible division of *Gulliver*, Part 3, also is tripartite. The first and last chapters, 1 and 11, deal with the Dutch and the Japanese. Chapters 2 through 6, by and large, treat natural scientists who foster music and mathematics in Laputa, manoeuvre the flying island, and run the grand Academy of Projectors in Lagado. A final group of chapters, 7 through 10, describes the revival of the ancients in Glubbdubdrib and the Struldbruggs— another sort of ancients, these past reviving—in the despotic land of Luggnagg. From this rough summary, a prima facie case exists, I think, for associating the crucifix-trampling Dutch with some form of inverted divine history, a loss in faith; for relating the Laputan and Balnibarbian scientists to some form of inverted natural history, a loss in knowledge; and for referring the ancients, the King of Luggnagg, and the immortal Struldbruggs, finally, to what is at least a sceptical form of human history, a loss in prudence. Prudence looks to the future, but neither the dead ancients nor the Struldbruggs have one. Prudence assumes that history is not random, but hopelessly garbled ancient and modern chronicles, the hidden springs of malice in Luggnagg, and the bad luck in being born a Struldbrugg do not help one with informed predictions.

Such a comprehensive grouping presents a text in which the sections complement each other but in which none, like the vivid chapters on the projectors or the Struldbruggs, has anomalous weight placed upon it. In this respect, Part 3 begins to look structurally more like Parts 1, 2, and 4. If one treats chapter 6, about the political projectors of Lagado, as a transition between projects and politics, that is, between knowledge and prudence, natural and human history, Part 3 even takes on a surprising degree of symmetry. Before chapter 6, we have two chapters each on Laputa and Balnibarbi, and after it two chapters each on events in Glubbdubdrib and Luggnagg respectively, with the two chapters on the Dutch and Japanese at the two ends. But I am afraid that such chapter-counting sounds too much like Martinus Scriblerus, so I shall not pursue this subject.

To read Part 3 as history offers more than an underlying structure. It offers a rationale for the superficial fragmentation that derives from the examples of Lucian's *True History* and of Rabelais's *Chroniques*.[6] These earlier texts mock history writing. The fragmented narrative peculiarly suits the genre of Part 3, then, though it would have no such decorum in Parts 1, 2, or 4. Moreover, like his predecessors, Swift gives such fragmentation cognitive force. Part 3, far more than Parts 1, 2, or 4, is about discontinuity, about the severance of that which is current from that which is old, since we are in the realm of history. The new science defines itself by either its novelty or its ahistoricity; the ancients in Glubbdubdrib have been cut off from our world by historians' misreporting; Struldbruggs have decayed memories; the Dutch have reverted to heathenism. No wonder we see separate clots of people, even within the islands on which they live. Laputans inhabit a mobile satellite, projectors stay in a group of institutional houses divided from each other and internally divided into individual apartments and classrooms, and the ancients rise from another world of immateriality and death. The Struldbruggs are marked and ostracized creatures, and the occidental Dutch live in an oriental world. Seen as history, then, this voyage of islands, as in Rabelais's Fifth Book, has its own symbolic rationale, as well as stylistic decorum.

Let me begin with the ends of this archipelago, the two chapters, 1 and 11, where the Dutch appear. In the former, the Dutch confederate of a Japanese pirate shows his fellow Protestant Gulliver less *charity* than does the heathen pirate; in the latter, the Dutch traders deny their Christian *faith* by trampling on the crucifix. (The missing third virtue, hope, is supplied in chapter 1 by the name of the ship on which Gulliver has set out, the *Hopewell*.) Swift's inclusion of this satire in Part 3, where for the only time in the *Travels* he sets the scene in a real country, Japan, and attacks a nation, Holland, without a pseudonym, has an explanation in the principle of inverting divine history. Divine history moves with, toward, and by Providence and salvation, types pointing to the antitype of the Messiah, man redeemed through the grace of Christ's sacrifice and the spreading of His Word through the apostles.

Japanese history let Swift allude to a real paradigm of the opposite pattern. According to seventeenth-century historians, Christianity might have been adopted in Japan but for the self-serving malignity of the Dutch, who secured a trading hegemony by convincing the Emperor, with the help of a forged letter in Portuguese, that the Christian missionaries and their allies planned a revolt against him. In the resulting combat and persecution, over sixty thousand Christians died. Before 1650, Christianity had been wholly abolished in Japan, according to Jean-Baptiste Tavernier, whose account I have been following.[7] Chapter 11, then, brings together this apostolic faithlessness and its symbol, the trampling on the sign of Christian faith. Here, Gulliver must assume a false identity and elaborate a pretended history for himself, in consonance with the world of infidelity; Swift documents the need for this by naming the Dutch vessel *Amboyna* to recall atrocities committed upon Englishmen by oriental Dutch traders in 1623, just the time of the deconversion, so to speak, of Japan.[8]

The division of the theme of divine history into two widely separated chapters gave it shorter shrift than natural or human history. I suggest that chapters 9 and 10, about the King of Luggnagg and the Struldbruggs, respectively, deal with this disproportion by alluding to the divine within their context of human history, of prudence. The Struldbrugg episode is at least coloured by homiletic tradition, where death was seen as justice because of the Fall and as grace because it could bring release from a vale of tears and real immortality in Heaven.[9] In this light, the deadly but never mortal spot on the Struldbruggs' foreheads is a material mark of a material analogue to election—the mark is compared to "a Silver Threepence" and "an *English* Shilling" (11:207)—and the Struldbruggs' peevish, amnesiac, and disenfranchised lives invert that vision of beatitude and infinite learning, a richer Eden, foreseen by many eighteenth-century writers as the lot of the saved. By God's law, Christians live on through dying; Struldbruggs die, by Luggnagg's law, through living on.

Such a reading of chapter 10 casts light on chapter 9. Immortality is a Christian promise as a sequel to dispensation of divine rewards and punishments. But while men are the subjects of God, the Struldbruggs are subjects of the King of Luggnagg, who presides over a court where debasement and death are in ambush. Great Lords suffer humiliation if they "have powerful Enemies" there, and the unpunished malice of a page murders "a young Lord of great Hopes" (11:204–5). What is needed to complete the inversion is that the King of Luggnagg should appear as a sort of material God, just as the Struldbruggs have material versions of salvation. Therefore, Swift gives us, to complement the king's absolutism, expressions with biblical flavour like "*lick the Dust before his Footstool*" or the seal that shows him "*lifting up a lame Beggar from the Earth*" (11:204, 216). I *Samuel* 2, 8 tells us that the Lord "raiseth up the poor out of the dust, and lifteth up the beggar from the dunghill," and in Christ's name or person the lame are healed in *Matthew*

15, 30–31 and *Acts* 3, 1–11. *Psalm* 72, 9 announces of God, "They that dwell in the wilderness shall bow before him; and his enemies shall lick the dust," and, of course, the serpent in *Genesis* 3, 14 is sentenced to go upon his belly and eat the dust, as Gulliver is "commanded to crawl upon my Belly, and lick the Floor as I advanced" (11:204). The Lord says in *Isaiah* 66, 1 that "the earth is my footstool." But I do not want to brandish biblical allusions, just to make clear a context that the king's image of himself puts into play. His footstool and dust are literal as the Bible's are metaphoric; his charity, whether to the nobles he discreetly poisons or to the beggar he is only pictured lifting up, exists simply in representations, words or pictures, unlike that of the Bible. Like the Dutch and the Struldbruggs, he shows divine history, incarnated in human life, savagely parodying itself.

As the kings of Laputa and Luggnagg raise, in a new context, political issues that had occupied Swift in the voyage to Lilliput, so the scientists raise, again in a new context, issues about the order of nature which shape the voyage to Brobdingnag. There, Swift challenges an orthodox taxonomy of nature, sometimes by methods familiar nowadays from the practice of those modern philosophic saboteurs, the deconstructionists: he pursues a train of logic to bizarre ends, as when a monkey follows maternal instinct, often praised as part of God's great plan, and almost stifles tiny Gulliver, or he reveals what the standard system ignores or tries to hide, like the blotchy, blemished skin of fine ladies. By contrast, the section about natural history in Part 3 measures aberrations by the taxonomy of nature. Nicolson and Mohler's generally convincing argument about this section—that Swift wrote parts of it with specific work of the Royal Society in view—is also an argument that the Laputans' and projectors' antics have a basis in an orthodox taxonomy and its logic, which is what the Royal Society presumably began with.[10] These unexamined norms do more than define what flouts common sense, what marks the impractical zaniness that every reader recognizes in a projector. They also let Swift pursue his strategy of reversals and parodies when he employs this well-known, elaborately hierarchical system which connects physical fact and value.

To read the satire, one is to assume that getting sunbeams from cucumbers instead of, say, leeks is particularly absurd because cucumbers are cooling vegetables; that making fire malleable debases a nobler element into a more material one; that turning excrement into food makes an end a beginning; that building houses downward from the roof degrades man to aping the animals; and that putting a sundial on the weather vane subjects the orderly annual and diurnal motions of the planets to something lower because more transient. The filthy, like human excrement, spiders, swine, or a dog's anus, now becomes prized; what is traditionally below, the material, replaces what is above, the mental, when books are written by mechanical accident, when dumbshow with objects ousts language, and when students literally swallow their mathematics on paper wafers inked with propositions. By striving for mathematical and musical order, the Laputans' world thereby promotes the reign of the disorderly and material: the flappers' unmusical noise, the wives' carnal appetites, the fears of material destruction of the planet. Systematic reversals of what is ontologically given present the same sort of pattern earlier observed in Swift's treatment of divine history.

This analysis can be extended to such practices as softening marble for pincushions, for example, if one recalls that natural history from the time of Pliny into the eighteenth century, although diminishingly, included the *use* of objects as part of their taxonomic place. Such ideas even affect the *Histoire Naturelle* of Buffon, a generation or more after Swift; their presence in Pliny's *Historia Naturalis* accounts for much space devoted to the arts, for instance, or pharmacology. This teleological impulse is so powerful that Charles Rollin, an almost exact contemporary of Swift's, can praise Providence, first, for having made fish nimble and prolific enough to maintain their species despite the carnivorousness of other fish, and then, paradoxically, for having made them the prey of human carnivores: "such [fish] as are most fit for the use of man, draw near the coasts, to offer themselves in a manner to him, whilst a great many others, which are useless to him, affect a remoteness from him."[11] If the proper use of an object is included in one's sense of its place in the order of nature, the development of naked sheep, soft marble pincushions, and farms of chaff rewrites natural history. The denaturing of such objects lowers them on the taxonomic scale.

My argument also implies that Swift satirizes the Royal Society for offering a socially canonized arena where the historiography of nature may be abused. The actual oddities of the Society and its famous, absent-minded President gave him sitting ducks to shoot, and he fired away. But he makes his attack at once both more and less devastating by taking several of his more flamboyant examples from previous mock-histories. The dog pumped with air through his anus and the trapping of sunbeams in vials occur in *Don Quixote*. In Rabelais, human excrement produces an elixir of life and a dog's turd produces honey. Fire is cut into stakes with a knife. Swift's air condensed "into a dry tangible Substance, by extracting the Nitre" (11:182) only varies the air squeezed into a cup to afford people "a Liquor much resembling Dew"; this occurs in Lucian.[12] If Swift's allusiveness sharpens the attack on the Moderns, in that they take seriously what earlier writers had only dreamed up as incredible fictions, the obliqueness of the allusions, in that Swift's readers could hardly have recognized borrowings from the *Transactions of the Royal Society*, also broadens the attack from the Moderns in particular to more general corruptions in writing the history of nature.

False history implies the denaturing of figures within history. In chapters 1 and 11, the Dutch have denatured themselves by removing themselves from their own Christian history, and they have reversed the dialectic of divine history in exploiting the Japanese. In chapters 2 through 5, Laputans and Lagadans have denatured themselves by enslaving themselves to the fad of the New Learning, and their treatment of the world reverses the taxonomic and utilitarian criteria that Swift's contemporaries thought integral to the order of natural history. Behind these actions, of course, lies self-interest, what a post-Nietzschean might call a "will to power." Swift, a reader of La Rochefoucauld, could have understood that phrase: in *Gulliver* 3, self-interest involves power in and through an ordering of the world with the self as point of fixed reference. This is precisely what the process of history contravenes; the historical self figures as a *product* of other actions and events.

Swift manages to show both perspectives. As narrated by Gulliver, Part 3 becomes a chronicle of pure obsessives, unlike anything else in the *Travels*. Characters fix their eyes and energies on that which abstracts them from the world at large, and we meet each of them only in the one performance that defines him. But the voyage also groups these figures, so that there are many Laputans and projectors, created by their societies; there are many ancients and many Struldbruggs, created by the accidents of their lives; the tyrant of Laputa is matched by the tyrant of Luggnagg, created by the positions into which they were born. Individual freedom, from this perspective, is an illusion. Thus, as rank and degree are central metaphors for the politics of Part 1, and the body for the natural order of Part 2, various mechanisms, functionally devoted but unfree, are central in Part 3. These are obvious in Laputa and Balnibarbi, most strikingly in chapter 6, where they are applied to people taken as machines: purges, pinches, hacking off halves of heads, and scrutinizing excrement are all devices to keep politicians ruly through their bodies. After this chapter, the mechanisms become signs or formulas, all coercive, like the magical turn of a finger which compels the spirits in Glubbdubdrib, the court gibberish of Luggnagg, perhaps the Struldbruggs' chromatic mark, and certainly the trampling on the crucifix. These, too, have to do with the issues of power and freedom.

A measure of this dual perspective occurs near the beginning of Part 3. In the next-to-last chapter of Part 2, Swift mentions gunpowder and printing where these inventions help define man's intellectual nature. Gunpowder and printing were two of the three signs of scientific progress most often boasted about by Moderns; the third was the use of the lodestone, or compass, which Swift introduces near the beginning of Part 3 for other navigatory ends, as the motor that manoeuvres Laputa. With it, the Laputans make themselves into forces of nature; that is, their own astronomical fears have to do with contact and deprivation, in worries that the earth will be swallowed up by the sun or incinerated by a comet, and that the sun will stop shedding light. Therefore, what they threaten to the Balnibarbians is annihilation by contact, pelting with stones or being squashed by the island itself, and deprivation of light and rain through the island's shadowing action. Gunpowder and printing are likely to be abused by men, as is the lodestone, but unlike them, it is abused in a way that makes people mere transmitters of forces, threatening unto others what celestial mechanics threatens unto them. As with other mechanisms in Part 3, the abuse of and subjection to, the new world of physics parodies the continuity of history—here, natural history—so as to produce discontinuity and loss.

Almost all the characters in Part 3 see themselves as free, in a simpler vision than Swift's. Except for those who are mere staffage, they work at the exercise of personal power, sometimes by force and over people (piracy, the tyranny of the floating island) and sometimes by invention and over the environment (the scientists). Swift alternates between these two sorts of power: as we read, the pirates and the tyrant sandwich the Laputan astronomers and are followed by the Lagadan projectors. Chapter 6, the centre of this Part, joins the two types by setting before us the school of political projectors, who pursue both scientific projects and the "wild impossible Chimæras" (11:187) of reform in the political system. Similarly, they get from Gulliver an account of the transcoding by which the English system of justice, with scientific mechanisms, wilfully creates "meaning" to frame its victims. The rest of Part 3 roughly continues this alternation. Chapter 7 ends with Gulliver in Glubbdubdrib, feeding his "Eyes with beholding the Destroyers of Tyrants and Usurpers, and the Restorers of Liberty to oppressed and injured Nations" (11:196), and Chapter 9 deals with the sinister King of Luggnagg, who poisons his subjects. Chapters 8 and 10 have to do with blocks to knowing and organizing one's heritage. In Chapter 8, Swift explodes critical and intellectual systems, and the pretensions of modern historians to be telling the truth. Chapter 10 exhibits the Struldbruggs, whose present state, once they have aged, puts them out of touch with the history of their selves or their times. They have literally forgotten what they are, thus offering a materialized metaphor for the state of almost everyone else in Part 3. They sum up the voyage in its penultimate chapter.

Munodi, the Ancients, and the Struldbruggs, alone in Part 3, understand themselves as creatures of history, and might be exceptions to the rule of self-interest. Swift, though, grants exceptions with a miser's fist. Before thirty, the Struldbruggs seem to be no better than other citizens, and after thirty, they start a decline into egoistic melancholy with "Envy and impotent Desires" as their "prevailing Passions" (11:212). The Ancients, many of whom were vicious or foolish while alive, now have no self-interest because they have no selves to be interested in. Just because they cannot aggrandize themselves, they can reassert historical truth against their denaturing by bad historians. Munodi faces innovators who want to abolish history, the settled and satisfactory ways of keeping his estate, and so has normative force for the satire. But he is not exempt from it. Unlike Swift the Drapier or, more to the point, the brave citizens of Lindalino at the end of the directly preceding chapter, Munodi fears to "incur the Censure of Pride, Singularity, Affectation, Ignorance, Caprice; and perhaps encrease his Majesty's Displeasure" (11:176). Although he does not choose to destroy and redefine history around himself, he acquiesces in self-betrayal and betraying his tenants, all for the selfishness of avoiding the imputation of being selfish. He follows the Ancients' material practice in agriculture and architecture, but not the spiritual practice of the imprudent, self-sacrificial "sextumvirate" praised by name in chapter 7: the two Brutuses, Socrates, Epaminondas, Cato Uticensis, and Thomas More.

In discussing the sections about divine and natural history, I have also commented on the human history presented in Glubbdubdrib and Luggnagg. These chapters acutely present a question implicit throughout: if true history in Part 3 is forever being avoided or abused, what can *we* learn about our own place? As an "objective" taxonomic order, history is supposed to teach us by example, and yet, like the historical line of individual memory in the Struldbruggs, the historical line of communal memory has been corrupted. We can know only that we had better be sceptics. Moreover, the idea of the exemplary implies that some kind of order, some kind of causal order, persists through time, but as Gulliver discovers, vile "Springs and Motives" have led to "great Enterprizes and Revolutions in the World," and these have "owed their Success" in turn to "contemptible Accidents" (11:199). These ideas of degeneration with time and of arbitrariness, which Chapter 8 presents as a general condition of mankind, are again emblematized in Chapter 10, the account of the Struldbruggs. If all that historians fumble away by their failures of communal memory is a rather seamy chaos, human history, as traditionally conceived, is impossible. *Exempla* can exist in fiction, which may have a causal structure precisely because it is false in its own way; but *exempla* can exist in history only if it is false in a way not its own, only if it is false in the way of fiction.

By another act of negation, Swift underlines the flimsiness of didactic pretensions for history. He fills Part 3 of *Gulliver* almost solely with *exempla* of failure, except for political rebels who battle authority. The role of history, through *exempla*, is to bring the contingent under the rule of the calculable; but the characters in Part 3 create their version of history through misdirected intentionality and the loss of the calculable. Each exercise of power implies loss. The Laputans' learning makes them cowards and cuckolds. Politically, they do not dare try to squash Balnibarbi. Only the Balnibarbians' projects are less fertile than their farms. Deeds are maimed in the telling by their chroniclers. The proud king of Luggnagg cannot control secret assassins in his court. Struldbruggs straggle into the valley of the shadow of dotage and camp there forever. Even the Dutch have mixed luck in handling the Japanese. An exemplar can be imitated only in terms of intentions, the reader's intentions, but Swift shows almost everyone too blind or hampered to exercise them. Part 3, moreover, presents few positive models; and, in this fragmented fictional history, the negative models seem "projectible," that is, cases suitable for generalization, only to those who are already convinced that they are projectible.

Other fictional histories, like *Tom Jones* or Gulliver's voyages to Lilliput and Brobdingnag, do offer a sense of projectible actions with worlds something like ours, worlds with enough internal logic and verisimilitude to permit one to make analogies and frame paradigms. The discontinuousness of Part 3 does not permit that. Act and outcome have weak connections, each being marked by some mode of logically undetermined failure within the text. (Failure in the other voyages mostly lies outside the written text, in us eighteenth-century Europeans as the written text forces us to see ourselves.) Where historians traditionally do find *exempla*, in classical heroes, Swift counters with direct, wilful denial—Hannibal did not erode the Alps with vinegar—or with an obvious fiction, that Caesar and Brutus are now "in good Intelligence with each other" (11:196). In most of Part 3, figures who might appear in our history books, real people, not pygmies, giants, or talking horses, behave in a way too arbitrarily contrived to teach behaviour to us. Their fates do reiterate to us, of course, the revenge that history takes upon those who would rewrite it with the self as its centre.

When I use "history" in this context, I am referring to something that in *Gulliver's Travels* is at least partly inaccessible, something that is known in terms of resistance, of Spinozan necessity. This is, as Fredric Jameson says, "History [as] what hurts . . . what refuses desire and sets inexorable limits to individual as well as collective praxis, which its 'ruses' turn into grisly and ironic reversals of their overt intention."[13] The other sense in which I have been using the word "history" has to do with an epistemological and discursive practice, the thing that historians write. This second sense lies behind the division of Part 3 into divine, natural, and human history, because it depends on a human focus of attention and desire, on the terms in which people try to tailor the world around them. In the first sense of history, a largely unseen and impregnable environment of resistances, all events are part of divine history, and all human history can be seen as documentation for parts of natural history. The use of natural objects, for example, and the propensities of man are subjects of natural history for which human history provides instances. This is especially true in the context of voyages, with their invitation to compare the pasts of disconnected cultures. Moreover, natural history, the realm of knowledge in Bodin's terms, underlies the exemplary function of human history, Bodin's realm of prudence. My discussion of Part 3, although it has been based on the form of the voyage and therefore on the tripartite division, has also reflected the overlap among the three kinds of history. With the discursive and the environmental senses both in mind and without disentangling them further, let me, then, summarize what seem to me the uses of history in *Gulliver 3*.

First, Swift could produce the illusion of unsystematic completeness by drawing on two traditions of discursive history. Orthodox doctrine let him cover the field by expanding upon the divine, the natural, and the human modes of history, each of them inverted. Literary history, in turn, offered a way of parodying the practice of historians. Lucian, Rabelais, and Quevedo provided Swift with models of disorganization and fragmentation; through these, he aligned himself with his own ancestors as a satirist, and he expressed the thematic fragmentation of Part 3. He also concealed the underlying formal pattern of the voyage in favour of something more apparently ingenuous and unpredictable, much of it a launching into fantasy without any single assumption governing its narrative logic. The mode of discourse with which Swift allies his work makes no claims to a fixed, quasi-allegorical relationship between its statements and any outside world, real or extrapolable from the real in the manner, say, of Lilliput. Nor does he tie Part 3 to another kind of outside world, a specific text with which he maintains continuing allusions as, for instance, in his poetic imitations of Horace or, as I have argued elsewhere, to the tale of Tom Thumb in Part 2 of *Gulliver*.

Part 3, like the other voyages, does operate by a single procedure, that of inverting taxonomic principles. In Part 1, the great world, that of politics, is made small. In Part 2, the lord of the creation in the order of nature becomes a pet or toy, or a naturally disgusting object. In Part 4, *equus* defies the logic books to appear as *animal rationale*, and *homo* defies any reason as Gulliver whinnies away in his stables, imitating what is most accidental and transient about the Houyhnhnms, a perfect *animal hinnibile*. So in Part 3, if one accepts my thesis, Swift sets inversions against the pattern of divine history: we witness the mercantile evangelism of the Dutch, the inability of the scientists to read the Book of Nature accurately and/or usefully, the virtue of the ancient pagans degenerating in the Christian moderns, and parodies of the divine in the King of Luggnagg and the Struldbruggs, his subjects. As with the realm of faith, so with that of knowledge. Swift's natural history shows people useless or harmful to themselves and others, so much so, paradoxically, that the real heroes of Part 3 are those who make proper use of their capacity to destroy the power of others: the rebels in Lindalino and the spectral tyrannicides in Glubbdubdrib. In the realm of prudence, human history, we find incalculability about cause and effect, the enfeebling of inferences from *exempla*, self-delusion, and a lack of success in action even in terms that the characters set for themselves.

Swift gives an extra fillip to this by having Gulliver, who has witnessed the multiple failures of Part 3, fly into raptures and moralizing, too, over the good fortune of the Struldbruggs, with the wish that he might be like them. In an orgy of emulative self-aggrandizement, he casts himself as "the wealthiest Man in the Kingdom," the man who "excel[s] all others in Learning," "the Oracle of the Nation," mentor to the young and patron to his peers, a historian and a scientist, in short, as the best and brightest of all those randomly born Struldbruggs (11:209–11). As in the earlier voyages, Gulliver is ridiculous here because of his own historical self, that of an average provincial Englishman, but as has not been true earlier, his folly has to do with his willingness to lose that historical self, produce self-serving causal arguments, set himself up as a historical *exemplum*, and hypothesize a future in which intention and result tally with one another. From what he has seen about wealth, knowledge, generosity, history, and science in this voyage, he has learned, appropriately, nothing. Those who have a sanguine turn of mind may think that *that* is an *exemplum* from Swift's pen, teaching one what to avoid, but I do not find much hope in Part 3, or the rest of *Gulliver's Travels* for that matter, that such follies as Gulliver's, given the natural and human history we share with him, are curable.

Written and oral history, as a source, supplies Swift with topical material. Part 3 contains a series of vignettes about absent-minded Newtonians, the Royal Society, the Dutch and the Japanese, and Ancients whose lives and work were schoolboy stuff. These anamorphic versions of known particulars, more frequent in Part 3 than elsewhere in the *Travels*, document Swift's case; and since he takes his referents from different periods of time and from other satiric works, which in turn refer to still different periods of time, he can generalize. His mingling of the historians' history and fiction-writers' history, of Livy and Lucian, helps him in an act of reversal: he turns reported history into his fiction so as to prove the fictionality of what purports to be history. All written history, given the force of self-interest, is fictionalized, and Swift's professed fiction may be more historical—indeed, in Glubbdubdrib it pretends to be more historical—than the discourse that passes for history. If true history is the Spinozan realm of necessity, the history that historians write reflects the illusory freedom of desire, despite its claim to be bound by facts; and the fiction that Swift writes, despite its looser relation to factuality, is what reaffirms the historical truth, the realm of necessity.

Let me put this into the larger satiric context most important for *Gulliver's Travels*. Humans take pride in the systems—politics, natural philosophy, history, logic—by which they mediate the world for human understanding. Swift, scarifying that pride, shows the wilfulness of these systems of mediation and therefore their inadequacy. He does not try to offer a better substitute and thus promote himself to an occasion for praising the human mind. Because he will not, to the distress of compromise-loving and upward-looking benevolists or F. R. Leavis, Swift's satire must be "negative." His positive figures all stand for the limitation, not the extension, of human power. From the anti-systematic fantasy of *Gulliver's Travels*, he shines an inexorable light upon whatever the system-makers are likely to find most damningly inconvenient. He does not pretend to be "true," but more "true" than they. For this end, the treatment of history in Part 3 is indispensable.

My approach to *Gulliver's Travels* implies that differences in subject matter from voyage to voyage are functions of conceptual difference; in theory, all the voyages might treat roughly the same subject matter, and to a large extent they do. By emphasizing sameness of subject matter, provisionality of norms, and human limits, however, I do not mean to deny development in *Gulliver's Travels*; the taxonomic models to which I have pointed increase in scope as Gulliver moves along. Politics has an armature of positive law, which is supposed to depend on prior, more basic tenets of natural law: Part 1 is conceptually enclosed in Part 2. In Part 3, the order of nature is made temporal, natural history, by relating it to human use and embracing it within a context of temporal movement. And the reason and logic of Part 4 obviously encompass the conceptual structures of history, for they define all conceptual structures. The argument here, I should stress, is about classifications, not reality. Real politics is rarely based on natural law and the order of nature, nor is history a child of reason and logic. But the discipline of politics, what modern jargon calls "political science," pretended to be based on natural law, and reason and logic, as disciplines, were supposed to reign over other systems of understanding.

The more these systems pretend to, the more fully and plainly they exhibit their own inadequacy. Gulliver, defined by the systems, suffers increasingly profound enfeeblement. Powerful and able to escape the political nastiness of Lilliput, he dwindles to a passive, frustrated curiosity in Brobdingnag; on the islands of Part 3, he has lost the familial and friendly relationships which he had in Part 2, and which the Brobdingnagians themselves enjoy. He wanders essentially alone, watching individuals construct their egocentric histories, a situation that anticipates his own chosen, radical exile in Part 4. Unable to be the breed of Houyhnhnm which he has always been told he is, an *animal rationale*, and appalled to be the cousin to the Yahoos which he sees he is, he loses self-definition in a muddle of anger, disgust, and pride. A retraction of individual power or communicativeness accompanies each enlargement of conceptual scheme. This is a procedure to which Part 3 trains the reader to be alert. Gulliver mirrors his species in this as in all other regards, so that the four voyages also define a progressive alienation of mankind from power over, or understanding of, itself and its world. The polity of Part 1 is a comprehensible artifact of human creation; the natural order of Part 2 is not, but it has its laws, admittedly instanced by unpredictable contingencies; these contingencies, in turn, become the iron and ironic law or principle of Part 3; and finally, in Part 4, reason and logic, definition and inference, are turned upside down and embodied in creatures who are not human and whom humans can barely and rarely imitate.

I would, then, give Part 3, like each Part of *Gulliver's Travels*, its own place in these movements towards greater conceptual scope and less human power. If these movements occur and if the subject matter of the *Travels* remains roughly the same, one would expect a good deal of incremental repetition. Thus, the imperialist longings of the Lilliputians recur in the gunpowder episode of Part 2, directly tainting the "odious little Vermin" of Europe, and recur once more in the minatory use of the flying island. Although the King of Laputa has limited political success, Laputa has made an intellectual conquest of Balnibarbi: forty years of striving for the promised land of ease, permanence, and control have created a nation of misery and want. Lilliputian court ceremonies and factions reappear with the grovelling courtiers of Luggnagg; but whereas the narrative of Part 1 gives at least proximate explanations for animosities, that of Part 3 leaves them unexplained, so that Luggnagg is more arbitrary, as well as more dangerous and degrading. Historical degeneration first comes up in the "original Institutions" of Lilliput, which have since fallen into "scandalous Corruptions" (11:60). Swift makes almost nothing of the idea there, reintroduces it in the comedy of tiny Gulliver's reading about the dwindling size of Brobdingnagians (it bears on the folly of moralists who reason about the "Laws of Nature" [(11:137]), and then presents it bitingly when he and we arrive in Glubbdubdrib, flanked as that episode is by those about the decline of Balnibarbi and of individual Struldbruggs. These three motifs—imperialism, ceremonial rank, and historical degeneration—return in Part 4. By that time, the satire around each has swollen, so that not even Gulliver can sustain a role as apologist for Europe. Part 3 has been so telling, in its own sweep and its growth from Parts 1 and 2, that Swift's incremental development of the motifs requires and legitimates a reversal in narrative voice.

This incremental devastation may or may not have accorded with Swift's serious opinions, conscious or unconscious, about his species at one time or another while he was writing *Gulliver*. The same is true of the radical scepticism about history in Part 3. (Swift did, after all, write history himself, and did so for readers.) For my purposes, what has been important is that a strategy of scepticism made *Gulliver* the satire on man which Swift thought he was writing.[14] In that frame of reference, his genius exploited the possibilities he could draw on in the 1720s, or, as another historically minded group of readers would prefer, the possibilities of the 1720s exploited the genius of Swift so as to find articulation. But I am not imposing on Swift a scepticism that he would have found alien. As W. A. Speck points out, Swift as a historian seizes on self-interest as a major principle of causation, always quitting historical process (below the level of the narrative, that is) in favour of the individual, the accidental, the historically inexplicable.[15] Where sophisticated history demands depth and complication, he provides simple but terminal accusations, along the lines provided him by chroniclers of the Machiavellian Dutch and the jealous, duped Japanese. This practice makes for impoverished history, but it can feed brilliant satire, where one is to be brought face to face with the leer of something to be hated or scorned, not explained.

This way of reading *Gulliver's Travels* and Part 3 accords, then, with Swift's inclinations. It aligns them with other contemporary practice: for Part 3 the traditional modes of historical writing, for *Gulliver's Travels* the use of a priori models—a genre, a classical text, a personal interpretative system—to be imitated and criticized in a piece of fiction. It also rescues them from being taken as casually or unevenly constructed, and it lets one talk about the design of the Part without thereby reducing the text's heterogeneity. It offers a rationale for many particulars. Admittedly, it has made me venture my own systems for the work, but I have been willing to do that in treating the *Travels* as an intentional artifact, marked by a formal and conceptual logic contrived by a mind something like ours. (By this principle of caution, the characters in the book who treat the real world as their interpretable text implicitly anthropomorphize God or deify themselves.) But even with this focus of mine, I recognize two dangers in my systematizing. First, the thematic paradoxes of fiction and history, order and disorder remain inconclusive enough and perhaps superficial enough to make their heuristic value uncertain, maybe too uncertain for some of the inferences I have drawn from them. Second, my emphasis on an overall purpose may misrepresent the degree to which Swift's text is best read as linear sequence. As such, it is a vehicle for heterogeneity, the local, the splenetic, the surprising, what Swift always wanted to say but had no good place to exhibit. I offer my reading as fuller than its competitors, as far as I know, only with these warning labels. I do not know what the spectre of Swift would have to add if I were to meet him in the court of the magician's palace in Glubbdubdrib.

Notes

1.   For this reading of the Houyhnhnms, see the paper by Hermann J. Real and Heinz J. Vienken, "The Structure of *Gulliver's Travels*" in *Proceedings of the First Münster Symposium on Jonathan Swift*, eds. Hermann J. Real and Heinz J. Vienken (München: Wilhelm Fink Verlag, 1985), 199–208. For a fuller discussion, see Hermann J. Real and Heinz J. Vienken, *Jonathan Swift: "Gulliver's Travels"* (München, 1984), 108–11. Foundations for a reading of Part 4 and logic were fixed by R. S. Crane, "The Houyhnhnms, the Yahoos, and the History of Ideas," *Reason and the Imagination: Studies in the History of Ideas*, 1600–1800, ed. J. A. Mazzeo (New York and London, 1962), 231–53.

2.   My discussion of Part 2 here and, below, of interpretative systems in fiction derive, respectively, from an article and a book of mine: "In Brobdingnag: Captain Gulliver, Dr. Derham, and Master Tom Thumb," *EA* 37 (1984): 129–41; and *Systems of Order and Inquiry in Later Eighteenth-Century Fiction* (Berkeley, Los Angeles, London, 1975).

3.   *The Prose Works of Jonathan Swift*, ed. Herbert Davis, 14 vols. (Oxford: Basil Blackwell, 1939–68), 11: 132. Citations from this edition of *Gulliver's Travels* are incorporated into the text.

4.   Erving Goffman, *Frame Analysis: An Essay on the Organization of Experience* (New York, 1974), 31. For the shows of London and *Gulliver* 2, see Aline Mackenzie Taylor, "Sights and Monsters and Gulliver's *Voyage to Brobdingnag*," TSE 7 (1957): 29–82.

5.   Degory Wheare, *The Method and Order of Reading Both Civil and Ecclesiastical Histories*, 3rd ed., tr. and ed. Edmund Bohun (London, 1698), 16; George H. Nadel ("Philosophy of History before Historicism," *History and Theory* 3 [1964]: 291–315) presents Bodin's division as typifying "the Renaissance humanist viewpoint" (306). Nadel also discusses the exemplary function of history. See also Myrddin Jones, "A Living Treasury of Knowledge and Wisdom: Some Comments on Swift's Attitude to the Writing of History," *DUJ* 67 (1974–75): 180–88.

6.   The most comprehensive, if challengeable, discussion of these debts remains William A. Eddy, *"Gulliver's Travels": A Critical Study* (Gloucester, Mass., 1963 [1923]).

7. Tavernier's "Relation du Japon" appears in his *Recueil de Plusieurs Relations et Traitez Singuliers & Curieux* (Paris, *s.a.*); an abridged account, professedly from Tavernier, appears in Louis Moréri's *Grand Dictionnaire Historique* (Paris, 1707), *s.v.* "Japon," with the heading "Etat du Christianisme au Japon," and a still shorter version in Jeremy Collier's English translation (London, 1701), which remarks "Thus Christianity was destroy'd by Trade, and the cursed Idolatry of Money" (*s. v.* "Japan").

8. See William J. Brown, "Gulliver's Passage on the Dutch *Amboyna*," *ELN* 1 (1963–64): 262–64; and also on this and other points of scholarly and critical discussion, the relevant pages and documentation in Real-Vienken, *Gulliver's Travels*, 84–86.

9. For such homiletic interpretations, see J. Leeds Barroll, III, "Gulliver and the Struldbruggs," *PMLA* 73 (1958): 43–50, and Roberta Sarfatt Borkat, "Pride, Progress, and Swift's Struldbruggs," *DUJ* 68 (1975–76): 126–34. An article that tries with some success and a number of acute insights to trace a more general religious allusiveness in Part 3 is Dennis Todd, "Laputa, the Whore of Babylon, and the Idols of Science," *SP* 75 (1978): 93–120. Todd offers a reading of the Struldbruggs' marks which I would be as willing to accept as the one I offer, that they allude to the marks on the foreheads of the righteous in *Ezechiel* 9,4 and *Revelation* 7,1–4; these are earned assurances of God's grace.

10. Marjorie Nicolson and Nora M. Mohler, "The Scientific Background of Swift's *Voyage to Laputa*" (1937), *Fair Liberty Was All His Cry: A Tercentenary Tribute to Jonathan Swift, 1667–1745*, ed. A. Norman Jeffares (London, Melbourne, Toronto, New York, 1967), 226–69.

11. Charles Rollin, *The Method of Teaching and Studying the Belles Lettres*, 3 vols., 6th ed. (London, 1769), 3: 295. Rollin's French original began to be published in the same year as *Gulliver's Travels*, 1726; it incidentally adopts the tripartite division of history into sacred, profane (i.e., human), and "philosophy" (i.e., natural).

12. The examples I cite, and they do not exhaust the possibilities, are from the Author's Preface to Part 2, Book 3 of *Don Quixote*, Rabelais's Fifth Book, ch. 22, and Lucian's *True History* in *The Works*, 4 vols. (London, 1711), 3: 138–39. For some more examples, see John M. Hill, "Corpuscular Fundament: Swift and the Mechanical Philosophy," *EnlE* 6, no. 1 (1975): 37–49.

13. Fredric Jameson, *The Political Unconscious: Narrative as a Socially Symbolic Act* (Ithaca, 1981), 102.

14. See Phillip Harth, "Swift's Self-Image as a Writer," in *Proceedings of the First Münster Symposium*, ed. Real and Vienken, 113–21, which discusses Swift's well-known letters to Pope about *Gulliver* in terms of Swift's casting himself in the role of satirist upon man, with the chief end of vexing the world.

15. See W. A. Speak, "Swift and the Historian," *Proceedings of the First Münster Symposium*, ed. Real and Vienken, 257–68.

Reading Race and Gender: Jonathan Swift

Laura Brown

To say the truth, I had conceived a few scruples with relation to the distributive justice of princes upon those occasions. For instance, a crew of pirates are driven by a storm they know not whither, at length a boy discovers land from the topmast, they go on shore to rob and plunder, they see an harmless people, are entertained with kindness, they give the country a new name, they take formal possession of it for the king . . . they murder two or three dozen of the natives . . . return home, and get their pardon . . . Ships are sent with the first opportunity, the natives driven out or destroyed, their princes tortured to discover their gold . . . and this execrable crew of butchers employed in so pious an expedition, is a modern colony sent to convert and civilize an idolatrous and babarous people.

But this description, I confess, doth by no means affect the British nation.
—Jonathan Swift, *Gulliver's Travels*[1]

The works of Jonathan Swift provide a test case for political criticism and a proving ground for the nature of the "politics" of such a criticism. An explicit misogynist and also an explicit anti-colonialist, Swift poses a distinct political problem: a critique from the perspective of gender would seem to point toward a political assessment diametrically opposed to that suggested by a critique from the perspective of race or colonialism. In other words, Swift's texts lend themselves equally well to a negative and a positive hermeneutic, and a critic concerned with the political aim of her readings of literary culture might well pause between the exposure of misogyny in the canon and the discovery of an early ally in the struggle against colonialism. Which to choose? What is a marxist/feminist to do? By arguing for the mutual interaction of gender and race in Swift's works, I want to provide a working example of a critical position that distinguishes itself from that of most American Foucauldians, whose historical analyses emphasize the coercive strategies of structures of power to the exclusion of effective opposition. The paradigm provided by Swift's problematic texts suggests the political utility of bringing positive and negative hermeneutics together, and defines what I see to be the necessary intimacy of structures of oppression and liberation in eigh-

From *Eighteenth-Century Studies* 23, no.4 (1990): 425–43. Reprinted with the permission of the American Society for Eighteenth-Century Studies.

teenth-century culture and thus the relevance of a method that seeks to link the categories of the oppressed under the rubric of a radical political critique of ideology.

1

From a feminist point of view, the oppression is not hard to find, and recent feminist critics have found much of interest in Swift's writing.[2] Aside from topical political subjects, the single most significant theme in Swift's poetry is the attack on women. These misogynist poems—"The Progress of Beauty," the dressing room poems, "Strephon and Chloe," "Cassinus and Peter," and others—were written between 1719 and 1731, the decade of *Gulliver's Travels* (1726), *A Modest Proposal* (1729), *The Drapier's Letters* (1724–25), and Swift's most energetic defense of Ireland against British colonialist policies. These poems belong to that venerable tradition of misogynist verse, long associated with Juvenal, whose most recent exemplars included Rochester, Mandeville, and Pope. They focus on the corruption and decay of the female body, on painting and dressing, on excrement and disease.

"The Lady's Dressing Room" provides a good example of their typical structure. It begins with a description of the artifice by which the true, corrupt nature of the female body is concealed:

> Five Hours, (and who can do it less in?)
> By haughty *Celia* spent in Dressing;
> The Goddess from her chamber issues,
> Array'd in Lace, Brocades and Tissues.[3]
> (1–4)

When Celia leaves the scene, the poem proceeds to undress her in her absence through an account of the contents of her dressing room, which climaxes in the most memorable passage in eighteenth-century misogyny:

> Thus finishing his grand Survey,
> Disgusted *Strephon* stole away
> Repeating in his amourous Fits,
> Oh! *Celia, Celia, Celia* shits!
> (125–28)

The degeneration of the absent Celia ends with the mock-advice to Strephon:

> I pity wretched *Strephon* blind
> To all the Charms of Female Kind;
> Should I the Queen of Love refuse,

Because she rose from stinking Ooze?
. . .
When *Celia* in her Glory shows,
If *Strephon* would but stop his Nose;
. . .
He soon would learn to think like me,
And bless his ravisht Sight to see
Such Order from Confusion sprung,
Such gaudy Tulips rais'd from Dung.

(115–44)

When Gulliver stops his nose with rue to avoid the nauseous scent of his wife at the end of Book 4 of *Gulliver's Travels,* he is taking the advice the poet gives to Strephon in this poem, and aspiring—though with a pointed lack of success—to the ironically liberated position of the speaker here, enacting the very extent of his disgust by claiming to accept the inevitability and essentiality of a gendered corruption.

Celia and the much-neglected Mrs. Gulliver are the absent objects of an attack that clearly exceeds their own poor power to offend. Though the female body is the purported locus of corruption in the misogynist poetry, it seems often to be slipping from sight, like the Celia of "The Progress of Beauty," who melts away piece by piece, a hideous victim of syphilis, so that by the end of the poem,

When Mercury her Tresses mows
To think of Oyl and Soot, is vain,
No Painting can restore a Nose,
Nor will her Teeth return again.

Two Balls of Glass may serve for Eyes,
While Lead can plaister up a Cleft,
But these alas, are poor Supplies
If neither Cheeks, nor Lips be left.

(109–16)

In fact there is no woman left at all in these attacks on women. The place of the female body is occupied by the materials with which it is adorned, or ultimately shored up: from dress to paint to plaster, "Crystal Eyes," and "artificial Hair" ("A Beautiful Young Nymph," 10–11). What is the status of a misogyny that, while claiming to condemn an essential corruption, so quickly substitutes the accoutrements or adornments of the female body for the woman herself? Or rather, what is the ideological status of this purported essentiality?

The attack on female painting is a trope of misogynist literature, as we all know, but in eighteenth-century England the representation of female adornment and dress has a very specific and consistent social referent: it evokes the products of mercantile capitalism. Joseph Addison, for example, in a passage in the *Spectator* papers typical of his description of women, turns the same topic to celebratory ends: "I consider woman as a beautiful, romantic animal, that may be adorned with furs and feathers, pearls and diamonds, ores and silks. The lynx shall cast its skin at her feet to make her a tippet; the peacock, parrot, and swan shall *pay contribution* to her muff; the sea shall be searched for shells, and the rocks for gems; and every part of nature furnish out its share towards the embellishment of a creature that is the most consummate work of it."[4] Addison's female figure, though undeniably more attractive than Swift's Celia, is like Celia in being defined by and subsumed in the materials with which she is adorned. But unlike Swift's misogynist poetry, Addison's image of female beauty gives us a hint of the source of that adornment. For Addison, all of nature cooperates in dressing womankind; in the discourse of eighteenth-century mercantile expansion, this is the most common trope of all, by which the agency of the acquisitive subject and the urgency of accumulation are concealed and deflected through the fantasy of a universal collaboration in the adornment of the female figure.

The Rape of the Lock (1712, 1714, 1717) supplies the locus classicus of this theme. In particular, Belinda's dressing room scene makes the economic context of Swift's misogynist dressing rooms explicit: the artifice through which Belinda's beauty is either created or awakened is attributed to the products of trade and defined through a catalogue of commodities for female consumption: "glitt'ring Spoil," "*India*'s glowing Gems," Arabian scents, tortoise shell, and ivory (1:129–36).[5] Elsewhere in the literary culture of this period, too, tortoise shell and ivory, the spices of Arabia, gems, gold, and silk are made to represent the primary objectives of mercantile capitalism, and these commodities in turn appear exclusively as the materials of the female toilet and wardrobe.[6] Thus, in the literature of mercantile capitalist apologia and even more broadly in the representation of women in general in the early eighteenth century, the richly adorned female figure is identified first of all with the products of trade and prosperity, and then with the whole male enterprise of commerce that generates those commodities. Indeed, a kind of reversal of object and agent becomes naturalized in the literary culture of this period, such that navigation, trade, and expansion all seem to be arranged solely for the delectation and profit of womankind. The activities and motives of the male adventurers and profiteers, and the systematic dimensions of imperialist expansion disappear behind the figure of the woman; in effect, because women wear the products of accumulation, they are by metonymy made to bear responsibility for the system by which they are adorned.

In short, the association of women with the process and products of mercantile capitalism is a strong cultural motif in this period of England's first major imperial expansion, and the obsession with female adornment and dress is a prominent expression of that association. In fact, a recent study of "the commercialization of English culture" designates female fashion and dress as the century's prototype for commodification. As Neil McKendrick says, "Clothes were the first mass consumer products to be noticed by contemporary observers." "Fashion and dress are often used almost interchangeably. From Mandeville onwards special attention was given to the role of clothes in this process of social and economic change."[7] The implicit cultural designation of dress as a synechdoche for mercantile capitalism is not surprising, since one of the earliest economic sources of the expansion and capitalization of the English economy was the textile industry, specifically the wool trade. So central was this notion, that Defoe used dress quite literally as the condition of English imperialism: for him English prosperity began with the textile industry, and would be sustained by the spread of English dress around the world. He even fantasized that the civilizing powers of English culture would bring clothing to the naked Africans, thereby promoting civilization, dress, and the English economy all at once.[8]

It is only one quick step from the equation of women and commodities to an attack on the hypocritical female as the embodiment of cultural corruption, the visceral epitome of the alienating effects of commodification and the disorienting social consequences of capitalist accumulation. This ideological fixation on female dress and adornment is expressed with the most direct vehemence by Bernard Mandeville when he describes "the silly and capricious Invention of Hoop'd and Quilted Petticoats" as one of the most important changes in English history, barely surpassed in significance by the Reformation.[9] He argues at length "that a considerable Portion of what the Prosperity of *London* and Trade in general, and consequently the Honour, Strength, Safety, and all the worldly Interest of the Nation consist in, depends entirely on the Deceit and vile Stratagems of Women" in their consumption of a "vast quantity" of trinkets and apparel which they "come at by . . . pinching their Families . . . and other ways of cheating and pilfering from their Husbands," and by "ever teazing their Spouses, tire them into Compliance," or "by downright Noise and Scolding bully their tame Fools out of any thing they have a mind to." For Mandeville "Humility, Content, Meekness, Obedience to reasonable Husbands, Frugality, and all the Virtues together, if they were possess'd of them in the most eminent Degree, could not possibly be a thousandth Part so serviceable, to make an opulent, powerful, and what we call a flourishing Kingdom, than their most hateful Qualities," that is, the taste for luxury, "the Consumption of Superfluities" (225–28).

Mandeville associates female luxury quite directly with the stimulation of a capitalist economy. Though his comments on women are partly satirical, that satire, like the poet's ironic acceptance of female corruption in "The Lady's Dressing Room," indicates the extent and inevitability of the problem. It is not surprising, in this context, to find in Swift's Irish tracts "A Proposal to the Ladies of Ireland" (1729), which suggests that the distresses of the Irish economy, caused by the colonialist trade restrictions imposed by England, can only be remedied by a restriction in turn upon "the importation of all unnecessary commodities," namely and specifically those for female consumption. Here Swift too takes for granted an intimate connection between female luxury and capitalism. But in this case the benefits of the accumulation of manufactured goods accrue to the English economy, not the Irish, and thus Swift draws the opposite conclusions from Mandeville:

> It is to gratify the vanity and pride, and luxury of the women . . . that we owe this unsupportable grievance of bringing in the instruments of our ruin. There is annually brought over to this kingdom near ninety thousand pounds worth of silk, whereof the greater part is manufactured: Thirty thousand pounds more is expended in muslin, holland, cambric, and callico . . . If the ladies, till better times, will not be content to go in their own country shifts, I wish they may go in rags. Let them vie with each other in the fineness of their native linen: Their beauty and gentleness will as well appear, as if they were covered over with diamonds and brocade.[10]

Elsewhere in the Irish tracts, economic and misogynist sentiments come even more directly into synchrony:

> Is it not the highest Indignity to human nature, that men should be such poltroons as to suffer the Kingdom and themselves to be undone, by the Vanity, the Folly, the Pride, and Wontonness of their Wives, who under their present Corruptions seem to be a kind of animal suffered for our sins to be sent into the world for the Destruction of Familyes, Societyes, and Kingdoms; and whose whole study seems directed to be as expensive as they possibly can in every useless article of living, who by long practice can reconcile the most pernicious forein Drugs to their health and pleasure, provided they are but expensive; as Starlings grow fat with henbane: who contract a Robustness by meer practice of Sloth and Luxury: who can play deep severall hours after midnight, sleep beyond noon, revel upon Indian poisons, and spend the revenue of a moderate family to adorn a nauseus unwholesom living Carcase.[11]

This passage makes the same economic assumptions about female adornment that we have associated with mercantile capitalist ideology, and with the same reversal of agency and object typical of the celebratory versions of that ideology. But here the attack on female luxury concludes with an attack on the body of the woman. Easily and unobtrusively, by the end of this passage the female body, rather than her dress, becomes the locus of cultural corruption, and this "nauseus unwholesom living Carcase" brings us back to the revolting female body that stands behind the representation of women in the misogynist poetry. The reversal of cause and effect at work here is characteristic of Swift's misogyny throughout his corpus. Through a kind of metonymy, the products of mercantile capitalism with which women surround and adorn themselves come to be implicated with the female body itself. That is, the pernicious corruptions of an expansionist culture are so intimately and inevitably associated with the figure of the woman that they are represented as internal rather than external to her; the nauseousness of the female body is thus a visceral representation of what Mandeville, and Swift himself in the Irish tracts, describe as an economic and social corruption. Even when the woman is absent, melted away by the disease she embodies, or when she is supplanted altogether by the products that she wears, we see her body as the epitome of essential corruption. And reciprocally, when she is present but undressed—presumably stripped of the corrupting commodity—she still appears as the essential incarnation of the evils of luxury and accumulation. Present or absent, dressed or undressed, the figure of the woman is made to bear responsibility for the cultural crisis of mercantile capitalism and imperial expansion. Thus, though the evidence of the Irish tracts suggests that Celia's corruption originates in the products of her adornment, her dress, in the misogynist poetry those products appear no longer as a cause of corruption; instead they are an innocent adjunct, an effect of Celia's essential corruption, simply absorbing the stench that arises directly from the inherent corruption of the "Female Kind":

> So Things, which must not be exprest,
> When plumpt into the reeking Chest;
> Send up an excremental Smell
> To taint the Parts from whence they fell.
> The Pettycoats and Gown perfume,
> Which waft a Stink round every Room.[12]

Excrement taints the female body, then her dress, then "every Room" she visits, so that the world inhabited by this female figure seems to receive corruption from her rather than bestow it upon her.

If we use the Irish tracts to locate Swift's misogyny in relation to the widespread contemporary discourse of women and commodities, then, we can begin to see—beneath the claim of essential female corruption that dominates the poetry—the fundamental implication of Swift's misogyny with mercantile capitalism. In the poetry, this implication is unacknowledged and probably unconscious, but it supplies us with one way of understanding the seemingly supererogatory violence of Swift's attack on women; and one way of placing misogyny in the context of Swift's corpus. In short, it enables us to provide a particular account of the historical status and ideological significance of these otherwise anomalous texts. The misogynist poetry records the cultural consequences of the historical crisis of this period with a vehemence and horror that is significantly absent from any explicit contemporary commentary. In other words, at a time of comparative ideological consensus in England, when the benefits of empire were rarely disputed,

Swift's misogyny occupies the place of a critique of mercantile capitalist expansion. This observation is not a justification for misogyny, but it complicates a political reading of Swift, and more important, it leads us to other images and other critiques of imperialism elsewhere in Swift's writing.

2

If we bring this reading of the misogynist poetry to bear upon *Gulliver's Travels*, we can move from the ideological status of women in Swift's writing and the connection of the representation of women with capitalist expansion to the historical problem of colonialism as it shapes the most important satire of the eighteenth century, and we can begin to see the mutual interaction of race and gender in Swift's major satire. Predictably, Gulliver's account of female luxury in Book 4 reproduces the economic trope of the Irish tracts and of Mandeville's more fully-faceted account of capitalism: "I assured him, that this whole globe of earth must be at least three times gone round, before one of our better female yahoos could get her breakfast, or a cup to put it in" (203).

But Book 2 supplies the famous images of the gigantic female body which put Gulliver in precisely the place of Strephon in "The Lady's Dressing Room" when he picks up the magnifying mirror:

> The Virtues we must not let pass,
> Of *Celia's* magnifying Glass.
> When frighted *Strephon* cast his Eye on't
> It shew'd the Visage of a Gyant.
> A Glass that can to Sight disclose,
> The smallest Worm in *Celia's* Nose,
> And faithfully direct her Nail
> To squeeze it out from Head to Tail.
> (59–66)

Brobdingnagian gigantism is intimately linked to misogyny. Indeed, the scenes that emphasize the scale of size in Book 2 are all centered around the female figure. The hideous, gigantic corporeality of the Brobdingnagian women is represented first in the anti-madonna scene that Gulliver witnesses almost upon his arrival in Brobdingnag—the woman nursing her child:

The nurse to quiet her babe made use of a rattle . . . but all in vain, so that she was forced to apply the last remedy by giving it suck. I must confess no object ever disgusted me so much as the sight of her monstrous breast, which I cannot tell what to compare with, so as to give the curious reader an idea of its bulk, shape and colour. It stood prominent six foot, and could not be less than sixteen in circumference. The nipple was about half the bigness of my head, and the hue both of that and the dug so varified with spots, pimples, and freckles, that nothing could appear more nauseous . . . This made me reflect upon the fair skins of our English ladies, who appear so beautiful to us, only because they are of our own size, and their defects not to be seen but through a magnifying glass. (74)

The nauseous scent against which Strephon ought to stop his nose almost overwhelms Gulliver in the apartments of the maids of honour: "They would often strip me naked from top to toe, and lay me at full length in their bosoms; wherewith I was much disgusted; because, to say the truth, a very offensive smell came from their skin" (95). And disease, like that which wastes Celia in "The Progress of Beauty," gives Gulliver his most horrific fantasy of female corruption in Brobdingnag: "One day the governess ordered our coachman to stop at several shops, where the beggars, watching their opportunity, crowded to the sides of the coach, and gave me the most horrible spectacles that ever an European eye beheld. There was a woman with a cancer in her breast, swelled to a monstrous size, full of holes, in two or three of which I could have easily crept, and covered my whole body" (90). Though Gulliver thinks to stop his nose with rue only at the end of Book 4, the nauseous scent, the disease and corruption, and the hideous corporeality that we have seen elsewhere in Swift's texts to be so powerfully and specifically associated with the female figure pervade the second book of his *Travels*. But if we look to the fourth book, we can see all these qualities again embodied in the Yahoos: their offensive smell, their naked corporeality, their connection with disease, and their uncontrolled sexuality are, as we have seen, the essential attributes of the female figure. From this perspective, the whole context of Book 4 takes on a new significance. The Yahoos are the prototypical women of Swift's works.

But Gulliver's relationship with the Yahoos themselves suggests another dimension to the role of the woman in the *Travels*. Gulliver begins at a seemingly unbridgeable distance from the Yahoos, which are represented as some species of monkey, perhaps, having little in common with the human. But the main import of Book 4 is the increasing proximity and eventual identification between the Yahoo and the human, despite Gulliver's own resistance and disgust. This process of association with the creatures that seem at first utterly and hideously other suggests a dynamic of aversion and identification that we will find to be central to the ideological significance of the satire. In Book 2, likewise, Gulliver's disgust with the maids of honor is balanced by a titillating voyeurism that singles out the "handsomest" and suggests that he is sexually implicated in the scene: figuratively, in the sense that he is evidently desirous himself, but also—and more grotesquely— physically, in that once we entertain the fantasy of a sexual connection between Gulliver and the maids of honor, we are implicitly invited to imagine the actual physical incorporation of the tiny male figure into the sexual body of the woman: "The handsomest among these maids of honor, a pleasant frolicsome girl of sixteen, would sometimes set me astride upon one of her nipples, with many other tricks, wherein the reader will excuse me for not being over particular" (96). The story of the cancerous breast, in this context, supplies a parallel image of explicit incorporation, in which Gulliver responds to the sight of female corruption with the extraordinary and unexpected fantasy of creeping inside and covering his whole body in the "nauseus unwholesom living Carcase" of the diseased woman.

In fact, Gulliver actually does take the place of the female figure at more than one prominent point in the *Travels*. In the relativist comparison between Gulliver's own form as a giant in Lilliput and his encounter with the giants of Brobdingnag, he repeatedly occupies the position of a woman. The overpowering scent of the Brobdingnagian maids of honor puts Gulliver in mind of the occasion in Lilliput when "an intimate friend of mine . . . took the freedom, in a warm day, when I had used a good deal of exercise, to complain of a strong smell about me . . . I suppose his faculty of smelling was as nice with regard to me, as mine was to that of this people." (95). And similarly, in the anti-madonna scene, after describing the "spots, pimples and freckles" of the nursing woman's skin, Gulliver provides a Lilliputian account of his own skin for comparison:

> an intimate friend of mine . . . said that my face appeared much fairer and smoother when he looked on me from the ground, than it did upon a nearer view when I took him up in my hand, and brought him close, which he confessed was at first a very shocking sight. He said he could discover great holes in my skin . . . and my complexion made up of several colours altogether disagreeable . . . On the other side discoursing of the ladies in that emperor's court, he used to tell me, one had freckles, another too wide a mouth, a third too large a nose, nothing of which I was able to distinguish.
>
> (74–75)

These comparisons too establish a routine and consistent interchangeability between Gulliver and the female figures of his narrative.

Similarly, in Book 2 Gulliver is dressed by his little nurse, Glumdal-clitch, in a manner that would have evoked a common contemporary female image. As Neil McKendrick has shown, the fashion doll was the major implement of the rise and popularization of female fashion in the eighteenth century. Originally imported singly from Paris and displayed in the London shops wearing the latest Parisian dress, these life-sized dolls were subsequently miniaturized and made widely available in rural as well as urban parts of England. Supplied with sample suits of the latest fashion, they were dressed both by clothing merchants and by children and adult women, and served as a major means of teaching the new and unfamiliar concept of rapidly changing styles of dress, and of spreading the notion of a market-conditioned obsolescence.[13] In Brobdingnag, Gulliver plays precisely this role; for Glumdalclitch and the contemporary reader he takes the place of this miniature commodified female figure.

To say that Gulliver occupies the place of the woman at recurrent moments in the *Travels* is not to say that Gulliver is the same as a woman, but to suggest a systematic pattern of implication, which moves from the various forms of interchangeability that we have seen in Gulliver's connection with the fashion doll and the Yahoos to a full incorporation like that offered by Gulliver's relation to the cancerous breast and the maids of honor, and which begins to problematize Swift's attack on women and to complicate our understanding of his relation with the female other. Gulliver's implicit identification with the female figure—a figure which we have seen to be systematically underlying the ideology of mercantile capitalism—suggests that his *Travels* must be read in the context of that major historical conjuncture. Those panegyrics on women that I cited earlier to exemplify the mercantile capitalist context of Swift's misogyny unconsciously function, as we saw, to displace responsibility for the historical consequences of capitalism upon womankind, to make her a locus for the male anxieties of empire. Swift's Irish tracts certainly participate in this common assumption of displaced responsibility, though with a different valuation. But the implicit dynamic of aversion and identification that we have begun to discern in *Gulliver's Travels* suggests that in this major text that effort of displacement partly fails, that the shifting status of the male observer (which we have been taught by formalist criticism of Swift to describe as the "persona controversy") makes the designation of a separable other, upon whom the anxieties and responsibilities of mercantile capitalism and imperialism can be displaced, symptomatically impossible.

3

But symptomatic of what? Here in order to invoke the dialectical connection of gender and race toward which I have been aiming, we must turn to another fictional account, contemporary with *Gulliver's Travels*, at least as disturbing, and much more offensive. This is the account that we can construct from the writings of travellers, naturalists, and colonialists of the nature and society of the Negro in what they describe as his native habitat in Africa or under slavery in the colonies of the New World. Unlike *Gulliver's Travels*, of course, this fiction was accepted as objective testimony in the travel literature and ultimately encoded as science in the most widely read volumes of travel and natural history through the middle of the next century.[14] At stake was the status of the Negro on the chain of being, his proximity of man or ape. And those two standards of deviation determined the definition of the Negro race.

Janet Schaw, in her journal of a voyage to the West Indies and North Carolina (1774), spontaneously reproduces, in her account of her first sight of Negro children upon her arrival in Antigua, an association quite typical of the period: "Just as we got into the lane, a number of pigs run out at a door, and after them a parcel of monkeys. This not a little surprised me, but I found what I took for monkeys were negro children, naked as they were born."[15]

If we juxtapose the details of two prominent contemporary accounts which served as compendia of seventeenth- and eighteenth-century observations of the inhabitants of Africa, we can set the context for Janet Schaw's predictable mistake. George Louis Leclerc Buffon's massive and influential *Natural History* (relevant volumes in French, 1749–60) and Edward Long's *History of Jamaica* (1774) both summarize accounts of the Negro from earlier writings in French and English dating from the early seventeenth century on.[16] Buffon and Long actually take opposite positions on Negroes, Buffon arguing, against contemporary sentiment, that they are of the same species as the European, and Long arguing, against Buffon, that "they are a different species of the same *genus*" (356): "Let us not then doubt, but that every member of the creation is wisely fitted and adapted to the certain uses, and confined within the certain bounds, to which it was ordained by the Divine Fabricator. The measure of the several orders and varieties of these Blacks may be as compleat as that of any other race of mortals; filling up that space, or degree, beyond which they are not destined to pass; and discriminating them from the rest of men, not in *kind*, but in *species*" (375).[17]

But though they arrive at very different conclusions, Long and Buffon produce very similar accounts. Buffon sets up the comparison between apes and Negroes most explicitly:

> To form a proper judgment between them, a savage man and an ape should be viewed together; for we have no just idea of man in a pure state of nature. The head covered with bristly hairs, or with curled wool; the face partly hid by a long beard, and still longer hairs in the front, which surround his eyes, and make them appear sunk in his head, like those of the brutes; the lips thick and projecting, the nose flat, the aspect wild or stupid; the ears, body, and limbs are covered with hair, the nails long, thick, and crooked . . . the breasts of the female long and flabby, and the skin of her belly hanging down to her knees; the children wallowing in filth, and crawling on their hands and feet; and, in short, the adults sitting on their hams, forming an hideous appearance, rendered more so by being smeared all over with stinking grease. This sketch, drawn from a savage Hottentot [a Negro], is still a flattering portrait, for there is as great a distance between a man in a pure state of nature and a Hottentot, as there is between a Hottentot and us. But if we wish to compare the human species with that of the ape, we must add to it the affinities of organization, the agreements of temperament, the vehement desire of the males for the females, the like conformation of the genitals in both sexes, the

periodic emanations of the females, the compulsive or voluntary intermixture of the negresses with the apes, the produce of which has united into both species; and then consider, supposing them not of the same species, how difficult it is to discover the interval by which they are separated.[18]

Buffon, unlike Long, ultimately dismisses the argument that apes and Negroes are of the same species; in other words, this passage indicates the position of a defender of the Negro's humanity.

The themes of nakedness, filth, and stench are persistent in this and in Long's account, alongside claims for nimbleness in climbing, running, or swimming (Long, 365). Long describes as one of the Negro's distinctive features: "Their bestial or fetid smell" (352). Buffon argues that the Hottentots are not true Negroes, but rather whites who make themselves dirty by wallowing in filth, noting that "they seldom live longer than 40 years; and this short duration of life is doubtless caused by their being continually covered with filth, and living chiefly upon meat that is corrupted" (298–99). Numerous reports summarized by these writers describe the Negro's habit of eating carrion: according to Long, "They are most brutal in their manners and uncleanly in their diet, eating flesh almost raw by choice, though intolerably putrid and full of maggots" (382); "at their meals they tear the meat with their talons, and chuck it by handfulls down their throats with all the voracity of wild beasts" (383).

Buffon's and Long's accounts agree that Negroes are incapable of civil government. According to Long: "In general, they are void of genius, and seem almost incapable of making any progress in civility or science. They have no plan or system of morality among them . . . They have no moral sensations" (353). "In regard to their laws and government, these may, with them, be more properly ranged under the title of customs and manners; they have no regulations dictated by foresight . . . they seem to have no polity, nor any comprehension of the use of civil institutions" (378). "Their genius (if it can be so called) consists alone in trick and cunning, enabling them, like monkies and apes, to be thievish and mischievous, with a peculiar dexterity. They seem unable to combine ideas, or pursue a chain of reasoning" (377). In short, they are "a brutish, ignorant, idle, crafty, treacherous, bloody, thievish, mistrustful, and superstitious people" (354).

Buffon summarizes various visitors' explanations for the difference between the facial features of Negroes and those of white Europeans; blacks have flat noses and faces from being carried against their mother's chests:

While at work or travelling, the Negro-women almost always carry their infants on their backs. To this custom some travellers ascribe the flat nose and big bellies among Negroes; since the woman, from necessarily giving sudden jerks, is apt to strike the nose of the child against her back; who in order to avoid the blow, keeps its head back by pushing its belly forward . . . Father

du Tertre says expressly, that if most negroes are flat-nosed, it is because the
parents crush the noses of their children . . . and that those who escape these
operations, their features are as comely as those of the Europeans.

(282–83)

One need not be a close reader of Book 4 of *Gulliver's Travels* to pick
up the numerous echoes there of this other major eighteenth-century fantasy
of difference: Swift's Yahoos are "prodigiously nimble from their infancy"
(214); their countenances, too, are "flat and broad, the nose depressed, the
lips large, and the mouth wide . . . distorted by . . . suffering their infants
to lie grovelling on the earth, or by carrying them on their backs, nuzzling
with their face against the mother's shoulders" (186). The picture that
Gulliver provides upon his first glimpse of the Yahoos sounds very much
like Buffon's image of the natural man or the Hottentot:

Their heads and breasts were covered with a thick hair, some frizzled and
others lank; they had beards like goats . . . they climbed high trees, as
nimbly as a squirrel, for they had strong extended claws before and behind,
terminating in sharp points, and hooked. They would often spring, and bound,
and leap with prodigious agility. The females were not so large as the males;
they had long lank hair on their heads, and only a sort of down on the rest of
their bodies. . . . Their dugs hung between their fore-feet, and often reached
almost to the ground as they walked. . . . Upon the whole, I never beheld in
all my travels so disagreeable an animal, or one against which I naturally
conceived so strong antipathy.

(181)

Gulliver makes much of their nakedness, distinguishing himself from the
Yahoos by emphasizing his own clothes. Their bodily hair, their "strange
disposition to nastiness and dirt" (212), their stench—especially the "offensive smell" of the female Yahoos (213)—all belong to the eighteenth-century
accounts of racial difference focusing on the Negro.

Furthermore, the Yahoos feed mainly upon raw flesh: "I saw three of
those detestable creatures . . . feeding upon . . . the flesh of some animals,
which I afterwards found to be that of asses and dogs, and now and then a
cow dead by accident or disease. . . . they held their food between the claws
of their forefeet, and tore it will their teeth. . . . [the Houyhnhnm] brought
out of the yahoo's kennel a piece of ass's flesh, but it smelt so offensively that
I turned from it with loathing: he then threw it to the yahoo, by whom it
was greedily devoured" (186). And they are by definition incapable of reason
or government; according to Gulliver "the yahoos appear to be the most
unteachable of all animals, their capacities never reaching higher than to
draw or carry burthens. Yet I am of opinion this defect ariseth chiefly from
a perverse, restive disposition. For they are cunning, malicious, treacherous

and revengeful. They are strong and hardy, but of a cowardly spirit, and by consequence insolent, abject, and cruel" (214–15).

But perhaps one of the most commonplace anecdotes of eighteenth-century racial fantasy was that of the sexual connection between Negroes and apes or orangutans alluded to in those arguments about the species of the Negro. These stories represent a kind of radical trans-species miscegenation that evidently captured the imagination of Swift's contemporaries. We can encounter several versions of the story retold by both Buffon and Long. Long's conclusions summarize his notion that whites and Negroes are different species, since the import of this story is that Negroes and apes are the same: "it is also averred, that [orangutans] sometimes endeavour to surprize and carry off Negroe women into their woody retreats, in order to enjoy them. . . . that they conceive a Passion for the Negroe women, and hence must be supposed to covet their embraces from a natural impulse of desire, such as inclines one animal towards another of the same species, or which has a conformity in the organs of generation. . . . [this is taken as proof that] the oran-outang and some races of black men are very nearly allied" (360, 364, 370). At this point, we need hardly remind ourselves of the encounter that teaches Gulliver that he is "a real yahoo in every limb and feature":

> [As he is bathing in a stream], a young female yahoo, standing behind a bank . . . and inflamed by desire . . . came running with all speed, and leaped into the water within five yards of the place where I bathed. I was never in my life so terribly frighted . . . She embraced me after a most fulsome manner; I roared as loud as I could and the nag [his protector] came galloping towards me, whereupon she quitted her grasp, with the utmost reluctancy, and leaped upon the opposite bank, where she stood gazing and howling all the time I was putting on my clothes. . . . now I could no longer deny that I was a real yahoo . . . since the females had a natural propensity to me as one of their own species.
>
> (215)

The Yahoos' greatest threat to Gulliver is here epitomized in the figure of the female whose sexuality stands as proof of the identification with the other that Gulliver abhors.

In short, Book 4 of *Gulliver's Travels* is pervasively connected with—indeed essentially compiled from—contemporary evidence of racial difference derived from accounts of the race that was in this period most immediately and visibly the object and human implement of mercantile capitalist expansion. This is not to say that the Yahoos are meant to stand for African blacks in any straightforward allegorical fashion. Indeed, the Houyhnhnms also participate in this general allusion to the cultural experience of imperialism: their aversion to untruth is modeled upon the common contemporary notion that native peoples cannot lie.[19] What we have observed in Book 4 of the *Travels* is not an allegory, but a pervasive contextualization in which the shifting status of the male observer, the dynamic of aversion and implication, difference and incorporation, that we have already observed in Swift's satire is given a specific historical referent: English imperialism and the trade in slaves.

Swift's miscegenation scene—in which the female Yahoo sets upon the male European—gives us an opportunity to define the mutual interaction of gender and race that shapes this text's relation to history. In this period, and even into the nineteenth century, accounts of the sexual attraction between apes and Negroes were invariably represented as exchanges between a male ape or orangutan and a Negro woman.[20] The anecdote in Swift's text—where the human male is set upon by an apparently bestial female—stands out for its evident violation of the sexual categories of this racist fantasy. Why, at this point, should Swift's text tamper with the materials that constitute the satire's representation of difference? The reversal of sexual roles in this scene could be seen as part of the persistent dynamic of identification or inter-changeability that we found in Gulliver's relation to the female figure else-where in the *Travels*: once again Gulliver is taking the place that the woman would occupy in the contemporary imagination. Or is he? Isn't it equally relevant to read this reversal as a racial interchangeability, where the white European Gulliver takes the place of the Negro, while the Yahoo takes the place of the ape, and the question of species is ironically restated? To see Gulliver as the Negro here, when the Yahoo has so consistently taken that role, is a striking new version of interchangeability that figures this reversal of the construction of racial difference. Programmatically, if in contemporary racist ideology the ape's lust for the Negro is supposed to prove them to be of the same species—non-human, then by the logic of Swift's satire the Yahoo's lust for Gulliver—the Negro's for the white European—proves them to be of the same species as well, equally human or non-human. In placing Gulliver in the position of the woman, then, this scene simultaneously puts him in the place of the Negro.

Like the female other in relation to the male observer in Books 1 and 2 of the *Travels* and in the misogynist poetry, the native other of Book 4 stands in a contradictory relationship with the colonialist, a relationship of aversion and implication, difference and incorporation. And Gulliver's posi-tion in this voyage—simultaneously identified with and absolutely differenti-ated from the Yahoo—itself suggests the contradictory nature of identity in Swift's redaction of the colonialist fantasy. The colonialist, for that reason, cannot reconcile himself to his own reflection in the mirror: "When I hap-pened to behold the reflection of my own form in a lake or fountain, I turned away my face in horror and detestation of myself, and could better endure the sight of a common yahoo, than of my own person" (225). The dynamic of difference and incorporation that characterizes this text makes it inevitable that Gulliver's ultimate efforts "to behold my figure often in a glass, and thus if possible habituate myself by time to tolerate the sight of a human creature" (238) must by definition be futile. On the one hand, the fourth voyage brings Gulliver into contact with an absolutely alien and hideous other, in the face of which all the brutality of colonialist repression—genocide included—must seem justified. On the other hand, it proposes an intense identification with and incorporation by the native that destabilizes any secure constitution of a distinct colonialist subject and even suggests an implicit critique of such a position.

The mutual interaction of the native and the woman through the mediation of the fictional Gulliver reproduces the historical relationship between imperialist exploitation abroad—with its economic dependence on slavery—and commodification at home—with its ideological emphasis on the figure of the woman. Thus Swift's satire registers the complex interdependency of categories of the oppressed in this period of English imperialism, and the interchangeability figured in Book 4 enables us to move beyond misogyny in itself or racism in itself to a dialectical critique that provides equal priority to both gender and race. Neither Swift's contemporaries nor Swift himself would have been able to move, as I have done here, from the misogynist attack on women to an understanding of its historical basis in commodification and trade. On the other hand, the active undermining of the ideology of racial superiority that we have observed in *Gulliver's Travels* certainly would have been accessible to an eighteenth-century audience. Contemporary readers—steeped in the racist images associated with English colonialism in that period and indeed through the mid-nineteenth-century—would have been much more ready than modern ones to register the crucial evocations of racial difference in Book 4, and much quicker than we are to pick up that text's pervasive playing with ideas of racial superiority and its perverse leveling of whites and non-whites to one common depravity. Indeed, the vitality and cultural power of *Gulliver's Travels*—and perhaps even its longevity in the canon of English literature—may be explained in part by the fact that it represented a challenge to an ideology that itself had a vital and powerful current function.

4

Let me return to the problem of the "politics" of political criticism. Let's say that this essay shows that Swift's misogyny is appropriately understood in the context of mercantile capitalism, that the structure of that misogyny opens up a critique of the treatment of racial difference which is essential to Swift's strategy in a crucial part of *Gulliver's Travels* and which was accessible from the moment of its publication. Why should we see these conclusions as radical, as opposed to other arguments that might be equally subtle in their use of historical context? This argument describes a certain odd configuration within a dominant ideology, certain surprising articulations among misogyny, imperialism, and racism. It should be no surprise to find that eighteenth-century imperialism is both misogynist and racist. The political utility might arise first through seeing that different forms of oppression—misogyny and racism—are not independent variables within the complex of a hegemony, but interdependent categories with mutualities of their own. But this reading of Swift also suggests that a basis for opposition can arise out of the interdependence of different forms of oppression: the unpromising materials of misogyny enable us to perceive the critique of racism. The sacrifice of women might seem a high price to pay for the problematization of racial difference. Ironically, though, it is this price that distinguishes a literary criticism of a distinctly liberationist cast from one more generally committed to a politicized thematic. The extreme case of Swift that I have been pursuing here is the rule rather than the exception; its ultimate political utility, as I see it, is as a positive model and not as a negative lesson. The lesson it might teach some critics is to infer from the compromised or problematic historical situation in which we always find ourselves the appropriateness of defeatism or despair. This lesson authorizes a criticism of withdrawal. But the model it provides is one of articulation and interdependence—the difficult negotiations that are the point of departure of a liberationist politics.

Let's say that Swift's travesty of true consciousness is the true radical political criticism.

Notes

1. *Gulliver's Travels*, in *Gulliver's Travels and Other Writings*, ed. Louis A. Landa (Boston: Houghton Mifflin, 1960), 237.

2. See Felicity A. Nussbaum, *The Brink of All We Hate: English Satires on Women*, 1660–1750 (Lexington: Univ. of Kentucky Press, 1984); Ellen Pollak, *The Poetics of Sexual Myth: Gender and Ideology in the Verse of Swift and Pope* (Chicago: Univ. of Chicago Press, 1985); Penelope Wilson, "Feminism and the Augustans: Some Readings and Problems," *Critical Quarterly* 28 (1986): 80–92, and Katherine M. Rogers, *The Troublesome Helpmate: A History of Misogyny in Literature* (Seattle: Univ. of Washington Press, 1966), and *Feminism in Eighteenth-Century England* (Urbana: Univ. of Illinois Press, 1982). The difficulty Swift presents for a feminist reading is suggested by the fact that Rogers' first book sees Swift as a misogynist and her second as a feminist, on the identical evidence (174 and 61, respectively).

3. *The Poems of Jonathan Swift*, ed. Harold Williams (Oxford: Clarendon Press, 1937). References by line to Swift's poems will be included parenthetically in the text.

4. Joseph Addison, *Tatler*, no. 116, 5 January 1709/10. Also quoted in Louis A. Landa, "Of Silkworms and Farthingales and the Will of God," in *Studies in the Eighteenth Century II: Essays presented at the Second David Nichol Smith Memorial Seminar*, ed. R. F. Brissenden (Toronto: Univ. of Toronto Press, 1973), 267–68.

5. For Pope and many other writers of this period, the connection between women and trade is direct and explicit, such that commerce itself and the process of production seem

organized for female adornment and consumption. See my *Alexander Pope* (Oxford: Basil Blackwell, 1985), ch. 1.

6. See James Ralph, *Clarinda, or the Fair Libertine* (London, 1729), 37–38; Soame Jenyns, *The Art of Dancing* (1730), in *Poems* (London, 1752), 7; John Durant Breval, *The Art of Dress* (London, 1717), 17; and Nicholas Rowe, *Jane Shore*, in *British Dramatists from Dryden to Sheridan*, ed. George H. Nettleton and Arthur E. Case, rev. ed. George Winchester Stone (Carbondale: Southern Illinois Univ. Press, 1959), V.i.111–16. Ralph, Jenyns, and Breval are discussed at greater length in Louis A. Landa, "Pope's Belinda, the General Emporie of the World and the Wondrous Worm," *South Atlantic Quarterly* 70 (1971): 223.

7. Neil McKendrick, "The Commercialization of Fashion," in McKendrick, John Brewer, and J. H. Plumb, *The Birth of a Consumer Society: The Commercialization of Eighteenth-Century England* (Bloomington: Indiana Univ. Press, 1982), 53 and 51.

8. Peter Earle, "The Economics of Stability: The Views of Daniel Defoe," in *Trade, Government and Economy in Pre-Industrial England*, ed. D. C. Coleman and A. H. John (London: Weidenfeld & Nicolson, 1976), 274–92, esp. 280. Earle's is a broadly synthetic article; as particularly relevant to this point, however, he cites Defoe's *General History of Discoveries and Improvements in Useful Arts* (1726–27), 79–152, and *A Plan of the English Commerce* (1728), 312–30 and 337–43.

9. Bernard Mandeville, *The Fable of the Bees: or, Private Vices, Publick Benefits*, ed. F. B. Kaye (Oxford: Clarendon Press, 1924), 1:356. Subsequent references will be cited in the text.

10. "A Proposal that All the Ladies and Women of Ireland should appear constantly in Irish Manufactures," *Prose Works*, ed. H. Davis (Oxford: Oxford Univ. Press, 1951), 12:126–27.

11. "Answer to Several Letters from Unknown Persons," *Prose Works*, 22:80.

12. Swift, "The Lady's Dressing Room," in *The Poems of Jonathan Swift*, ed. Harold Williams (Oxford: Clarendon Press, 1937), 524–30.

13. McKendrick, 43–49.

14. See Sander Gilman, "Black Bodies, White Bodies: Toward an Iconography of Female Sexuality in Late Nineteenth-Century Art, Medicine, and Literature," in *Critical Inquiry* 12, 1 (1985):204–42.

15. *Journal of a Lady of Quality; Being the Narrative of a Journey from Scotland to the West Indies . . . 1774 to 1776*, ed. Evangeline Walker Andrews and Charles McLean Andrews (New Haven: Yale Univ. Press, 1922), 78.

16. Among the relevant additional sources are Wouter Schouten, *Voyages de Gautier Schouten aux Indes orientales, commence l'an 1658 & fini l'an 1665* (Paris, 1725), 2 vols. (trans. from the Dutch); Claude Counte de Forbin, *Memoires du Compte de Forbin* (1729); Pierre Françoise Xavier de Charlevoix, *Histoire de L'isle Espagnole ou de S. Domingue* (Paris, 1730–31), *History of Paraguay* (London, 1769) [original French publication 1757], *Histoire de la Nouvelle France* (Paris, 1744); Jean Baptiste Dutertre, *Histoire Generale des Antilles* (Paris, 1654); Willem Bosman, *New and Accurate Description of the Coast of Guinea* (London, 1705; rpt. 1721) [English trans. from the Dutch]; Hans Sloane, *A Voyage To the Islands Madera, Barbados, Nieves, S. Christophers and Jamaica . . .* (London, 1707). Furthermore, A. H. Mackinnon describes the Augustans' fascination with the native "other" as depicted particularly in the narratives of William Dampier, *A New Voyage Round the World* (1697), François Leguat, *A New Voyage to the East Indies* (1708), and Woodes Rogers, *A Cruizing Voyage Round the World* (1712); he suggests that Swift may have been influenced by Dampier and Woodes Rogers. See "The Augustan Intellectual and the Ignoble Savage: Houynhym versus Hottentot" in J. Bakker and J. A. Verleun, ed., *Essays on English and American Literature and a Sheaf of Poems* (Amsterdam: Rodopi, 1987).

17. Edward Long, *The History of Jamaica. . . ,* 3 vols., (London, 1774), 1:356, 375. Subsequent references will be cited parenthetically in the text.

18.   George Louis Leclerc Buffon, *Buffon's Natural History, Containing a Theory of the Earth, A General History of Man, of the Brute Creation, and of Vegetables, Minerals, etc.*, 10 vols. (London, 1797), 9:136–37. Subsequent references will be noted parenthetically in the text. A recent note suggesting a contemporary influence upon Swift's depiction of the Yahoo suggests another sort of connection between Yahoo and Hottentot in terms of the debate over the "natural man"; this Hottentot, however, represents a philosophical rather than a racial category. See Daniel Eilon, "Swift's Yahoo and Leslie's Hottentot," *Notes and Queries* (December 1983): 510–12.

19.   For instance, of the Mosquitos Indians, "there is nothing more hateful to them than breach of Promise, or telling an Untruth, their Words being inviolable." Sloane, *A Voyage To the Islands Madera, Barbados, Nieves, S. Christophers and Jamaica. . .* , I, lxxvii.

20.   See Sander Gilman for a description of the focus on the sexuality of the female Negro, with the corollary absence of any interest at all in the sexuality of the Negro male.

A TALE OF A TUB AND EIGHTEENTH-CENTURY LITERATURE

◆

A *Tale of a Tub* and *Clarissa*:
A Battling of Books

EVERETT ZIMMERMAN

A Tale of a Tub and *Clarissa* are unlikely yokemates, yet as Swift perceived, opposites are prone to meet. The incongruousness in the relationship of these books is indicative of aspects of the ancients and moderns controversy, the clashes of the two books exemplifying conflicting elements of the arguments of Sir William Temple and William Wotton. While Richardson was less directly engaged in these issues than Swift, he explicitly acknowledged his antagonism to his predecessor. Nearly a half century after the publication of the *Tale*, Richardson represented in *Clarissa* his rejection of Swift, once directly in a footnote and elsewhere by allusions associating the *Tale* with Lovelace's interpretive program.[1] Richardson later encouraged the writing of, and then published, one of the final salvos of the ancients and moderns controversy, Young's *Conjectures on Original Composition*, which repeatedly cites Swift denigratingly, while extolling the moderns' potential for greatness and including Richardson among examples of modern excellence.

An apparent point of entry into the complex system of differences that divides and unites these figures is through their responses to the contemporary literary establishment, which was increasingly molded by the social and economic consequences of the technology of printing.[2] Printing was, of course, a significant part of Richardson's identity. He managed his professional life, which included aspects of what we would now call publishing as well as printing, with consummate skill, and as author he benefited from his own ministrations.[3] The proliferation of prefaces, dedications, notes, and other addenda that Swift replicated scornfully as evidence of the corruptions brought by the press (although Swift found similar corruptions resulting from patronage too) were skillfully manipulated by Richardson for the advantage of his own reputation and what he thought of as the proper reception of his works. A *Pamela* and especially a *Clarissa*, with all their accretions, look much like *A Tale of a Tub*, but what Richardson regards as support of his text is by Swift regarded as a symptom of textual spuriousness, a failing effort to nudge inconsequential writing into significance. And running through Swift's writings are the irritable whines of authors or putative authors

This essay was written specifically for this volume and appears here for the first time.

directed at booksellers and printers, who lose manuscripts, print the names wrong, make promises they can't or won't keep, and see the purpose of making books as selling them.[4]

Attitudes toward the significance and consequences of the printing press mark important points of divergence between Temple and Wotton in the controversy that led up to the *Tale*. In *An Essay upon the Ancient and Modern Learning* (1690), Temple represents the press as irrelevant to the propagation of true knowledge, believing that much could have been transmitted through oral tradition and also that books are "dead instructors," a terminology suggesting his prepossession in favor of presence.[5] Despite the destruction of many ancient writings, existing books are often repetitious: "few . . . can pretend to be authors rather than transcribers or commentators of the ancient learning" (Temple, 41). Wotton in contrast emphasizes the crucial importance of modern technology for the advancement and mediation of learning, including the telescope, microscope, engraving, and, most important of all, printing: "The Use of *Printing* has been so vast, that every thing else wherein the Moderns have pretended to excel the Ancients, is almost entirely owing to it."[6] Included among the conventional advantages of books over manuscripts are that they are cheaper, more easily read, and the text better preserved. Among the less conventionally prominent conveniences of books that Wotton cites are that notices of their publication are dispersed, thus bringing them to the attention of those seeking learning, and that they often include indexes and "other necessary divisions" too cumbersome for manuscripts, which enable desired information to be found expeditiously (Wotton, 171–72). Even critical philology with its aim of recovering a true past is dependent upon the press. This characteristic branch of modern study relies heavily on the examination and comparison of historical claims and their evidentiary bases. With printing, books that were available previously only in a relatively few manuscripts could now be examined and compared with ease (Wotton, 312).

The multiplication of books is not, however, without its own problems. The responses of Temple and Wotten can both be regarded as attempts to subdue the anxieties produced by a proliferation of books. Temple's wish to accept a canon that reduces modern books to relative unimportance and that calmly acquiesces in the irrecoverability of large portions of antiquity is a way of keeping learning within boundaries that are masterable. Not only need he not deal with the large numbers of modern books that are inevitably repetitious, but he may also safely ignore those modern books that question the boundaries of the canon that he accepts: such questioning in Temple's view is highly conjectural and merely pedantic. But if modern critical philology in Wotten's sense is taken seriously, antiquity is rendered an unsteady concept requiring constant adjustment, the fragmentary not safely confined to the irrecoverable nor the seemingly whole sequestered from potential fragmentation. Temple's very acquiescence in loss stabilizes a canon by placing limits on what may be learned about it. For Wotton, on the other hand, critical philology can potentially incorporate a new ancient world into the remarkably expanded modern one. But just as Temple wishes to reduce the modern intellectual world to manageable dimensions by setting up against it an overshadowing but ungraspable, and thus unchangeable, ancient world, Wotton too must find ways to comprehend the overwhelming modern world that he is constituting. The question incipient in Temple and Wotton is this: Who can possibly encompass the knowledge that is claimed in potentiality?

Wotton's own book is a compendium of others' achievements, designed to give a survey of all the kingdoms of knowledge, ancient and modern. His remarkably confident purpose is to facilitate the identification of those areas of investigation that may be most profitably pursued, "by which Means, Knowledge, in all its Parts, might at last be compleated" (Wotton, Preface). But even as he praises the achievements of modernity, he betrays an anxiety about their quantity that is not fully allayed by modern skills in abridgment and indexing. As, for example, he describes the achievements of philology, he expresses both a sense of plenitude and of loss of control: "The *Bodleyan* and *Leyden* Libraries can witness what vast Heaps of *Eastern MSS.* have been brought . . . into *Europe*," a description that introduces disorder into the manuscript divisions of these libraries. And this implied loss of controlled access is followed by a reflection on the difficulties of summarizing the vast achievements of modern philology in response to this heaping of manuscripts: "One would think I were drawing up a Catalogue . . . if I were to enumerate the Books which have been printed about the *Oriental* Learning, within these last Seventy Years" (Wotton, 314). His own survey, even if at times summary of summary, is hard pressed to comprehend the volume of modern learning. As we moderns know too well, inaccessible or unassimilable information is only another form of ignorance. However complete in a theoretical way knowledge may be, it counts only to the extent that it is appropriated. As Wotten praises the increase of knowledge, he is also observing its approaching disjuncture. The possibility of the completion of knowledge that he, like Bacon and others, asserts is a way of imagining a static state that coheres without disintegrating. This conception avoids acknowledging the paradox implicit in a too rapid increase of knowledge: information exceeding any possible appropriation is reduced to the fragments from which it issued. Wotten *and* Temple are seeking a form of "sufficiency," the vice Temple finds particularly characteristic of moderns and their motive for attempting to detach themselves from the ancients.

For the purposes of his satire, Swift represents both Wotton's quantitative estimate of the proliferation of modern books and Temple's qualitative views about the repetitiousness of modern learning, a combination that Swift expresses by reducing modern books literally and figuratively to bales of paper, which metonymically constitute two additional metaphors, both alimentary: books are a bare livelihood or, ultimately, mere refuse, depending on whether the paper is used as bread wrapping or ends in a jakes.[7] Grub Street is the world of the garret, of fasting, and of the overwhelming need to sell: *"considering my urgent necessities*, what . . . might be acceptable this month" (*Tale*, 207). The modern learning garnered from books and needed to produce them is acquired by reading titles or, preferably, getting "a thorough Insight into the *Index*, by which the whole Book is governed" (*Tale*, 145). Indexes are characterized as *"Back-Door"* learning, the usually shameful but nevertheless urgent end of the human trunk, which end is shared with the source of the sole modern contribution to writing, "deducing Similitudes, Allusions, and Applications . . . from the *Pudenda* of either Sex" (*Tale*, 147). As the "Digression in Praise of Digressions" illustrates in form and content, the applauded modern production of books is enabled by indexes, compendiums, quotations, lexicons, systems, and abstracts—all seemingly second-order forms of information ordering and retrieval that Wotton regards as facilitators of progress but that Swift represents as degenerative repetition.

Yet for quantitative reasons, these books are not, despite their seeming evanescence, benignly biodegradable. The regularizing of the new forms of learning has increased the number of writers, thus allowing their existence as quantity to withstand their self-cancelling repetitiveness. However vacuous, airy, or elusive modern books are in the *Tale*, they are also an oppressive presence, from their representation as "Bales of Paper" in the "Epistle Dedicatory" (*Tale*, 35) through the proliferation of titles in the course of the narration. Although books have many ways of leaving the world, they are also a swarming if useless presence within it. For example, the *Tale*'s opening includes a list of 11 treatises written by its author and waiting to be published, which titles the narrator reiterates as extensions or preemptions of topics discussed throughout the succeeding text; and in the "Introduction," a competing modern, John Dunton, is announced to be preparing the publication of 12 folio volumes of the speeches of condemned criminals (*Tale*, 59). Combined with the constant references to multitudinous other productions of Grub Street and the acknowledgement of the vast numbers of volumes that are ransacked to produce even one volume, such persistent reference to the burgeoning of books evokes a claustrophobic sense of a paper world closing in on nature, truly creating a need for a tale of a tub to amuse those dangerous wits "appointed . . . with Pen, Ink, and Paper" (*Tale*, 39).

Swift's satiric conflation of modern repetitiveness and productiveness—the worst composition of Temple and Wotton—leads to a version of the human mind and endeavor that is both energetic and circular: "the mind of Man . . . sallies out into both extreams of High and Low" but eventually the extremes meet "like one who travels the *East* into the *West*; or like a strait Line drawn by its own Length into a Circle" (*Tale*, 157–58). The circular image is also one of imprisonment within a restrictive pattern that permits no escape from Temple's world, Wotton's version of supercession being merely fruitless emulation. As W. B. Carnochan remarks, "This parody of the happy prison comes close to being the real thing."[8] "The Digression concerning . . . Madness" presents innovation as the effort of an overturned reason, while "the Brain in its natural Position . . . disposeth its Owner to pass his Life in the common Forms" (*Tale*, 171), presumably without any serious desires to escape from this confinement. Yet happiness is dependent on delusion, *"the Possession of being well deceived"* (*Tale*, 174). The treadmill of language that results from Swift's conflation of Temple's static world and Wotton's world of unceasing endeavor is unbearable.

The culminating subject of the *Tale* is exhaustion—of narrator and of the narrated, but perhaps not of narration itself: "I am now trying an Experiment very frequent among Modern Authors; which is, *to write upon Nothing*; When the Subject is utterly exhausted, to let the Pen still move on" (*Tale*, 208). The writing meanders until it concludes in the decision to "here pause awhile, till I find, by feeling the World's Pulse, and my own, that it will be of absolute Necessity for us both to resume my Pen" (*Tale*, 210). Exhaustiveness generates exhaustion, but in a world of repetitiveness not necessarily completion. Exhaustiveness may be achieved either by the multiplication of summaries or the extension of commentary. The book can recapitulate the many texts of the larger world or it can imply the complexities of the seemingly inert single text. The aim of the *Tale* as announced in the "Epistle Dedicatory" is to give to posterity a "faithful Abstract, drawn from the Universal Body of all Arts and Sciences" (*Tale*, 38), an aim that betrays its limitations even as it is stated: abstracts are linked to past texts and can be made to encompass posterity only through the constant interpretive efforts of human beings, which are figured as the Word, the book as person. The attempt to include all—the fixities of summary, inclusive but also closed, as well as the dynamics of the person, limited but also continuing—are metaphorically implied by having books reduced to a material form, which is then embodied in a person who reproduces, or excretes, a summary: "an universal System, in a small portable Volume, of all Things that are to be known, or Believed, or Imagined, or Practised in Life" is to be produced through the distilling of books into an elixir, which when snuffed up the nose creates a perception in the head of "Abstracts, Summaries, Compendiums, Extracts, Collections, Medulla's, Excerpta, quaedam's, Florilegias, *and the like, all disposed into great Order, and reducible upon Paper"* (*Tale*, 125, 126–27).

When Homer, like many epic poets thought to be a master of the learning of his time, is dealt with as if a summarizer, the narrator finds many omissions (*Tale*, 127). He demands that the *Tale* be accorded a different treatment: he has opened his vein for the universal benefit of mankind, and he invites his readers to find in his book whatever meanings they need: "the Reader truly *Learned* . . . will here find sufficient Matter to employ his Speculations for the rest of his Life. . . . *seven* ample Commentaries on this comprehensive Discourse . . . will be all, without the least Distortion, manifestly deduceable from the Text" (*Tale*, 184, 185). His text, embodying him, is to be treated like a sacred text in which through commentary all essential meanings are to be found. Thus the *Tale* will contain a summary of all past knowledge and will also exfoliate all future knowledge through the efforts of the skilled reader. Although digressions and tale are not systematically discriminated by theme, the digressions, especially those "in the Modern Kind" and "in Praise of Digressions" tend to explore the possibilities and liabilities of repetitiveness, of summary, while the allegorical tale of the three brothers explores the possibilities, and liabilities, of commentary.[9]

Elizabeth L. Eisenstein remarks that the multiplication of books made possible by printing allowed scholars to be less "engrossed by a single text. . . . The era of the glossator and commentator came to an end" and was succeeded by comparison and compilation as more characteristic scholarly activities.[10] In the *Tale* Swift finds both kinds of activity to be similarly perverted by the desire for totalization, a version of "sufficiency." The brothers are in the position of having to use what we take to be an allegory as if it were an encyclopedia. The aim of the encyclopedia is to be all-encompassing and discursive, to arrange all available knowledge according to a scheme that will make portions of it accessible for any purpose. Allegoresis allows a single text to imply increasing complexity, but it does not permit totality unless founded upon a radically allegorical conception of reality in which any element of the world is connected to every element—the kind of allegory Augustine implies when he finds that words point to things and that things, including words, each have their own meanings, all connected to that totality of conception that is God's.[11] In such a schema even the alphabet has a meaning, but not in Swift's *Tale*: here the dissolution of words leads to an alphabet that is incomplete and from which the only meaning derivable is that which is constructed by the desire of the moment. Swift has created a text in which summary and commentary are in conflict. The summarizing characteristic of an encyclopedia enjoins a literalistic interpretation, but a single narrative (as opposed to multiple entries each arranged under their proper topic) demands expansion by commentary in order to engage by allegory the manifold exigencies of life. Martin and Jack reject the irresponsible allegorizing that characterizes Peter's assertion of self above the literal meaning of the will. Yet Jack's subsequent behavior shows the limits of the will in a literal interpretation. Not finding an authentic phrase from the will for inquiring the way to a jakes, he soils himself, but he will not clean himself because of the scriptural phrase "he which is filthy, let him be filthy still," a dubious phrase that may have been "foisted in by the Transcriber" (*Tale*, 191). Here even the details of the text, the will that is the basis for interpretation, literal or allegorical, is of limited authority.

Foucault's definition of a shift from resemblance to representation is relevant to these conflicts of interpretation. The preclassical episteme assumes no sharp division between reality and the language used to present it. Resemblances can be discovered between words and the things they designate; indeed understanding is dependent on discovering resemblances that connect all. In the classical episteme, however, language facilitates an analytical understanding that assumes a separation of the representation from its object, the analytical tool from what is analyzed. In Foucault's sense, the preclassical episteme is based on repetition, the connection of all into a great web in which the resemblance is apparent through some kind of similarity; adjacency is not adventitious.[12] In the sense implied by Swift's *Tale*, the classical episteme too is based on repetition because the modern learning is merely a disguised repetition of that already achieved by the ancients. The summary that is characteristic of a book like Wotton's is for Swift a tendency of all knowledge; the aim at completeness of knowledge turns into an encyclopedic repetition of one disconnected fragment of knowledge after another. But a return to interpretation by resemblance is also rejected in the *Tale*. Allegoresis, which is the expansion of meaning by resemblance, avoids the discursiveness of fragmented summary, but for Swift it is in practice governed by desire and thus, unless institutionally sanctioned, a private aberration that evades the common forms. Systems, totalizing schemes, are also in Swift's sense governed by resemblance, no matter how "modern" they appear. The placement of disparate fragments within a context that clarifies their meaning (as in the "cabinet of curiosities" of an eighteenth-century antiquarian or natural philosopher) if seen in Swiftian terms is the creation of arbitrary meaning by the imposition of contiguity and the discovery of elements of resemblance; in contrast, the "modern" sees it as an attempt to generate meaning by means of a system of classification that is distinct from the fragments. While attacking the classical episteme, Swift grants no alternative validity to the preclassical episteme: when language is reduced to an alphabet, or to things, meaning vanishes because the analytical device for ordering and representing meaning has been dissolved. It is not in itself meaningful.[13] The brothers thus have a will that may be admirable but much of the interpretation that extends it to new times and circumstances reflects either the ludicrous literalization of regressive summary, as sometimes exemplified in Jack, or uncontrolled resemblance, as sometimes exemplified in Peter; each of these interpretive moves is a willful distortion motivated by private desire.

Martin, of course, represents the preferable alternative to Peter and Jack, yet his behavior does not validate the demand for literality implied by the interpretive excesses mocked in the satire. His response is related to a uniformitarian history that accepts neither a radical difference of past from present nor the past's identity with the present. He stops short of attending precisely to the will's instructions, and thus he avoids destroying the "substance" of the coat, a violation of the will justified as according with its "true intent and meaning" (*Tale*, 65). Jack's ripping and tearing in opposition to

Peter is an attempt to recover some pristine original state, a denial of his history, while Martin's less fervent response acknowledges his experience, which has brought about an irreparable distancing from the will. Although his coat continues to harbor the signs of his alienating history, it also creates some connection to an essential meaning that has power even when no longer literally applicable. Jack's tearing is analogous to Swift's version of a modern like Bentley whose meticulous analysis of the ancients reduces them to shreds, while Peter's desertion of the will in order to facilitate his own advancement is analogous to Wotton's rejection of dependency on the ancients.[14] Martin's response to the will thus represents an acknowledgement of history—a connection to the past, but a rejection of a historicism that would make the difference of the past centrally important. The "phlegmatic" Martin shapes his conduct as much by a concern for the continuity of "common forms" as by a stringent view of the will's meaning.

The institutions of book, encyclopedia, and archive are related to the form of the *Tale*, or perhaps more properly to the strains on its apparent formal organization. The notion of creating the "bulk" of a book by summarizing others and digressing from oneself suggests that the work is a book only in terms of material form, yet the metaphoric expansion to authorial body creates a putative organic unity. However, the topical multiplicity, the unrestrained inclusiveness, leads to the analogy of book to world, which implies an order but imposes an impossible demand in a "modern" world with unassimilable amounts of information. Allegoresis is used to supplement these textual deficiencies, but it fragments the book by its introduction of conflicting and unrationalized interpretive norms. The demands of inclusiveness subvert order and result in the reader being empowered to remove a digression "into any other Corner he pleases" (149), a move toward the arbitrary order necessitated by an encyclopedic goal.[15] But eventually the book moves toward an archival self-conception, as the narrator tries to create significance for his commonplace book by emptying it into the *Tale* and as Swift in subsequent editions adds footnotes, including material from Wotton's attack. The *Tale* simulates a modern text and a modern version of an ancient text simultaneously. It is ragged with missing passages, defaced pages, and editorial explanations, as well as with multiplications of prefatory materials and excerpts from others' commentary that change from one edition to another. It becomes a lopsided, stuffed collection of papers, and it implies a conception of its potentiality that requires the reordering, indexing, and storage that are not possible within the covers that are the convential demarcations of books.[16] Swift's parodic version of a book responds to the modern's conception of an uncontrolled increase in knowledge that finds its salient manifestation in the printing industry; its exemplary contrast is the concise book that expresses conclusions, rather than exploring the conditions for its own hegemony, and that has a limited coherent scheme with a controlled and controlling narration. Such values imply a canon and a library as their larger models. The canon negotiates a compromise that reduces mere repetition and avoids conflicts of values, thus keeping the library small and free of battles, not the library of Babel but Temple's library.

A summary of some conventional differences between archive and library may be useful for identifying issues in the historical outlook of ancients and moderns that are relevant to understanding the contrasts between Swift and Richardson. Although the terms *archive* and *library* overlap and are even sometimes used synonymously, T. R. Schellenberg's summary of differences reveals disparities of function and, consequently, differing standards of relevance. Library materials are often chosen for their cultural significance, "whereas the cultural significance of archival materials may be incidental."[17] The archive exists to documents a particular institution, not a large cultural configuration, and therefore all items are more closely related to each other than are those of a library, which tends to consist of discrete items "whose significance is wholly independent of their relationship to other items" (Schellenberg, 17). Because the archive exists to preserve the shape and articulation of the particular institution it serves, its significance lies in the preservation of structures, not single documents but the relationships of parts. Thus the arrangement of the archive must differ from that of the library. A library groups items "in accordance to a predetermined logical scheme," while the archive must preserve items in their context, using a "classification that is dictated by the original circumstances of creation." The librarian preserves discrete items, trying to keep like things together, but "the significance of a particular item will not necessarily be lost if it is not classified in a certain place" (Schellenberg, 22). The archivist, in contrast, deals with units that "derive their significance, in large part at least, from their relation to one another" (Schellenberg, 23).

The attempt at modern exhaustiveness that Wotton displays and Swift parodies has a generalizing aspect that seemingly has more in common with the library and the encyclopedia than with the limited institutional nature of the archive. Yet the modern concern for part to whole relationships resembles the conception of the archive. Wotton's understanding of a classical civilization that exists in dispersal and fragmentation but that can be brought to coherence through careful comparison and criticism of existing texts is an archival analogy. Texts are not so much independent monuments, as in Temple, but pieces whose significance lies in the proper arrangement that will bring the historical order of classical civilization into clearer outline. Swift's parodic version of this conception represents it as a process that creates confusion (as in Bentley's destroying of the position of Aesop and Phalaris in the canon) and replaces existing wholeness with fragmentation. The rearrangements of the archive turn the discrete order of the library into a multiplicity that in Swift's version is a battle for dominance, not a move toward increased understanding. *A Tale of a Tub* is an archive of modernism, representing it not only in statement but also in its formal confusion, so stuffed with its own ambitions that nothing can be eliminated, its writing having required the "perusing of hundreds of prefaces" (*Tale*, 20).

Richardson uses the archival conception that Swift parodies as a governing fiction for *Clarissa*: masses of documents, written for varying purposes, are all brought together for mutual illumination in service of the institution (ultimately monument) that Clarissa makes of herself. In themselves the letters are fragments; in their arrangement a "history." But to his consternation, Richardson's archival fiction was interpreted diversely, thus calling into question the very sense of documentary objectivity that is advanced by the conception of an archive. Some aspects of these interpretive conflicts may be articulated more clearly through an examination of the concept of the archive itself in relationship to its constituting "traces" and its epistemological ambitions. The archive's contents are documents, the materials evoking and supporting a conception of the institution to which the archive is responsible. Only assertions warranted by the archival documents are considered valid. But as Paul Ricoeur points out, archives are also monuments, their contents consisting of what was thought worthy of being preserved, and thus already a product of institutional conception or self-conception rather than its basis.[18] A differing understanding of the document may be achieved by its placement within a broader and/or markedly differing context from that of the archive, where the monumental function may exclude much. As a consequence the monumentally proffered document requires interrogation and interpretation, achieving its status as warrant only by means of the uncertainties and partialities of argument and not by mere existence. Thus the document is a "trace," having the characteristic absence or partiality of context that thwarts interpretation and also the apparent connection to an absent context that provokes interpretation. A trace exists in the present as a remnant of something past and is thus in itself the survival of the past, yet as Ricoeur, following Levinas, suggests, its connection is to a "passing," as a footprint is a trace of an animal that calls attention to a former act of passage; it implies absence (from knowledge as well as the present) but tantalizes with hints of recoverability. The archive is an organization of traces with the purpose of providing the mutual contextualizing that leads to documentary usefulness. It is in that respect like those "cabinets of curiosities" built by seventeenth-and eighteenth-century artisans to hold the artifacts of the virtuosos—each little compartment holding its own separate item, yet the arrangement of items designed to shed light on each other, the classification system itself leading to understanding.[19] The monument, of course, depicts finalities, while the "cabinet of curiosities" and the archive also have the possibility of constant rearrangement as contexts are altered or expand.

The limits of the monumental archive (of which *Clarissa* is a fictional example) and the kind of history to which it is related are discussed in Foucault's *The Archeology of Knowledge*, which defines and rejects the critical history that moves from document/trace to totality (the history Wotton praised as a salient modern achievement). Foucault rejects the history that has as its purpose the transformation of the monumental into the documentary through the interrogation of its biases and designs; instead "in our time, history . . . transforms documents into monuments" by rejecting the assumption that the documentary can be disinterred from its monumental function and converted to a link in an existing continuity.[20] The problem, in his view, is not to overcome discontinuity but to make it a "working concept": discontinuity is an instrument as well as an object of research (Foucault, 8–9). As a consequence the possibility of "total history" disappears and "general history" emerges. Total history is the ambition of the moderns, seeking as it does to "reconstitute the overall form of a civilization" (Foucault, 9), while general history questions the possibility of connecting perceived discontinuities and takes the very constitution of series, rather than the filling in of already established series, as its problem. The archives, then, are not for Foucault those "institutions, which, in a given society, make it possible to record and preserve those discourses that one wishes to remember and keep in circulation," but instead "the law of what can be said. . . . *the system of its functioning*" (Foucault, 129). Archival study is not properly "a question of rediscovering what might legitimize an assertion, but of freeing the conditions of emergence of statements" (Foucault, 127). An implication of Foucault's views is that the apparent cacophony of voices within a culture cannot be ordered validly to show an underlying continuity of perspective or hierarchy of values but that, nevertheless, the very discontinuities that constitute the cacophony can be seen to be authorized by "discourse"; the conflicts of content are not resolvable in the monumental archive of documents but can be comprehended by the Foucaultian archive of discourse, in which is sought not the resolution of conflicts but the conditions that govern their articulation.

Foucault's analysis of the archive brings into relief the import of Richardson's attempt to make his fictional monument documentary. Making optimistic assumptions like Wotton's about the powers of a totalizing history, Richardson expects that which is fragmentary in itself to yield a full meaning in context. He obtrudes the fragmentation of both perspective and form: the writers have limited knowledge and letters themselves begin and end in medias res. Richardson's method, therefore, demands continuity as an end and an instrument of analysis, for if this presupposition is changed to discontinuity, the gaps within and between letters enlarge. Reduced from documents to traces, the letters raise questions about their grounding. Placed in the context of other traces, a trace may document a much expanded conception of a "passing," yet the question of the character or characteristics of the cause of the trace remains unexhausted in any scrutiny of the effect, the mark. The "passing" of Lovelace and Clarissa is documented by the collection of letters, but their precise relationship to their writings is never fully resolved. To argue that such questions about a fictional work must be resolved by asking the questions of authors rather than of characters is to add another layer to the analysis but not to dissolve the question itself. In following the epistolary fiction of archival representation and reconstruction, Richardson himself recognizes the problematical relationship of writer to letter, of cause to mark. Such complexities are part of the fiction, not bracketed out by it. Designating Lovelace as a Proteus and subjecting Clarissa's feelings about him to sustained and contradictory analysis raises the question of the relationship of trace to cause, of letter to writer, rather than suppressing it.[21] Foucault remarks that "making historical analysis the discourse of the continuous and making human consciousness the original subject of all historical development and all action are the two sides of the same system of thought" (Foucault, 12), a system of thought Foucault rejects as an attempt at "total history." Richardson's project enmeshed him in the difficulties of such thinking, and many elements of the structure and content of *Clarissa* are related to his attempt to make the archive yield continuity and human consciousness.

Clarissa's writing of letters includes the intention of preserving them to reify and thus vindicate her conduct after it and its occasions have vanished.[22] The letters have other purposes too—ranging from ordinary instrumental uses to the expression and relief of feelings—but their monumental use is what requires their collection; if they are to serve as monument to her, preserving and organizing are of equal importance with writing and sending. As has often been noted, the production of writing is a central topic of Richardson's fiction; *Clarissa* adds the duties of archivist to production. In *Pamela* too, it is true, letters require disposal, yet it is perhaps of significance that the major cache of Pamela's writing surrounds her person beneath her garments, whereas Clarissa's letters are far too voluminous and have too explicitly public a rationale for such presentation. Clarissa herself functions in a limited way as archivist in the book, but the demands on that role expand until ultimately Belford must undertake the increased collecting, arranging, and providing access that are required because of the need for multiple perspectives and multiple correspondences in the interest of completeness.[23]

Before becoming *Clarissa*, Clarissa needs one more mediator—the editor. A vast collection of letters, erratically delivered and circulated among a diversity of recipients, is brought toward coherence by the efforts of Clarissa and then completed by Belford when her efforts at compiling apparently are doomed to insufficiency. Yet much of this material is repetitious, containing originals and interpolated copies that have been variously circulated for varying purposes, a mass of papers presenting repeated descriptions of the same events. Without the efforts of an information manager, this book would be even longer than the longest novel in English. And what mere reader could have the simultaneous grasp of the facts and implications of widely separated letters that is needed to arrive unescorted at a just understanding of every episode and implication, the objective truth that is assumed to emerge merely from archival completeness? An increasingly more interpretive, in contrast to a solely textual, version of the editor gradually emerges, one who appears to be in control of a vast store of papers, deciding which are needed, which can be excerpted, and which can be left out. This editor remains notably scrupulous in indicating textual provenance and defining any alterations, yet the alterations influence the book's texture significantly, sometimes seeming to move it from the participant's toward the editor's provenance.[24]

The print world of *Clarissa* intersects aspects of the satire of Swift's *Tale*, especially in relation to Swift's reduction to absurdity of Wotton's praise of the proliferation of modern books and the devices of modern information management that allow their appropriation. Swift rejects modern claims to significant originality, but the fragmentation that Swift finds characteristic of the exhaustion of the moderns is in Richardson presented as the result of a minute view of human character in conflict. The collecting of the fragments of *Clarissa* presumably results then not in contradiction but in the construction of continuity. As a consequence, those devices of arrangement and summary, seen by Swift as degenerative repetition, function in Richardson as enablers of an insight into the larger patterns of continuity and organization within the fragmentation. Swift and Richardson share a "modern" world on which they have markedly different perspectives. Yet the anxieties and ambiguities that emerge from their perceptions also have notable points of similarity.

Clarissa shows Lovelace's virtuosity in using the common forms for individualistic purposes. On display is an archive of textual devices for manipulative deception, as if Richardson's earlier *Letters Written to and for Particular Friends on the Most Important Occasions* (1741) had been rewritten for a counterfeiter, who delights in textual deceit and uses the epistolary forms for reasons unrelated to their ostensible purposes. Richardson and Clarissa finally present a textually defined truth through Belford's compilement, yet despite Richardson's intentions and resistance, he saw in his readers' questions the muddling of that truth too. Lovelace is Richardson's version of the taleteller, who, in Swift's conception, links modern writing wholly to desire, eliminating any values beyond the self. As a consequence, Swift's parodic version of the modern embraces any contradiction that will minister to his desires, thus eventually evacuating any self other than what inheres in appetite. Severed from any clear identity of person, textual meaning in the service of desire is evanescent, linked to no external stabilities. Richardson counters by making text itself weighty, its convolutions supporting the illusion of self-groundedness.[25] Lovelace represents the subversions of text in *Clarissa*, and rejecting him implies a repudiation of that fragmentation that occurs when no stable consciousness underwrites the text.[26] Richardson represents him as a forger, one who literally counterfeits letters but also one who counterfeits himself, presenting versions of Lovelace that have no continuous existence external to the words from which they are inferred. He and the version of textuality that he implies are associated with *A Tale of a Tub* and made into an aberration. Richardson thus provides a defense of the archival fiction, which posits the stabilizing of meaning through completeness of documentation, individual aberration refuted by comparative analysis.

Swift appears in *Clarissa* as the author of "The Lady's Dressing Room," the *Travels*, and, most notably, the *Tale*.[27] The most directly antagonistic comment about Swift occurs in a note to Belford's description of his visit to the dying Mrs. Sinclair, which Richardson uses to congratulate himself on having presented a "not only more natural but more decent painting" than that in "The Lady's Dressing Room."[28] Belford himself compares the "profligate women" he describes to "one of Swift's Yahoos, or Virgil's obscene Harpies." References to the *Tale* are more frequent and primarily Lovelace's. He alludes to the *Tale* in warning Belford that if he interferes between him and Clarissa, he will "be a madder Jack than him in the *Tale of a Tub*" (*Clarissa*, no. 370, p. 1144). This warning comes after his ridicule of Belford's efforts at reforming him, which he compares to the interpretive efforts of the enthusiasts in a passage reminiscent of a satiric point from the *Tale*: "As enthusiasts do by Scripture, so dost thou by the poets thou hast read: anything that carries the most distant allusion by *either* to the case in hand, is put down by both for gospel, however incongruous to the general scope of either." Rather than connecting Belford to the dissenters, however, such hermeneutical skepticism connects Lovelace to a blinding empiricism. Clarissa's subsequent ambiguous reference to her expected departure for "my father's house" where "I am bid to hope that he will receive his poor penitent with a goodness peculiar to himself" (*Clarissa* no. 421.1, p. 1233) is read by Lovelace with a numbed univocality that is responsive only to his desires. His eventual suspicions about her meaning and his interpretation of it lead to a comparison of her figural use of her "father's house" to what "Gulliver in his abominable Yahoo story" calls "saying the *thing that is not*" (*Clarissa*, no. 439, p. 1270). This Gulliverian literalism is exemplified in his earlier perverse interpretation of her meditation "on being hunted after by the enemy of my soul": "She says she has *eaten ashes like bread*—a sad mistake to be sure!—*and mingled her drink with weeping*—sweet maudlin soul! should I say to anyone confessing this but Miss Harlowe" (*Clarissa*, no. 418, p. 1221).

Lovelace characterizes his deceptions of Clarissa as throwing "a tub to a whale" (*Clarissa*, no. 103, p. 412), and he justifies deceit by paraphrasing "The Digression Concerning . . . Madness": "Are we not told that in being *well* deceived consists the whole of human happiness" (*Clarissa*, no.218, p. 700). His allusions to the *Tale* take a formal turn as he describes Hickman's speech as Tubbian: "parenthesis within parenthesis, apologizing for apologies, in imitation I suppose of Swift's Digressions in Praise of Digressions" (*Clarissa*, no. 346, p. 1091). Possible but scattered and less explicit allusions to *The Battle of the Books* also occur: a reference to Phalaris and his bull, and a comparison of Clarissa's counterplotting to "a spider . . . spinning only a cobweb" (*Clarissa*, no. 252, p. 865; no. 256, p. 879). But more important than the bare allusive reference is Richardson's fascinated construction of one for whom writing is not presence, nor presence any more definitive than writing, who is characterized as unfixed, a threat to any conception of text that, in Richardson's terms, is justifiable.[29]

Lovelace is in some respects a composite of Peter and the tale-teller, exhibiting an appetite that consumes all voluntary restraints and losing any consistency except that conferred by desire. "I will draw out from this letter an alphabet," is Lovelace's preface to forgery, a statement displaying the overt domination of meaning that the brothers of the *Tale* attempt to conceal as they reassemble the alphabet of their father's will (*Clarissa*, no. 229 p. 754). Lovelace's encroachments on others' meanings are evident throughout, but they reach a notable involution when he annotates his own letter to Belford, "that I may not break in upon my narrative" (*Clarissa*, no. 233 p. 774). His machinations have reached a complexity that cannot be easily contained in narrative, an excess that perhaps implies that such doubling of text in narrative and commentary cannot be grounded in a unitary consciousness. When Lovelace's climactic attempt at domination, the rape, fails, he is left without any rationale for his incoherent self, which has only power over others as its structuring object: "I will take an airing, and try to fly from myself—Do not thou upbraid me on my weak fits—on my contradictory purposes—on my irresolution . . ." (*Clarissa*, no. 274 p. 930). Clarissa conceives of her rape as having occasioned a multiplication and loathing of self: "Once more have I escaped—but alas! I, my *best self*, have not escaped. . . . What a tale have I to unfold!—But still upon *self*, this vile, this hated *self*" (*Clarissa*, no. 295, p. 974). She, however, moves from textual fragmentation toward unity and coherence as she constructs the archive that will define her story.[30] Lovelace in contrast increasingly manifests the textual incoherence that is presupposed by his radical selfishness.

Lovelace conceives of his plotting as narration—as turning bits and pieces into a story that has the shape required by his desires. His letters thus represent his plots more closely than by analogy alone. Writing to Belford of his elaborate charades at Hampstead, he boasts: "Now, Belford, for the narrative of narratives. I will continue it as I have opportunity; and that so dextrously, that if I break off twenty times, thou shalt not discern where I piece my thread" (*Clarissa*, no. 233, p. 767). But when his plotting fails, his narration does also, and he increasingly replicates the narrative failures of Swift's tale-teller. He convicts himself of writing upon nothing: "Wilt thou, or wilt thou not, take this for a letter? There's quantity, I am sure— How have I filled a sheet (not a shorthand one indeed) without a subject" (*Clarissa*, no. 321, p. 1024). He sees his writing as an escape from the burdens of a self that is no longer ordered by his pursuit of Clarissa: "I am ashamed of my ramblings: but what would'st have me do?—Seest thou not that I am but seeking to run out of myself in hope to lose myself; yet that I am unable to do either?" (*Clarissa*, no. 472, p. 1347). Lovelace's verdict on his own recently written letter late in the book is that it borders on insanity: "Were I to have continued but one week more in the way I was in when I wrote the latter part of it, I should have been confined, and in straw the next" (*Clarissa*, no. 512, p. 1431).

In Richardson's scheme, this debility of text is to be regarded as symptomatic of Lovelace's character and thus without reflection on Clarissa's text. In the latter case, the writing is grounded on a principled character, and in the former, on an appetitive consciousness. Thus, in this view, the meaning of Swift's *Tale* must be relegated to the disorders of the tale-teller and not to a modern consciousness that is exemplified in the writing of what we now know as the novel. The tale-teller and Lovelace are to be contrasted to Clarissa, whose story is to be connected to those "common forms" that provide a stability of character to underwrite a coherent text. Yet Clarissa as well as Lovelace is an example of radical subjectivity, her writing the product of sustained and intense self-scrutiny and, as plausibly as the tale-teller's, a product of possible physiological need. Some who confuse the simplicity of Swift with simplemindedness may see the attack of the *Tale* as a limited one on the obvious deficiencies of Temple's enemies. The implication of the *Tale*, however, are not easily confined to those modern examples that he cites (Vaughan, Dryden, Wotton, Bentley, and so on); he seems more generally to be denominating what Pope later described as "the Itch of Verse and Praise" ("Epistle to Dr. Arbuthnot," 1. 224), an obsession with text that is associated with narcissism, an obsession Swift too suffered from and made into an other by calling it Grub Street.[31] *Clarissa* stands as an exemplification of the modern consciousness that Swift parodically represented in the *Tale*; Richardson diverts Swift's indictment to Lovelace, with whom he associates Swift.

In 1759 Richardson printed Edward Young's *Conjectures on Original Composition, in a Letter to the Author of "Sir Charles Grandison,"* a work he had helped Young revise.[32] "*Know thyself,*" "*Reverence thyself,*" commands Young. "Dive deep into thy bosom; learn the depth, extent, biass, and full fort of thy mind; contract full intimacy with the stranger within thee; excite, and cherish every spark of Intellectual light and heat" (Young, 879). Not unexpectedly for someone expressing such sentiments, he admires Richardson's writings and uses Swift as an opposing example of modern failure. According to Young, Swift's was "an Infantine Genius; a Genius, which, like other Infants, must be nursed, and educated, or it will come to nought" (Young, 876). The genius he admires "has ever been supposed to partake of something Divine" and does not require learning (Young, 875). The reason for any modern inferiority to the ancients derives, in Young's view, from imitating them rather than from not knowing them. Originality is for him the preeminent quality: "Born *Originals*, how comes it to pass that we die *Copies*. That meddling Ape *Imitation*, as soon as we come to years of *Indiscretion* (so let me speak), snatches the Pen" (Young, 878). Swift's negative views of human capabilities are inimical to the true possibilities of the moderns, who as "heaven's latest editions of the human mind may be the most correct and fair" (Young, 883). But in making the Houyhnhnms (who cannot write) superior to mankind, Swift "blasphemed a nature little lower than that of Angels" (Young, 881). "Some are of Opinion," Young writes, "that the Press is overcharged"; he however believes that within the restraints of virtue "the more Composition the better" (Young, 871, 872). This late salvo in the ancients and moderns controversy brings Swift and Richardson, satire and the novel, to the center of the controversy where the printing press has been at least since Wotton. But the press that Young evokes duplicates originals that come into being without essential reference to each other. In contrast to the books of Swift's *Tale*, these do not necessarily "interfere constantly with each other" (146) but may proceed from an individual and oblivious genius. There is thus no need for the accumulative efforts of indexes, summaries, and encyclopedias, the detritus of modernism. The anxieties of appropriation are replaced by the anxieties of influence. Where Swift saw repetition, Young saw the originality of self that might be saved from the contamination occasioned by engagement with the proliferations of the other. The inundations of text continue but, for the true modern, the need for comprehension is dissipated.

Notes

1.   John Carroll, "Richardson at Work: Revisions, Allusions, and Quotations in *Clarissa*," from *Studies in the Eighteenth Century II: Papers presented at the Second David Nichol Smith Memorial Seminar, Canberra, 1970*, ed. R. F. Brissenden (Toronto: University of Toronto Press, 1973), remarks that "in both his letters and his novels, Richardson clearly stood on the side of the moderns in the battle of the books" (65). Carroll also notes that the direct criticism of Swift was supplemented in the third edition of *Clarissa* (1751) by having Anna Howe record Clarissa's chiding of Swift "for so employing his admirable pen, that a pure eye was afraid of looking into his works, and a pure ear of hearing anything quoted from them [*Clarissa*, 1751, viii, 214]" (75).

2.   Alvin Kernan, *Printing Technology, Letters, and Samuel Johnson* (Princeton, N.J.: Princeton University Press, 1987), argues that the full social impact of the invention of printing was not felt until the late seventeenth and early eighteenth centuries when "the more advanced countries of Europe [were transformed] from oral into print societies, reordering the entire social world, and restructuring rather than merely modifying letters" (9). Mark Rose, "The Author as Proprieter: Donaldson v. Becket and the Genealogy of Modern Authorship," *Representations* 23 (1988), provides an analysis of "conflicting assumptions" about "the author's role in society, a matter that was rapidly changing in the years immediately preceeding *Donaldson v. Becket* [1774] as patronage was declining and authors were becoming independent professionals able to support themselves by writing for the enormously increased reading public" (54).

3. William M. Sale, Jr., *Samuel Richardson: Master Printer* (Ithaca, N.Y.: Cornell University Press, 1950), surveys major aspects of Richardson's printing career and lists books known to have been printed by his press.

4. Pat Rogers, *Grub Street: Studies in a Subculture* (London: Methuen, 1972), studies the satirists' responses to the writing and publishing culture of the early eighteenth century that was known as "Grubstreet." He deals specifically with Swift's responses to hack writers in *A Tale of a Tub* in the chapter entitled "Swift and the Scribbler" (220–35). Angus Ross, "The Books in the *Tale*: Swift and Reading in *A Tale of a Tub*," in *Proceedings of the First Münster Symposium on Jonathan Swift*, ed. Hermann J. Real and Hans J. Vienken (München: Wilhelm Fink, 1985), 209–16, examines the "sense of a world of books" in the *Tale*.

5. William Temple, *Five Miscellaneous Essays by Sir William Temple*, ed. Samuel Holt Monk (Ann Arbor: University of Michigan Press, 1963), 41; hereafter cited in text.

6. William Wotton, *Reflections upon Ancient and Modern Learning* (London, 1694), 170–71. All quotations are from the facsimile of this edition published by Georg Olms (Hildesheim, 1968); hereafter cited in text.

7. *A Tale of a Tub*, ed. A. C. Guthkelch and D. Nichol Smith, 2d ed. (Oxford: Clarendon Press, 1958), 35–36; hereafter cited in text as *Tale*.

8. W. B. Carnochan, *Confinement and Flight: An Essay on English Literature of the Eighteenth Century* (Berkeley: University of California Press, 1977), 91.

9. Richard Nash, "Entrapment and Ironic Modes in *A Tale of a Tub*," *Eighteenth-Century Studies* 24 (1991), makes a related point: "While the allegorical mode of the parable encourages the reader's submission to the text, the narrative mode of the digressions encourages the reader to interpret the text against its ostensible meaning" (423).

10. Elizabeth L. Eisenstein, *The Printing Revolution in Early Modern Europe* (Cambridge: Cambridge University Press, 1983), 42.

11. See Augustine, *On Christian Doctrine*, trans. D. W. Robertson, Jr. (Indianapolis, Ind.: Bobbs-Merrill, 1958), Bk. 1, sec. 2; Bk. 2, sec. 1; Bk. 2, sec. 28.

12. See Michel Foucault, *The Order of Things*, trans. of *Les Mots et les choses* (New York: Random House, 1971), 46–77.

13. Frank Palmeri, in "The Satiric Footnotes of Swift and Gibbon," finds that "Swift satirizes the paradigm of criticism and representation in the footnotes to *A Tale of a Tub* (5th ed., 1710)," p. 191 in this volume. In some of the notes, Palmeri concludes, "Swift seems to undermine his own text by extending its uncertainties rather than resolving them" (197).

14. Joseph M. Levine, *The Battle of the Books: History and Literature in the Augustan Age* (Ithaca, N.Y.: Cornell University Press, 1991), discusses the historical dimensions of the ancients and moderns controversy in depth, finding that "it was clear that the controversy was above all about history, about how to read and understand past authors, and about how to recapture and represent past customs, institutions, and events" (267).

15. Richard Yeo, "Reading Encyclopedias: Science and the Organization of Knowledge in British Dictionaries of Arts and Sciences, 1730–1850," *Isis* 82 (1991), points out the "apparent absurdity" confronting those who attempt encyclopedic organization, "the combination of universal knowledge and alphabetical order" (24). Yeo notes that the eighteenth century has been identified as both an age of encyclopedias and of classification, both characteristics reflected in, for example, Chambers's *Cyclopaedia* and the *Encyclopédie* (26–27). The interest in encyclopedias is a response to the proliferation of knowledge: "Chambers warned that 'a reduction of the body of learning' in the form of an encyclopedia was 'growing every day more necessary' " (27).

16. For an extension of some of the concepts discussed here into the realm of recent technology, see George P. Landow and Paul Delaney, "Hypertext, Hypermedia, and Literary Studies: The State of the Art," in *Hypermedia and Literary Studies* (Cambridge: MIT Press, 1991), 3–50.

17. T. R. Schellenberg, *Modern Archives: Principles and Techniques* (Chicago: University of Chicago Press, 1956), 17; hereafter cited in text.

18. I am indebted in my discussion of monuments and traces to Paul Ricoeur, *Time and Narrative*, trans. Kathleen Blamey and David Pellauer, vol. 3 (Chicago: University of Chicago Press, 1985), 116–26. Ricoeur acknowledges indebtedness to Emmanuel Levinas for his discussion of the trace as a passing.

19. Amy Boesky, " 'Outlandish-Fruits': Commissioning Nature for the Museum of Man," *ELH* 58 (1991), studies the beginnings of the Ashmolean Museum, suggesting that "the collections or 'cabinets' of the sixteenth and seventeenth centuries were not so distinct from the great national museums of the eighteenth and nineteenth centuries" (307). She argues that "every collection, however haphazard or random it may (anachronistically) appear, is in its own right an allegory—of salvage, of teleology, of the masterpiece, of classification" (309).

20. Michel Foucault, *The Archeology of Knowledge*, trans. A. M. Sheridan Smith (New York: Harper & Row, 1972), 7; hereafter cited in text.

21. John A. Dussinger, "Truth and Storytelling in *Clarissa*," in *Samuel Richardson: Tercentenary Essays*, ed. Margaret Anne Doody and Peter Sabor (New York: Cambridge University Press, 1989), examines the status of Clarissa's moral sentiments, concluding that "role-playing, as Clarissa discovers, is the requisite condition of being in the world, inescapable not only in talking to others but also in setting pen to paper" (50).

22. William Beatty Warner, *Reading "Clarissa": The Struggles of Interpretation* (New Haven, Conn.: Yale University Press, 1979), discusses, in the chapter entitled "Building a Book into an Empire of Meaning," the power created by Clarissa's construction of her book. Terry Castle, *Clarissa's Cyphers: Meaning and Disruption in Richardson's "Clarissa"* (Ithaca, N.Y.: Cornell University Press, 1982), presents a different perspective: "Clarissa is without force: as a woman she is without the kinds of power available to Lovelace" and must thus "enact the fantasies of her persecutor" (25). Surely both views have merit. Through her book, Clarissa triumphs over Lovelace, although at the expense of her life. Yet Lovelace's manipulations of Clarissa are rarely thwarted as he controls her sources of information and supports his will by threats and force. It is perhaps worth noting that Clarissa's book can be prepared definitively only with the power that Belford lends to her cause.

23. Robert A. Erickson, *Mother Midnight: Birth, Sex, and Fate in Eighteenth-Century Fiction* (New York: AMS Press, 1986), comments on the relationship between Belford and Richardson: Belford becomes "a kind of ideal editor, the artistic role Richardson finds most congenial for himself" (180).

24. William Beatty Warner studies Richardson's "much more aggressive use of the role of editor in the second and third editions of *Clarissa*" (130) and considers also the controlling effects of Richardson's index/summary that was placed in the second edition (180–96). Mark Kinkaid-Weekes, "*Clarissa* Restored?" *Review of English Studies* 10 (1959): 156–71, finds that much of the material that Richardson claimed to be "restoring" to *Clarissa* in the second and the third editions was in fact new composition designed to combat what he thought of as erroneous interpretations of the novel.

25. John Preston, *The Created Self: The Reader's Role in Eighteenth-Century Fiction* (New York: Barnes & Noble, 1970), writes of the isolation of the reading and writing experience in *Clarissa*: "The event narrated is at a distance, the act of narrating is immediate, and inseparable from the act of reading. The only realities for the writers are those concerned with telling" (55). A related and often discussed issue in the interpretation of *Clarissa* is the tension between isolation and community in the book. Such discussion impinges on both hermeneutical and social issues. Christina Marsdon Gillis, *The Paradox of Privacy: Epistolary Form in "Clarissa"* (Gainesville: University Presses of Florida, 1984), finds that despite the element of privacy in Richardson's use of the epistolary form, Clarissa's faith "in her own

collection or 'story' " implies that "letter texts are finally to be read, reliably, within context, by a community of readers" (3, 3–4). Leopold Damrosch, Jr., *God's Plot and Man's Stories: Studies in the Fictional Imagination from Milton to Fielding* (Chicago: University of Chicago Press, 1985), focuses on the nature of Clarissa's social experience and concludes: "*Pamela* had its origin in conduct books, including Richardson's own *Familiar Letters*, which were designed to help people integrate themselves into society. *Clarissa* stands utterly outside of such a structure" (221).

26. Terry Eagleton, *The Rape of Clarissa* (Minneapolis: University of Minnesota Press, 1982), describes the differing attitudes to text of Clarissa and Lovelace: "Lovelace's writing is mercurial, diffuse, exuberant. Clarissa's letters brook no contradiction. Behind them stands a transcendental subject, apparently unscathed by her own slips and evasions, whose relationship to writing is dominative and instrumental. Lovelace, by contrast, lives on the interior of his prose, generating a provisional identity from the folds of his text, luxuriating in multiple modes of being" (53).

27. T. C. Duncan Eaves and Ben D. Kimpel, *Samuel Richardson: A Biography* (Oxford: Clarendon Press, 1971), state that "the prose writers [Richardson] mentions most often are, not surprisingly, Addison and Swift. Swift is almost always mentioned with great reservations" (579). Richardson's antagonism to Swift appears to be at least in part a response to what W. Jackson Bate identifies as the burden of the past: a sense, especially fostered by neoclassicism, that the great achievements of the past leave little for the modern to do (*The Burden of the Past and the English Poet* [Cambridge: Harvard University Press, 1970]). In his satires Swift explicitly expresses the view that little remains for the modern to do, yet at the same time he exhibits his mastery of a form of literature that subsequent moderns must also compete with. Harold Bloom, *The Anxiety of Influence: A Theory of Poetry* (New York: Oxford University Press, 1973), presents categories of response to the burden of the past that illuminate some of the duplicity in Richardson's response, that is, his use as well as rejection of the earlier writer. The Bloomian terminology ranges from the *clinamen*, a poetic misreading that differentiates a writer from a predecessor, to the *Apophrades*, the "return of the dead," which makes it seem to us "as though the later poet himself had written the precursor's characteristic work" (14–16).

28. *Clarissa*, ed. Angus Ross (New York: Penguin, 1985), no. 499, p. 1388. All subsequent references are to this text, which is based on the first edition. Letter and page numbers are cited. While this paper is confined to discussing the first edition, footnote 1 referencing Carroll and footnote 24 referencing Kinkaid-Weekes and Warner call attention to relevant issues from later editions.

29. In a now well-known letter to Sophia Westcombe in 1746, Richardson writes: "While I read [your letter], I have you before me in person. . . . who then shall decline the converse of the pen? The pen that makes distance, presence; and brings back to sweet remembrance all the delights of presence; which makes even presence but body, while absence becomes the soul" (*Selected Letters of Samuel Richardson*, ed. John Carroll [Oxford: Clarendon Press, 1964], 65).

30. Jonathan Lamb, "The Fragmentation of Originals and Clarissa," *Studies in English Literature* 28 (1988), discusses two uses of fragments—pleonasm or "fragments on fragments" and tautology or "fragment as fragment." Pleonasm can be "the consoling mockery of ruin—pieces on pieces" while tautology is "ruin itself—pieces as pieces." After her rape, "nine of Clarissa's written fragments are continuous with destruction, fragments as fragments; but the tenth, consisting of ten fragments of poetry, makes fragments of [on?] fragments by matching each bit of wreckage with a quotation" (453).

31. C. J. Rawson, *Gulliver and the Gentle Reader: Studies in Swift and Our Time* (London: Routledge & Kegan Paul, 1973), characterizes the *Tale* as follows: "The *Tale's* whole narrative method of self-posturing cannot be entirely accounted for by its ostensible purpose, which is

to mock those modern authors . . . who write this sort of book straight. For the *Tale* has at the same time a vitality of sheer performance which suggests that a strong self-conscious pressure of primary self-display on Swift's own part is also at work" (2).

32. The text of Young's work is quoted from *Eighteenth-Century English Literature*, ed. Geoffrey Tillotson, Paul Fussell, Jr., and Marshall Waingrow (New York: Harcourt, Brace & World, 1969), a text based on the first edition but including substantive variants of the second edition. T. C. Duncan Eaves and Ben Kimpel discuss the extent of Richardson's influence on Young's work, Richardson having read a draft in response to which he made relatively extensive suggestions to Young (432–36).

Swift and Sterne: Two Tales, Several Sermons, and a Relationship Revisited

MELVYN NEW

> Once *School-Divines* this zealous Isle o'erspread;
> Who knew most *Sentences* was *deepest* read. . . .
> *Scotists* and *Thomists*, now, in Peace remain,
> Amidst their *kindred Cobwebs* in *Duck-Lane*.
> —Alexander Pope, *An Essay on Criticism*

The particular *"kindred Cobwebs"* I would like to weave together in this reconsideration of the Swift-Sterne nexus have primarily to do with the presence of *A Tale of a Tub* in Sterne's "Slawkenbergius's Tale," which occupies some 36 pages at the beginning of volume 4 of *Tristram Shandy*— and perhaps another 15 pages of introductory comments at the end of volume 3.[1] I can recall few similar discussions in the long annals of those who have commented upon the Swift-Sterne relationship, but some similarities seem readily apparent, for example, the respective play on ears and noses, the satire on scholasticism and "school-divines," the parodic squabbles between Catholics and Protestants, the polar opposition between curiosity and complacency, the attack on false learning and textual abuse, and, above all, the undercurrents of sexuality that both Sterne and Swift seem consistently to employ whenever the learned gather[2]—all are points of obvious contact. While I shall probably touch upon most of these subjects, I will concentrate this reexamination on the authors' shared interest in problems of truth, particularly religious truth. In doing so, I hope to suggest yet another reason why Sterne singled out Swift among the writers of the preceding generation as a model for his own work—a predilection that has caused infinite trouble for those who readily hear tonal differences between the two but are unable (or unwilling) to comprehend the shared intellectual base that makes Sterne the last true heir of Swift.

◆

Let me digress—of course. The Florida editors of *Tristram Shandy* note that while Sterne's motto to volumes 1 and 2 of *Tristram* comes originally from

This essay was written specifically for this volume and appears here for the first time.

Epictetus, it perhaps reached Sterne via one of his favorite authors (and one of Swift's favorites as well), Michel de Montaigne, where it provides the opening sentence for his essay, "That the Relish of Goods and Evils, does, in a great measure, depend upon the Opinion we have of them." Cotton translates the sentence: "MEN (says an ancient *Greek* Sentence) are tormented with the Opinions they have of Things, and not by the Things themselves."[3] Clearly Sterne intends his motto to reflect the "life and opinions" of his title, but a stoical sentence occurring in a discussion of the philosopher's imperviousness to death seems oddly out of tune with the book that follows. Donald Greene has noted this oddity and has suggested that we look more closely at the Greek original, provided by Sterne; he provides a transliteration into the Roman alphabet and an interlinear translation of its rearranged text that casts interesting new light on the motto—and, as well, on Montaigne's interest in it:

> Ou ta Pragmata tarassei tous Anthrōpous,
> Not practicalities trouble human beings,
> alla ta Dogmata peri tōn Pragmatōn.
> but dogmas concerning practicalities.

Greene concludes: "It seems to me that the epigraph will be closer to what Sterne wanted us to read if we give it a more modern rendering: what is needed is pragmatism, not dogmatism; it is not reality that causes most trouble for the human race but far-fetched, thin-spun, rigidly held theories imposed on reality by pride in the human capacity for ratiocination."[4]

Interestingly, where Swift and Sterne sound most alike on the question of dogmatism is in their sermons, where both define Anglicanism as a middle position between the dogmatism of Roman Catholicism on one side and dissent or Methodism on the other. Clearly, they are not alone in doing so; rather, they practice the rhetorical strategy of the Latitudinarians, John Tillotson in particular. I cannot resolve the ongoing debate over the "orthodoxy" of Latitudinarianism,[5] but perhaps the issue is moot outside of the confines of Christian belief; a more historical perspective might suggest that the "dogma of the middle," adopted by the English church as a necessary tactical (or pragmatic) means of survival after a century of debilitating religious warfare, is always orthodox in intention, its aim being to preserve the institution at the center of a community's social, religious, and political life. The heart of the Anglican strategy was to define the church not in its own right but in comparison with the perceived errors of excess and omission by others; it was a strategy of the Aristotelian mean or the Pyrrhonic suspension, an interesting surrender of theology to philosophy, faith to suspicion. Swift's practice of the strategy can be related directly to the history of religious warfare in the seventeenth century, Sterne's to the dominant reaction to that strategy in the eighteenth century, the Methodist movement, which recognized that Anglicanism, by eschewing zeal, had argued itself into a quite vulnerable silence: "For points obscure are of small use to learn: / But *Common quiet* is *Mankind's concern.*"[6]

In many ways, *A Tale of a Tub* is about that "Common quiet" or, more specifically, about the disturbers of it; from its opening discussion of the engines of oratory to its conclusion in *The Mechanical Operation of the Spirit*, Swift is concerned with the powers of persuasiveness, the making of proselytizers and proselytes. One useful gloss on this concern is found in his few surviving sermons; we might turn, for example, to "On the Testimony of Conscience," from which Sterne borrowed for his "Abuses of Conscience" sermon inserted into volume 2 of *Tristram Shandy*.[7] Swift begins by criticizing the term "Liberty of Conscience," which "is now-a-days not only understood to be the Liberty of believing what Men please, but also of endeavouring to propagate the Belief as much as they can," and the issue is still on his mind at the end: "Besides, it is certain, that Men who profess to have no Religion, are full as zealous to bring over Proselytes as any Papist or Fanatick can be."[8] In "On the Trinity" he again opens with a condemnation of those not content to "possess their own Infidelity in Silence, without communicating it to the Disturbance of Mankind," those who "follow the Trade of seducing others" (*Tracts*, 159). Such an attack is particularly apropos of the doctrine of the Trinity, a mystery that invites silence rather than comment: "the Apostle telleth us, *We see but in part, and we know but in part*; and yet we would comprehend all the secret Ways and Workings of God" (*Tracts*, 162). Behind Swift's attack, from the pulpit or in *A Tale of a Tub*, is the rather simple scriptural lesson that we see the world "through a glass darkly"—and, indeed, Swift quotes the verse a few paragraphs later (*Tracts*, 165). What makes his preaching of it particularly interesting is the inescapable play of dogma in the midst of his attack on certainty, his need, that is, to assert the *absolute* truth of a triune God, even while he condemns the mode of proselytizing certitude that 1700 years earlier had *revolutionized* Jewish faith in a unitary God. It is a paradox neither Swift nor Sterne ever completely negotiates.

Swift returns to the theme once again in "On the Trinity," this time echoing *A Tale of a Tub* quite closely in condemning those who "are zealous to bring over as many others as they can to their own Opinions; because it is some kind of imaginary Comfort to have a Multitude on their Side" (*Tracts*, 165). In "On Brotherly Love," Swift still is harping on the same issue; he attributes dissensions in the world to the spreading of errors and heresies by "designing Men," who "have been the Cause of infinite Calamities, as well as Corruptions of Faith and Manners, in the Christian World" (*Tracts*, 171). In particular, Swift says that "this Nation of ours hath for an Hundred Years past, been infested by two Enemies, the Papists and Fanaticks . . ." (*Tracts*, 172), and he touches upon the demagoguery of both, the way in which they have made the "lower Sort" their "Tools and Instruments" to "work their Designs," putting "Words into [their] Mouths" they "do not understand"

and addressing them with an "ungoverned Zeal" that is at once self-serving and deceptive. Yet here again the paradox of self-implication arises, although more consciously than in "On the Trinity." Swift notes plaintively that those who "preach with any Zeal and Vehemence against the Sin or Danger of Schism" are censured as being "hot and high-flying . . . [and] an Enemy to Moderation" and hence are forced to "widen their Bottom, by sacrificing their Principles . . ." (*Tracts*, 172–73). Landa notes "the irony in the title of this violent and uncharitable invective against the dissenters" (*Tracts*, 119), but I believe the problem runs deeper than Swift's defense of high churchmen against low. The key to defending the Anglican position was the rhetorical strategy of holding the pragmatic middle ground against the dogmatists of the extremes; it is, then, a splendid counter gambit by one "extreme" to point out that the centrist position is itself not immune from the zeal that seems to infect all persuasion, all proselytizing—and Swift seems to admire the argument even while he laments its effective strike against his own position. To be forced to distinguish between "Zeal" and "ungoverned Zeal" (*Tracts*, 173) is untenable; the implied oxymoron ("governed Zeal") indicates Swift's difficulty, quite similar to the difficulty noted earlier of maintaining the absolute truth of the Trinity.[9]

In this as in other sermons, Swift images forth the situation of the opening of *A Tale of a Tub*, where an orator sways a malleable crowd. Such orators are, among other labels, "cunning Men" (*Tracts*, 173) or simply "Leaders" (*Tracts*, 177) and the crowd is "the lower Sort" (*Tracts*, 173, 177), "the Generality of Mankind," the "poor deluded Multitude" (*Tracts*, 179). Behind such imagery are the fundamental questions of the *Tale*: first, why do innovators "advance new systems with such an eager zeal"; and, second, "to what quality of human nature [have] these grand innovators . . . been indebted for their number of disciples?"[10] The answer Swift provides is well known, appearing in famous passages such as "But when a man's fancy gets *astride* on his reason," etc., which Sterne echoes in his own theory of the hobbyhorse: "WHEN a man gives himself up to the government of a ruling passion,——or, in other words, when his HOBBY-HORSE grows headstrong,——farewell cool reason and fair discretion!" (*TS* 2:5:106)[11] In the sermon "On False Witness," however, Swift adds a key element to the landscape he is exploring when he suggests the need to eschew not merely zeal but the entire enterprise of what today we would call the "exchange of ideas": "AVOID, as much as possible, the Conversation of those People, who are given to talk of publick Persons and Affairs, especially of those whose Opinions in such Matters are different from yours. I never once knew any Disputes of this Kind managed with tolerable Temper; but on both Sides they only agree as much as possible to provoke the Passions of each other" (*Tracts*, 187). Behind this advocacy of withdrawal and silence is Swift's portrait of Martin. In a work filled with mad assertiveness, whether in the allegory or the digressions, Martin stands uniquely alone in his quietness;

while Peter and Jack merge into one and are themselves echoed by the hack and all the literary "noise" he represents, Martin is positioned as an entity eschewing debate.[12] We are told that he is "extremely phlegmatic and sedate," speaking only in observation of the "rules prescribed in their father's Will" and working only toward "the advance of unity" rather than the "increase of contradiction" (*Tale*, 67).

Swift's suspicion of theological eloquence is made clear in several of his writings; for example, in the sermon "Upon Sleeping in Church," he tells us not to blame preachers for "neglecting human Oratory to move the Passions, which is not the Business of a Christian Orator, whose Office it is only to work upon Faith and Reason. All other Eloquence hath been a perfect Cheat, to stir up Men's Passions against Truth and Justice, for the Service of a Faction, to put false Colours upon Things, and by an Amusement of agreeable Words, make the worse Reason appear to be the better" (*Tracts*, 214).[13] This is, of course, eloquently stated, and Swift is never blind to the persuasiveness of his own rhetoric. The "plain and simple style" is a trope, and indeed simplicity is a mode of the sublime. More than that, "sweet reasonableness" is a devastating political weapon, which is why Jack responds to Martin's coolness with rage: "And as in scholastic disputes nothing serves to rouse the spleen of him that *opposes*, so much as a kind of pedantic affected calmness in the *respondent* . . . so it happened here" (*Tale*, 67–68). Martin's position, despite its privilege, is indeed part of a "scholastic dispute," even, perhaps, a cunning rhetorical ploy, and Swift undercuts his own centrism, his own silence, with the acerbic phrase, "a kind of pedantic affected calmness."

Just how "affected" that calmness is appears in his version of a Thirtieth of January sermon (commemorating the martyrdom of Charles I), a litmus-test occasion for eighteenth-century clergy. Echoes of *A Tale of a Tub* abound:

> Some general knowledge of this horrid rebellion and murder, with the consequences they had upon these nations, may be a warning to our people not to believe a lie, and to mistrust those deluding spirits, who . . . would lead them [astray]. . . . If his religion be different from that of his country . . . he ought to be fully satisfied, and give no offence, by writing or discourse, to the worship established, as the dissenting preachers are too apt to do. But, if he hath any new visions of his own, it is his duty to be quiet, and possess them in silence, without disturbing the community by a furious zeal for making proselytes.
>
> (*Tracts*, 227)

Swift then specifically condemns the "antient Puritan fanatics" who propagated "whatever wild or wicked opinions" they held, under the cover that all proceeded from the "Holy Ghost."[14]

Significantly, in *A Tale of a Tub* Swift marginalizes the two discussions closest to the path that has led us to the "Holy Ghost," once by discarding draft material and a second time by relegating his discussion to a coda to the *Tale* itself. *The Mechanical Operation of the Spirit* serves as a commentary on the allegory of the three coats, much as *The Battle of the Books* comments on the digressions. The subject is one I have suggested is central to Swift's concerns in the *Tale*: "by what methods this *teacher* arrives at his *gifts*, or *spirit*, or *light*; and by what intercourse between him and his assembly it is cultivated and supported" (*Tale*, 128). That Swift is talking here not about ideas in general, but about the very specific ideas generated by divine inspiration, is suggested by his beginning with Mahomet's rise to paradise on an ass and confirmed when he separates the "*fanatic* strain, or tincture of *enthusiasm*," in the "fields of *empire* and of *knowledge*" from its appearance "upon *holy ground*," where it has "fixed deeper and spread yet further" (*Tale*, 128–29).

The validity of revelation weighs heavily on Swift's mind, I suspect, because it is the fundamental question left unanswered by the *Tale*—culpably unanswered, since the failure to do so undercuts Swift's desire to hold the middle ground without irony. Swift the Anglican and sermon writer must assign inspired language to the center, while Swift the satirist undercuts all such claims to inspiration. The untenable position cuts very deep indeed. Swift distinguishes between enthusiasm that "is the immediate act of God, and is called *prophecy* or *inspiration*," and that which is the "immediate act of the Devil, and is termed *possession*" (*Tale*, 129). The passive construction embodies the dilemma, for the agent of the "calling," the man of "labels" if you will, must have grounds of judgment, must be inspired—must, as we have already seen, be able to distinguish between "governed" and "ungoverned" Zeal. But precisely that capacity is what Swift has thrown into great disrepute, although he is too self-conscious a writer, too dramatic a portrayer of voices, not to have had his own glimmer of insight into the gulf opening around him.

The basic situation I have isolated as the *Tale's* primary image, a man persuaded first of his own truth and in turn persuading others, is the situation of Christ on earth, the Word incarnate; and the entire proselytizing urge that so concerns Swift was Christ's own message (and, to be sure, that of the prophets before him), which is why Swift so carefully privileges "*prophecy* or *inspiration*": "And it shall come to pass in the last days, saith God, I will pour out of my Spirit upon all flesh: and your sons and your daughters shall prophesy, and your young men shall see visions, and your old men shall dream dreams" (Acts 2:17).[15] The second chapter of Acts, so important to all shades of Christian dissent in the seventeenth century, is on Swift's mind in *Mechanical Operation*, and he speaks of a "very dangerous objection" that "must, if possible, be removed," namely, that the "primitive way" of inspiration and the modern way are the same (*Tale*, 130–31). He is, however, unable to distinguish between the two, except on the dubious grounds of language, the manifestation of spirit; where the early apostles were given the gift of tongues (Acts 2:3–4), the modern saints "neither understand propriety of words or phrases." To reduce the distinction between prophecy and possession to a question of style (grammar?) moves Swift away from an answer to his impasse in that he continues to celebrate language, the fleshly and hence corrupting manifestation of the Word, the breakdown of the "Common quiet."

It is no surprise, therefore, that in his next paragraph Swift sidesteps the distinction by falsely dismissing it as a "different acceptation of the word *spirit*" (*Tale*, 131) from that which concerns him. And in section 2 of *Mechanical Operation*, he completely abandons his confrontation with these dangerous questions, instead integrating the coda with the *Tale* proper by rejecting enthusiasm of any kind whatsoever, without regard to counterclaims of legitimacy, except in the most primitive religion (that of "wild Indians") where the sole religious instinct is to keep good and evil distinct:

> Not so with us, who pretending by the lines and measures of our reason to extend the dominion of one invisible power and contract that of the other, have discovered a gross ignorance in the natures of good and evil, and most horribly confounded the frontiers of both. . . . I laugh aloud to see these reasoners . . . engaged in wise dispute about certain walks and purlieus, whether they are in the verge of God or the devil. . . . Of the like nature is the disquisition before us. It hath continued these hundred years an even debate whether the deportment and the cant of our English enthusiastic preachers were *possession* or *inspiration*, and a world of argument has been drained on either side, perhaps to little purpose.
>
> (*Tale*, 133)

There is a note of despair in this passage that suggests to me Swift's clearest insight into the pathos of the center, the infinite regression of language in the face of conflicting ideologies (dogma versus dogma) to a point of absolutely minimal articulation, the barest emergence from primal silence. All else is the destructive warfare of conflicting positions, which Swift so brilliantly ridicules and condemns, even though he cannot himself avoid the battle.[16]

The second marginalized text connected to *A Tale of a Tub* consists of several draft fragments elaborating a plan for the character of Martin as a historical entity, parallel to the histories provided for Peter and Jack. As Swift writes this plan, however, it becomes clear that Martin's claim to the Word is as fragile, as flawed, as the claims of Jack or Peter; he becomes no more than the political creature of Harry Huff and Lady Bess. Once again, Swift perceives the danger, and once again he evades the disappearance of the center:

> How the Author finds himself embarassed for having introduced into his History a new Sect, different from the three he had undertaken to treat of; & how his inviolable respect to the sacred number *three* obliges him to reduce these four, as he intends to doe all other things, to that number; & for that

end to drop the former *Martin*, & to substitute in his place Lady *Besses* Institution, which is to pass under the name of *Martin* in the sequel of this true History. This weighty point being clear'd, the Author goes on & describes mighty quarrels and squables between *Jack* and *Martin*. . . .

(Tale, 144)

Three is indeed an important number for Swift's antidogmatism, insofar as it allows him always to define his own position as between extremes. When the middle proves no different from the extremes, however, the argument collapses—most particularly, the argument that the Church of England embodies the primitive church, as close to the Holy Ghost as possible. Rather, it is seen quarreling and squabbling, part of the problem and not its resolution; yet another position must be defined. Significantly, Swift's draft at this point offers a digression *"on the nature{,} usefulness & necessity of Wars & Quarels,"* which concludes: "The greatest part of Mankind loves War more than peace: They are but few & mean spirited that live in peace with all men. The modest & meek of all kinds always a prey to those of more noble or stronger apetites" (*Tale*, 145). Swift indicates here, in outline, the "new" Martin—agreeable, meek, modest, and mild, outside the ideological dogmatism that marks the human way with ideas. This is indeed the Martin of the *Tale* as we have it, whom Swift created not by adding to the portrait but instead by wisely rejecting the elaborations of the drafts. He is portrayed, in an essential way, outside history, outside language, certainly closer to the "wild Indian" of *Mechanical Operation* than to the Anglican church Swift had set out to defend. Further, I suggest he also resembles Don Diego, the well-endowed hero of Sterne's Slawkenbergian tale.

In both marginalized texts, Swift glimpses the fact that his irony had diminished his own position as well as his enemy's, and he controls his finished piece so that the weakness is more or less concealed. In doing so, he instructs us most powerfully about our way with opinions, for Swift himself is a masterful orator with an audience to persuade—and he does so with pleasing deceptions, satire being that particular form of literature authorized to persuade as well as to instruct and delight. Neither a man to "live in peace with all men" nor a "modest and meek" prey to others, Swift is a master of language, a prophet and satirist, a dogmatist who tries to convince us that his quarrel with the world is God's quarrel. Swift is a man with a position to maintain; he comes to realize that the only certain insight he has into that position is that it cannot be defined without becoming equivalent to the position he argues against: definition destroys transcendence.

"For by the word *Nose*, throughout all this long chapter of noses, and in every other part of my work, where the word *Nose* occurs,—I declare, by that word I mean a Nose, and nothing more, or less" (*TS*, 3:31:258). Sterne's leaky tautology is embodied in the figure of Don Diego, whose own deep silence concerning his journey to the "Promontory of Noses" is in stark contrast to the noise of interpretation surrounding him. I certainly do not want to allegorize "Slawkenbergius's Tale" into a parallel to Swift's religious allegory, but there is something about Sterne's procedure that invites a reader to do so; that is to say, the "Tale" is prefaced first by the marbled page with its invitation (via Rabelais's discussion of the allegory of his work) to penetrate its moral ("mostly emblem of my work!")[17] and then by a discussion of the excesses of "verbal criticism." Walter as a pedant armed with certainty of "meaning" on the one hand and a penknife on the other is both a echo of Peter (and Martinus Scriblerus) and a foreshadowing of the "Tale" and its readers; as the Strasbourgers attempt to "read" Diego's "nose," indulging their zealous curiosity even while they lose their good sense and their city, so readers are tempted to interpretation even by the warnings against it. As with tautological definition ("a nose is a nose," "I am that I am") a sense of the interpretative inadequacy of others is—in Swift's terms—a tickling we do not, perhaps cannot, leave unscratched.[18] And as with Swift, Sterne's eschewing of definition (interpretation) is at best paradoxical. The silence and subsequent absence of Don Diego seem to be Sterne's attempt to establish his potency above all others. What he has received remains a mystery that we are not allowed to penetrate; the age of miracles has passed, and the "voice" from the "promontory" is silent before us. But precisely for this reason, Don Diego is the potent *center* of attention, the cynosure of all interpretation and ultimately the measure of its validity. The substance of "Slawkenbergius's Tale" reflects a habit of thinking we find, not surprisingly, anticipated in Sterne's sermons, which reflect the same Anglican centrist indoctrination and strategy as Swift's, along with a dislike of zeal that seems both traditional and personal.

During the 1740s Sterne engaged in some local political writing, the full scope of which is only now being uncovered;[19] still, I suspect nothing will challenge the drift of a letter he wrote to a rival paper, the *York Courant*, at the end of some particularly bitter exchanges; "Sir, I find by some late Preferments, that it may not be improper to change Sides; therefore I beg the Favour of you to inform the Publick, that I sincerely beg Pardon for the abusive Gazetteers I wrote during the late contested Election. . . ."[20] Years later in volume 8 of *Tristram Shandy* Sterne would write:

I have no
   Zeal or Anger——or
   Anger or Zeal——
And till gods and men agree together to call it by the same name———the errantest TARTUFFE, in science—in politics—or in religion, shall never kindle a spark within me.

(TS, 8:2:657)

Sterne, it seems to me, maintained throughout his life this refusal to become involved—so *unlike* Swift—in the pressing issues of his own day, as well as a concomitant toleration ("latitude") for the opinions and foibles of others. Just as important, however, and often overlooked, this toleration was in constant tension with an opposing characteristic, a persistent intolerance of the dogmatic and self-indulgent (self-"interested" in eighteenth-century moral terms). The play in the motto to *Tristram Shandy*, wherein—as explored above—the Greek *Dogmata* lends itself to translation as both *dogmas* and *opinions*, embodies this tension, because Sterne's attention is so often drawn, as is Swift's, to the human inability to hold "opinions" undogmatically: "What could be wanting in my father but to have wrote a book to publish this notion of his to the world? Little boots it to the subtle speculatist to stand single in his opinions,----unless he gives them proper vent" (*TS*, 1:19:63). Several of Sterne's sermons (and, to be sure, his praise and imitation of Swift, the keystone of this reexamination) suggest a context for this typically Shandean comment—with its Swiftian "vent" at the end.

As we saw in Swift, any discussion of Anglicanism in relationship to other modes of Christian practice (and it is difficult to find pulpit discussions of Anglicanism that are *not* comparative in nature) tends in Sterne to drive toward questions concerning the Holy Spirit—that is, "governed Zeal." versus "ungoverned Zeal." His treatment of Roman Catholicism in relationship to the Spirit is both dull and traditional: the Church has taken control of all possible visitation by imposing itself between God and the worshipper; here demagoguery is portrayed in a routine and somewhat anachronistic manner—as in, for example, his description of the Inquisition in "Abuses of Conscience."[21] His treatment of the opposite extreme, the "dissenting" dogmatism of the Methodists, is more imaginative although by no means unique. As Albert Lyles pointed out many years ago, the attack on Methodism adopted the tactics and language of the earlier attack on dissent.[22] Who could safely say, for example, whether the target of this passage is a Methodist or a Puritan: "'Tis no new error—but one which has misled thousands before these days wherever enthusiasm has got footing,——and that is,——the attempting to prove their works, by that very argument which is the greatest proof of their weakness and superstition;—I mean that extraordinary impulse and intercourse with the Spirit of God which they pretend to, and whose operations (if you trust them) are so sensibly felt in their hearts and souls, as to render at once all other proofs of their works needless to themselves."[23] Interestingly, we see here (in the question of proving works) the same mode of tautological definition that tempts us toward clarification in the "Tale"; it is, indeed, the consistent mode by which Sterne challenges Methodism. As had happened to Swift before him, however, his strategy also implicates his own centrist position in the debate. The longest such discussion is in his sermon, "Humility":

Now there is this inconvenience on our side, That there is no arguing with a frenzy of this kind; . . . for if you should enquire upon what evidence so

strange a persuasion is grounded?——they will tell you, "They feel it is
so."——if you reply, That this is no conviction to you, who do not feel it
like them, and therefore would wish to be satisfied by what tokens they are
able to be distinguish such emotions from those of fancy and complexion?
they will answer, That the manner of it is incommunicable by human language,——but 'tis a matter of fact. . . .

(Sermons, 4: 130–31; sermon 25)

But what is here treated as both an irrational response and, in the following
paragraphs, the result of a "disorder'd body" and an "empty mind," is not
really distinguishable from that visitation of the Holy Spirit that Sterne
describes a few pages earlier as acceptable to the Anglican communion: "That
the influence and assistance of GOD's spirit in a way imperceptible to us,
does enable us to render him an acceptable service, we learn from scripture—
in what particular manner this is effected . . . the scripture says not: we
know only the account is so; but as for any sensible demonstrations of it's
workings to be felt as such within us—————the word of GOD is utterly
silent; nor can that silence be supplied by any experience (*Sermons* 125–26;
sermon 25). To attempt to distinguish a visitation that is "imperceptible"
from one that is "incommunicable" is to confront Swift's dilemma between
proper and improper zeal; it is, in short, an argumentative gambit, largely
unconscious I suspect, by which Sterne replays the Anglican strategy that
had been Swift's strategy as well—to define one's position as the middle
ground between extremes and to move toward a "silence" that suggests the
end of human argument although it turns out to be, always, only another
beginning.

One additional sermon is worth our attention, Sterne's most elaborate
discussion of the issues we have raised. "On Enthusiasm" begins with the
question of the Holy Spirit, "the influence and communications of God,"
and argues that "there is scarce any point in our religion wherein men have
run into such violent extremes as in the senses given" to the concept of
inspired truth; his aim is to "reduce both the extremes . . . to reason . . .
[and] to mark the safe and true doctrine of our church concerning the
promised influences and operations of the spirit" (*Sermons*, 6: 119–21; sermon
38). As with Swift, an exploration of the topic leads Sterne invariably to
Acts 2:3–4 and the necessary voice given to the apostles and then to an
attempt to distinguish that original visitation from what is now available,
an inner gift which "graciously kept us from falling, and enabled us to
perform the holy professions of our religion" (*Sermons*, 6:126, sermon 38).
The distinction is not much more useful than Swift's claim that he meant
"spirit" in a "different acceptation," and the weakness of Sterne's argument
is suggested by his attempt, throughout the sermon, to define his position
as "consistent with reason and common sense," which means, of course,
different from the extreme positions he assigns to deists (freethinkers) on the

one hand, Methodists on the other.[24] The deist position is particularly interesting, both because it occupies the ground where one usually finds Roman Catholics in Sterne's (and Anglican) polemics and because it offers an argument that undermines quite dramatically the Anglican assault on the other extreme, Methodist enthusiasm. In brief, Sterne must undo the idea (so clearly implied by the division of "spirits" he has tried to make) that the modern "spirit" simply applies to the "rational soul," a concept that "concerns us no farther as *christians*, than as we are *men*" (*Sermons*, 6:128; sermon 38). This is, I would suggest, a revisiting of Swift's "wild Indians," although Sterne used instead the "heathen philosophers" who at least understood that "nothing great and exalted can be atchieved, sine divino afflatu" (*Sermons* 6:135; sermon 38).[25] They could not, however, understand the particular "grace" made necessary by the fall, and possible through Christ—that is, the particular gift of the "Holy Spirit" first offered to the apostles and, in reality, not easily—if at all—distinguishable from what is offered through communion in the Anglican church: "The Holy Ghost, proceeding from the Father and the Son, is of one substance, majesty, and glory, with the Father and the Son, very and eternal God" (article 5 of the *Thirty-Nine Articles*). Sterne's attempt to interpret the silence of God can find no middle ground between a deistic (or heathen) denial of the triune God of the New Testament and an acceptance of it (that is, of a concept of spiritual visitation that necessarily involves the divine drama of spiritual death and rebirth through Christ); but acceptance immediately raises the same issue of proselytization that we examined in Swift—when did the Holy Ghost stop producing in the human being the true zeal of the apostles? It was the question Whitefield and Wesley never tried of asking across the length and breadth of England, to the great embarrassment of the mid-century Anglican establishment.

To Sterne's credit, he seems to recognize the pit he has dug for himself, and before delivering a long, intolerant, and uncharitable attack on the Methodists, he returns to the silence of God, the pinprick of knowledge, beyond which all is dogmatism: "Our Saviour hath thought proper to mortify all scrupulous enquiries into operations of this kind, by comparing them to the wind, *which bloweth where it listeth; and thou hearest the sound thereof, but canst not tell whence it cometh, or whither it goeth:—so is every one that is born of the spirit.*—Let humble gratitude acknowledge the effect, unprompted by an idle curiosity to explain the cause" (*Sermons* 6: 139–40; sermon 38).[26] To Sterne's default, this "wisdom" does not prevent him from turning all his satirical weapons on the "mistaken enthusiast" (in contrast to the "sober-minded christian")[27] and then concluding with a tribute to the "rational, sober, and consistent institution" of the Anglican church, in contrast with the "two opposite errors" he has examined (*Sermons* 6: 141, 149; sermon 38).[28]

How far away from Don Diego's triumphant ride through the streets of Strasbourg do we seem! And yet, not very far at all, for we can recognize distinct traces of our discussion thus far in Sterne's introduction to Slawkenbergius's "grand FOLIO":

> Tell me . . . what secret impulse was it? what intonation of voice? whence came it? how did it sound in thy ears?—art thou sure thou heard'st it?—which first cried out to thee [to write his great work] . . .
>
> How the communication was conveyed into *Slawkenbergius*'s sensorium,——so that *Slawkenbergius* should know whose finger touch'd the key——and whose hand it was that blew the bellows . . . we can only raise conjectures.
>
> *Slawkenbergius* was play'd upon, for aught I know, like one of *Whitfield*'s disciples,——that is, with such a distinct intelligence, Sir, of which of the two *masters* it was, that had been practising upon his *instrument*,——as to make all reasoning upon it needless.
>
> (*TS*, 3:38:272–73)

The sudden appearance of Whitefield is only one clue of several that Sterne's context is religious (opinionative) enthusiasm and its concomitants, visitation and authentication.[29] The image of the organ ("finger touch'd the key . . . hand . . . blew the bellows") is pregnant with the imagery surrounding *inspir*ation or *enthusi*asm one finds in *A Tale of a Tub*; and the question of the "two *masters*" restates Swift's observation concerning the distinction between *possession* and *inspiration*: "I laugh aloud to see these reasoners . . . engaged in wise dispute about . . . whether they are in the verge of God or the devil" (*Tale*, 133). Moreover, Slawkenbergius's justification for writing is suspiciously pious; ever since he had arrived at the age of discernment and was able "to sit down coolly, and consider within himself the true state and condition of man, and distinguish the main end and design of his being . . . [he has] felt a strong impulse, with a mighty and an unresistible call within. . . , to gird up" for this undertaking (*TS*, 3:38:273–74). Sterne opens his sermon "Trust in God" (*Sermons*, 6:3; sermon 34) with the sentence: "WHOEVER seriously reflects upon the state and condition of man," and toward the sermon's end comments upon "whoever cooly sits down and reflects upon the many accidents . . . which have befallen him" (24); in both instances the result is a belief in a providential God. And the first sentence of the sermon "Follow Peace" (*Sermons*, 7:33; sermon 41) is "THE great end and design of our holy religion, next to the main view of reconciling us to God, was to reconcile us to each other."[30] Further, the "girding of himself" is, of course, a biblical commonplace, as, for example, in a particularly apropos verse, Jer. 1:17: "Thou therefore gird up thy lions, and arise, and speak unto them all that I command thee"—the voice of God to one of the *inspired* prophets. Finally, one might note that Slawkenbergius takes as his cue for readiness the tautological knowledge of "what was what" (*TS*, 3:38:274); again, it is tautological definition, the reflection of interpretative inadequacy, that serves as a midwife to the "prolix" offerings of the human mind.

As a writer, Slawkenbergius is the archetypal scholastic philosopher, a point Sterne makes by telling us his book "may properly be considered, not only as a model,—but as a thorough-stitch'd DIGEST and regular institute of *noses*; comprehending in it, all that is, or can be needful to be known about them" (*TS*, 3:38:274). The idea of an "institute" is one of Sterne's favorites: he describes Ernulphus's curse as an "institute of swearing" (*TS*, 3:12:215) and the *Tristrapædia* in a similar fashion (*TS*, 5:16:445); and in his "Rabelaisian Fragment," the intention is to collect the scattered rules of sermon writing into one "Code . . . by way of a regular Institute."[31] The Scriblerian suggestion that the perfect gathering of *all* available information will result in systems of perfect knowledge is as ludicrous to Sterne as it was to Swift.

This context of scholasticism prepares us for the digression that follows, the quarrel between Prignitz and Scroderus, who anticipate in their debate (whether fancy begets the nose, or the nose begets the fancy) the debate of the Strasbourg logicians whether the man belongs to the nose or the nose to the man; in both instances, Sterne parodies philosophy's long interest in efficient and accidental causes, substances and attributes, and other Aristotelian subjects to which he gave little credence. That Walter resolves the debate by alluding to material lifted from Rabelais (on Ambrose Paré) is another clue to the scholastic context of the discussion; and Sterne's style at this point imitates Rabelais's (and Swift's) noisy redundancy and excess of language madly pursuing truth: "his nose was so snubb'd, so rebuff'd, so rebated, and so refrigerated" and "the nose was comforted, nourish'd, plump'd up, refresh'd, refocillated, and set a growing for ever" (*TS*, 3:38:277). Tristram calls attention to the "utmost chastity and decorum of expression" (*TS*, 277) used by Slawkenbergius, since he is focussed (and wants us to focus) on Paré's bawdy possibilities; Sterne, I suspect, would like us to admire, instead, the exuberant fecundity of a style that offers—as in Rabelais and Swift—so devastating a comparison to the emptiness of its content, the futility of its attempt to organize the richness of experience. Equally important, the argument of Ambrose Paré overthrows "the peace and harmony" of the Shandy family. Why this happens we are never told, because Tristram runs out of time; the pattern of debate and disturbance will be repeated, however, in the "Tale" itself.

Still we are not into the "Tale" proper as Sterne's "introduction" to it begins to take on the atmospherics of Swift's prefatory matter to *A Tale of a Tub*. That Walter's imagination is "heated" by "long noses" (*TS*, 3:39:279) we can, by this time, readily accept; he is, like Slawkenbergius, an enthusiast; what remains is that he proselytize: "Nothing would serve him but to heat my uncle *Toby*'s [imagination] too." Lighting the "*damp* tinder" of Toby's brain is, however, no easy task, not even for the "warmer paroxisms of [Walter's] zeal." The result is a confrontation that reenacts Sterne's strategy in the sermon "On Enthusiasm"; the clash of ideas brings one to silence: "Let humble gratitude acknowledge the effect, unprompted by an idle curiosity to explain the cause" (*Sermons*: 6:140; sermon 38). Toby's "solution" to the problem of long noses—"God pleases to have it so" (*TS*, 3:41:284)—comes to us via Rabelais ("That is *Grangousier*'s solution, said my father"),[32] which reinforces, I believe, its skeptical insight within a Christian framework. Like Sterne, Toby allows the titans of ideas to clash above his head, while the business of a Christian's life is pursued elsewhere; the whole of *Tristram Shandy*—and its longest interpolated episode, "Slawkenbergius's Tale"— might well be considered words to accompany Toby's response to Walter's "idle curiosity," a more than usually *zealous* whistling of Lillabullero (*TS*, 3:41:285).

The "Tale" appears, for the first part, in Latin and English on fronting pages, a tautological presentation that Sterne employs on only one other occasion, "Ernulphus's Curse," a splendid example—from Sterne's Anglican perspective—of Roman Catholic "scholasticsm" ("thoroughness"). I said above that I do not want to allegorize the "Tale," and I will not do so. Yet there is Don Diego parading through the center of Strasbourg, pummelled by theories from one side of the street and the other—a splendidly facetious rendering, if I *were* allegorizing, of Swift's Peter-Martin-Jack. Better still, Sterne chose Strasbourg not only because of its "untimely demise" at the hands of Louis XIV but even more, I suspect, because it was a city he could neatly divide between Lutherans and Roman Catholics—Strasbourg was, geographically and theologically, an important Protestant thrust into Catholic France. Finally, were one to squeeze the text to its utmost, I might point to the fact that when Diego alights for his walk around town and dons his crimson satin breeches with the silver-fringed cod-piece, the facing translation gives us the Greek *Perizomate* (a word Tristram says he dare not translate but does so with "cod-piece" in the next phrase), a girdle worn round the loins and appearing in such scriptural phrases—in the Greek translation— as "Thou therefore gird up thy loins, and arise, and speak unto them all that I command thee" (Jer. 1:17).

But of course Diego speaks very little and rather than prophesying to or proselytizing the people, he makes it a point of honor to refuse them any "conviction" concerning the *truth* of his nose; and his quick departure prevents the main disputants from seeing him (as do the townspeople) or overhearing his several conversations on the road (as do the readers). Yet those who do see require "touch" for certainty and those who overhear are more interested in what is *unsaid* than said. The incomplete sentence or word is Diego's most characteristic style—*climaxing*, one might suggest, in Julia's lament that she will die "*un——*" (*TS*, 4:S[lawkenbergius's] T[ale]:321). Despite the editors of the Florida edition who believe *undone* would best complete the sentence, Diego's offering of *"unconvinced"* ought not be dismissed.[33] Much in the "Tale" revolves around the problem of *conviction* in its peculiarly Anglican guise as faced by both Swift and Sterne in their pulpits. Diego's journey is designed to produce a *conviction* of potency in Julia; its result is an obsessive search for *conviction* among the Strasbourgers and a loss of potency as they are penetrated by the French.

The attempt to understand Diego parallels, I have suggested, Walter's way with Erasmus's text and our way with the "Tale." But having described the sleeplessness of the female church dignitaries and the "restlessness and disquietude" of the males (in both instances, replete with sexual allusions that weave a Swiftian web of erotic curiosity and appetite around our need for knowledge and certainty), Sterne offers another parallel: "Such a zealous inquiry into the cause of that restlessness, had never happened in *Strasburg*, since *Martin Luther*, with his doctrines, had turned the city up-side down" (*TS*, 4:ST:303). Swift's difficulty with "Martin," we recall, is that his real name should be "Lady *Besses* Institution"; only by suppressing this honest insight is Swift able to maintain the centrist position of Anglicanism. Sterne, I would suggest, overcomes the same problem by simply allowing the historical Strasbourg to speak for itself; the two universities, one Catholic, one Protestant, divide the town and eventually divide themselves into numerous sects; but Don Diego remains untouched by their quarrels and divisions, not merely silent or aloof, but absent. He is, we might say, the center of attention but not of the discourse—and, indeed, if we listen carefully to that discourse, we come to realize how Swiftian Sterne can be in deploring what the human mind does with its gifts. There is much celebration of the "democracy of minds" among modern readers of Sterne, but it is difficult to see anything but rejection and repudiation in his handling of "the riot and disorder" of the city and the futility of the learned, who argue "so many strange things, with equal confidence on all sides, and with equal eloquence in all places" (*TS*, 4:ST:303). Swift and Sterne listen very carefully to the noise of the human discourse, which produces their capacity to parody it with great brilliance. Parody here is not—pace some recent readings—approval. Within the context provided by the sermons, both authors discover the need to replace such discourse with silence, self-assurance with humility, self-assertion with self-doubt. Curiosity and pride were, after all, the sins in the garden.

Strasbourg is turned into a city much like that pictured in *A Tale of a Tub*, in that an advocate of the "truth" preaches on every street corner to the ready ears of the populace. The most popular is the "trumpeter's wife," who stands "upon a stool in the middle of the great parade"—"but when a demonstrator in philosophy (cries *Slawkenbergius*) has a *trumpet* for an apparatus, pray what rival in science can pretend to be heard besides him" (*TS*, 4:ST:305). The medical faculty, the logicians, the lawyers, all have their say on the matter, but their wildly different discussions all share, significantly enough, a common mode of argumentation; whatever one side opines the other side offers a counteropinion. What attracts Sterne is clearly not the substance of any one argument but rather its calling forth a counterargument. Swift's metaphors of extremism (high and low, depth and height) are translated by Sterne into a particularly mechanical operation of the intellect whereby each argument comes into existence only as a counter to the preceding:

> He dies of a plethora, said they . . .
> —It happens otherways—replied the opponents.———
> It ought not, said they.
>
> (*TS*, 4:ST:308)

or:

> Now death, continued the logician, being nothing but the stagnation of the blood—
> I deny the definition—Death is the separation of the soul from the body, said his antagonist—Then we don't agree about our weapon, said the logician—Then there is an end of the dispute, replied the antagonist.
>
> (*TS*, 4:ST:309)[34]

Despite the "scientific" content of these exchanges, their model is clearly theological scholasticism and we are not surprised when the ecclesiastic court underwrites its first decision (significantly, an allegorical "reading" of "Promontory of NOSES") with a footnote of legalistic gibberish; as D. W. Jefferson noted long ago, the satire of learned wit considers the various faculties and the church as interchangeable targets.[35]

Better yet, Sterne is able to locate two universities in Strasbourg—one Lutheran, the other "Popish"[36]—and he sets them the problem of Martin Luther's birthdate, using materials garnered from that magnificent repository of seventeenth-century skepticism, Bayle's *Dictionary*.[37] The reappearance of Luther as the subject of dispute (and founder of one school) is useful in that it once again indicates Sterne's alternation of Swift's tripartite schema. The third party to these quarrels is both absent and silent, having left behind a powerful image—or an image of power; being ourselves dialecticians we will never determine the precise nature of Diego's legacy. Unlike Swift's Martin, Diego is the cause of historical events but out of history, the cause of historical events but out of history, the cause of positions and counterpositions but not a participant—even a quiet or calm one—in the debate. There is a potency of tranquillity in Diego that suggests as much of skeptical *ataraxia* as of Anglican compromise.

The arguments of the Catholics and Lutherans are dim reflections of very real theological (and philosophical) disputes, but I believe the Florida annotation to the passage is correct: "It seems . . . probable that this entire section is a . . . generalized satire on scholasticism, for which Chambers is as useful a supporting document as any particular theologian or philosopher. . . . [U]nder *Scholastic*, he delivers this opinion: 'the school began to be wholly taken up in frivolous questions. They disputed, with great heat, about mere formalities; and even raised phantoms on purpose to combat withal. The *school divinity* is now fallen into the last contempt' " (*Notes*, 3:293, n. to 314.5–6).[38] If we refocus our attention to aspects of the debate other than content, we can note three themes that help embellish the web I have been weaving from the strands of Swift and Sterne, sermons and "tales." First, the theologians lose track of the object under study: "The stranger's nose was no more heard of in the dispute—it just served as a frigate to launch them into the gulph of school-divinity" (*TS*, 4:ST:315). The important word is "school-divinity," Chambers's dismissal of which was just quoted; here, it ties Sterne's purpose to other passages in *Tristram Shandy* where he distinguishes between "practical" and "polemic" divinity. It is the sort of division Swift is alert to, not only as a question of style, as in "Upon Sleeping in Church," but in the advice he gives to a neophyte clergyman:

> SOME Gentlemen abounding in their University Erudition, are apt to fill their Sermons with philosophical Terms, and Notions of the metaphysical or abstracted Kind; which generally have one Advantage, to be equally understood by the Wise, the Vulgar, and the Preacher himself. I have been better entertained, and more informed by a Chapter in the *Pilgrim's Progress*, than by a long Discourse upon the *Will* and the *Intellect*, and *simple* or *complex Ideas* . . .
>
> I DO not find that you are any where directed in the Canons, or Articles, to attempt explaining the Mysteries of the Christian Religion. And, indeed, since Providence intended there should be Mysteries; I do not see how it can be agreeable to *Piety*, *Orthodoxy*, or good *Sense*, to go about such a Work.[39]

Sterne's own similar views are twice expressed in *Tristram Shandy*, the first time in the same volume in which the "Tale" appears: "To preach, to shew the extent of our reading, or the subtleties of our wit—to parade it in the eyes of the vulgar with the beggarly accounts of a little learning, tinseled over with a few words which glitter, but convey little light and less warmth—is a dishonest use of the poor single half hour in a week which is put into our hands—'Tis not preaching the gospel—but ourselves—For my own part, continued *Yorick*, I had rather direct five words point blank to the heart—" (*TS*, 4:26:377).[40] And a year later, in volume 5, Sterne devotes a full chapter (chap. 29) to quoting a ludicrous passage from Rabelais (Gymnast's acrobatic feats on his horse) because Yorick considers it a description of "polemic divines": "I wish there was not a polemic divine, said *Yorick*, in the kingdom;—one ounce of practical divinity—is worth a painted ship load of all their reverences have imported these fifty years" (*TS*, 5:28:462).

The second theme emerging from the debates of the school divines is the sectarian nature of their strife. Sterne indicates this in a subtle and comical manner, first positing Nosarian and Antinosarian sides and then, as the parishioners are inflamed and "left in all the distresses of desire unsatisfied," the Protestants split even further into *Parchmentarians*, *Brassarians*, and *Turpentarians* (*TS*, 4:ST:315). Had Sterne consulted Ephraim Chambers under *Lutheranism*, he would have found 39 such sects listed, including the Confessionists, Antinomians, Samosatenses, Antiswenkfeldians and Antiosiandrians. The world of position and counterposition opens us to never-ending divisiveness. The warfare of dogma, of ideology, is, indeed, the history of the modern world.

Sterne points us to a final theme in two of those wonderfully abrupt and pointed sentences that so often punctuate the seemingly random and undisciplined "drift" of his narrative style. The first is a commonplace yet devastating aphorism: "Heat is in proportion to the want of true knowledge" (*TS*, 4:ST:315). The second, the climax of the "Tale," where Slawkenbergius himself locates the end of the "Catastasis": "—The poor Strasburgers left upon the beach!" (*TS*, 4:ST:315; cf. 317). For both Swift and Sterne, guardians of the Anglican establishment, the result of zeal, dogma, and demagoguery was public danger. Swift most feared the manipulation of the mob, the proselytizing of an "ignorant herd" by devious and insane enthusiasts; his historical horizon was bounded, obviously, by the Interregnum. Sterne, on the other hand, seems to have been aroused more by the futility, comic and tragic, of the human desire for certainty and conviction; somewhere among Montaigne, Locke, Bayle, Chambers, Rabelais, and Swift, he sought a skeptical stance that would deny the absolutism of dogmatists while preserving his own (and his congregation's) capacity to believe in the concept of Truth. For neither Swift nor Sterne could—or would—abandon their own certainty concerning Anglican centrism, and I believe it is essential to understand this common commitment when we consider Sterne's interest in Swift or when we read *Tristram Shandy*. While protecting their congregations from the errors of zeal and zealots, they invested "moderation" and "silence" with considerable power, a source of determinacy and measurement that distinguishes their world from our own.[41] Thus, "Slawkenbergius's Tale" is framed by significant images of "Truth." Before it begins, Tristram defines the "great and principal act of ratiocination in man" as the "finding out the agreement or disagreement of two ideas one with another, by the intervention of a third; (called the *medius terminus*) just as a man, as *Locke* well observes, by a yard, finds two mens nine-pin-alleys to be of the same length, which could not be brought together, to measure their equality, by *juxta-position*" (*TS*, 3:40:281). At the conclusion of the "Tale," Slawkenbergius dismisses the various theories concerning the demise of Strasbourg in this manner: "It is the lot of few to trace out the true springs of this and such like revolutions—The vulgar look too high for them—Statesmen look too low—Truth (for once) lies in the middle" (*TS*, 4:ST:323). That Sterne alters Locke's "two Houses" to "two mens nine-pin-alleys," setting up a rather bawdy possibility because of "yard" (penis), and that he parenthetically adds "for once" in the second statement suggests to me the same insight I attributed to Swift: a recognition of the irony of his own ideological position, the pathos of the center in infinite regression from conflicting ideologies. Both writers then suppress all signs of that recognition. Surely Sterne understood the irony of a faith that had to be embodied in the potency of absence and silence; but given the impotent surrender of the Strasbourgers to "the grand system of Universal Monarchy" (triumphant dogmatism) and, indeed, the impotence that hovers everywhere in the Shandy world, certainly the figure of Don Diego is a force to be reckoned with. Whether he represents the "power of love" as Julia would find him, or the "state of rest and quietness" to which Slawkenbergius, seeing the world as a stage, finally brings his hero, we need not determine; an Anglican clergyman—Swift or Sterne—would be at home with either text: it is, after all, the "peace" of their God, which "passeth all understanding" (Phil. 4:7).

Notes

1. All citations from *Tristram Shandy* are from the Florida edition, ed. Melvyn New and Joan New, vols. 1 and 2 (Gainesville: University of Florida Press, 1978). Hereafter cited as *TS*, with original volume and chapter numbers.

2. The Visitation dinner toward the end of volume 4 is just one further example; the warmth Phutatorius feels in his groin from the hot chestnut strikes me as a particularly telling and Swiftian dismissal of academic forums.

3. *Notes to Tristram Shandy,* ed. Melvyn New, with Richard A. Davies and W. G. Day, vol. 3 (Gainesville: University of Florida Press, 1984), 37; hereafter cited as *Notes.* Montaigne is quoted from the Charles Cotton translation, 5th ed. (1738), 1:40:285.

4. Donald Greene, "Pragmatism versus Dogmatism: The Ideology of *Tristram Shandy,*" in *Approaches to Teaching Sterne's "Tristram Shandy,"* (New York: Modern Language Association, 1989), 110, 105–6. On "opinion," see Samuel Butler, *The Genuine Remains in Verse and Prose* (1759), 1:241.

5. A good summary is provided by Frans De Bruyn, "Latitudinarianism and its Importance as a Precursor of Sensibility," *JEGP* 80 (1981): 349–68; and an excellent analysis by Gerard Reedy, S. J., *The Bible and Reason: Anglicans and Scripture in Late Seventeenth-Century England* (Philadelphia: University of Pennsylvania Press, 1985). See also Irvin Ehrenpreis's discussion of Tillotson and Swift in "The Doctrine of *A Tale of a Tub*" in *Proceedings of the First Münster Symposium on Jonathan Swift,* ed. Hermann J. Real and Heinz J. Vienken (München: Wilhelm Fink, 1985), 69–71; Ehrenpreis convincingly maintains that Tillotson was for Swift "a spokesman for uncontroversial central doctrine."

6. John Dryden, *Religio Laici*, ll. 449–50.

7. See *Notes*, 3:178, 180; nn. to 154.12–16, 157.14ff. See also my essay "Swift and Sterne: Sermons and Satire," *MLQ*, 30 (1969): 198–211. Most commentary on *Tristram Shandy* ignores Swift's influence on the "Abuses of Conscience" sermon, perhaps because the borrowings so vividly highlight an antisolipsism that embarrasses many "modern" readings.

8.   Jonathan Swift, *Irish Tracts, 1720–1723, and Sermons*, ed. Herbert Davis and Louis Landa (Oxford: Basil Blackwell, 1963), 151, 157; hereafter cited in text as *Tracts*.

9.   In the sermon "On False Witness," Swift talks about "mad Zeal" and "mistaken Zeal" (*Tracts*, 180, 181), opposing them to "true Zeal" (*Tracts*, 184, 185).

10.   Swift, *A Tale of A Tub and Other Works*, ed. Angus Ross and David Woolley (Oxford: Oxford University Press, 1986), 80; hereafter cited in text as *Tale*.

11.   Behind both passages one suspects Montaigne, 3:2:293–94.

12.   Cf. Ehrenpreis, "Doctrine," 61: "The weakness of the characterization of Martin . . . suggests the author's awareness of how sadly the Church of England lacked the simplicity, purity, and stability that Swift would have liked to attribute to it in an age of ferocious religious dissension."

13.   Cf. Locke's famous attack on figurative language (*Essay Concerning Human Understanding*, 3:10:34), which Swift seems to echo: "But yet, if we would speak of Things as they are, we must allow, that all the Art of Rhetorick, besides Order and Clearness, . . . hath invented, are for nothing else but to insinuate wrong *Ideas*, move the Passions, and thereby mislead the Judgment; and so indeed are perfect cheat: And therefore however laudable or allowable Oratory may render them in Harangues and popular Addresses, they are certainly, in all Discourses that pretend to inform or instruct, wholly to be avoided" (ed. Peter H. Nidditch [Oxford: Clarendon Press, 1975], 508). The political rather than epistemological implications of such statements—Locke's and Swift's—ought to be stressed.

14.   Swift's difficulty with this position emerges in several ways as the sermon progresses; for example, in any good nation, citizens want to live in peace and obedience rather than rebel against authority—except "where the vulgar are deluded by false preachers," as in the instance of Charles I. But not, he hastens to add, in the instance of James II, who "would have forced a false religion upon his subjects." The key is to avoid "all broachers and preachers of new-fangled doctrines in the church" and *"meddle not with those who are given to change"* (*Tracts*, 229–31). The original evangelical nature of Christianity is not so much forgotten as papered over in such statements.

15.   The verse repeats the prophecy from Joel 2:28. The discussion of *A Tale of a Tub* at this point borrows from my essay "Jonathan Swift and Thomas Mann: The Irony of Ideology" in *Telling New Lies: Seven Essays in Fiction, Past and Present* (Gainesville: University Press of Florida, 1992), 163–88.

16.   I do not necessarily disagree with Ross and Woolley that section 1 of *Mechanical Operation* was written by Thomas Swift, Jonathan's cousin; if that was indeed the case, Swift spotted the danger in his cousin's work, tried to rectify it in section 2, and then shrewdly dropped both sections from the *Tale* proper. See *Tale*, xvi–xvii and appendix B, 192–201; and R. M. Adams, "Jonathan Swift, Thomas Swift, and the Authorship of *A Tale of a Tub*," *MP* 64 (1967): 198–232.

17.   See *Notes*, 3:269, n. to 268.8–10.

18.   Cf. Jonathan Lamb, *Sterne's Fiction and the Double Principle* (Cambridge: Cambridge University Press, 1989), 100, where Lamb comments upon the "Tale," Le Fever's story, and Toby's amours, as "three [stories] about the need to find out, about the torment of knowing only a portion of the whole . . . [and about] the methods taken to solve this problem." My interest in Sterne's mode of "tautological definition" was triggered by Lamb's many examples of "doubling" ("pleonasm") and especially 49–50; our conclusions differ, however.

19.   See Kenneth Monkman's contributions to *The Shandean: An Annual of the Laurence Sterne Trust*, vols. 1 (1990) and 2 (1991).

20.   Quoted from Arthur H. Cash, *Laurence Sterne: The Early and Middle Years* (London: Methuen, 1975), 111.

21.   Sterne actually borrows his description from earlier writers; see *Notes*, 3:183–84, n. to 160.3ff.

22.　Albert M. Lyles, *Methodism Mocked: The Satiric Reaction to Methodism in the Eighteenth Century* (London: Epworth, 1960), passim.

23.　Laurence Sterne, *The Sermons of Mr. Yorick* (London, 1760–69), 2:205–6 (sermon 14, "Self-Examination"); hereafter cited in text as *Sermons*, from the first edition of the seven volumes; the sermon number represents the consecutive numbering of all 45 sermons.

24.　It is unfair to blame Sterne for the weakness of his argument since one can find numerous similar discussions in Anglican sermons and tracts; indeed, Sterne appears in this sermon to have borrowed heavily from George Hickes's *The Spirit of Enthusiasm Exorcised* (1680). Hickes's text is 1 Cor. 12:4: "Now there are diversities of gifts, but the same Spirit," and the bulk of the argument, ignored by Sterne, is a careful delineation of the several miraculous gifts made available to the apostles but falsely claimed by modern "Saints." Few issues were more important to early Anglican centrists than delimiting the notion of individual inspiration while retaining the fundamental doctrine of the Holy Spirit—no easy task, politically or theologically. Methodism had returned the issue to primacy by the mid-eighteenth century.

25.　Sterne offers two quotations to this effect: the one quoted here is borrowed from Cicero; the other, from Seneca.

26.　Sterne quotes John 3:8.

27.　Interestingly, Sterne's diatribe against the "modern enthusiasts" is abetted by linking them to Roman Catholics—as Swift does in *A Tale of a Tub* and Hickes in *Enthusiasm Exorcised*. Sterne echoes Hickes (44) verbatim in this passage: "Already [the Methodists have] taught us . . . much blasphemous language;—and, if it goes on, by the samples given us in their journals, will fill us with as many legendary accounts of visions and revelations, as we have formerly had from the church of Rome" (147–48). Hickes, of course, is talking about dissenters. Lyles, 88–89, calls attention to the labeling of Methodist leaders "Sons of Loyola" and "Bedlam-Popes."

28.　The phrasing is borrowed from Hickes, 46.

29.　James E. Swearingen is one of the few Sterne critics who has paid attention to "Slawkenbergius's Tale," and his conclusion seems quite useful to me: "The conspicuous question in all the disputes is the central issue of modern thought: the nature, limits, and test of knowledge. The parody is of the reductionist tendency inherent in all specialized systems, legal, medical, logical, or what have you; none provide [*sic*] valid accounts of the world." (*Reflexivity in Tristram Shandy: An Essay in Phenomenological Criticism* [New Haven: Yale University Press, 1977], 201).

30.　Cf. the opening of chapter 7 of volume 4: "WHEN I reflect, brother *Toby* [says Walter], upon MAN; and take a view of that dark side of him which represents his life as open to so many causes of trouble . . ." (332). Walter searches for the "hidden resources" that enable us to withstand troubles, while Toby repeats the conclusion he reaches at the end of the present discussion, Grangousier's "solution": "'Tis by the assistance of Almighty God" (See n. 32, below).

31.　See Melvyn New, "Sterne's Rabelaisian Fragment: A Text from the Holograph Manuscript," *PMLA* 87 (1972): 1088, 11. 38–42; cf. Alexander Pope, *Peri Bathous:* "THEREFORE to supply our former Defect, I purpose to collect the scatter'd Rules of our Art into regular Institutes" (ed. E. L. Steeves [New York: King's Crown Press, 1952], 7).

32.　Rabelais, *The Works*, trans. Thomas Urquhart and Peter Motteux, with notes by John Ozell (London, 1750), 1:40:319: "What is the cause, said Gargantua, that friar John hath such a goodly nose? Because, said Grangousier, that God would have it so. . . ." See *Notes*, 3:277–78, n. to 284.17–20.

33.　See *Notes*, 3:297, n. to 321.16–18; 9:28:796 is cited for the usage of *undone* the editors consider appropriate.

34.　Cf. Sterne's mechanical metaphor for the work of the learned: "[They were] busy in pumping her [truth] up thro' the conduits of dialect induction—they concerned themselves not with facts—they reasoned" (306).

35. *"Tristram Shandy* and the Tradition of Learned Wit," *Essays in Criticism* 1 (1951): 225–48. Sterne borrowed many of the abbreviations and citations of the note from the margins of Henry Swinburne's *A Briefe Treatise of Testaments and Last Willes*; see textual note to 310.20ff in *TS*, 2:852–53.

36. See *Notes*, 3:288–90, n. to 310.10–12.

37. See *Notes*, 3:290–91, n. to 310.15–311.30. The reference is to Bayle's "Luther" entry.

38. For Sterne's use of Ephraim Chambers's *Cyclopaedia: or an Universal Dictionary of Arts and Sciences* in constructing the Strasbourgers' arguments, see, for example, notes to 307.1–20 (the argument on nutriment for such a nose), 309.1–5 (the definitions of death), and 314.5–6 (on "implying contradictions") (*Notes*, 3:286–93).

39. Jonathan Swift, "A Letter to a Young Gentleman, Lately entered into Holy Orders," in *Tracts*, 76–77; see also his comments on simple words, 68–69. I agree with David Nokes's observation that Swift, "having started from the axiom that the Church of England has a monopoly of truth and light," occupies a "middle position" with the "inevitable unease of all bargains struck between God and the Devil" (*Jonathan Swift: A Hypocrite Reversed* [Oxford: Oxford University Press, 1985], 93). Nokes is too quick, however, to doubt Swift's religious commitment.

40. Swift and Sterne would seem to separate on the issue of "head" versus "heart," Swift warning against "the Art of wetting the Handkerchiefs of a whole Congregation" ("Letter," 70); still, he goes on to talk about "as moving a Manner as the Nature of the Subject will properly admit" ("governed Zeal"?), and I suspect that both are arguing essentially the same point: a preaching that is direct and forceful, simple and orthodox.

41. R. D. Stock, in *The Flutes of Dionysus: Daemonic Enthrallment in Literature* (Lincoln: University of Nebraska Press, 1989), reads the relationship between *A Tale of a Tub* and "Slawkenbergius's Tale" in a diametrically opposite fashion; for example, "in Swift subjectivity is nasty, destructive, alienating, whereas in Sterne it is not alienating but protective from the world," and "Walter finds solace in his obscure books on noses. That protuberance, which in Swift is the despicable instrument of the enthusiast preacher . . . here affords a benign excitement, a reason to live" (217, 219). Stock senses in *Tristram Shandy* an "implied relativism that aligns it with much modern literature" (221); that sense enables him to observe the allusion to Whitefield, for one example, without assigning meaning to it.

The Satiric Footnotes of Swift and Gibbon

FRANK PALMERI

The transition from the use of marginal glosses or citations to the use of footnotes or endnotes signals a shift from a paradigm organized around relations of resemblance and acts of commentary to one that produces representations and acts of criticism. Michel Foucault has argued that the earlier paradigm of discourse and thought holds from the Renaissance through the middle of the seventeenth century, when the latter comes to predominate.[1] I focus here on developments in forms of annotation that exemplify this shift, in particular on the opposite possibilities of very dense or very thin footnoting in the later paradigm. I propose that the footnotes of Swift and Gibbon discover satiric and ironic ways of eluding these alternate extremes in the paradigm of criticism and representation. Their satiric footnotes make use of what Mikhail Bakhtin has characterized as dialogical parody; their ironies exploit what Jacques Derrida has analyzed as the paradoxes of supplementarity.

1

The practice of marginal glossing presumes an analogy between Scripture and natural history, considering both to be the writing of God. Through exfoliating commentary on the divine text, the human text discovers signifying resemblances between nature or history and itself. In medieval texts, Scripture occupies the central position and human glosses fill the margins; by the sixteenth and seventeenth centuries, the human text occupies the center of the page, and the margins contain references to the divine text of the Bible which parallel the assertions made in the text. The relation of figure to ground becomes reversed, but the paradigm of resemblance informs both textual practices. In this paradigm, the divine text of Scripture and the human text both possess a comparable status as glosses on the world as a text, and in this way testify to the authority of God.[2]

Although Sir Thomas Browne's works do not make extensive use of

This essay was first published in *The Eighteenth Century: Theory and Interpretation*, vol. 31:3, Texas Tech University Press, Lubbock, TX 79409–1037. Used by permission of Texas Tech University Press.

marginal glosses or citations, they exemplify this conception of the world as text, and the practice of writing as the discovery of signifying patterns in the hieroglyphics of nature and history. The elaborate rhetoric of a work such as *The Garden of Cyrus* (1658) draws attention to the resemblance between patterns in natural and human history and patterns in the text that comments on them. In Bunyan's *Pilgrim's Progress* (1678), the marginal citations from Scripture indicate clearly the parallels between Bunyan's text and the text that was authoritative for his culture. Thomas Burnet's *Sacred Theory of the Earth* (1679) describes the tearing and crinkling of the earth's originally smooth, egg-like surface through the eruption of the Flood from within, like the breaking of waters during childbirth (2:7). The glosses provide authoritative confirmations for this account in Scripture, and, to a lesser extent, in the classics and Church fathers. The first two books of Hobbes's *Leviathan* (1651) construct an argument that dispenses with the need for a divine author for earthly sovereigns; instead of accepting any resemblance between the divine and the human king, Hobbes founds civil society on an agreement among individuals to have one authority who will *represent* their will to have peace (1:16). Hobbes's work thus prepares for the diminished cultural authority of the Bible in the following century; nevertheless, the frequent marginal notes in his last two books on the Christian commonwealth and the kingdom of darkness reveal that he continued to work within the paradigm of resemblance and commentary.

The new paradigm of criticism emerges in Bayle's *Dictionnaire Historique et Critique* (1696), whose enormous footnotes investigate skeptically whatever of relevance has been written on a historical subject in order to establish a few incontrovertible facts stated in the text above.[3] In Bayle, wondering commentary like Browne's gives way to skeptical, ironic criticism. Yet in its continued use of marginal citations, Bayle's *Dictionary* remains transitional. Although the extent to which the footnotes overwhelm and displace the entries to become the primary text of Bayle's *Dictionary* may be idiosyncratic, it also reveals an extreme to which the paradigm of annotated representations can lead. Unlike in the earlier paradigm, which insisted upon the materiality of the text in its resemblance to the world, in this paradigm the textual representation of the world attempts to render itself transparent. This shift from resemblances to representations coincides with the displacement of undisputed divine authority; it inaugurates the practice of establishing textual authority by critical dispute with other texts of merely human authority.[4] The imperative of representational transparency requires that such disputes be relegated to notes; in their placement at the bottom of the page or the end of the text, such notes should support without obscuring the text's transparent representation.[5] Their subordinate position indicates the reduction of extratextual cultural authority to a secondary status. The attempt of eighteenth-century texts to establish their own authority by supplanting other textual authorities points to the question of doubtful cultural authority that informs this period of criticism, a question that hardly arises in the preceding period of textual commentary.

The complementary relation between text and gloss that characterized this earlier period thus gives way to an antagonistic relation between the text and the limited, partial, or mistaken authorities it refers to in its notes. The new relation between text and notes leads to one of two opposed tendencies: either antiquarian compilations, like Bayle's *Critical and Historical Dictionary*, consisting almost entirely of critical controversies and citations, which overwhelm narrative coherence as they strain to establish their few main assertions; or philosophical histories, such as Hume's *History of England*, implicitly asserting their own authority, and making almost no references to dubious authorities, sources, or predecessors, in order to establish a seamless and coherent narrative. These tendencies within the paradigm receive major emphasis in succession: skeptical criticism predominates from the 1690's into the 1730's; perspicuous narrative coherence predominates through the 1780's.

Like Bayle's *Dictionary*, Robert Brady's *Introduction to the History of England* (1684) evinces an absence of narrative and a sharply critical skepticism as it aims to establish a very few indubitable facts. Brady does not employ footnotes, but his appendices, his glossary, and all his investigations of the exact meanings of words in old English statutes and records resemble a series of skeptical footnotes that contradict the Whig notion of the ancient constitution and support his two theses about the late origin of Parliament. Brady's few theses appear at the head of his volume, just as Bayle's few facts appear above his notes. Despite its close critical analysis of documentary evidence, however, Brady's argument lacks narrative coherence, and was neglected until Hume made extensive use of it in the medieval volumes of his *History of England*. Although the popular Whig *History of England* by Paul Rapin-Thoyras (1725, trans., with additional notes by N. Tindal, 1732) comes closer to attaining narrative coherence than do works such as Brady's, Rapin still shows affinities with the early compilers in the frequency with which he inserts entire documents into his text. Because they occupy approximately equal space in the text, one might say either that the documents interrupt his narrative, or that his narrative interrupts the statutes, speeches, petitions, and negotiations he quotes entire and verbatim. Historical documents remain obtrusive and undigested in Rapin's historical narrative.

With the *History of England* (1754–62), Hume became the foremost British writer of philosophical history, which seeks to derive a few general truths from historical particulars, and to demonstrate that similar causes will produce similar results throughout history. Hume's *History* thus exemplifies the preeminent value placed on narrative coherence in the latter half of the paradigm of representation. In order to avoid "the prolix, tedious Style of . . . modern Compilers" like Brady and Rapin, Hume explained, "I have inserted no original Papers, and enter'd into no Detail of minute, uninteresting Facts."[6] The paucity of notes and documentation, especially in Hume's first volumes on the Stuarts, shows his reaction against the fragmentary compilations of the critical antiquarians and his affirmation of an opposite ideal of the text as an unbroken, transparent representation. Hume soon modified his avoidance of documentation in response to criticism by Horace Walpole, among others, and accordingly included numerous citations on each page of the Tudor and medieval volumes, later providing comparable citations for the Stuart volumes also.[7] The addition of both short references and long explanatory notes demonstrates that Hume did not entirely avoid critical controversy or neglect factual accuracy; he pursued research in documents available to him when they concerned a point of importance for his argument.[8] Hume's changing practices of annotation point to the impossibility under this paradigm of avoiding documentation entirely, and the difficulty of determining the number and form of notes appropriate to a philosophical history interested in the transparent representation of general arguments.

This difficulty underlies the various combinations of philosophical history and critical documentation that William Robertson employed in his works. He splits his *History of Scotland* (1759) evenly between the two: a narrative entirely without notes, and fifty-three appendices consisting entirely of documents. His *History of Charles V* (1769), also containing no notes, remains pure philosophical history. But it is preceded by a "View of the Progress of Society in Europe, From the Subversion of the Roman Empire, to the Beginning of the Sixteenth Century," to which Robertson attaches full references and expanded considerations of points made in his text. Only in his last work, *The History of America* (1777), published after Gibbon's first volume, does Robertson find an approximate balance between narrative and documentation, mentioning short references at the bottom of each page, and placing in endnotes more extended considerations of, for example, the population of Mexico or the origin of syphilis.

Gibbon was indebted to the examples of Hume and Robertson in many ways.[9] However, he found a more productive solution to the contradictions between lucid philosophical representations and obscure critical controversies, which had left many earlier works either starkly divided or, like Voltaire's histories, thinly documented. Gibbon developed the forms of irony appropriate both to philosophical history and to critical notes. In his sweeping historical narrative, he wields his "grave and temperate" irony;[10] but in his notes, following in the critical tradition of Bayle, he registers combative satiric judgments of previous partial or bigoted authorities. The notes of Robertson and Hume generally maintain an elevated propriety—Robertson apologizes uncomfortably for discussing syphilis, for example, and Hume descends, once, to detail a medieval noble household's domestic expenses—but Gibbon's footnotes frequently include such satiric elements as grotesque detail, low humor, and references to bodily functions. Gibbon includes in the footnotes that anchor his narrative not only extensive documentation and detailed critical disputes but also barbed satiric characterizations of other historians. Through this satiric and ironic dialogue with preceding authorities in his footnotes, and through the dialogue between his notes and his narrative, Gibbon conjoins philosophical history and critical controversy.

If Gibbon's footnotes undercut both the ideal of a coherent, autonomous text and the laborious researches of antiquarian compilers, Swift satirizes the paradigm of criticism and representation in the footnotes to A *Tale of a Tub* (5th ed., 1710). Appropriating as footnotes excerpts from a hostile critical explication of the *Tale*, Swift allows the modern critic, a "Discoverer and Collector of Writers Faults" (95), to exhibit himself as one who rifles texts to seize on a few meanings for condemnation.[11] Swift's own parodic notes to his text also mock the early critical project of considering interpretations as facts (e.g., "I do not well understand what the Author aims at here" [159]). Through the multiple ironies and parodies of the *Tale*'s footnotes and digressions, which defeat such simple critical conceptions of meaning, Swift satirizes the paradigm of critical skepticism as arbiter of cultural authority. Above and outside these footnotes, in his satiric history of Christianity, Swift also satirizes the earlier belief in God as the author of the script of all things natural and human.[12] Swift thus satirizes all the available criteria of cultural authority. Explicitly rejecting criticism and implicitly rejecting God as anchors of cultural authority, his parodic use of forms suggests that satiric narrative may offer a source of authority and perspective more promising than either.[13]

Texts that exhibit such ironic, divided authority provide striking instances of the phenomena that Mikhail Bakhtin has analyzed as dialogicality and heteroglossia, in which meaning emerges indirectly from the patterns of interference between conflicting voices and languages, each of which carries its own presuppositions, interests, and view of the world.[14] The paradoxical, supplementary relation between footnotes and narrative in these two texts may also serve to exemplify the supplementarity that Jacques Derrida has analyzed in Rousseau.[15] Swift's notes more readily illustrate Bakhtin's categories, as Gibbon's illustrate Derrida's; the congruence between the ironies and self-parody of these two sets of notes marks a convergence between the categories and theories of Bakhtin and Derrida.[16] Bakhtin contrasts the urge toward unitary language with the centrifugal energies and multiple voices of heteroglot and dialogical texts; Derrida contrasts the satisfying but unavailable plenitude of origin with the unending chain of imperfect signifiers that determines the supplementarity of all language and texts.

Whereas Swift's parodies authorize neither the newly emerging paradigm nor the earlier one of resemblance and commentary, Gibbon's ironies synthesize both the narrative representation and criticism of the later paradigm. Nevertheless, both authors use the same means of satiric footnoting to question the presumptions of the reigning paradigm of representation and criticism. Their satiric footnotes serve not to acknowledge or establish authorities, but to undercut the authority of their opponents and predecessors. Swift cities modern writers and Gibbon cites Christian saints *as if* they were authorities. Moreover, Swift and Gibbon imply affinities between their own tests and those of the authorities they satirize. Paradoxically, both also adopt the methods of their adversaries in their footnotes: Swift in satirizing Puritans, and Gibbon in satirizing Church historians. As a result of such self-parody, neither claims more than a dubious authority for himself. Turning their irony on themselves, both appear to subvert their own texts; but in fact, such self-parody enables the satiric texts to establish their authority indirectly. As Bakhtin and Derrida assert, claims to an unambiguous, unified language express a desire for political or theological absolutism, but the multiplication and dispersion of sites of limited authority implies a vital fragmentation of social and philosophical centralism. Through their deliberate supplementarity, the satiric footnotes of Swift and Gibbon contest the cultural authority of other texts, engaging them in sharply parodic but open-ended dialogue.

2

Although Swift's satiric strategies have been analyzed from many points of view, the ingenious footnotes in *A Tale of a Tub* have not received attention as major instruments of his parodic satire.[17] Some commentators have noted that Gibbon's footnotes contribute substantially to the total effect of the *Decline and Fall*, but few have analyzed the relations between the footnotes and his text. Moreover, since Gibbon's history has hardly begun to be examined as a satiric work, focusing on his footnotes as sites of irony and satire opens a possibility of analyzing the *Decline and Fall* from a largely new perspective.[18]

The first four editions (1704–5) of *A Tale of a Tub* contain no footnotes and only a few marginal references, such as "Herodot L.4." In the text of these anonymously published editions, Swift mocked William Wotton as a typically pedantic and literal-minded modern critic. Wotton responded in the next edition of his *Reflections on Ancient and Modern Learning* (1705) with a hostile but plodding explication of the allegorical narrative of the brothers as Christian churches, and with an attack on the *Tale* as a satire of the Anglican church. Swift prefaced the fifth (still anonymously published) edition of the *Tale* (1710) with an "Apology for the Etc.," in which he responded to Wotton and other critics, defending the *Tale* as a satire not of religion itself but of religious delusions, and asserting its conformity with the doctrines of the Church of England. Swift also added to this edition scores of footnotes, about a quarter of which consist of extracts quoted directly from Wotton's own antagonistic commentary on the *Tale*. These notes constitute a more searching parodic response to Wotton's attack than the "Apology." Swift grants a provisional degree of authority to Wotton in the footnotes in order further to satirize him and other modern critics as dull annotators. Appropriating Wotton's explications, Swift represents him as a solemn, pedestrian annotator of a text in which Wotton's own writings and ideas figure among the main objects of the satiric humor. In addition to these footnotes taken from Wotton, Swift's own added footnotes often parody passages in the *Tale*; both sets of notes satirize the kind of annotation that characterizes the early stage of footnoting—the critical and skeptical annotation of adversaries' texts.

Swift employs Wotton in the footnotes for the inglorious task of explaining the obvious; Wotton's notes make explicit the uncomplicated, one-to-one correspondences between the history of Christianity and the history of the three brothers in Swift's allegory. For example, Wotton identifies the sons when they first appear: "*By these three Sons, *Peter, Martyn* and *Jack; Popery*, the *Church* of *England*, and our Protestant *Dissenters* are designed. *W. Wotton*" (73).

Thus repeated, "W. Wotton" comes to designate a mechanical, unimaginative but self-important annotator. The second note that Swift borrows from Wotton concerns the coats the brothers inherit from their father: "By his Coats which he gave his Sons, the Garments of the Israelites. *W. Wotton*." But what follows calls attention to Wotton's incompetence even as the self-appointed intepreter of a simple allegory: "An Error (with Submission) of the learned Commentator; for by the Coats are meant the Doctrine and Faith of *Christianity*, by the Wisdom of the Divine Founder fitted to all Times, Places and Circumstances" (73). Although Swift ascribes this note to "Lambin" (a dead French scholar), thus obscuring his own part in the satiric dialogue, he has clearly subverted Wotton's role as the "learned Commentator."

In the first section of the *Tale*, just a few pages before these two footnotes from Wotton, Swift offers ironic praise for a number of modern authors, including the author of "an Abstract" (of *The Wise Men of Gotham*) that "hath been lately published by a *worthy Member*" of the modern school. Swift's footnote identifies this "Abstract" as "Mr. *W-tt-n*'s Discourse of Antient and Modern Learning" (69). That Wotton should be thus repeatedly satirized in the very work to which he contributes grave explanatory notes gives Swift his satiric revenge.

Speaking only through others' voices in A *Tale of a Tub*, Swift subordinates those voices to his own purposive inflections; but he also subordinates his own discursive purposes to the words of others, including William Wotton. Swift's parodic appropriations, therefore, register a "degree of dialogic resistance of the parodied discourse."[19] Incorporating Wotton's words into his work, Swift intensifies his satire of Wotton, but he also grants the object of his satire an authoritative standing; he makes Wotton his collaborator, a co-author of A *Tale of a Tub*. Unlike referential or explanatory footnotes,

Swift's parodic footnotes do not resolve the ironies of the *Tale* into a single authoritative voice. Rather, the dialogic tension between the voice of Wotton in the footnotes and the satire of Wotton in the text extends the unresolved dialogue between opposite positions and languages in the *Tale*.

In appropriating for footnotes to the *Tale* passages from Wotton's commentary on the *Tale*, in thus juxtaposing competing languages, Swift illustrates Bakhtin's notion of heteroglossia. In the *Reflections*, Wotton presumes that the meaning of Swift's *Tale* is self-evident, and that his own critical language provides an adequate and direct access to the truth of other texts. But Wotton mistakes all but the broadest satire in the *Tale* and neglects irony and parody almost entirely. His language thus joins the other languages in the *Tale* that are parodied for their claim to give an adequate account of the world—the languages of scholarly criticism, literal interpretation, and experimental materialism. In addition to parodying these languages and their implied systems of belief, Swift parodies as well the earlier and opposite presumptions in the languages of neoplatonism, typological interpretation, and alchemical transformation. In this way, Swift achieves an extreme, doubly parodic dialogicality in the *Tale*.[20] He never speaks in his own voice or directly expresses his own position, but leaves it to be extrapolated from the intersection of parodied voices. What Bakhtin says of Rabelais also applies to Swift here: "the truth that might oppose such falsity [as that of conventional ideological discourse] receives almost no direct intentional and verbal expression in Rabelais, it does not receive its *own* word—it reverberates only in the parodic and unmasking accents in which the lie is present."[21]

Like Swift, Gibbon turns his opponents' texts to satiric purposes in his footnotes; his aim of providing an accurate historical narrative in the *Decline and Fall of the Roman Empire* requires him to rely on authors from whom he differs substantially. His first footnote in his chapter on monasticism exemplifies the combination of precise citation and ironic evaluation that consequently characterizes his footnotes: "[1]The origin of the monastic institution has been laboriously discussed by Thomassin (Discipline de l'Eglise, tom. i. p. 1419–1426) and Helyot (Hist. des Ordres Monastiques, tom i. p. 1–66). These authors are very learned and tolerably honest, and their difference of opinion shows the subject in its full extent."[22] Observing the convention of learned usage by referring to particular titles and page numbers, Gibbon slyly subverts it by ironically indicating his judgment of his authorities' exceptional labor and merely moderate honesty.

Gibbon's notes almost always contain such an ironic turn: citations of author, title, and page number without any comment occur very rarely. Occasionally, a footnote lacks any reference to a printed work, and consists solely of comment: "[58]I have somewhere heard or read the frank confession of a Benedictine abbot: 'My vow of poverty has given me an hundred thousand crowns a year; my vow of obedience has raised me to the rank of a sovereign prince.'—I forget the consequences of his vow of chastity" (37;4:76). While the previous note conforms to developing scholarly convention, this one takes the form of a witty anecdote that might appear in conversation rather than at the bottom of a page.

The infrequency of such examples, either of pure citation or of purely ironic commentary, highlights Gibbon's habitual practice of combining the two in his footnotes. Harold Bond argues that Gibbon's assumed role "as impartial historian enables him to quote the adversaries on either side against each other and produce the exact measure of approbation he wishes."[23] Gibbon's footnotes often show him arbitrating between preceding and conflicting accounts of historical matters. However, rather than judiciously balancing differing authorities on either side of a particular issue, Gibbon typically goes further and ironically undermines his predecessors, including credulous ecclesiastical historians and high Christian authorities. For instance, Gibbon points out the superstitious credulity of Sts. Jerome and Augustine, two of the most learned Fathers of the early Church: "[81]The presbyter Vigilantius, the protestant of his age, firmly, though ineffectually, withstood the superstition of monks, relics, saints, fasts, &c., for which Jerom compares him to the Hydra, Cerberus, the Centaurs, &c., and considers him only as the organ of the daemon (tom.ii. p. 120–126). Whoever will peruse the controversy of St. Jerom and Vigilantius, and St. Augustin's account of the miracles of St. Stephen, may speedily gain some idea of the spirit of the Fathers" (28;3:221). Gibbon's skeptical intelligence makes use of unreliable partisan testimonies not as sources of information about Vigilantius or Stephen, but as evidence of the strength of superstition in the Church that regarded Jerome and Augustine as authorities.

In order to illuminate the contradictions and illogicalities among Christian authorities, Gibbon frequently juxtaposes them satirically in his footnotes. In ironic perplexity about when to fix the cessation of miracles, for example, Gibbon observes: "[83]It may seem somewhat remarkable that Bernard of Clairvaux, who records so many miracles of his friend St. Malachi, never takes any notice of his own, which, in their turn, however, are carefully related by his companions and disciples. In the long series of ecclesiastical history, does there exist a single instance of a saint asserting that he himself possessed the gift of miracles?" (15;2:32). Here and throughout the *Decline and Fall*, Gibbon strategically turns his opponents' words upon themselves. What Bernard and St. Malachi each omit to say about themselves casts doubt on what each says about the other, and Gibbon's rhetorical question derives a definite implausibility from juxtaposing the accounts of two esteemed authorities.

In a similar undermining of his superstitious sources, Gibbon points out that several historians of the early Church credit not only the sign of the Labarum that is said to have appeared to Constantine the night before his decisive victory at the Milvian bridge, but also the angel said to have appeared to Constantine's opponent, Licinius: "[41]. . . Yet even this angel is favourably entertained by Pagi, Tillemont, Fleury, &c., who are fond of increasing their stock of miracles" (20;2:31). Tillemont's large compilation of ecclesiastical history constitutes a principal source that Gibbon mines throughout the *Decline and Fall*, but Gibbon frequently arraigns Tillemont for his willingness to believe in miracles and relics. Here Tillemont and other ecclesiastical historians credit not only the miraculous vision of the first Christian emperor but also the similar vision of his adversary, as though, Gibbon implies, God were betting on both sides. As with the juxtaposition of saintly authorities in the previous note, the citation here of numerous authors, which usually works to redouble their authority, has the opposite effect of undermining their credibility. Gibbon often mocks other authorities in notes such as this; however, he cannot discredit them entirely, since he must base his work on that of his predecessors, among them historians of the Church.

Footnotes attempt to ground the authority of a text on other texts construed as authoritative, but such a strategy uncovers a lack of authority in the text itself. Thus, although Gibbon's *History* possesses a monumental structure and a stately syntax, which implicitly assert its indisputable authority, its footnotes, as additions that bring to light a previously existing lack, possess the paradoxical structure of the supplement that Derrida has described. Gibbon establishes the authority of his historical narrative on his citation of, among others, authorities on ecclesiastical history; however, in his footnotes he also undermines the assertions of these predecessors, whom he finds wanting in reliability or judgment. His footnotes thus provide the site of an intensely satiric dialogue between the religious historians who constitute Gibbon's sources and the skeptical philosophical historian who inverts their celebration of the rise of Christianity by regretting the subversion of the pagan empire by the Church.

Although Gibbon, like other scholars, uses footnotes to assert his learning, complete his text, and establish his authority, his footnotes lead him into unresolved dialogues with competing authorities, revealing the contingent, embattled nature of his text. Such extended dialogues with predecessors question the presumed primacy of text and the subordinate status of footnotes. The footnotes establish and authorize the historical narrative. But, alternatively, the entire text may prove to be a footnote to other texts: the *Decline and Fall* can be read as a polemical footnote that seeks to reverse more than thirteen hundred years of Christian history.[24] As the distinction between footnotes and text becomes fainter, however, the relation of supplementarity remains. Derrida's statement concerning Rousseau applies here: "there have never been anything but supplements, substitutive significations, which could only come forth in a chain of differential references."[25] There is no single origin and source of authority, but only the struggle between imperfect, limited, and multiple writings.

The *Decline and Fall* and *Tale of a Tub* thus share a dialogic tension that results from citing objects of their satire as authorities in their footnotes.

Swift aims to satirize modern criticism in *A Tale of a Tub*, yet in his footnotes he makes use of a modern critic, Wotton; in the *Decline and Fall*, Gibbon intends to satirize religious enthusiasm, yet he cites saints in his notes. Both refer to authorities in support of positions that implicitly or explicitly attack the authorities themselves. Facing the impossibility of establishing their authority directly in such parodic and satiric texts, Swift and Gibbon use the supplementary relation between footnotes and text, and the dialogical contestation of other authorities in their footnotes, to establish their own authority indirectly.

3

Swift and Gibbon extend their indirection even to self-parody. In addition to including Wotton's comments, Swift added many footnotes to the 1710 edition of the *Tale* in which he parodies his own enigmatic text.[26] Some of these notes perform the same function as Wotton's by identifying an element in the allegory: "By this Rupture [between the brothers] is meant the Reformation" (119). Others comically frustrate the expectation of similar clarification, for example: "I cannot guess the Author's meaning here, which I would be very glad to know, because it seems to be of Importance" (191). In such notes, Swift seems to undermine his own text by extending its uncertainties rather than resolving them. Parodying the vacuity of pretentious hermetic authors, he abdicates the authority that footnotes make available to him, and gives the reader a greater share in determining the meaning of his text.

In a different kind of self-parody, Swift appropriates with aggressive ventriloquism the voices of those he satirizes. In Section 1 of the *Tale*, the narrator claims that his "Physico-logical Scheme of Oratorical Receptacles or Machines contains a great Mystery, being a Type, a Sign, an Emblem, a Shadow, a Symbol, bearing Analogy to the Spacious Commonwealth of Writers" (61). To support this absurd claim, the author explains that modern pulpits consist of rotten wood for two reasons:

> Because it is the Quality of rotten Wood to give *Light* in the Dark: And secondly, Because its Cavities are full of Worms: which is a *Type with a Pair of Handles, having a Respect to the two principal Qualifications of the Orator, and the two different Fates attending upon his Works.

> *The Two Principal Qualifications of a Phanatick Preacher are, his Inward Light, and his Head full of Maggots, and the Two different Fates of his writings are, to be burnt or Worm eaten.

> (62)

This ludicrously far-fetched typology actually makes satiric sense; yet what it signifies, the meaning of the mysterious "pair of handles," can only be understood from the footnote. There, the satiric type of rotten wood exhibits a notable precision, brevity, and point. Providing ingenious and comically satisfying explications in such notes, Swift engages in the same typological discourse that he parodies. But Swift not only masters his opponents' mode; he surpasses them by using their own rhetoric to reveal the potential for deceit in all rhetoric of mystery. In this and similar passages, Swift and Gibbon seek to establish textual authority through parodic and subversive adoption of the voices of their opponents.

Gibbon's work moves toward a similar self-parody in its ironic praise of other historians, which reveals Gibbon's anxiety about his own history. In a note, he commends St. Jerome's biographies of saints, but only for their aesthetic qualities: "the only defect of these pleasing compositions is the want of truth and common sense" (37;4:66). Of course, Jerome's narrative does not intend to be pleasing, but it does claim to be true. Yet, Gibbon finds himself in a position similar to Jerome's in a footnote on Christian apocalyptic visions: "[71]On this subject every reader of taste will be entertained with the third part of Burnet's Sacred Theory. He blends philosophy, scripture, and tradition, into one magnificent system; in the description of which he displays a strength of fancy not inferior to that of Milton himself" (15;2:28). Gibbon ironically commends for their "strength of fancy" both the works of saints and a modern history of the earth that anchors itself in Scripture. He deflates Burnet by judging his *Sacred Theory* suitable for "every reader of taste," but a very similar judgment has occasionally been brought against Gibbon himself. As Burnet did within the preceding paradigm, Gibbon constructs in his narrative a "magnificent system" that may contain more imaginative power than explanatory force. Precisely through his urbane irony, Gibbon himself appeals to readers of taste of his time.

Further self-parody arises from Gibbon's ironic treatment of religious historians for "insinuating" desired allegorical interpretations of Scripture into their works. On the early Christians' belief in the imminence of Christ's second coming, Gibbon notes: "[62]This expectation was countenanced by the twenty-fourth chapter of St. Matthew and by the first epistle of St. Paul to the Thessalonians. Erasmus removes the difficulty by the help of allegory and metaphor, and the learned Grotius ventures to insinuate that, for wise purposes, the pious deception was permitted to take place" (15;2:25). Gibbon may believe that Christian teachers knowingly have fostered unjustified expectations of the end of the world, or that Christian apologists have resorted in bad faith to allegorical readings of the Bible. However, his pose as impartial historian does not allow him to make such assertions directly. Gibbon's insinuating, ironic method of satirizing Christian historians in fact provides a near equivalent to Grotius's insinuation of an allegorical meaning into the sacred text. Gibbon mocks Erasmus and Grotius for a kind of interpretation very close to his own: interpretation as slyly aggressive appropriation.[27]

Gibbon's relation to insinuating historians resembles Swift's relation to Puritan typologists: each satirist appropriates the voices of his adversaries, employing the rhetoric of those he satirizes with only the minimal variation or exaggeration necessary to turn the original meaning on its head. In these dialogical texts, all the voices—the satirized as well as the satirizing—are qualified by parodic intonations. This parodic dialogicality provides Swift and Gibbon with the means of establishing an indirect and ironic authority greater than that of the univocal authorities cited in their footnotes.

Footnotes conventionally serve as repositories of authority, where creditable sources may be cited to support an author's argument; they also provide sites for anchoring an author's voice so that the appended comments and explanations will validate and complete the text. However, when that voice is ironic and satiric, withholding unmediated expression of a single position, the author challenges the reader's involvement in interpreting the open-ended text. Indeed, subsequent readers and editors have added their own footnotes to Swift's and Gibbon's text and notes, including A. C. Guthkelch and David Nichol Smith, editors of the authoritative edition of the *Tale*, and J. B. Bury, the historian of the ancient world and editor of the standard edition of the *Decline and Fall*. Annotations to Swift's *Tale* possess the peculiarity of tracking down many quotations that are nonsensical or lack an origin in other texts; Swift has sent his annotators on wild goose chases as if he were continuing to satirize his critical annotators. Adding notes to Gibbon's own can similarly make one an unwitting object of his satire. In his *Idea of History*, R. G. Collingwood points out that Bury's project attempts "the very strange feat of bringing Gibbon up to date by means of footnotes, adding to the aggregate of knowledge already contained in his pages the numerous facts that had been ascertained in the meantime without suspecting that the very discovery of these facts resulted from an historical mentality so different from Gibbon's own that the result was not unlike adding a saxophone obbligato to an Elizabethan madrigal."[28] Collingwood underscores the contingent nature of ideas of historical understanding. As a philosophical historian, Gibbon attempts to understand and evaluate the patterns connecting widely separate eras. Bury, however, presumes that the goal of historical work consists of ascertaining facts, and hence that one can establish irrefutable historical truths. This positivism informs Bury's notes, which appear to acknowledge but actually contest Gibbon's authority by offering to update and correct the *Decline and Fall*. It determines as well Bury's inability to revise Gibbon's arguments; no accumulation of discrete facts can alter the shape or implications of Gibbon's narrative.

Bury's supplemental notes to the *Decline and Fall* also aim to make Gibbon's history acceptable to Christians, a project Bury shares with a series of nineteenth-century editors (including Guizot, Milman, and Smeaton) who abandoned the early direct attacks on Gibbon's history and instead attempted to appropriate the *Decline and Fall* for orthodox religious opinion. These editors dedicate their notes to updating the historian's facts when they can, and more frequently to disapproving of his pointed ironies and earthy satire. The pious have been from the first among the readers most troubled by both Swift's *Tale* and Gibbon's *History*; their attacks seek to controvert a crucial implication of both texts.[29]

Unlike the marginal glosses and references to Scripture in Burnet's *Sacred Theory* or Bunyan's *Pilgrim's Progress*, the satiric footnotes in Swift and Gibbon do not recognize a sacred authority or a delegated representative; by ironically citing authorities who are unhallowed, fallen, and debunked, these footnotes imply that no source of indisputable spiritual or cultural authority exists. As Derrida asserts, the chain of compensatory supplemental signifiers carries as a corollary "the absence of the referent or transcendental signified."[30] In these texts, the divine and nature, the origin and fullness of meaning, remain conspicuously absent. Bakhtin likewise predicates his analysis on the absence of unity and a center, noting for example that even "monoglossia is always in essence relative," as is monologism.[31] Thus, for both Bakhtin and Derrida, the absence of a transcendent origin and an authoritative discourse defines the conditions of meaning. The absence of a transcendent origin certainly determines the texts of Gibbon and Swift in the discursive paradigm of criticism and representation. The narratives in both the *Decline and Fall* and the *Tale of a Tub* recount satirically inverted histories of Christianity, designating the absence rather than presence of the authoritative, divine discourse that served as the origin of Christian history and interpretation. In consonance with such narratives, their satiric and self-parodic footnotes register an absence of sacred authority, and establish their disputable, divided authority in the realm of the supplementary, the secular, and the dialogical.

Notes

1. Michel Foucault, *The Order of Things* (New York, 1973), 58–71, 78–81.

2. On the theory of the marginal gloss, I am indebted to Lawrence Lipking's "The Marginal Gloss," *Critical Inquiry* 3 (1977): 609–55. Lipking concentrates on the marginal gloss, rather than, as I do here, the marginal citation; but his observations on the function of both helped me formulate the relation between paradigms of discourse and forms of notation.

3. Lipking remarks on the "thin rivulet" of certainty in the text that "flows over the great depths of the footnotes" in Bayle's *Dictionary* ("Marginal Gloss," 626).

4. Lipking maintains that "modern footnotes and modern theories of progress were introduced at the same time and in the same context: the late seventeenth-century war between Ancients and Moderns" ("Marginal Gloss," 638).

5. On the desire for transparency in the language of the late seventeenth and eighteenth centuries, see Foucault, *Order of Things*, 117.

6. *The Letters of David Hume*, ed. J. Y. T. Greig (Oxford, 1932), 1:179, 193.

7. See *Letters* 1:284–85.

8. For a good example of Hume's concern with factual accuracy, see his extended discussion of the authenticity of Mary's letter to Bothwell, *History of England* (London, 1778; rpt. Indianapolis, 1983), vol. 4, note K, 390–93.

9. For the first sentence of the *Decline and Fall*, Gibbon echoed, with significant inversions, a sentence near the opening of Robertson's "View": "If a man were called to fix upon the period, in the history of the world, during which the condition of the human race was most calamitous and afflicted, he would without hesitation, name that which elapsed from the death of Theodosius the Great, to the establishment of the Lombards in Italy" (A.D. 395–571). *History of the Reign of Charles V* (London, 1770), 1:8. Hume gave Gibbon strong encouragement after reading the first volume of the *Decline and Fall*. He also suggested that the printer place Gibbon's notes at the bottom of the page rather than the end of the volume. This change facilitated Gibbon's development of the distinctive dialogue between his footnotes and his text in later editions and volumes of his history (Hume, *Letters*, 2:313).

10. *The Autobiographies of Edward Gibbon*, ed. John Murray (London, 1896), 143.

11. This definition of the "true Critick" comes from Section 3 of the *Tale*, the "Digression Concerning Critics"; the prototype of the modern critic is the spider in The *Battle of the Books*. Jonathan Swift, A *Tale of a Tub*, ed. A. C. Guthkelch and D. Nichol Smith (1920; 2nd ed., Oxford, 1958), 228, 232. Further citations from this edition appear in the text.

12. For discussion of such satire, see Everett Zimmerman, *Swift's Narrative Satires: Author and Authority* (Ithaca, 1983), 172–73, who relates Swift's practices to Foucault's theories in two ways: he discerns satire of the paradigm of commentary in the allegorical narrative of A *Tale of a Tub*, and satire of the presumed possibility of transparent representations in *Gulliver's Travels*. However, Zimmerman does not analyze the footnotes and digressive sections in the *Tale* as parodies of the emerging paradigm of criticism and representation.

13. In "At the Margin of Discourse: Footnotes in the Fictional Text," PMLA 98 (1983): 207, 209, Shari Benstock argues that footnotes in fictional texts do not, like scholarly footnotes, refer outward to external authority, but rather act self-reflexively to draw readers into the fictional work. Significantly, the footnotes she considers as antecedents for Joyce's practice in *Finnegans Wake* appear in satiric narratives of the mid-eighteenth century: *Tom Jones* and *Tristram Shandy*.

14. In *The Dialogic Imagination*, ed. Michael Holquist, trans. Caryl Emerson and Michael Holquist (Austin, 1981), Bakhtin designates as heteroglossia the multiplicity of languages in any society and the struggle among languages that reflects antagonisms among social strata: language "represents the co-existence of socio-ideological contradictions between the present and the past, between different epochs of the past, between different socio-ideological groups in the present, between tendencies, schools, circles and so forth, all given a bodily form. These 'languages' of heteroglossia intersect each other in a variety of ways, forming new socially typifying 'languages' " (291). On heteroglossia, see also 60–67, 288–96, 314. By dialogicality, Bakhtin means the similarly open-ended intersection of diverse voices in a single discourse. For Bakhtin, parody necessarily consists of a dialogical hybrid of voices (*The Dialogic Imagination*, 76, 308–14, 358–66).

15. In Derrida's analysis, which proceeds from Rousseau's *Confessions*, the supplement arises as an addition to natural pleasures and satisfactions, but, being exterior to what is natural, it reveals a lack in nature's presumed perfection. The supplement provides a surplus, an enrichment, but at the same time uncovers a previous insufficiency. Moreover, there is no escape from supplementarity; Derrida argues that in Rousseau's text, what makes meaning and language possible is the disappearance of natural presence: "the absolute present, Nature, that which words like 'real mother' name, have always already escaped, have never existed" (*Of Grammatology*, trans. Gayatri Chakravorty Spivak [Baltimore, 1976], 159). On supplementarity, see also 144–64. In Derrida's analysis, Rousseau never recognizes the ontological impossibility of gaining access to natural presence.

16. In "Bakhtin, Marxism, and Post-Structuralism," in *Literature, Politics, and Theory,*

202 ♦ FRANK PALMERI

ed. Francis Barker, Peter Hulme, et al. (London, 1986), 104–25, Graham Pechey analyzes the development of Bakhtin's theories as a deconstruction of Russian Formalism in the direction of Marxism, and thus shows a commonality between the methods of Bakhtin and of Derrida.

17. Hugh Kenner's discussion of footnotes in *The Stoic Comedians* (Berkeley, 1962), 39–40, takes *A Tale of a Tub* as its point of departure. On Satiric strategies in *A Tale of a Tub*, see Miriam Starkman, *Swift's Satire on Learning in "A Tale of a Tub"* (Princeton, 1950): Ronald Paulson, *Theme and Structure in Swift's "A Tale of a Tub"* (New Haven, 1960); Edward Rosenheim, *Swift and the Satirist's Art* (Chicago, 1963), 189–206; John Clark, *Form and Frenzy in "A Tale of a Tub"* (Ithaca, 1970); Michael Seidel, *Satiric Inheritance: Rabelais to Sterne* (Princeton, 1979), 169–200; and Zimmerman, *Swift's Narrative Satires*. In "The Irony of Swift," in *The Common Pursuit* (New York, 1952), 73–87, F. R. Leavis contrasted the "essentially negative" irony of Swift with what he considered the positive values underlying Gibbon's irony. A. E. Dyson similarly opposes the two as he concentrates on Gibbon's "urbane assurance" in "A Note on Dismissive Irony," *English* 11 (1957): 222–25. William Frost reverses Leavis's valuation of Gibbon's self-assurance over Swift's fierceness in "The Irony of Swift and Gibbon: A Reply to F. R. Leavis," *Essays in Criticism* 17 (1967): 41–47.

18. James D. Garrison has investigated the relation between Gibbon's satiric footnotes and the authority of his historical project in two important articles. In "Gibbon and the 'Treacherous Language of Panegyrics,' " *Eighteenth-Century Studies* 11 (1977): 40–62, Garrison analyzes how Gibbon "distilled solid evidence from such discredited materials as the panegyrics addressed to the later Roman emperors." In "Lively and Laborious: Characterization in Gibbon's Metahistory," *Modern Philology* 76 (1978): 163–78, he shows that Gibbon defines his model philosophical historian through satiric characterization of earlier historians in his footnotes. Leo Braudy points out that, in addition to the "voluminous documentation" they supply, Gibbon's footnotes in later chapters refer to earlier chapters and notes in the *Decline and Fall* as authoritative sources, in *Narrative Form in History and Fiction: Hume, Fielding, and Gibbon* (Princeton, 1970), 250, 257, 260. Lipking observes Gibbon's ingenuity in setting up ironic dialogues between his footnotes and his overarching narrative ("Marginal Gloss," 626). Lionel Gossman discusses Gibbon's notes as a "privileged place" for establishing a personal and informal relationship with his reader, in *The Empire Unpossess'd* (Cambridge, 1981), 76, 93. In "The Art of the Footnote," *The American Scholar* 53 (Winter 1983–84): 54–62, G. W. Bowerstock considers Gibbon a master of the footnote because he is able to acknowledge simultaneously his "indebtedness to an ancient source and his poor opinion of that source."

19. Bakhtin, *Dialogic Imagination*, 413.

20. On Swift's use of double parody, endorsing opposite sets of values in order to satirize both, see my *Satire in Narrative* (Austin, 1990).

21. *Dialogic Imagination*, 309.

22. Edward Gibbon, *The Decline and Fall of the Roman Empire*, ed. J. B. Bury (London, 1909–14; rpt. New York, 1974), ch. 37, vol. 4, p. 62. Further citations from this edition appear in the text.

23. Harold Bond, *The Literary Art of Edward Gibbon* (Oxford, 1960), 123.

24. In *Gibbon and His Roman Empire* (Urbana, 1971), 157–58, David Jordan discusses Gibbon's project in the *History* as an overturning of Augustine's project in *The City of God*.

25. *Of Grammatology*, 159.

26. All the evidence indicates that these notes are by Swift; see Guthkelch and Nichol Smith, xxii–xxiv.

27. Lipking points out that in controversial writings, the footnote frequently "appears less a means of forcing disputants to demonstrate their proofs, more a means of cleverly asserting the priority of the [footnoted] text" ("Marginal Gloss," 639).

28. R. G. Collingwood, *The Idea of History* (Oxford, 1946), 147.

29. James Boswell, for one, complained that Gibbon "should have warned us of our

danger before we entered his garden of flowery eloquence, by advertising 'Spring-guns and men-traps set here.' " Boswell's injured tone testifies to the success of Gibbon's strategies. Reported in the *Life of Johnson*, ed. Birkbeck-Hill (Oxford, 1934–50), 2: 512–13, quoted in Jordan, *Gibbon and His Roman Empire*, 224.

30. *Of Grammatology*, 158.

31. *Dialogic Imagination*, 66.

POETRY

◆

The Difference in Swift

ELLEN POLLAK

> Women have served all these centuries as looking-glasses possessing the magic
> and delicious power of reflecting the figure of man at twice its natural size.
> —Virginia Woolf, *A Room of One's Own*

The difference between Swift and Pope has to do with the respective ways
the two writers represent the concept of difference in their texts. With
Swift, even more persistently than Pope, the issue of gender cannot be fully
disentangled from the larger network of textual relations inscribing selfhood,
representation, and the more general notion of difference.

I have elsewhere sought to explore the socioeconomic determinants of
what, by the early eighteenth century, had become a culturally dominant
sexual mythology. Being ideologically overdetermined, however, that mythology may be illuminated by psychosexual as well as sociocultural analysis.
And since it is precisely such a psychosexual approach that Swift's obscene
and "excremental" poems about women seem to demand, I shall introduce
a more psychoanalytic framework for my discussion in the present chapter
than I have in others. I should perhaps make clear from the outset that, in
doing so, I operate on the full conviction that the myths of psychoanalysis
may be brought to bear fruitfully on the analysis of literary texts and of the
models of desire they assume without necessitating a lapse either into a
narrowly psychobiographical use of literary discourse or into a critical indifference to the broadly ideological implications of the psychosexual norms that
condition a culture's literary productions.

In the following pages, the concept of the fetish becomes central to my
discussion of the difference between Swift and Pope. What I shall be arguing
is that while Pope fetishizes the female as a way of eliminating visible traces
of anxiety and violence from the interior of his texts, Swift is intent on
exposing not only the male anxiety engendered by the fact of sexual difference, but also the process by which the fetishized female "normally" displaces
masculine fear. Pope accommodates women comfortably within his texts by
objectifying them in such a way that they give him back the image of himself
he wants to see. In Swift's texts, however, women are unrecuperated; within

From *The Poetics of Sexual Myth: Gender and Ideology in the Verse of Swift and Pope*, 1985. Reprinted with
the permission of the University of Chicago Press and the author.

the symbolic system Swift exploits they represent the active principle of difference itself, and this principle in turn becomes the motivating structure of Swift's art.

The difference in Swift's and Pope's representations of sexual difference is, I shall argue further, intimately related to the conceptions of authorship that underwrite their texts. In Pope, the concept of authorial presence (a concept which Derrida has sought to dismantle as one of the totalizing myths of a metaphysics predicated on the suppression of difference)[1] is stabilized by the opposing inscription of woman as absence, lack; in Swift, no such unifying equilibrium is ever comfortably achieved. Swift's mind, ever negative, ever fiercely analytic, was constantly resistant to the stasis of ideological cliché. Indeed, his writing both centers on and derives its energy from precisely the perception and exploitation of the problematic nature of authorship in a culture that erected the stability of the notion of selfhood on the exquisite instability of an ideology of difference.

◆

What is becoming increasingly apparent as scholars bring feminist imperatives to bear on the analysis of Western literary culture is the extent to which the principle of fetishistic displacement operates as a poetic and narrative convention in literary representations of the female "subject." Michel Foucault, in his history of modern sexuality as it has evolved since the eighteenth century, has suggested the dialectical nature of the relationship between sexual pathology and norms; within the economy of power/pleasure established by bourgeois sexual codes, perversions are extensions, not subversions, of social morality. They are what Foucault calls "implantations" within the very discourse that defines their negative relation to the norm.[2] Questions of gender, however, occupy a less than marginal status in Foucault's analysis, and the fetish per se, although Foucault calls it the "model perversion,"[3] is nonetheless only one among several forms of illicit pleasure that he names. For a feminist perspective on the ways in which fetishism has become a moral, aesthetic, and erotic imperative in literary representation, we must turn to the work of such critics as Peggy Kamuf and Nancy Vickers.

Writing on Rousseau's *Julie*, Kamuf identifies the designation of proxies as an underlying principle of the exchange of letters in the epistolary novel.[4] Saint Preux's desire, she demonstrates, is fetishistic; but according to her analysis that fetishism is, instead of a perversion, a mark of his normality within the conventions of eighteenth-century fictional discourse. Deconstructing the opposition between normality and perversion, she shows how fetishism is both dependent on and an outgrowth of a particular code of sexual morality: "Radical perversion cannot be sustained outside the structure that houses normality. It is found inside the house, and inside the inside—in the closets. A perversion *of* convention, *of* normality is the fetishist's prerogative. Since his gratification is not obtained by transgressing the prohibition which regulates access to the normal erotic object, the field of his sexual pleasure is not restricted by this obstacle but given sanction and reinforcement. . . . Fetishism exploits the erotic possibilities of the law which normally restricts and limits erotic pleasure."[5] Similarly, Nancy Vickers has shown how the Petrarchan mode of figuring the female body is generated by a process of fetishistic overdetermination; Petrarch's figuring of Laura as a "scattered woman" in the "scattered rhymes" of his *Canzones* marks, in Vickers's terms, "a decisive stage in the development of a code of beauty . . . that causes us to view the fetishized body as a norm."[6]

In its anthropological meaning, the fetish is a material object believed, among certain primitive tribes, to represent a supernatural being; the possession of this object is supposed to give the possessor the power to control that being. Marx writes of the process by which commodities become fetishized in capitalist society: as man-made objects become alien to their creators, a relation between men assumes "the fantastic form of a relation between things."[7] But Foucault, Kamuf, and Vickers all use the concept of fetishism in the sense in which Freud defined it in 1927 to refer to a sexual perversion symptomatic of unresolved castration anxiety. According to the Freudian analysis, the fetish is any object (frequently a part of the female body, sometimes an appurtenance of it, such as a piece of clothing) onto which the male subject displaces libidinal feelings that, in the course of the "normal" development of heterosexual masculinity, would be invested in the "full sexual identity" of the female object.[8]

The fetishized object, Freud says, is actually a substitute for the maternal phallus. When the male child, operating on the infantile, narcissistic assumption that the female body must mirror his own, discovers the fact of sexual difference (presumably by means of the visual perception of the mother's genitals), he not only perceives the female as castrated but construes that perception as a shocking proof of the possibility that his body may be in jeopardy as well. The child must thus seek some way to repair the wound to his narcissism precipitated by this confrontation with the "other" and concretized in his own feared dismemberment.

The fetish enables the male to restore the specular status of the female by supplying her with the phallus that she "lacks." As Kamuf explains in her discussion of the fetishistic function of female clothing in *Julie*, the article of a woman's clothing, like feminine modesty itself, increases the erotic value of the female for Saint Preux by serving as both a cover and a substitute for the absence of a phallus. The fetishized garment at once diverts attention from this absence and "redresses" it; "re-covering" the assumed castration of the female, it mitigates the status of female difference as a dire threat to men.[9]

As Freud is quick to note, however, a fetishistic disavowal of reality embodies the seeds of its own contradiction. The perception of difference as lack is intransigently embedded in the very process by which that difference would be effaced. Thus even as the fetish seeks to reconstitute lack as presence, it functions stubbornly as a sign of absence within the economy of a masculine desire that seeks its own completion. The female body must be figured metonymically because it cannot be looked upon directly; the substitution may reassure, but the gaze must be perpetually averted. The "horror of castration," writes Freud, "has set up a memorial to itself in the creation of this substitute."[10]

The Perseus myth is the prototype of the Freudian narrative. Perseus's task is to decapitate the Medusa, one of three gorgons the sight of whom is death; whoever looks upon these female monsters turns to stone. With the aid of a shield given him by Athena, Perseus is able to accomplish his murderous feat; by looking into his shield instead of directly at his prey, he sees the Medusa reflected "as in a mirror." The Medusa's severed head, which Perseus appropriates as a prize of battle, now becomes a private source of power; by exposing it to the eyes of his enemies, he is able to turn them into stone.

In the Freudian reading, the Medusa's head is a fetishistic rendering of the female genitals.[11] A part of the female body is made to stand for the absent phallus; the appropriation of this symbolic phallus by the male is commensurate with his mastery of the threat of the castration it conceals. But like the shield which renders its appropriation possible, the gorgon's head also signifies the very lack it would deny; its presence affirms the terror which it protects Perseus from confronting directly.[12] In the Perseus narrative, the opposition between mastery and apprehension is collapsed in the act of decapitation, which is at once an enactment of the castration the hero fears and the execution of his triumph against that threat.

◆

What I have been observing in Pope's representations of women is precisely the operation of this dynamic. It is visible perhaps most patently in the *Rape*, where Pope affirms women's status as objects even as he attacks the dehumanizing values of commercial culture. Pope's attack on a world where, to borrow Marx's terms, a relation between men assumes the fantastic form of a relation between things is, I have argued, evidenced both in his depiction of a universe where "Wigs with Wigs, with Sword-knots Sword-knots strive" (1: 101) and in his underworld inversion of that objectification in the Cave of Spleen, where inanimate objects are humanized.[13] But this attack on a fetishistic society is also a pretext for Pope's own fetishization of the female. As Leo Braudy suggests, Pope's Baron may be barren,[14] may be mocked for his sterile obsession with possessing and exposing the plait of a woman's hair, but at the same time Pope himself celebrates Belinda's lock as the emblem of an essentially self-mutilating art. For in this text, dress—which is imaged as the coquette's armor against man—is also the very basis of the conversion of her power and visibility into his. Her self-adornment may seduce, but only within the viciously circular economy of a masculine desire that inexorably defines women as its objects. The seduction is reflexive, and Belinda doubles back upon herself, inevitably seducing the Baron into victimizing her. The lock is thus doubly fetishized, and doubly identified as lack. For her beauty—insofar as it is symbolized by her phallic lock—is not only represented as a form of masculinity, but this obscuring of sexual difference is replicated in the narrative sequence by which the masculinized/ emasculating woman is "refeminized" in terms that assure her complicity with a phallocentric norm. The Baron's appropriation of the lock, in other words, is imaged not as the appropriation of something of Belinda's, but as the reappropriation, or reclaiming, of something that already belongs to him.[15] Whether the lock is "enclosed" by the Baron's weapon, or whether, in that same proprietary gesture, Belinda as "glitt'ring Forfex" is voyeuristically "spread," a masculine subjectivity always activates Pope's verbs.

This textual economy perfectly suits what Vickers calls a code of beauty in which the fetishized body is the norm, in which the fear of castration triggered by the fact of sexual difference is allayed by the dismemberment of women.[16] A certain identity is asserted between the glitter of a ravishing exterior and the naked female body it conceals. For whether arrayed or disarrayed (which is what Belinda is both literally and metaphorically at the moment of the rape), Belinda is discreetly covered in the image of a man. Contained by a discourse in which, like the Hindu figure Draupadi, she is "infinitely clothed," she may be stripped and still be safely gazed upon.[17]

As in "To a Lady," the sight of woman—which is, in one sense, the emblem of her "art"—is repeatedly made the occasion in the *Rape* for her possession by a man. For only the removal of that power which is visible can confer a proper "femininity," can bestow that invisible charm, the "power" that legitimizes woman even as it excludes her from self-representation. If Martha rules, she never "shows" she rules; her sway is a negativity, an empowerment that by remaining interior to a masculine prerogative is ever doomed to cancel itself out: "Charms by accepting, by submitting sways, / Yet has her humour most, when she obeys." Like Richardson's Clarissa who, despite (if not because of) her vow that her hand and heart would never be separated, is destined at last to banish self from self, Pope's Martha and Belinda are subject to a psychic and physical fracturing that "places" them at the service of a wholeness not their own. A woman's peculiar charm in Pope resides not in her difference from the other, but rather in her difference from herself.

Pope uses Belinda and Martha as occasions for his own self-representation. Their enshrinement in his writing is, for him, proof both of his own linguistic prowess and of the self-sustaining power of his art. Women, associated with the fallen world, may, like that world, be linguistically "reformed" and thus be made to mirror man (to paraphrase my epigraph from Woolf in a fashion perhaps too literal for Pope) at twice his natural size. They may, like Martha Blount, despite their historicity, be "made over" in Pope's image of the feminine ideal. Like a fetish, the Word—by dressing woman to advantage—would redeem her.[18]

◆

It is this conventional fetishization of the female that Swift inverts in his so-called "excremental" verse, where he seems precisely to reverse the process that Freud describes. Here, instead of finding idealizations that, by masking, redress shock, we witness an unmasking and undressing that sorely test male sanity. In "The Lady's Dressing Room," shocking discovery is concretized by Swift in a nauseating version of the fetishist's dream of finding himself alone in his lover's dressing room; instead of delighting in what he finds, poor Strephon must confront the awful evidence of a shared humanity. Rather than possessing Celia through an appropriation of her parts, Strephon himself becomes possessed—indeed forever prepossessed—by the unrelenting memory of her stench. That to shit, i.e., to be human or *like men*, is identified in a woman as a horrid crime against men merely reminds one that the threat of castration is embedded in the idea of *be(com)ing like* a woman.[19] In "A Beautiful Young Nymph Going to Bed," the implications of that threat resonate in images of physical dismemberment; the removal of Corinna's parts is commensurate with the discovery of her underlying incompleteness— of the basic mutilation beneath her beauty's artifice. But whether disfigurement or defecation is the most immediate theme, what these poems have in common is their demonstration of the condition of male distress when the magic of the fetish is removed, when the accessories of the female no longer rectify her "failings" but are divested of the power to repair.

In "Cassinus and Peter," for example, we discover a series of suggestive mirrorings. Cassy is the first "Sight" that we encounter in this text (9), presumably become such by the horrid "Fact" that he has visually beheld ("These Eyes, these Eyes beheld the Fact" [98]). And, like the sight he has seen, Cassinus appears in disarray, in dishabille:

> He seem'd as just crept out of Bed;
> One greasy Stocking round his Head,
>
> . . . .
> His Breeches torn exposing wide
> A ragged Shirt, and tawny Hyde.
> Scorcht were his Shins, his Legs were bare,
> But, well embrown'd with Dirt and Hair.
>
> (11–18)

The excretory suggestions are important here. This is the first of a series of narrative anticlimaxes in the text. We learn that something is exposed by the hole in Cassy's pants *before* we are made privy to exactly what that something is. What we are invited to imagine is much worse than what we get. The narrative deflects our view to shirt, skin, shins, and legs. No decorum is breached; but the anal and fecal overtones are strong, and we are inclined to recall the yahoos' nether parts, also well embrowned with dirt and hair.

The next in Swift's series of narrative reversals involves the position of the lovesick Cassy's jordan, or chamber-pot. Standing "in Manner fitting / Between his Legs," it seems appropriately placed for urination or ejaculation; specification of its actual use, however, is subtly delayed, allowing the text temporarily to breed suggestions that finally are not substantially borne out. The series of images evoked nonetheless proves apt for a poem that is, finally, about sexual nausea. The picture of Cassy throwing up in the vessel that might otherwise receive the offerings of his autoerotic lust is a figuring of masculine sexual fantasy turned sour. Nor should we be surprised to find a suggestion of this sort in the work of a writer who so archly and insistently named Gulliver's shipmaster Master Bates and who, in a mock-panegyric on himself, described both the making of butter and the writing of lampoons in distinctly onanistic imagery.[20] Indeed, even within "Cassinus and Peter" the seminal metaphor reappears in a climatic and melodramatic moment of self-loathing on Cassy's part. Threatening to die unconfessed (unpurged) of his awful (pressing) secret, Cassy hallucinates a series of threatening, underworld encounters at a point in his text that seems to signal at once orgasm and suicide:

> I come, I come—*Medusa*, see,
> Her Serpents hiss direct at me.
> Begone; unhand me, hellish Fry;
> Avaunt—ye cannot say 'twas I.
> (85–88)

And just as in "A Panegyric on the Dean," sexual innuendo in this poem modulates into pure scatology.[21] For no sooner do we make the mental adjustment required to turn erotic pleasure into sexual disgust, than Cassy's phallic pipe (its pleasures only half enjoyed) is described in a vaguely excremental way:

> His Jordan stood in Manner fitting
> Between his Legs, to spew or spit in.
> His antient Pipe in Sable dy'd,
> And half unsmoakt, lay by his side. . . .
> (21–24)

Swift is mercilessly attentive to detail. Like Celia's "blackest of all Female Deeds" (106), the pipe is sable, black. Cassinus is surrounded by fecal matter.

His very food cannot escape the association, which the poet at once invites and disavows: "The Leavings of his last Night's Pot / On Embers plac'd, to drink it hot" (27–28).

As Cassy himself tells us, the purity of his passion is contaminated, betrayed by the carnality of its object (58). Anality is like contagion; when the loved one is mortal, desire becomes a function of the body. Why else should *he* fear punishment for *her* crime? Cassy actually imagines that knowledge of Celia's deed will bring upon *him* the retribution of Alecto and Medusa. With whip of scorpions and snaky hair, these two mythological figures quite faithfully fulfill the requirements of Freud's vengeful "phallic mother," representative at once of the "castrated" female—fantasmatically recuperated by the multiplication of penis symbols—and symbolic avenger of infantile autoerotic play and fantasy.

For Cassy, in short, the threat of castration is consequent on visual knowledge of "the Fact," of woman's body (also fantasmatically reversed by Swift as the discovery of her identity with him). Swift has robbed his young man of the power of that shield in which the body of Medusa could be viewed by Perseus, that mirror which by deflecting the sight of woman could serve at least to dissipate her threat. Through his "unmediated" vision, Cassinus confronts the horror at once of the possibility of his own dismemberment and of the soiling passion for which it threatens punishment. And this knowledge is so abhorrent, so alien to his sense of who he is, that—having entered through his eyes—it ultimately cannot be contained. Mortality, as imaged by Charon's wherry, is the "leaky" vessel of the body (83), and Celia reminds Cassinus of his own, of his essential alienation from himself.

Ultimately Cassinus must "force . . . out" (95) the secret that, like an alien presence, poisons his repose. Like poor Gulliver, he does not have indefinite control: "Now, bend thine Ear; since out it must" (99). But Celia's secret(ion) has become Cassinus's secret(ion) nonetheless. And the youth's parting injunction to his friend Peter to contain what he imparts bespeaks an acceptance of *her* shame upon himself.

Thematic discussion of this poem is not complete, however, without a conditioning analysis of the tactics of authorship by which Swift toys with, but never responsibly commits, his transgressions of decorum. Indeed, despite the text's thematic obsession with expressing the "inexpressible," neither Cassy nor his poet ever finally utters the unutterable "Shits." Instead, the anticlimactic climax of Cassy's speech is converted to an injunction not to speak ("sh––"), leaving the worst it suggests to the reader's imagination. In other words, as in his series of earlier narrative swerves from indecency, or as in the telling silence of *Cadenus and Vanessa*'s "conscious Muse," Swift at last evades in the writing of this text the gross necessity that he creates so irresistibly in the reading. Taking guilty pleasure in rubbing his readers' faces in the most unthinkable of thoughts, he still (with a certain arch, and even libertine, devotion to the literal technicalities of the law) manages to come out smelling like a rose. As Swift would say of himself in the voice of Lady Acheson—with irony, but also seriousness—he always judged "so nicely to a Hair / How far to go, and when to spare" ("Panegyric on the Dean," 115–16).

What is accomplished by this teasing narrative technique, this disingenuous strategy of approach and withdrawal? Among other things, it effects a certain characteristic multiplying of Swift's targets of attack. Sometimes these butts are mutually exclusive. Here, for example, Swift manages at once to sanction and explode the terms of the decorum by which Celia so very monstrously falls short. Indeed, the "excremental" verse in general seems to blame the female body for failing to fulfill its promise as much as it blames the promise for being empty and absurd.

The force of this contradiction has managed to generate considerable scholarly debate. Are the poems expressions of or satires on misogyny?[22] There is virtually no textual certainty. Indeed, it seems to be precisely one of Swift's tactics of authorship to have left this very question unresolved. In "Cassinus and Peter," the thematics of incontinence (in which the distinction between inside and outside Cassy starts to blur as his knowledge of Celia's crime makes him into a mirror of what he witnesses and hates so much in her) is played out too in the poem's continually deferred significance, in its critical indeterminacy, its rather self-conscious failure to function as a container, or receptacle, of "truth." Just as the Dean at once invites and mocks indecency, he at once elicits and embarrasses exegesis.[23]

◆

Let me pursue this matter of indeterminacy through the analysis of another short poem that, like "Cassinus and Peter," leads into an interpretive culde-sac. This is Swift's "Verses Wrote in a Lady's Ivory Table-Book." Like his "excremental" verse, it is about the annihilating force of incarnate woman, only the concern about male physical and rhetorical impotence occasioned by exposure to the female genitals is more graphically and directly imaged here, where textuality—in the form of a female body "literally" inscribed by a phallic "tool"—is conceived as permanently "under erasure."

The poem has been read as Swift's version of *The Rape of the Lock*, his satire on the superficial values of a fashionable society in which men foolishly seek "permanence in matter . . . rather than through it."[24] For all the material "hardness" of its ivory, the table-book—like the heart of the woman to whom it belongs (and which, along with her genitals, it is made to symbolize)—is changeable, impenetrable. In its infinite, indiscriminate receptivity to the press of phallic scrawls, it will not retain a permanent impression. Even the wise man is a fool because the creative "Issue" he delivers between its vaginal "Leaves" (1) will be superseded, blotted out, by the next fool to "Clap his . . . Nonsense in the place" (24).

The mutability of texts and women's hearts—which in their "hardness" partake of the corruption of all matter—is emblematic here of the poet's broader concern with the fate of writing in an effeminate, modern culture where, as Swift conceives it, not even satire can redeem. Pope never despairs of the power of the word in quite this way; in the fourth book of *The Dunciad* itself, history still promises vengeance on a barbarous age, and satire sustains a fainting, comic muse (39–42). Pope's very use, albeit inverted, of classical poetic form is confident. But the speaker of Swift's text is helplessly drawn into the vortex of the physical and rhetorical sterility he attacks. Even as he makes this book—this metaphorical body of a woman—speak for him, he expects in the very act to be erased. The blank page that is woman here is both the site of authorial inscription and that which threatens legibility, relentlessly asserting itself against the written word.[25] There is no fetish here, no magic by which this blankness can be subsumed, incorporated by, placed at the service of a stable authorial "masculinity." Instead, the voice of the poet in this text and the deconstitutive force that blots him out seem to be simultaneously separate and of a piece; they continually differentiate and merge. "Peruse my Leaves thro' ev'ry Part, / And think thou seest my owners Heart, / Scrawl'd o'er with Trifles thus, and quite / As hard, as sensless, and as light" (1–4); the book, speaking for Swift, attacks its female owner. "Who that had Wit would place it here / For every peeping Fop to Jear" (17–18); the book, speaking for Swift, attacks all wits, including Swift. "Whoe're expects to hold his part / In such a Book and such a Heart, / If he be Wealthy and a Fool / Is in all Points the fittest Tool" (25–28); speaking for Swift, the book, now become one with the woman it attacks, attacks itself as well as those who, like Swift, expect to survive (expect their "part[s]" to last) within its leaves.

One might, with John Irwin Fischer, dismiss the bottomlessness of Swift's writing, what Terry Castle calls the "hermeneutic nightmare" of his texts, as the mark of poetic failure.[26] One might explain it simply as the perverse malice of a mind that seeks to vex.[27] Or one might legitimately argue that this mode of writing which deconstitutes itself in the very moment of inscription is precisely the fulfillment of the metaphor by which woman is made the emblem of nonmeaning, of at once the silence and the babel of the uncreating word. As Susan Gubar has written, "The female [in Augustan satire] is despised and feared because she obliterates all distinctions, forecasts the onrushing apocalypse." A world where the "dreaded female has triumphed,"[28] is one characterized by the emasculation of culture, by the crippling of the possibility of form, by a monstrous and self-replicating textuality that has lost all connection with the authority of an originary voice, where the very practice of writing is corrupt.[29] Thus Swift's fictions become variants of Pope's, expressions of the anxiety that the latter's more veiled misogyny obscures, representations of the imagined nightmare that Pope's texts would disavow. In them we see the failure (perhaps refusal) of those repressions that enable the more elegant Popeian renderings of women.

However persuasive, though, no one of these analyses alone takes the matter of Swift's authorial tactics far enough. For it is by the Dean's very surrender to the dismantling of form, by the stubbornness of his refusal of the balanced economy of a discourse in which "propriety" is established when an authorial presence appropriates otherness as "proper" to itself, that his texts achieve their most idiosyncratic and intractable results. Even as he assails the "hardness" of language—its temporality, its materiality, its lack of contact with the purity of authorial intent—it is the very "hardness" of his own writing, the obstinacy with which it disables exegesis, relentlessly and even merrily exploiting the infinitely receding promise of a pure significance, that opens the way to his undoing of a metaphysics in which the female plays no part except as a negativity that must be summarily either mastered or absorbed. If it is the womblike tendency of written language to breed interpretation that Swift hates, it is nonetheless through his own reveling in the fecundity of texts that he asserts himself most indelibly against annihilation. If it is the falseness of decorum that enrages him, it is by the very blasting of decorums (both social and linguistic) that he aspires to outdo their treachery, mastering his disappointment by becoming its very agent, basking in the condition that he hates.

◆

Thus where Pope's linguistic prowess consists in his sense of his own power as a satirist to use language to "reform" a fallen world, Swift's resides in the bravado, even aggression, with which he authorizes the abandonment of form; he murders language with his very rage against its failing powers, avoids being condemned to silence by imposing a form of silence on himself.[30] If he despairs over the radical instability of written language, over the ease with which it can be alienated from authorial intent, it is nonetheless a positive, characterizing feature of his own work to create an undecidable confusion over the question of exactly "who is speaking" in his texts. One need only skim the literature on Swift to discover the persistence with which this question has been asked, and variously answered, by critics who have fallen into what Grant Holly and Terry Castle both would regard as a typical Swiftian hermeneutic trap.[31] But though Swift's "intent" may be, in part, to let the radical instability of his texts stand as the fulfillment of his most dreaded fantasy, the very logic by which he exploits the impurity of voice that he attacks also establishes that instability as the most compelling basis of his art. As we see perhaps most plainly in A Tale of a Tub, even as it laments the instability of writing, Swift's own writing invites its reader to keep pondering what is impossible to decipher; it makes its reader excessively exegetical by very virtue of defying exegesis.

In short, if Swift's savagely reactionary response to modern discourse reflects an aversion to an all-absorbing textuality for which woman is a central metaphor, it is also—paradoxically—the grounds for his own production of a mode of writing that ultimately embraces the ontological and epistemological premises of modern discourse more joyfully than Pope's optimistic literary conservatism ever would. The very violence of Swift's resistance to transition becomes a form of capitulation in his work. By donning the literary vestures of the modern exegete and hack and appropriating them for his own satiric uses through irony, he managed to mourn the passing of a culture in the very act of becoming a modern writer. Pope's more accommodating response to "modernism" would attempt to conquer the encroachments of the new by exploiting them in the interest of reestablishing old forms. But Swift's productions refuse those immunizing accommodations that protect established systems against subversion.[32] By destabilizing the very signifying structures he exploits (or by insistently exposing their inherent instability), he destroys all grounds for the reconstitution—through the infusion of new strains—of the balanced economy of classical forms. Thus, both more and less than Pope, he surrenders to the conditions of the new.

◆

What I have been suggesting is that although Swift continues to use certain standard physical metaphors to disparage modern writing, even repeating debased and debasing images of the female apparently casually in his texts, there is also a sense in which such repetitions in his work are always somewhat less than casual. Let me conclude my discussion of this aspect of Swift by examining a passage from the Dean's most sophisticated prose attack on the late seventeenth-century tradition of the new, *A Tale of a Tub*. Here, in his famous "Digression in Praise of Digressions," Swift satirizes the modern craze for novelty by means of several anatomical images. Applauding the moderns' ingenious fabrication of subject matter in what seemed to them a shrinking universe of literary possibility, the narrator of the *Tale* becomes entangled in the contradictions of his own efforts to defend modern writing against the charge of sterility. As proof of the fertile wit of the moderns, he offers

> that highly celebrated Talent among the *Modern* Wits, of deducing Similitudes, Allusions, and Applications, very Surprizing, Agreeable, and Apposite, from the *Pudenda* of either Sex, together with *their proper Uses*. And truly, having observed how little Invention bears any Vogue, besides what is derived into these *Channels*, I have sometimes had a Thought, That the happy Genius of our Age and Country, was prophetically held forth by that ancient typical Description of the *Indian* Pygmies; *whose Stature did not exceed above two Foot; Sed quorum pudenda crassa, & ad talos usque pertingentia*. Now, I have been very curious to inspect the late Productions, wherein the Beauties of this kind have most prominently appeared. And altho' this *Vein* hath bled so freely, and all Endeavours have been used in the Power of Human Breath, to dilate, extend, and keep it open: Like the Scythians, *Who had a Custom, and an Instrument, to blow up the Privities of their Mares, that they might yield the more Milk*; Yet I am

under an Apprehension, it is near growing dry, and past all Recovery; And that either some new *Fonde* of Wit should, if possible, be provided, or else that we must e'en be content with Repetition here, as well as upon all other Occasions.[33]

Swift uses a number of physical images to communicate his distaste for modern discourse and its ultimately sterile predilections. And as Sherman Hawkins and Paul Korshin both observe, these figures are in their most manifest incarnations masculine.[34] Indeed, the modern practice of deducing similitudes and allusions from the pudenda of *either sex* seems significantly reduced in the figure the narrator chooses to typify the genius of his age, since—as Korshin notes—its source in Ctesias refers only to the "pudenda" of pigmy males.[35] Such a privileging of the male anatomy is consistent with Swift's imagistic practice in other texts, where the "seed" of visions and enthusiasms is conceived as literally, corporeally, seminal; as Hawkins notes, in the narrative economy of Swift's texts, ejaculation, eructation, defecation, and phlebotomy are virtually overlapping images of the excessive and wasteful production of modern wit.[36]

But, as we have also seen, Swift typically designs his own allusions to breed beyond the limits of their literal referents, so that—as Hawkins suggests—we never trust our own imaginations.[37] The reader has been primed to expect allusions to the pudenda of either sex, and those expectations do not go wholly unfulfilled. The female genitals may be imaged less conspicuously than the male, but their role here is not less significant. Like the ivory table-book, they are the animating source of male effusions, the catalyst for zealous but ineffectual modern schemes. Modern genius may be figured phallically, but "little [of its] Invention," as the tale-teller notes, "bears any Vogue, besides what is derived into . . . *Channels*" that are figured graphically as either anal or vaginal. As in the allegory of the *Tale*, where three ladies who fancy shoulder knots determine the wills of three young men to dismember patriarchal authority, female desire is here conceived as the incurably fickle arbiter of modern taste, of a culture grossly and unregenerately feminized.[38] In Swift's sexual economy, the modern writer's lack of mastery over even his own script is manifest precisely in the dismemberment of discourse.

Swift's corrupted coital image of modern fertility, furthermore, concludes in blood. Granted, what we have here finally is a sign not of generation but of death—an inversion of hymeneal imagery; but the inversion itself constitutes an indirect allusion to the very set of terms it would subvert. The kind of writing that Swift's narrator is defending demonstrates a preoccupation with the features and functions of human pudenda as disproportionate as the genitals of the Indian pigmies, whose penises are so large in relation to their total bodies that they hang almost all the way to the ground. The oversized male organ becomes the very type and emblem of wit "derived into" modern channels of this sort. Still, by the time the narrator has described this kind of writing as a freely bleeding vein, it is hardly plain which gender Swift has—or wishes us to have—in mind. When read in its entirety, the loosely constructed final sentence of Swift's passage technically yields the grosteque image of a phlebotomy likened to the artificially induced lactation of Scythian mares.[39] But Swift's convoluted syntax also encourages partial exegesis, prompting the reader to associate the freely bleeding vein of modern wit with female "privates" before the mammary connection is specified.

In a dizzying replication of the kind of aborted discourse it would expose, Swift's text perversely initiates a series of false starts, transiently conjuring images of virgin blood and menstruation only to retreat from its own suggestions by obscurely fusing them with a proliferating glut of other anatomical images. Hence arise those "false surmises" that invariably send Swift's commentators and editors "searching on the wrong track."[40] What is striking in this instance is that it is the female reproductive anatomy that figures as the route of misdirection, as that "false track" or "channel" that Swift at once lures his readers into and evades. Indeed, it is precisely woman's body that constitutes the final destination toward which the tale-teller's distended and overexcited narrative inclines, but which relentlessly eludes its mastery. In the *Rape*, the consummation of the Baron's desire for Belinda's lock, however transient it may be dramatically, is a formal precondition of the stability and the closure of Pope's text. Similarly, the internal structural logic of "To a Lady" depends on the masterful enclosing of woman's desire within man's. But in Swift's *Tale*, the moment of discursive mastery over woman never comes, the obsessively phallic text of modern genius inscribing the interminably unfulfilled desire of a masculine subjectivity dominated by the inappropriability of its object. It is in this sense, ultimately, that woman becomes the very emblem of the principle of excess in this treatise on the sterility of excess—becomes that breeding-place of insignificance that at once stands beyond the reach of narrative and, like a disembodied presence, pervades the very fabric of Swift's text. Indeed, it is a facet of the paradoxical logic of Swift's authorial strategy that the failure of modern writing to contain or to recuperate its own excess should manifest itself precisely in the castration or mutilation of discourse. In the absence of the fetishistic magic of the word, the body of the female is unredeemed. The source of an existential anxiety at once empowering and crippling, woman is the dark but inexhaustible "fonde" of an inspiration that can give rise only to the effusions of wasteful substance, to intellectual abortions, and to death.[41]

◆

On one level, Swift's aversion to modern discourse seems quite clear. While rejecting the doctrine of infinite matter, the moderns cling desperately to the idea of their own infinite virtuosity. Indeed, by exalting the modern ego as a source of infinitely self-generated meaning, they pervert the very idea of infinitude. Like the bleeding of a vein that cures the disease but kills the patient (as one projector using a bellows in Lagado does a dog), [42] the modern craze for novelty is ingenious but self-defeating, a perversion as wasteful and involuted as the onanistic spilling of male seed. Like menstruation, it is the sign of an unfertilized possibility that, if allowed to run too freely for too long without producing any vital progeny, will eventually incur the risk of running dry, "past all recovery."[43]

On another level, however, Swift's use of this cluster of debased and debasing images is complicated by the radical irony of the technique by which he shifts his own relation to the writing for which they serve as analogies. Swift's very use of the Indian pigmies to typify modern wit betrays this vexed relation to his objects of attack if one considers the ferocity and flagrancy of his own preoccupation with pudenda and their functions in *his* work. But there is another, yet more powerful, irony: Swift's attack on exhaustion here—in the perverse parasitism of its parodic strategy—finds infinitude in a panegyric on exhaustion; in a final twist of the central paradox of the text, the doctrine of exhaustion in the panegyric defeats itself even as its proponent exemplifies the sterility of all efforts to delimit, or escape from, repetition.

It is possible to read the conundrum unfolding here as a rather straight-forward example of the way Swift damns the modern voice through mock-defense; the modern who refuses to see the fruitful relation between repetition and infinity is doomed not only to infinite self-repetition, but to a repetition of the very tradition from which he declares his difference. But it creates the conditions, too, for an interminably expensive irony—an irony that serves as a demonstration by negative illumination of the merits of mental balance and by positive example of the absolute freedom negation can achieve from the inherent restraints of positivity. This kind of irony is quite the opposite of Pope's, which—as we have seen in several instances—delicately hangs two sides of a contradiction in a balance quite integral to itself and consistent with the terms of the ideological system it enshrines. Here, by contrast, the principle of permanence is constituted precisely at the point of instability, difference. Continuity and discontinuity originate at the same discursive moment.

Pope dissociated himself quite adamantly from such extravagant plays of wit in a letter he wrote to Swift in 1734. He is nearing the completion of *The Moral Essays* and reaffirms his commitment to the "Truth":

I am almost at the end of my Morals, as I've been, long ago, of my Wit; my system is a short one, and my circle narrow. Imagination has no limits, and that is a sphere in which you may move onto eternity; but where one is confined to Truth . . . we soon find the shortness of our Tether. Indeed by the help of a metaphysical chain of idæas, one may extend the circulation, go round and round for ever, without making any progress beyond the point to which Providence has pinn'd us: But this does not satisfy me, who would rather say a little to no purpose, than a great deal.[44]

Swift would seem to have paved the way for this assertion when, in the "Digression in Praise of Digressions," he made his narrator lament the consequences that would ensure "if Men were put upon making Books, with the fatal Confinement of delivering nothing beyond what is to the Purpose."[45] But there is a sense too in which, for Swift, such confinement would constitute a fatality indeed. For it is precisely this excess, this "beyond what is to the Purpose," that Swift exploits most powerfully as the condition of possibility in his work.

In a sense, through his own radical pursuit of negativity, Swift is more faithful to the principle of difference than even the mad modern whose discourse he seeks to dismantle though parody. Indeed, what he exposes in the *Tale* is precisely the contradiction at the heart of a modern ontology that, on the one hand, authorized singularity (difference) as the basis of selfhood and, on the other, predicated authorial presence on the reduction of difference—on the appropriation or exclusion of everything not proper to (but different from) the self. Thus the *Tale* is at once a way of bringing modern discourse to a radical consciousness of itself by making it betray its own internal difference from itself and a way of indirectly authorizing a discourse not enclosed by the ideological limits of modern thought. Indeed, it is the infinitely dynamic repetition of the contradictions that modern discourse normally sought to stabilize rhetorically (and thus obscure) that Swift exploits as the central poetic fulcrum of his texts.

Granted, there is something inherently equivocal in the process whereby Swift's own authorial voice merges (almost, but never fully, to the point of positive embrace) with the multivocal babel of infinite possibility that the tale-teller at once both replicates and resists. By the same token, there is something equivocal about the process by which Swift's texts exploit certain static sexual metaphors while assuming a dynamic relation to their terms. For even as the cluster of physical metaphors by which women, the body, and modern discourse are reciprocally disparaged remains intact within his texts, Swift nonetheless engages in a curious swirling around the stasis of those fixed analogies, so that the double negativity of his relation to modern writing and to the figures it assumes takes on the aspect of an affirmative attitude. Like his flirting with indecency in a poem like "Cassinus and Peter," Swift's toying with the rethinking of sexual metaphor is a possibility built into the infinitely negative pressure of his thought that he never quite responsibly embraced.

Thus Swift's texts manage to remain both open and closed at the same time. Inescapably confined within the metaphorical structures of the thought they would destroy, always walking the tightrope between transgression and complicity, between a departure from and a return to metaphysics, they are simultaneously occasions for the affirmation and cancellation of cultural codes.

◆

It is in this sense that Swift, thought he never fully departs from the terms of gender established by the standard metaphors of Western thought, delivers us before the opening out of unspoken possibilities more fully than Pope, whose textual concentricity is so systematically, so hermetically (en)closed. Indeed, Swift's whole discursive project seems intent on reminding us (as, despite its claims to "Tory gloom," Pope's generally happier verse really does not) of the inescapable, internal "otherness" of "selves." The fictions of Defoe and Richardson—indeed, of Pope—sought at once to accommodate and conceal the contradiction between singularity and its limits, and they did so in part by fetishistically metaphorizing woman, denying her "otherness" except as an object within (except as a "part" of) the economy of a masculine desire. Swift had difficulty with this conceptual strategy, not because he wanted to salvage the legitimacy of the female subject, but because he rejected the idea of the modern subject altogether.

Indeed, to Swift, no self was ever fully "proper" to itself. Rather, all identity as he conceived it was perforce, in part, extrinsically derived. Gulliver's experience is perhaps the essential parable of this belief. In him we discover the antithesis of the modern hero as embodied in the fiction of Defoe. For if Crusoe is the modern subject, not bogged down in circumstance but self-reliant and constantly on the move, becoming/defining himself by his ability to gain control over the savage in himself and in his world, Gulliver is the ultimately mastered and ultimately alienated soul. When Gulliver cuts himself off from society, he becomes not—as Crusoe does— an agent of self-creation but a slave both to his body and his own subjective needs. Indeed, by contrast to Crusoe, who gains identity through a sense of dominance over the world outside and antagonistic to the self, Gulliver finally is a mirror of the very otherness he most zealously resists; behaving like a Houyhnhnm, he epitomizes yahooistic pride. For Gulliver, the creation of an identity is an infinitely regressive enterprise; he is constantly absorbed by that which he defines himself as not.

So Cadenus, in his overzealous desire to be a "proper" wit, becomes the very image of a fool; so the narrator of Swift's *Tale* ratifies tradition in his effort to resist it; so Swift, in his resistance to modern discourse in that same narrative, becomes a modern; so Celia is the mirror of Cassinus. Satire, insofar as it is built on the assertion of difference, is the most self-effacing and self-implicating of rhetorical strategies; even as it distances what we hate, it reflects the very image of ourselves. "Satyr," wrote Swift in the preface to *The Battle of the Books*, "is a sort of *Glass*, wherein Beholders do generally discover every body's Face but their Own."[46]

◆

Ultimately, Swift's inclination to expose rather than hide his rhetorical dilemmas does not absolve him from nostalgia for the redemptive powers of a literary language in which Pope, as we have seen, sustained some faith. It was he, after all, who wrote, "In Pope I cannot read a Line, / But with a Sigh, I wish it mine" ("Verses on the Death of Dr. Swift," 47–48). What Swift's deconstitutive discourse does suggest is a certain crippling self-consciousness about accepting the "natural" limits of difference presupposed and sanctioned by modern thought. In this sense, of course, Swift is more nostalgic yet than Pope, whose integration of classical forms and bourgeois values was an empowering and forward-looking enterprise. The demise of traditional values never vexed Pope with the same intensity as it did Swift because the younger poet was able to imagine the forms of that tradition revitalized by the spirit of bourgeois myth. Clarissa's echo of Sarpedon in *The Rape of the Lock*, in which female self-sacrifice to patriarchal marriage is evoked as both a parody *and* an eighteenth-century analogue to the moral heroism of a culture now defunct, is a prime example of how Pope made this fusion (a kind of reinfusion) work. To Swift, however, the terms of modern culture seemed no more viable, and certainly less attractive, than the rhetoric and mythology of a former epic age. It was not that his yearning for a vital meta-discourse was not as powerful as Pope's, but that he never suffered it to be gratified by a compromise with the terms of modern myth.

Notes

1. This is Jacques Derrida's general project in *Of Grammatology*, trans. Gayatri Chakravorty Spivak (Baltimore: The Johns Hopkins University Press, 1974).

2. Michel Foucault, *The History of Sexuality*, vol. 1, *An Introduction*, trans. Robert Hurley (New York: Random House, 1978), 47–48

3. Foucault, 154. The designation of the fetish as such is a commonplace in psychoanalytic writing. See, for example, Robert C. Bak's reference to it as "the basic perversion" in "The Phallic Woman: The Ubiquitous Fantasy in Perversions," in *The Psychoanalytic Study of the Child*, vol. 23 (New York: International Universities Press, 1968), 17.

4. "Inside *Julie*'s Closet,"*The Romanic Review* 69, no. 4 (November 1978): 296–306.

5. Kamuf, "Inside *Julie*'s Closet," 303–4.

6. "Diana Described," 277.

7. Karl Marx, *Capital*, vol. 1, trans. Ben Fowkes (New York: Vintage Books, 1977), 165.

8. Sigmund Freud, "Fetishism," in *The Standard Edition of the Complete Psychological Works*, trans. James Strachey (London: Hogarth Press, 1961), 21:152–57.

The assumption in almost all the classic psychoanalytic literature on fetishism is that the subject is male, the object female. See, for example, Phyllis Greenacre's "Perversions: General Considerations Regarding Their Genetic and Dynamic Background," in *The Psychoanalytic Study of the Child*, 23: 47–62. See also examples cited by Mary Daly in *Gyn/Ecology* (Boston: Beacon Press, 1978), 232–36. I use quotation marks around "full sexual identity" in my text to suggest the unintended irony (also remarked by Daly, 234) in the standard restriction of fetishism to nongenital parts of the body. The restriction at once assumes that the "full sexual identity" of the female is concentrated in the genitals and denies the possibility that the female genitals may be fetishized.

9. Kamuf, 300–302.

10. Freud, "Fetishism," 154.

11. Freud analyzes the myth in "Medusa's Head" (1922), in *The Standard Edition of the Complete Psychological Works*, 18: 273–74.

12. The "multiplication of penis symbols," writes Freud, "signifies castration" ("Medusa's Head," 273).

13. In Marxian theory, the process of commodity fetishism is not only the process by which human relations are reduced to relations between things, but also the process by which commodities take on social characteristics, the products of human labor appearing as "autonomous figures endowed with a life of their own, and entering into relation both with one another and the human race" (*Capital*, 1:165).

14. Leo Braudy, "Penetration and Impenetrability in *Clarissa*," in *New Approaches to Eighteenth-Century Literature*, ed. Phillip Harth (New York: Columbia University Press, 1974), 177.

15. See Mary Daly's concept of the "*pre*possession" of the female, *Gyn/Ecology*, 232.

16. Nancy J. Vickers, "Diana Described: Scattered Woman and Scattered Rhyme," *Critical Inquiry* 8, no. 2 (Winter 1981): 273.

17. See Gayatri Chakravorty Spivak's foreword to the story "Draupadi" by Mahasveta Devi in *Critical Inquiry* 8, no. 2 (Winter 1981): 388.

18. For an interesting analysis of Pope's identification with women as an aspect of his neoclassical concept of the redemptive role of art, see Erica Mann [Jong], "The Theme of Women in the Poetry of Pope: A Study of Conventional Sexual Language and Imagery in *Eloise to Abelard*" (M.A. thesis, Columbia University, 1965). Jong's work is especially suggestive in the context of a discussion of fetishistic displacement, since its implication is that by covering woman's "lack," Pope aesthetically obviates his own. For further discussion, see my Epilogue.

19. According to Freud, the child associates feces and phallus in the anal period, the stool and the penis being linked as parts of the body and associated in both body area and form. If Norman O. Brown is right (as I think he is) that Swift anticipated many of what later became "Freudian" commonplaces, then Swift's preoccupation with female excretion in his verse is suggestive not only in its thematizing of issues of men's identification and differentiation from women, but also specifically for its imaging of defecation as a fantasied form of castration itself (see Brown's "The Excremental Vision," in *Life Against Death: The Psychoanalytical Meaning of History* [Middletown, Conn.: Wesleyan University Press, 1959], ch. 13).

20. I am thinking of "A Panegyrick on the D—N, in the Person of a Lady in the North," esp. lines 166–96.

21. Within 10 lines of Swift's description, in the "Panegyric," of his rather constipated mode of composition, the Dean has erected two temples in honor of the "gentle Goddess Cloacine" (205ff.).

22. For the range of readings that participate in and, in their several ways, define the terms of this debate, see Murry, 432–48; Quintana, 171 and 356; Herbert Davis, "A Modest Defence of 'The Lady's Dressing Room,' " in *Restoration and Eighteenth-Century Literature: Essays in Honor of Alan Dugald McKillop* (Chicago: University of Chicago Press, 1963), 39–48, and "Swift's View of Poetry" in *Fair Liberty Was All His Cry*, ed. A. Norman Jeffares (New York: St. Martin's Press, 1967), 62–97; Irvin Ehrenpreis, *The Personality of Jonathan Swift* (London: Methuen, 1958), ch.2; John M. Aden, "Corinna and the Sterner Muse of Swift," *English Language Notes* 4 (1966): 23–31, and "Those Gaudy Tulips: Swift's 'Unprintables,' " in *Quick Springs of Sense: Studies in the Eighteenth Century*, ed. Larry S. Champion (Athens, Ga.: University of Georgia Press, 1974), 15–32; Thomas B. Gilmore, "The Comedy of Swift's Scatological Poems," *PMLA* 91 (January 1976): 33–43; Donald Greene, "On Swift's Scatolog-

ical Poems,'" *Sewanee Review* 75, no. 4 (1967): 672–89; Jae Num Lee, *Swift and Scatological Satire* (Albuquerque: University of New Mexico Press, 1971); Brown, "The Excremental Vision"; and Gubar, "The Female Monster." For a summary of some of the arguments and another voice in the discussion, see Jaffe, 102–20.

23. Two articles which demonstrate such indeterminacy in other works by Swift are Terry J. Castle's "Why the Houyhnhnms Don't Write: Swift, Satire and the Fear of the Text," *Essays in Literature* 7 (Spring 1980): 31–44, reprinted in this volume, pp. 57–71, and Grant Holly's "Travel and Translation: Textuality in *Gulliver's Travels*," *Criticism* 21 (1979): 134–52.

24. John Irwin Fischer, *On Swift's Poetry* (Gainesville: University Presses of Florida, 1978), 58. On the same subject, see Schakel, 53–56.

25. For a related discussion of woman as text, see Gubar's " 'The Blank Page' and the Issues of Female Creativity," 243–47.

26. Fischer, 59; Castle, 35.

27. In a famous letter to Pope of 29 September 1725, Swift wrote, "the chief end I propose to my self in all my labors is to vex the world rather than divert it" (*The Correspondence of Jonathan Swift*, ed. Harold Williams [Oxford: The Clarendon Press, 1963–65], 2: 325).

28. Gubar, "The Female Monster," 392.

29. Castle, 35–36.

30. The resounding and sometimes cacophonous silence of Swift's texts may be compared to the silence of Gerard Genette's "ideologically transgressive" text as defined, in contradistinction to the "ideologically complicitous" text, by Nancy Miller in her adaptation of Genette's concept of textual mutism in "Emphasis Added: Plots and Plausibilities in Women's Fiction," *PMLA* 96, no. 1 (January 1981): 38.

31. Castle, 33; Holly, 134–35.

32. See Barthes's concept of the "inoculation," in *Mythologies*, 150–51.

33. *Tale*, 147.

34. Sherman Hawkins, "Swift's Physical Imagery" (Ph.D. diss., Princeton University, 1960), 412–24; Paul J. Korshin, *Typologies in England, 1650–1820* (Princeton; Princeton University Press, 1982), 295–303.

35. Korshin, 296. Korshin gives the Latin text of Photius's abridgement of Ctesias. The Latin of Photius is translated by J. W. McCrindle as follows: "He writes that in the middle of India are found the swarthy men called Pygmies. . . . They are very diminutive, the tallest of them being but two cubits in height, while the majority are only one and a half. They let their hair grow very long—down to their knees, and even lower. . . . Their privates are thick, and so large [the Latin says "longam"] that they depend even to their ancles" (*Ancient India as Described by Ktesias the Knidian* [London, 1882], 15–16).

36. Hawkins, 414–16.

37. Hawkins, 413.

38. *Tale*, 74ff. It is doubtful, moreover, that Swift would have expected all his readers to be familiar with the context of his quotation from Photius. Apart from that knowledge, the passage generates multiple, sexually ambiguous images. The reference to the lactation of mares later in the passage even makes Swift's pigmy image seem peculiarly like his description of the female yahoos in *Gulliver's Travels* some years later: "The females were not so large as the males; they had long lank hair on their heads, and only a sort of down on the rest of their bodies, except about the anus, and pudenda. Their dugs hung between their fore-feet, and often reached almost to the ground as they walked" (*Gulliver's Travels and Other Writings*, ed. Louis A. Landa [Boston: Houghton Mifflin, 1960], 181). Some of Swift's choices in amending Photius's Latin, moreover, seem striking ; e.g., the omission of the adjective "longam" and the substitution of the noun "pudenda" for "veretrum" in Photius. The first four editions of the *Tale* read "Genitals," the change to "Pudenda" in the fifth edition—which included the author's corrections—being one of what Guthkelch and Nichol Smith have called "a few minor alterations which do not extend beyond a word or a phrase and never affect the sense

of a passage" (*Tale*, xxii). But even if this change does not profoundly alter the significance of Swift's text, the use of "pudenda," with its traditionally stronger association with the female genitals, serves at the very least to enhance the ambiguity of the passage and the subliminal role of the female body in it. Swift made another interesting change of this nature in section 9 of the *Tale*, where he omitted "Cunnus" and capitalized the initial "t" in "teterrima" in the following passage:

> The very same Principle that influences a *Bully* to break the Windows of a Whore, who has jilted him, naturally stirs up a Great Prince to raise mighty Armies, and dream of nothing but Sieges, Battles, and Victories.
> —Cunnus teterrima belli Causa—
> Causa—
>
> (Tale, 165).

"Cunnus"—literally "the female genitals" and, by metonymy, "a whore"—is obscured as the offensive source of choler or inflammation in the male, indeed becomes quite palpably the "absent *Female*" who, just a few lines prior to Swift's Latin quotation, is cited as responsible for the vapors of a certain famous prince. (The Latin passage is from Horace, *Sat.* 1, 3, 107: "the lecherous life / Was lived long before fair Helen—the revolting cause / Of many a war was the crotch" (*The Satires and Epistles of Horace*, trans. Smith Palmer Bovie [Chicago: University of Chicago Press, 1959]). *Pudenda* is from the verb *pudere*, to be ashamed of; *veretrum* is from the verb *vere*, to revere or to fear.

39. "The Scythians blind their slaves, a practice in some way connected with the milk which they prepare for drinking in the following way: they insert a tube made of bone and shaped like a flute into the mare's genitals, and blow; and while one blows, another milks. According to them, the object of this is to inflate the mare's veins with air and so cause the udder to be forced down" (Herodotus, *The Histories*, trans. Aubrey de Sélincourt [Baltimore: Penguin Books, 1954], 242).

40. *Tale*, liv.

41. See also section 10 of the *Tale*, where obscure texts are compared to Night, "Mother of Things," and their commentators to midwives who deliver them "of Meanings, that the Authors themselves, perhaps, never conceived, and yet may very justly be allowed the Lawful Parents of them" (186) and section 12, where the narrator refers to writing that goes "*too long*" or "*too short*" as the cause of intellectual abortion (206).

42. *Gulliver's Travels*, 147.

43. An investigation of accepted views of sexual anatomy as described in popular midwifery books of the age reveals the commonplace belief that the female reproductive anatomy was modelled on the male's, indeed that, like the male genitals, the female genitals contained "Spermatick Vessels." For example, according to Nicholas Culpepper—whose *Directory of Midwives* of 1651 remained immensely popular throughout the eighteenth century—the spermatic vessels in both sexes are divided into the "Vasa Praeparantia" or preparing vessels, and the "Vasa Deferentia" or carrying vessels (Culpepper, *A Directory for Midwives or, A Guide for Women* [London: Cole, 1660], 5, 13, 30–31). Thus, whatever pun on the Latin noun "vas" Swift might have been exploiting in his image of the freely bleeding "vein" would have been equally applicable to the male and female anatomy. . . .

44. *Correspondence*, 3:445.

45. *Tale* 144.

46. *Tale*, 215. For an illuminating study of satire in terms of narrative inheritance, which offers both an excellent general discussion of the nature of satire and interesting readings of some of the same texts I cover here (but from another angle), see Michael Seidel, *Satiric Inheritance, Rabelais to Sterne* (Princeton: Princeton University Press, 1979), esp. ch. 1. and 6–8. See also pp. 75–90 in this volume.

Antipastoral Vision and Antipastoral Reality

CAROLE FABRICANT

Swift's anti-and mock-pastoral depictions constitute an important aspect of his continuing political and social commentary on contemporary society. His mock-pastoral verses are offered as one of the very few types of expression appropriate for an age witnessing the systematic debasement of the land. On the broadest level, the one especially evident in his writings before 1715, they form part of Swift's devastating critique of capitalism as the latter was beginning to develop and expand throughout the first half of the eighteenth century.[1] A number of his *Examiner* essays were written to expose both the corruptions and the disruptions produced by the new economic order—more specifically, to decry the consequences of the fact that "*Power*, which, according to the old Maxim, was used to follow *Land*, is now gone over to *Money*."[2] The formerly exalted status and importance of the land is progressively being destroyed by a society that now computes all value according to "the Rise and Fall of Stocks" (6): a society that is being ruled to an ever greater extent by a nouveau riche class composed of city bankers, stock jobbers, and the like, who are referred to variously as "assuming Upstarts" (151), "*Retailers of Fraud*" (137), and "Engrossers of Money" (169).

Several of the *Examiner* essays exploit the contrast between the stable, firmly fixed Tories ("in or out of Favour, you see no Alteration [in them]" [PW, 3:126]), and the "*high-flying Whigs*" (109), men "under the Dominion of the *Moon*, [who] are for perpetual *Changes,* and perpetual *Revolutions*" (147)—between a landed aristocracy rooted in the *terra firma* and a class of assorted "retailers," unpropertied beings associated with "transient or imaginary" things (119). In both prose and poetry, Swift demonstrates that the disappearance of paradise is the result, not only of Man's Fall, but also of the present age's economic folly, which is systematically converting the British soil into a wasteland: "The bold Encroachers on the Deep, / Gain by Degrees huge Tracts of Land, / 'Till Neptune with a Gen'ral Sweep / Turns all again to barren Strand" (*The Run upon the Bankers,* 1–4). A new breed of financial speculators—"new dextrous Men [introduced] into Business and Credit" (PW, 3:6)—has either directly appropriated or indirectly contami-

From Fabricant, Carole. *Swift's Landscape.* The Johns Hopkins University Press, Baltimore/London, 1983, pp. 72–82.

nated the physical terrain, with the result that the eminently solid and firmly rooted features of Eden become transformed into ambiguous shapes of watery illusion:

> Thus the deluded Bankrupt raves,
> Puts all upon a desp'rate Bett,
> Then plunges in the *Southern* Waves,
> Dipt over head and Ears—in Debt.
>
> So, by a Calenture misled,
> The Mariner with Rapture sees
> On the smooth Ocean's azure Bed
> Enamell'd Fields, and verdant Trees;
>
> With eager Hast he longs to rove
> In that fantastick Scene, and thinks
> It must be some enchanted Grove,
> And in he leaps, and down he sinks.
> (*The Bubble*, 21–32)

When the land is not dissolving into water, it is threatening to vanish in thin air. Swift in this regard exploits the symbolic and imagistic as well as the literal significance of the South Sea Bubble, the eighteenth century's first stock market crash.[3] He uses the myth of Icarus to emblematize the destructiveness of the new capitalist society and the folly of those who are seduced by it:

> On *Paper* Wings he takes his Flight,
> With *Wax* the *Father* bound them fast,
> The *Wax* is melted by the Height,
> And down the towring Boy is cast.
> (*The Bubble*, 37–40)

But the contrast Swift drew here between a landed gentry and a class of urban capitalists, between a stability associated with the soil and a mutability evidenced by fluctuating stocks, gradually gave way to his far more significant and original insight that, in the final analysis, the traditional distinction between country and city no longer applied. This is particularly relevant to our concerns here since, as Frank Kermode observes, "The first condition of pastoral poetry is that there should be a sharp difference between two ways of life, the rustic and the urban."[4] It may well be that originally (as Cowper put it) "God made the country and man made the town," but Swift's writings continually underscore the fact that in eighteenth-century England and Ireland, the country along with the town was being created (or, to be more precise, uncreated and then re-created) by man: with man's money, in man's own image, for man's self-interest. Swift's recurring historical perceptions serve to confirm Raymond Williams's analysis of the perversely reciprocal relationship between country and city in eighteenth-century England: "The exploitation of man and of nature, which takes place in the country, is realized and concentrated in the city. But also, the profits of other kinds of exploitation—the accumulating wealth of the merchant, the lawyer, the court favorite—come to penetrate the country. . . ."⁵ Swift repeatedly points to the way in which capitalist values have infiltrated country and town alike, destroying all alternative modes of existence. In his *Pastoral Dialogue between Richmond-Lodge and Marble-Hill,* he has the latter house foresee its own doom as a result of capitalism's encroachments:

> Some *South Sea* Broker from the City,
> Will purchase me, the more's the Pity,
> Lay all my fine Plantations waste,
> To fit them to his Vulgar Taste.
>
> (67–70)

The mansion's reminder that "My Groves, my Ecchoes, and my Birds, / Have taught [Pope] his poetick Words" (91–92) suggests that its own destruction will mean the demise of poetry (more specifically, pastoral poetry) as well. In light of the changes being perpetrated on the land by the inexorable movement from town to country, pastoral existence—and the literary genre associated with it—can be no more than an anachronistic fiction. It must necessarily give way to the contemporary reality of a land ravaged by the acquisitive and avaricious spirit characteristic of the new economy, typified by "The neighbouring Country Squires always watching like Crows for a Carcase over every Estate that was likely to be sold."⁶

In *Part of the Seventh Epistle of the First Book of Horace, Imitated,* Swift portrays himself attempting to establish a country seat in Ireland but becoming mired in degrading financial transactions that create an inevitable alienation from the soil and its former values:

> Now all the Doctor's Money's spent,
> His Tenants wrong him in his Rent;
> The Farmers, spightfully combin'd,
> Force him to take his Tythes in kind;
> And *Parvisol* discounts Arrears,
> By Bills for Taxes and Repairs.
>
> (107–12)

We see here the very antithesis of the traditional, idyllic (and, on another level, falsely romanticized) pastoral realm, marked by harmonious and joyful coexistence and functioning through a primitive but equitable economy—

what Poggioli calls "home economics in the literal sense of the term." As he explains it, "Pastoral economy seems to realize the contained self-sufficiency that is the ideal of the tribe, of the clan, of the family. . . . Money, credit, and debt have no place in an economy of this kind."[7] The economic relationships described by Swift therefore presuppose, by their very nature, an antipastoral mode of existence. Swift's rural world grotesquely mirrors the city's depersonalization of human relationships—its conversion of human values into monetary ones. Hence the conventional contrast between town and country (or garden and city) loses its meaning, for literary myth and political ideology alike. The Dean's "Seat" is a place of turmoil and class warfare, not cosmic harmony, and therefore fails to reflect even the faintest traces of Eden.

If Swift's country world reflects the influence of the city, his depictions of the city often mirror or parody aspects of country life. It is not coincidental that Swift sets his mock-eclogue, *A Description of the Morning,* and his mock-georgic, *A Description of a City Shower,* in decidedly urban environs, heralding in the former "Ruddy Morns Approach" (2) in the midst of London's squalor and substituting the turnkey's "Flock" (15) for the shepherd's. Moreover, in *A Beautiful Young Nymph Going to Bed,* Swift creates what is on at least one level a mock-pastoral set in the midst of eighteenth-century London's "inner city," describing the life of a most cosmopolitan "Nymph" who plies her trade in Drury Lane and then returns to her shabby fourth-story "Bow'r" (8).

Swift's later writings, growing directly out of his daily experiences while living in Ireland, remind us in other ways too of the perverse bonds existing between country and city. In his tract *Maxims Controlled in Ireland,* for example, Swift notes the "concourse to this beggarly city [Dublin]" of "miserable farmers and cottagers," who in their desperate attempt to escape the poverty of the countryside only wind up bringing it with them into their new urban surroundings (PW, 12:135). Likewise, in one of his sermons he decries the great masses of "Strolers [and Vagabonds] from the Country" who daily swarm into Dublin, intensifying its level of poverty (PW, 9:207). Finally one cannot distinguish between city and country, because they have become basically interchangeable embodiments of Ireland's wretchedness and general deterioration. The very terms "country" and "town" are often deliberately coupled, as in the allusion to "the vast Number of ragged and naked Children in Town and Country" (201). In the world described by Swift, it makes little difference whether one walks through the streets of Dublin or along isolated provincial roads; the sights one sees are fated to prove equally pitiable and repellent in either case.

As the preceding examples hint at, Swift's general critique of capitalism and its adverse effects upon the British landscape increasingly gave way to a more specific (as well as more impassioned) exposure of the ills inflicted on the Irish soil by England's colonialist policies. In his Irish tracts of the 1720s and 1730s, Swift dramatizes the consequences arising from England's treatment of Ireland precisely by showing how this treatment has changed a potential green world—"a Country so favoured by Nature as ours, both in Fruitfulness of Soil, and Temperature of Climate" (PW, 12:10)—into a devastated garden where, as he sarcastically described it in one tract, "the People live with Comfort on Potatoes and Bonnyclabber" (178). Swift's ironical description of Ireland in 1731 as a would-be arcadia boasting of blackberry bushes and potato beds (176) reminds us that the debased landscape inhabited by Sheelah and Dermot is not a satiric fiction so much as a comically heightened historical fact.

A similarly debased landscape reflecting historical fact appears in Swift's cynical exposures of the paradisal myths about the New World. Decrying "the strong delusion in [the Irish] by false allurement from America," he invokes the authority of Sir William Penn, who "did assure me that his Country wanted the shelter of mountains, which left it open to the Northern winds from Hudson's bay and the frozen sea, which destroyed all Plantations of Trees, and was even pernicious to all common vegetables" (PW, 12:78, 76). Pennsylvania, as described here, invites comparison with Holyhead's "bleaky shore," where "nature hardly seems alive" (*Holyhead. Sept. 25. 1727,* 29, 32) and with the wilds of Cavan, where "Air ripens not, nor Earth produces" (*To Quilca,* 6). Swift goes on to emphasize the connections between England's colonialist policies and the creation of an antipastoral landscape, between Edenic myths and political propaganda. If the Irish who remain in their homeland "live worse than *English* Beggars," without even "a House so convenient as an *English* Hog-sty, to receive them" (PW, 12:11, 10), then their fellow countrymen who leave for America in order to escape "their present insupportable Condition at home" find themselves in even more pitiable straits, compelled to perform the role of those "barbarous People, whom the *Romans* placed in their Armies, for no other Service than to blunt their Enemies Swords, and afterwards to fill up Trenches with their dead Bodies" (60). Within the context of eighteenth-century English colonialism, paradisal vision can at any moment turn into genocidal nightmare.

The niggardly and unproductive soil depicted throughout Swift's mock-pastoral verses, symbolic of postlapsarian starvation rather than Edenic feasting, was likewise a historical and topographical reality, however much this reality may have taken on certain heightened dimensions through the workings of Swift's consciousness. Again and again, Swift directed his reader's or correspondent's attention to the terrible famine engulfing the land, insisting upon the urgency of the situation. In a letter to Pope he notes that in Ireland "there have been three terrible years dearth of corn, and every place strowed with beggars," and concludes that "the kingdom is absolutely undone" (C, 3:341). Responding to the writer of a paper recommending as a solution to Ireland's food problem the importation of corn from plantations abroad, Swift counters with his own combined proposal and warning:

If you will propose a general Contribution, in supporting the Poor in *Potatoes* and *Butter-milk*, till the new Corn comes in, perhaps you may succeed better; because the Thing, at least, is possible: And, I think, if our Brethren in *England* would contribute, upon this Emergency, out of the Million they gain from us every Year, they would do a Piece of *Justice* as well as *Charity*. In the mean Time, go and preach to your own Tenants, to fall to the Plough as fast as they can; and prevail with your neighbouring 'Squires to do the same with theirs; or else die with the Guilt of having driven away half the Inhabitants, and starving the rest.

(PW, 12:22)

In a similar vein, the sermon *Causes of the Wretched Condition of Ireland* calls attention to the tragic fact that "our Tradesmen and Shop-keepers, who deal in Home-Goods, are left in a starving Condition" (PW, 9:201). The scarcity of food is attributable not to any inherent limitations of Ireland's terrain— which, as Swift stresses, "is capable of producing all Things necessary, and most Things convenient for Life, sufficient for the Support of four Times the Number of its Inhabitants" (199)—but rather, to man-made policies, particularly as they emanate directly from England's colonialist rule. The "Injured Lady," a personification of Ireland, laments that "we must send all our Goods to his [England's] Market just in their Naturals; the Milk immediately from the Cow without making it into Cheese or Butter; the Corn in the Ear; the Grass as it is mowed; the Wool as it cometh from the Sheeps Back; and bring the Fruit upon the Branch, that he might not be obliged to eat it after our filthy Hands" (6). Whereas in Marvell's garden world, "Luscious Clusters of the Vine" along with "The Nectaren, and curious Peach" eagerly submit themselves to man's mouth and reach (*The Garden*, 35–38),[8] in Swift's mock-arcadia, Ireland's milk, corn, and "Fruit upon the Branch" are in effect snatched away by England's grasping fingers, to vanish into England's ravenous maw. It is hardly surprising, therefore, that Swift's portrait of an English statesman is of

> A bloated M[iniste]r in all his Geer,
> With shameless Visage, and perfidious Leer,
> Two Rows of Teeth arm each devouring Jaw;
> And, *Ostrich*-like, his all-digesting Maw.
> (*To Mr. Gay*, 33–36)

This imagistic depiction occurs elsewhere. In *A Panegyric on the Reverend D——n S——t*, Swift notes that men like Swift and Delany "So long *unbishoprick'd* lie by" (147) while others (those sent or supported by England) "Devour the *Church's tiddest Bits*" (150), and in a contemporary tract he declares that "at this day there is hardly any reminder left of Dean and chapter lands in Ireland; that delicious morsel swallowed so greedily in England under the fanatick Usurpations" (PW, 12:185–86).

This latter reference to the "long wars between the Invaders and the Natives," during which "the Conquerors always seized what lands they could with little ceremony" (183), reminds us that underlying Swift's characterization of Ireland's plight was a long history of violence and oppression: a history rooted in the extremes of famine and devouring. Testimony to this fact appears in Spenser's *A View of the Present State of Ireland*, where Irenius's prediction of the outcome of the wars against the Desmonds (at which time the English would finally wipe out the "stout and obstinate rebels") paints a grisly picture of widespread starvation and the bestiality resulting from it:

> The end I assure me will be very short and much sooner than can be in so great a trouble (as it seemeth) hoped for. Although there should none of them fall by the sword, nor be slain by the soldier, yet thus being kept from manurance, and their cattle from running abroad by this hard restraint, they would quickly consume themselves and devour one another. The proof whereof I saw sufficiently ensampled in those late wars in Munster, for notwithstanding that the same was a most rich and plentiful country, full of corn and cattle, that you would have thought they would have been able to stand long, yet ere one year and a half they were brought to such wretchedness, as that any stony heart would have rued the same. Out of every corner of the woods and glens they came creeping forth upon their hands, for their legs could not bear them. They looked anatomies of death, they spake like ghosts crying out of their graves, they did eat of the dead carrions, happy were they could find them, yea and one another soon after in so much as the very carcasses they spared not to scrape out of their graves, and if they found a plot of water cress or shamrocks, there they flocked as to a feast for the time, yet not able long to continue therewithal, that in short space there were none almost left and a most populous and plentiful country suddenly left void of man or beast.[9]

On whatever level and to whatever extent this aspect of Irish history affected Swift's consciousness, the fact is that he repeatedly described the inherently exploitative relationship between England and Ireland, not only through references to starvation, but also through images suggesting perverted acts of eating, including cannibalism. In a poem attacking Lord Allen, for example, he asserts: "Hence he draws his daily Food, / From his Tenants vital Blood" (*Traulus, The Second Part*, 41–42). This image is reinforced elsewhere by the poetic persona representing St. Patrick, who grimly foresees in Ireland's future a time

> When Shells and Leather shall for Money pass,
> Nor thy oppressing Lords afford thee Brass.

> But all turn Leasers to that Mongril Breed,
> Who from thee sprung, yet on thy Vitals feed.
> (*Verses occasioned by the sudden drying up of*
> *St. Patrick's Well*, 93–96)

The "Mongril Breed" in this passage refers, as a contemporary footnote to the poem indicates, to "The Absentees, who spend the Income of their *Irish* Estates, Places and Pensions in *England.*"[10]

The hellish situation in which children feed themselves by devouring their mother's substance leads, with its own kind of satanic logic, to the situation described in *A Modest Proposal,* where parents must have recourse to eating their offspring: "A Child will make two Dishes at an Entertainment for Friends; and when the Family dines alone, the fore or hind Quarter will make a reasonable Dish; and seasoned with a little Pepper or Salt, will be very good Boiled on the fourth Day, especially in *Winter*" (PW, 12:112). We can, if we wish, discuss the preceding as a satiric fiction, but only if we simultaneously acknowledge its inextricable links to what was, for Swift, economic and political reality. Despite its gruesomely bizarre and surreal character, the image of a child served up as a family's evening repast it, viewed in the broadest perspective, only a slightly fictionalized extension of "those *voluntary Abortions*, and that horrid Practice of *Women murdering their Bastard Children* . . . sacrificing the *poor innocent Babes*, I doubt, more to avoid the Expence than the Shame" (110); it is no more monstrous or incredible than "that vast Number of poor People, who are Aged, Diseased, or Maimed" and who are "every Day *dying*, and *rotting*, by *Cold* and *Famine*, and *Filth*, and *Vermin*, as fast as can be reasonably expected" (114). Contrary to Oliver W. Ferguson's contention that Swift's wrath in this work was directed "not against England, or callous economists, or visionary projectors, but against Ireland herself,"[11] *A Modest Proposal* is governed by a central metaphor that for Swift automatically conveyed a definite political and eco-nomic—specifically anticolonialist—statement: one that assumed the exis-tence of close ties between Ireland's self-destructive tendencies and England's brutal oppressions. As Swift saw it, England's lawless seizure of Ireland's earthly produce, like Eve's willful plunder of the forbidden fruit, generated a fundamentally anarchic and predatory world founded upon a grotesque Chain of Devouring. It is a world in which parents consume children while themselves becoming the repast of others: "I grant this Food will be somewhat dear, and therefore very *proper for Landlords*; who, as they have already de-voured most of the Parents, seem to have the best Title to the Children" (112). Ultimately even the Irish landlords, along with their less fortunate countrymen, become potential food for another: ". . . this Kind of Commod-ity will not bear Exportation; the Flesh being of too tender a Consistence, to admit a long Continuance in Salt; *although, perhaps, I could name a Country, which would be glad to eat up our whole Nation without it*" (117).

Swift incorporated into his writings numerous variations on this basic vision of a cannibalistic world. His versified parable *Desire and Possession* concludes with a portrayal of Possession expiring beneath the heavy weight of his load:

> The Raven, Vulture, Owl, and Kite,
> At once upon his Carcase light;
> And strip his Hyde, and pick his Bones,
> Regardless of his dying Groans.
>
> (55–58)

On Poetry: A Rapsody presents a similar vision of bestiality:

> *Hobbes* clearly proves that ev'ry Creature
> Lives in a State of War by Nature.
> The Greater for the Smallest watch,
> But meddle seldom with their Match.
> A Whale of moderate Size will draw
> A Shole of Herrings down his Maw.
> A Fox with Geese his Belly crams;
> A Wolf destroys a thousand Lambs.
>
> (319–26)

The sea, like the land, functions on this principle of mutual devouring. Hence we have

> Anarchy at Sea,
> Where Fishes on each other prey;
> Where ev'ry Trout can make as high Rants
> O'er his Inferiors as our Tyrants.
>
> (*On a Printer's being sent to*
> *Newgate, by*—, 3–6)

The explicitly topical subject matter of this verse (the imprisonment of Swift's printer, George Faulkner, for a piece he had published) underscores the links between Swift's images of a predatory world and his perception of the contemporary political situation. As the counterpart to the piscatory world where the trout tyrannizes over his inferiors, though he "hide[s] his coward Snout in Mud" at the appearance of "a lordly Pike" (10, 8), we are elsewhere shown a human world rooted in *"universal Oppression,"* where *"Slaves* have a natural Disposition to be *Tyrants;* [so] that when my *Betters* give me a Kick, I am apt to revenge it with six upon my *Footman"*—even though, it is strongly implied, the real culprits are his superiors, in the figure of such as *"their Worships* the Landlords" (PW, 9:21). However much Swift's recurring images of a fiercely, often grotesquely predatory world may have grown out of satiric convention, and however much they may express a deep-seated Christian pessimism concerning man's fallen nature, on some (I would argue, profound) level they were shaped, imbued with a special cogency and force, by Swift's perception of the historical plight of Ireland, as a country being systematically devoured by her "superiors."

The *Verses occasioned by the sudden drying up of St. Patrick's Well* provides particularly powerful testimony to the historical basis of Swift's imagery. The curse incurred by man as a consequence of his sin finds its Swiftian counterpart in this poem, where the wrathful God-like speaker (St. Patrick) describes the sufferings he has imposed on the "spurious and degenerate Line" (101) now inhabiting Ireland—fallen creatures who "in Vice and Slavery are drown'd" (38). This piece vividly underscores Swift's simultaneous rage against the English for their oppressions and his disgust with the Irish for their cowardly acquiescence in their own enslavement. The poem presents Swift's version of the destruction of paradise—of the ". . . happy Island, *Pallas* call'd her own, / When haughty *Britain* was a Land Unknown" (9–10)—through a kind of serpentine infiltration by "base Invaders" (22) who gradually conquered the land:

> *Britain*, by thee we fell, ungrateful Isle!
> Not by thy Valour, but superior Guile:
> *Britain*, with Shame confess, this Land of mine
> First taught thee human Knowledge and divine;
> My Prelates and my Students, sent from hence,
> Made your Sons Converts both to God and Sense:
> Not like the Pastors of thy rav'nous Breed,
> Who come to fleece the Flocks, and not to feed.
> (25–32)

Swift metaphorically exploits here the historical fact that the well located near Trinity College suddenly dried up in 1729:

> Where is the sacred Well, that bore my Name?
> Fled to the Fountain back, from whence it came!
> Fair Freedom's Emblem once, which smoothly flows,
> And Blessings equally on all bestows.
> (65–68)

It is characteristic of Swift that he should have chosen to poetically commemorate the demise of the well rather than celebrate the renewal of its waters several years later, as did other contemporary versifiers. By placing the disappearance of St. Patrick's Well in a specifically political context, Swift emphasizes the fact that, for him, contemporary reenactments of Man's Fall were directly linked to England's colonialist policies and Ireland's colonized mentality.

Confronted with the spread of "Vice" and "Slavery" in his adopted isle (38), St. Patrick heralds forth a postlapsarian world where predatory creatures devour one another while the threat of barrenness and starvation looms ever larger:

> I sent the Magpye from the *British* Soil,
> With restless Beak thy blooming Fruit to spoil,
>
> . . . .
>
> See, where the new-devouring Vermin runs,
> Sent in my Anger from the Land of *Huns*;
> With harpy Claws it undermines the Ground,
> And sudden spreads a numerous Offspring round;
> Th' amphibious Tyrant, with his rav'nous Band,
> Drains all thy Lakes of Fish, of Fruits thy Land.
> (45–46, 59–64)

As the verse makes clear, Ireland does not lack harvests, but these are "waste[d] in Luxury" by those who systematically transport the country's "Treasures" to England, "yon rav'nous Isle" (97–98). This blatantly inequitable system has given rise to the spectre of famine amidst plenty, so that St. Patrick foresees the rapidly approaching time "When, for the Use of no *Hibernian* born, / Shall rise one Blade of Grass, one Ear of Corn" (91–92). The last line cited echoes almost verbatim part of Gulliver's description of Balnibarbi's countryside, where, "except in some very few Places," he "could not discover one Ear of Corn, or Blade of Grass" (PW, 11:175), once again directing our attention to the fact that even Swift's fictionalized depictions of landscape never stray very far afield from the actual landscape amidst which he spent his life.

Notes

1. The period following the Glorious Revolution witnessed radical innovations in Great Britain's economic system: the development of the Bank of England, the growth of the stock market, the accumulation of a huge national debt, and a growing dependency upon paper currency and credit, accompanied by a pervasive spirit of financial speculation symbolized for the Tory opposition by the South Sea Bubble. For background on the new economic situation, especially in terms of its effect upon writers of the period, see Isaac Kramnick, *Bolingbroke and His Circle: The Politics of Nostalgia in the Age of Walpole* (Cambridge, Mass.: Harvard University Press, 1968), 39–55, 188–235. For a more technical and detailed analysis, see Peter Dickson, *The Financial Revolution in England: A Study in the Development of Public Credit, 1688–1756* (New York: St. Martin's Press, 1967).

2. *The Prose Works of Jonathan Swift*, ed. Herbert Davis, 14 vols. (Oxford: Basil Backwell, 1939–68), 3:5. Further references to this edition will be given parenthetically in the text.

3. For a relevant discussion of the South Sea Bubble, see Howard Erskine-Hill, "Pope and the Financial Revolution," in *Writers and Their Background: Alexander Pope*, ed. Peter

Dixon (Athens: Ohio University Press, 1972), 200–229. See also John Carswell, *The South Sea Bubble* (Stanford, Calif.: Stanford University Press, 1960).

4. *English Pastoral Poetry from the Beginnings to Marvell*, ed. Frank Kermode (1952; New York: Norton, 1972), 228.

5. Williams, *The Country and the City* (New York: Oxford University Press, 1973), 48.

6. *The Correspondence of Jonathan Swift*, ed. Harold Williams, 5 vols. (Oxford: Clarendon Press, 1963–65), 4:319. Further reference to this edition will be given parenthetically in the text.

7. Renato Poggioli, *The Oaten Flute: Essays on Pastoral Poetry and the Pastoral Ideal* (Cambridge, Mass.: Harvard University Press, 1975), 4–5.

8. References to Marvell's poetry are to *The Poems and Letters of Andrew Marvell*, ed. H. M. Margoliouth, rev. by Pierre Legouis with E. E. Duncan-Jones (Oxford: Clarendon Press, 1971), vol. 1.

9. Spenser, *A View of the Present State of Ireland*, ed. W. L. Renwick (Oxford: Clarendon Press, 1970), 104. Various periods of famine in Ireland were accompanied by historically recorded instances of cannibalism, including child eating. Moreover, popular tradition (as well as Swift himself) linked the Irish with the Scythians, particularly in their alleged common practice of drinking human blood and engaging in other cannibalistic activities. These historical and legendary accounts undoubtedly informed and helped shape Swift's depictions. See C. J. Rawson, "A Reading of *A Modest Proposal*," in *Augustan Worlds: Essays in Honour of A. R. Humphreys*, ed. J. C. Hilson, M. M. B. Jones, and J. R. Watson (Leicester: Leicester University Press, 1978), pp. 37–38, 48; nn. 20, 22.

10. *The Poems of Jonathan Swift*, ed. Harold Williams, 3 vols. (Oxford: The Clarendon Press, 1958), 3:794.

11. Ferguson, *Jonathan Swift and Ireland* (Urbana: University of Illinois Press, 1962), 175.

"Suppose Me Dead": Swift's *Verses on the Death of Dr. Swift*

RONALD PAULSON

Two of Swift's most powerful symbols are the political hack writer who claims that he is unrewarded and shabby, his body battered with poxes and beatings, and the writer whose work is unread, unpreserved, and simply absent—whose own identity and existence themselves are therefore in jeopardy. The first returns in the poems about Swift himself and his close friends; the second in the *Verses on the Death of Dr. Swift* (written in the 1730s), where both body and writings deteriorate to the point of demise, in a grim recapitulation of the passage in *A Tale of a Tub* about the fruitless posting of modern writings: "The Originals were posted fresh upon all Gates and Corners of Streets; but returning in a very few Hours to take a Review, they were all torn down, and fresh ones in their Places: I enquired after them among Readers and Booksellers, but I enquired in vain, the *Memorial of them was lost among Men, their Place was no more to be found*."[1] In the *Verses* this becomes the scene following Swift's death:

> Some country squire to Lintot goes,
> Inquires for Swift in verse and prose:
> Says Lintot, "I have heard the name:
> He died a year ago." The same.
> He searcheth all his shop in vain;
> "Sir, you may find them in Duck Lane:
> I sent them with a load of books,
> Last Monday to the pastry-cook's.
> To fancy they could live a year!
> I find you're but a stranger here."
> (11. 253–62)

Each writer ends in the transient contingency of jakes, pie pans, and lanterns, and is (in the words of the *Verses*) "no more . . . missed, / Than if he never did exist." The emotional power of the two passages, from the beginning and the end of Swift's career, is equal: in the second he can be seen, having

From *Breaking and Remaking: Aesthetic Practice in England, 1700–1820*, by Ronald Paulson. © 1989 by Rutgers, The State University. Reprinted by permission of Rutgers University Press.

broken all the other idols, to have iconoclasted himself. He has proved himself the iconoclast (as every Protestant knew, only the most susceptible idolator) who first destroys external idols and at last the internal idol that may have served as point of origin for all the others.

Thus if goddesses and shepherdesses are reduced in Swift's poems (*A Description of the Morning*) to shabby London housemaids and prostitutes, and the Irish Parliament degenerates into a madhouse (as in *The Legion Club*), the figure of the poet himself, Swift or the Patriot-Drapier-Dean-Hero of the Irish, is treated no better.

This battered Swift has already emerged by 1713, even before the fall of the Tory Ministry, as the protagonist of his poems.[2] He is characterized as Dean (i.e., not-Bishop), penurious, deaf, vertiginous, aging, and all too conscious of his deteriorating body.

In his imitation of Horace's *Epistle* 1.7. (1713) Horace, Augustus, and Maecenas become Swift, Queen Anne, and Harley in a relationship quite different from the one Pope would employ in the 1730s: they are all, and Swift in particular, sad reminders, shabby modern equivalents of the great Augustans. He is "Poor Swift, with all his Losses vext," "Above a Thousand Pounds in debt," "so dirty, pale and thin," "so lean," and when he is asked why "neglect your Self"? he replies, not for "Pelf," but also not for selfless service, but simply because he has been put in such a difficult position—to be a dean in Dublin—that his only recourse is to concoct a classical parallel like this one, add rhyme, and make a poem out of his experience.

The message of the poem is that he has been taken from his true station in life, lifted up, in effect "idolized" by the Tory ministers, and thereby loaded with troubles, as if for Harley's "Jest" (anticipating the God of his *Day of Judgement* who says, "Go, go, you're bit"): "And since you now have done your worst, / Pray leave me where you found me first," that is, back on the streets of London.

This poor lean ragged figure recalls not only the Grub Street Hack of the *Tale of a Tub* but the poet-goose of *The Progress of Poetry* (1720), whose "cackle" is poetry, and whose poetic cackle is elicited only when he is hungry. As in *The Dunciad*, poetry, poverty, and hunger are directly related, but Swift leaves us not only with a comic paradox but with no alternative. There is no suggestion in these poems of the way another, supposedly better kind of poetry is to be made, or what it would consist of. Neither the ancient classical building nor the reasonably well-fed goose will serve. Poetry can be made now only from the representation of this paradox or from the imitation of the "lank and spare" goose's cackle. It is obvious that, being a satirist, Swift chooses the latter: to ridicule and destroy the cackle, but thereby incorporate it into his own mode. And the ruinous modern poem is directly represented, or reflected or echoed, in the poems by Swift's own "lank and spare" deteriorating body. What is produced with this "cackle"? In the case of the hungry goose,

> Her Body light, she tries her Wings,
> And scorns the Ground, and upward springs,
> While all the Parish, as she flies,
> Hear Sounds harmonious from the Skies.

And in the case of the hungry poet, "He singing flies, and flying sings, / While from below all Grub-street sings." In the same mode as Pope's later description of a poor poet in the *Epistle to Dr. Arbuthnot* ("high in Drury Lane / Lull'd by soft Zephyrs thro' the broken Pane"), these lines happen to be the most "beautiful" Swift allows himself in his poetry. "Beauty" equals poetic, flatulent verse.

In terms of the iconoclastic trope we can try another phrasing: Swift breaks and empties the idol and then climbs (or suspects that he climbs) inside the shell himself, becoming what he has broken now that it is clearly broken and no longer idolizable. What is, of course, unsettling about this proceeding is that Swift is made to fit precisely the image of the decrepit house or lantern in which the religious enthusiasts of the *Tale of a Tub* tried to manifest their spirit. In this as in other ways, Swift becomes his own Grub Street Hack. Ultimately, in the *Verses on the Death of Dr. Swift*, he is dead, his writings forgotten. But he cannot let go, and so (although Pope objected and made cuts in the London edition) he retains the memory of himself, as the form taken by his spiritual part. His deteriorating body is theoretically justified (as in the related case of his friend Stella's) by the elevation of mind or spirit, whatever transcends body; but this body comes very close to the sooty lantern of the enthusiast or the airy castle of the poetaster.

When all is broken and destroyed, what remains?—the spirit, though we are aware only of the materiality of the ruins in which it supposedly dwells, or from which it has been released, or around which hovers memory, or its external version, fame. Swift's *Verses* can be taken as a model for the transition from idol to tomb, from an iconoclastic to a memorial mode.

How is the tomb of the *Verses* arrived at? As one result of the famous Swiftean "irony," entombment is the logical outcome of a procedure of praise-by-blame (Stella is mean, cranky, and self-centered) which is the other half of blame-by-praise, the more viable, satiric half of irony. In other words, Swift's ironic and self-destructive blame (i.e., praise) embodies the imaginative truth of his ironic writing. Swift's works, his body, and his being are blamed (said to be self-centered, trivial, and ephemeral) and, in the end, are rendered nonexistent—by his friends, his enemies, himself. And by making them so, Swift acknowledges in the most poignant way that he is himself part of all that he has iconoclasted as Other—the world of the Grub Street Hack, which is in fact *our* world. But at the same time, as a function of praise-by-blame, he is actually all the opposites—heroic, immortal, and the only true friend, as at the end of the *Verses* he allows the "impartial voice" (to some readers' confusion) to verbalize.

The purpose of the "impartial" Man at the Rose is to refill the empty space of Swift's identity created by the almost infinite division of opinions that eventuated in dissolution. Likewise all those different interpretations of the *Verses* (one of the cruces of eighteenth-century scholarship) imply a dispersal of meaning and of self which is Swift's primary intention within the text itself. The self-ironies and contradictions pointed out by Barry Slepian and others are only a part of this dispersal, in the form of safety nets.[3] When Swift gives us once again the official story of "Dean Swift" which he has been rewriting in poems ever since 1713–14, he must put it in the mouth of one ironically referred to as "quite indifferent in the cause," who tends, for example, to praise Swift's originality in lines lifted from Denham and his public role in Ireland (genuinely heroic) in the jingling verses beginning "Fair Liberty was all his cry" which Swift himself would have spurned.

The point is that Swift's body is completely gone, and his works as well. What survives is his memory—what I once referred to as a platonic spirit but now see is more accurately summed up in Pope's terms "fame" or "character" or opinion.[4] The ironies thus demonstrate the instability of Swift's identity even here, or perhaps of all places here, in his "fame." In terms of the iconoclastic structure, his body has been destroyed and remade into something utilizable—an "example," no more real than the original, and indeed capable (as Swift's profoundest irony shows) of itself being turned into as much of an idol as the old broken one (or as the one Pope was laboriously constructing for himself on the other side of the Irish Sea out of his correspondence and portraits).

Swift's point, as throughout his poetic oeuvre, is that one must destroy in order to make: kill the body, destroy the (his own) literary works in order to replace the potential, the dead idol himself (to others, to himself, *like* Walpole an idol) with the living reality. This means replacing the abused, that is, worshiped icon with the unabused image of his memory expressed in the words of an "impartial voice." So the broken idol is replaced by memory and the poem becomes the funerary monument that expresses or represents the lifeless body as well as the memorial apotheosis. Or (as in Hogarth's procedure in *The Analysis of Beauty*, plate 1, fig. 3), you take Dean Swift, literally kill him, that is, empty the sign of its conventional iconographical meaning, and put it, now dead and empty, in another, an existential context—and so give it a different, and therefore a reenlivening meaning.

Notes

1. *The Prose Works of Jonathan Swift*, ed. Herbert Davis, 14 vols. (Oxford: Basil Blackwell, 1939–68), 9:34–35.

2. Both Swift and Pope write obsessively about themselves. There are many sources

for their foregrounding of the poet—Milton comes to mind, and in a way perhaps closer to Swift, the Earl of Rochester. But I suspect that the passage in *A Tale of a Tub* in which the Grub Street Hack, in the voice of Dryden, describes his sad career and sadder physical state, though parodic, nevertheless set the terms for Swift's own obsessive use of himself as the central symbol of his poetry. Revisions of Dryden—the Dryden of the late poetry, especially the confessional part of *The Hind and the Panther*, and the prose surrounding the *Aeneis*—permeate the text of the *Tale*.

3.　For a list of the interpretations of the *Verses*, see David Vieth, "The Mystery of Personal Identity: Swift's Verses on His Own Death," in *The Author in His Work*, ed. Louis L. Martz and Aubrey Williams (New Haven, 1978), 245–62; Barry Slepian's essay was "The Ironic Intention of Swift's Verses on His Own Death," *Review of English Studies*, n.s. 14 (1963): 249–56.

4.　See Paulson, "Swift, Stella, and Permanence," *ELH* 27 (1960): 298–314, and in *The Fictions of Satire* (Baltimore, 1967), 189–210.

NONFICTIONAL PROSE

◆

How Possibly to Improve Discourse: The Proposal for an Academy

ANN CLINE KELLY

I hope, when this Treatise of mine shall be translated into Foreign Languages . . . that the worthy Members of the several *Academies* abroad, especially those of *France* and *Italy*, will favorably accept these humble Offers, for the Advancement of Universal Knowledge.

—A Tale of a Tub[1]

In the mid- to late seventeenth century, the desirability of creating an academy to regulate language was generally accepted in England and on the Continent, where the French and Italians had already founded institutions for this purpose. Although Swift's *Proposal for Correcting, Improving, and Ascertaining the English Tongue* ostensibly argues that England ought to remedy her linguistic problems through the work of an academy, the document is confusing because it subverts its own arguments. The text and the subtext of the *Proposal* are at odds, reflecting Swift's own dualism, his wish on one hand for some regulation of language and on the other, his suspicion of instant (as opposed to ancient) institutions, such as an academy. Contradicting each other also are the national and personal goals that Swift simultaneously promotes in the essay.

THE TEXT

Swift's *Proposal*, contrived as an epistle to Robert Harley, articulates the need for a national institution to guide the development of the English language and to provide some method of standardizing it. Because Swift believed that preserving the common forms of language was necessary for national well-being, he urged the immediate implementation of plans for an academy. He refutes the idea that "*all such Thoughts must be deferred to a Time of Peace*: a Topick which some have carried so far, that they would not have us by any Means think of preserving our Civil or Religious Constitution, because we

From *Swift and the English Language*, 89–103, by Ann Cline Kelly. Copyright © 1988 by the University of Pennsylvania Press.

247

are engaged in a War abroad" (*Proposal, PW* 4:5–6). Here Swift argues against statements such as Dryden's that England not form an academy until "the quiet of the Nation . . . be secur'd; and a mutuall trust, betwixt Prince and people be renew'd."[2] Dryden may be echoing the sentiments of the French, who delayed the establishment of their academy until "publick tranquility" and "good order" were restored after civil and foreign wars, because they felt that the polishing of their language should occur only in a time of peace.[3] In contrast, Swift believed that the "Civil [and] Religious Constitution" and the English language expressing it must be maintained regardless of political distractions.

To this end, Swift advocated a bipartisan, nonpolitical academy, whose members would be selected without regard to "Quality, Party, or Profession" (14). To Stella he explains, "tis no Politicks, but a harmless Proposall about the Improvement of the Engl. Tongue."[4] At one point he wrote Archbishop William King that he and Harley had chosen ten men from each party for the academy.[5] And as a conciliatory gesture toward the Whigs, Swift praises Steele in the *Proposal*, later telling him "that, in the only thing I ever published with my name, I took care to celebrate you as much as I could" (*C* 1:360). Although he would be insulted at the comparison, Swift linguistic society is similar in concept to the Royal Society, which admitted people without consideration of religion, occupation, or nationality, so that, as Sprat says, "there will no one particular of them overweigh the other, or make the *Oracle* onely speak their *private* sence."[6] On one level, then, Swift saw the academy as a national conversation, ideally drawing all parts of society together in a matter of mutual concern. On another level Swift used the *Proposal* to establish certain partisan and personal stances that were at odds with the theme of unity.

The major functions of the academy, suggested by the *Proposal*'s title page, would be "Correcting, Improving, and Ascertaining the English Tongue." These actions are necessary, Swift implies, because increased publication had solidified into print many "Alterations" that violated traditional norms. In the past, when the world was less book-ridden, linguistic change was impeded by such works as the Bible and the *Book of Common Prayer*, which, because they were "perpetually read in Churches, have proved a Kind of Standard for Language, especially to the common People" (*Proposal, PW*, 4:15). In recent times, however, all sorts of solecisms were committed to print, a complaint of a purported letter-writer in one of Swift's *Tatlers*: "I would engage to furnish you with a Catalogue of English Books published within the Compass of seven Years past, which at first hand would cost you an hundred Pounds; wherein you shall not be able to find ten Lines together of common Grammar, or common Sense . . . Without some timely Remedy," he warns, the English language "will suffer more by the false Refinements of Twenty years past, than it hath been improved in the foregoing Hundred" (*Tatler, PW* 2:174; italics omitted). Swift expresses this opinion directly in the *Proposal* when he wonders whether "from that great Rebellion to this present Time [1712] . . . the Corruptions in our Language have not, at least, equalled the Refinements of it" (*PW* 4:9–10). Swift seemed to believe that an academy could slow the rate of linguistic corruption.

Abbreviation and faddish invention are two types of linguistic disintegration an academy might control. These are the vices allegorized in Peter's elaboration of his coat and Jack's shredding of his. In either case, the traditional fabric of language is rent by Moderns, like the men about town, "who had Credit enough to give Rise to some new Word, and propagate it in most Conversations; although it had neither Humour nor Significancy"; or poets, who create "Manglings and Abbreviations" to "fit [words] to the Measure of their Verses"; or university men, who "reckon all their Errors for Accomplishments, borrow the newest Set of Phrases; and if they take a Pen in their Hands, all the odd Words they have picked up in a Coffee-House, or a Gaming-ordinary, are produced as Flowers of Style; and the Orthography refined to the utmost" (10–12). Swift cites the self-styled elite as the source of linguistic pollution that will inevitably filter into that wellspring of pure language, the speech of common people.

In *An Argument against Abolishing Christianity*, Swift humorously describes the process by which fads emanate from the top of the social hierarchy, gradually trickle down, and ultimately disappear. The speaker here notes that abolishing Christianity may be a waste of time because no one believes in it anymore anyway: "I freely own, that all Appearances are against me. The System of the Gospel, after the Fate of other Systems is generally antiquated and exploded; and the Mass or Body of the common People, among whom it seems to have had its latest Credit, are now grown as much ashamed of it as their Betters: Opinions, like Fashions, always descending from those of Quality to the Middle Sort, and thence to the Vulgar, where at length they are dropt and vanish" (*PW* 2:27). In this apocalyptic vision, all common forms of religion are forgotten, but the common people are the last to let go of their memories.

To prevent the meaning of words from being "dropt" and vanishing, Swift, sharing the position of many early eighteenth-century linguists,[7] sees etymology as the anchor that stabilizes the language by linking it to its historical origins. He opposed concocted or mangled words because their etymologies were either illegitimate or indiscernible. The Modern, though, has so little concern for traditional forms that he sees the shortening of words as a step toward "Perfection," the ultimate "Perfection" being total annihilation: Swift satirizes this idea when he ironically declares, "Some Words are hitherto but fairly split; and therefore only in their Way to Perfection; as *Incog.* [for incognito] and *Plenipo's* [for plenipotentiaries]: But in a short Time, it is to be hoped, they will be further docked to *Inc* and *Plen*" (*Tatler, PW* 2:175–76). Equally vitiating are linguistic inventions, "such as *Banter, Bamboozle, Country Put, and Kidney* . . . some of which are now struggling for the Vogue, and others are in Possession of it" (176). Here is the process of verbal "uncreating" that horrified both Swift and Pope.

Swift, like most people, did not necessarily expect people to talk strictly in standard English, but he believed that those who committed their thoughts to print had an obligation to reinforce traditional linguistic practice. Swift was not alone in fearing that casual alterations of the language in conversation might find their way into print. John Dryden, for instance, worried that "so long as some affect to Speak them, there will not want others who will have the boldness to Write them."[8] When the *Tale*-teller fails to impress people with his conversation, he is inspired to set himself up as an author because print gives a certain cachet to his utterances, "For, I have remarked many a *towardly Word*, to be wholly neglected or despised in *Discourse*, which hath passed very smoothly, with some Consideration and Esteem, after its Preferment and Sanction in *Print*" (*PW* 1:134–35). Swift realized that an army of Moderns with easy access to printing presses could shortly destroy the language. Swift did not seem to agree with Samuel Johnson's opinion, expressed later in the century, that linguistic variations "will always be observed to grow fewer, and less different, as books are multiplied."[9] If all authors are as energetic and as entropic as the *Tale*-teller, who even as he is finishing one collection of fragments threatens an immediate sequel, the language is in great peril.

Although Swift is not explicit in the *Proposal*, one presumes Modern manglings and abbreviations are some of the "many Words that deserve to be utterly thrown out . . . [and] to be corrected." In addition, he notes that "the Grammar-part" of the language is "very defective" and that there are numerous other "gross Improprieties" to be remedied by the academy (*PW* 4:14).

To improve the language, Swift suggests that certain words be added. Indeed, incorporating new vocabulary to reflect new ideas is a feature of enduring cultures.

> Had the *Roman* Tongue continued vulgar in that City till this Time; it would have been absolutely necessary, from the mighty Changes that have been made in Law and Religion; from the many Terms of Art required in Trade and in War; from the new Inventions that have happened in the World; from the vast spreading of Navigation and Commerce; with many other obvious Circumstances, to have made great Additions to that Language; yet the Antients would still have been read, and understood with Pleasure and Ease. The *Greek* Tongue received many Enlargements between the Time of *Homer*, and that of *Plutarch*; yet the former Author was probably as well understood in *Trajan's* Time, as the latter. What *Horace* says of *Words going off, and perishing like Leaves, and new ones coming in their Place*, is a Misfortune he laments, rather than a Thing he approves: But I cannot see why this should be absolutely necessary, or if it were, what would have become of his *Monumentum ære perennius*.
>
> (15–16)

Swift emphasizes here that amplification of a language is a natural process, one that in no way lessens the intelligibility of literature to future generations. Exactly how he thinks words should be added to the lexicon is vague, but, judging from his stress on etymology, one would suppose he advocates the creation of words from recognizable roots. To maintain the currency of all works written in English, Swift asserts that no words should be dropped from the national lexicon because they are obsolete, an opinion that Samuel Johnson found ridiculous.

Improvements and corrections to the language, however, are not what Swift had "most at Heart" in the *Proposal*. His paramount interest was "in *Ascertaining* and *Fixing* our Language for ever, after such Alterations are made in it as shall be thought requisite" (14). The bulk of the epistle argues this point. Swift laments that the readership of English writers is "confined to these two Islands; and it is hard it should be limited in *Time* as much as *Place* by the perpetual Variations of our Speech" (14). Authors, particularly historians, will lose their incentive to write: "How . . . shall any Man . . . be able to undertake . . . a Work with Spirit and Cheerfulness, when he considers, that he will be read with Pleasure but a very few Years, and in an Age or two shall hardly be understood without an Interpreter?" (18). Without some standard, the literary relics of the past will be lost and future productions aborted by the fear of impermanence. The memoryless void the Struldbruggs or the *Tale*-brothers inhabit would soon be home for everyone.

How did Swift propose fixing and ascertaining the language? Perhaps he had in mind a dictionary such as the Académie Française sought to compile, but he does not suggest this, either in his *Proposal* or elsewhere. He is adamant, though, that English be "refined to a certain Standard" (9)— not a theoretical standard but one that could be effectively realized, for, he says, "it is better a Language should not be wholly perfect, than that it should be perpetually changing" (14). Samuel Johnson agreed that the anomalies of language cannot be eradicated but "require only to be registered, that they may not be increased, and ascertained, that they may not be confounded" and that "for the law to be *known*, is of more importance than to be right. . . . There is in constancy and stability a general and lasting advantage, which will always overbalance the slow improvements of gradual correction."[10]

Although he provides no details, one assumes that Swift would have the academy standardize the spelling of words. Otherwise basic aspects of language, corrupted by the vagaries of pronunciation, would slowly change from generation to generation. As a case in point, Swift notes that "the rude *Latin* of the *Monks* is still very intelligible; whereas, had their Records been delivered down only in the vulgar Tongue . . . so subject to continual succeeding Changes; they could not now be understood" (18). To guarantee a language's persistence over time and geography, Swift believed that consistency in graphic forms must be maintained. In this sense he wished to "fix and ascertain" English.

Swift told Harley that the events of Queen Anne's reign "ought to be recorded in Words more durable than Brass, and such as our Posterity may read a thousand Years hence" (17). He cites Chinese as an example of a language resistant to linguistic change; its characters are understood by all China's inhabitants, regardless of their regional speech differences, and have survived thousands of years. Swift argues that not only will a language with set graphic forms assure cultural continuity, but it will foster national unity by eliminating barriers of dialect. For this reason Swift opposes suggestions that spelling ought to conform to pronunciation: "Not only the several Towns and Counties of *England*, have a different Way of pronouncing, but even here in *London*, they clip Words after one Manner about the Court, another in the City, and a third in the Suburbs; and in a few Years, it is Probable, will all differ from themselves, as Fancy or Fashion shall direct" (11). London will crumble out to atomies, and the rest of the country will follow, unless a uniform spelling standard is enforced. Swift conviction that a standard written language would preserve the political and cultural unity of England explains his almost fanatic emphasis on proper spelling.

One of the first persons to focus on the uncertainties of English spelling was William Camden. He noted, as did most writers on this subject, that English spelling has a bewildering inconsistency. To illustrate the point, Camden cited the experiment of Sir John Price, who "reporteth that a sentence spoken by him in English, & penned out of his mouth by foure good Secretaries, severally, for trial of our Orthography, was so set downe by them, that they all differed one from the other in many letters."[11] For those who sought to ascertain the spelling of doubtful words two choices existed they would establish spelling to reflect either pronunciation or etymology. Some of the most radical proposals for spelling reform came from theorists who sought to make the graphic representations of words mirror current pronunciation. One of the first of these innovators was Sir Thomas Smith, Queen Elizabeth's secretary, who proposed resurrecting certain letters from Anglo-Saxon to express English sounds not adequately designated by Roman letters,[12] an idea that Ben Jonson and others supported.[13] Charles Butler suggested even more sweeping spelling revisions; a brief example is his expression of his belief that the language would be most easily fixed "if wee writ' [his system involves the use of apostrophes to signify certain sounds] altogether according to the sound nou generally received."[14]

In the first decades of the eighteenth century, spelling books were commonplace, the most popular being Thomas Dyche's *A Guide to the English Tongue* (1707); Dyche and other spelling book compilers wanted words to reflect their historical origin and thus grounded orthography in etymology,[15] a movement Swift supported. Decrying those who "spell as they speak," Swift sarcastically denounced pronunciation as a basis for written forms— "A noble Standard for Language!" (*Tatler, PW* 2:176). Swift elaborates this idea in *Proposal* when he condemns the "foolish Opinion . . . that we ought to spell exactly as we speak; which beside the obvious Inconvenience of utterly destroying our Etymology, would be a Thing we should never see the End of. . . . All which reduced to Writing, would entirely confound Orthography. [It would be just as wise to shape our Bodies to our Cloathes and not our Cloathes to our bodyes]" (*PW* 4: 11; brackets in the text). The sound of words is subject to the vagaries of time and place, but etymology is a historical constant. Samuel Johnson accepted this as a guiding principle in publishing his *Dictionary* (1755), which, more than anything else, standardized English spelling.

If spelling is to be regulated by etymology, how should definitions be determined? Again, Swift does not specify this in the *Proposal*. In his passing remarks on the subject elsewhere, Swift implies that meanings of words derive from a historical consensus. But what discourse should be the standard—that of the "best" or most educated speakers, as Quintilian, Ben Jonson, and John Dryden argued, or that of the "ordinary" speaker, as Cicero, Thomas Wilson, and Thomas Sprat argued? This debate about whose discourse should be the basis for a standard began in ancient times and continues to the present day.[16] Swift's satires against erudite definition as a means of obfuscation and his suspicion that the educated elite are an active force in shredding the language suggest that he would seek meaning among the common speakers of the language rather than the "best" speakers.

The following examples, multiplied for effect, show the pervasiveness in Swift's thought of the idea that the average, modestly rational English-speaker knows exactly what a certain word means in a certain context and that in ordinary discourse, words do not need definition: "Politicks, as the Word is *commonly understood*, are nothing but Corruptions" (*Thoughts on Various Subjects*, PW 4:246); "If those two Rivals were really no more than *Parties, according to the common Acceptation* of the Word" (*Examiner*, PW 3:122); "what we call *Whigs* in the Sense which by that Word is *general understood*" (*Drapier's Letters*, PW 10:132); "we are a free People, in the *Common Acceptation of that Word*" (100); "Liberty and Property are words of *known Use and Signification in this Kingdom*; and that the very Lawyers pretend to understand" (87); "and a man may be very loyal, in the *common sense* of the word, without one grain of public good at his heart" (*On Doing Good*, PW 9:233); "I believe him to be an honest Gentleman, as the Word *Honest* is *generally understood*" (*Advice to the Freemen of Dublin*, PW 13:84); "there is no Word more frequently in the Mouths of Men, than that of *Conscience*, and the Meaning of it is in some measure *generally understood*" (*Testimony of Conscience*, PW 9:150); "But that is not what in *common speech* we usually mean by Church" (*References to Tindall's Rights*, PW 2:87); "The whole Kingdom had given the same Interpretation that I had done . . . Friends and Enemies agreed in applying the word *Faction*" (*Some Remarks upon a Pamphlet*, PW 3:192) (some italics added; others deleted). One would suppose, therefore, that the members of Swift's proposed academy would not determine the definitions of words in the abstract but, rather, would somehow gather the particulars of everyday speech to establish meaning, although this operation, like most others, is not elaborated in the *Proposal*.

THE SUBTEXT

The *Proposal for Correcting, Improving, and Ascertaining the English Tongue* is a strange document because its factional rhetoric is at odds with Swift's vision of a bipartisan academy. Although no theory satisfactorily explains the odd combination of assertions in the *Proposal*, one might conclude that the creation of an English academy was not his main object in publishing the piece. Indeed, the academy and its methods are barely mentioned. If the academy is not the focus of the *Proposal*, what is?

Louis Landa suggests that the "red flags" in the document—the insults to the Whigs, the fulsome praise of Harley, and Swift's signature—indicate that he wanted to accentuate its Tory bias so as to "provoke opposition and to avoid any leaven of Whiggism in the . . . Academy." In other words, Swift "wished the Whigs to dissociate themselves from the project [so that] entire credit for the founding of the Academy should rest with Harley and Harley's supporters."[17] This interpretation of Swift's motives is also offered by Irvin Ehrenpreis who believes that Swift wanted to cast a "permanent lustre on his friends' political administration" by making sure all knew that this was a Tory idea.[18] Yet Swift seems to acknowledge that without general support, the British academy could not function because he praises Steele, a Whig spokesman, and asserts their agreement on matters linguistic. At the same time, though, Swift pointedly offends the Whigs in his praise of Harley as a man who saved England from ruin "by a *foreign War*, and a *domestick Faction*" (18).

Creation of an academy in the *Proposal* may be secondary to Swift's interest in using it as a means to patch up the quarrel between the Lord Treasurer, Harley, and the Secretary of State, Bolingbroke, that threatened the stability of the Tory ministry. Swift could argue to himself that if the Tories lost power, England's cultural integrity would be imperiled by the rapacious moneyed class with its latitudinarian prejudices. Knowing that both Harley and Bolingbroke would concur on the importance of correcting, improving, and ascertaining the English language, Swift seems to have used the proposal for an academy as an excuse to involve them in an issue he hoped was bigger than their petty feud, all the while reminding them of their common enemy, the Whigs. Swift describes the process to Archbishop King:

> I have been engaging my Lord Treasurer and the other great Men in a Project of my own, which they tell me they will embrace, especially his Lordship. He

is to erect some kind of Society or Academy under the Patronage of the Ministers, and Protection of the Queen, for correcting, enlarging, polishing, and fixing our Language. The Methods must be left to the Society . . . I am writing . . . some general Hints, which I design to publish. . . . All this may come to nothing, although, I find, the ingenious and learned Men of all my Acquaintance fall readily in with it.

(C 1:239)

Unfortunately, the two men he was most concerned to enlist in his project, Harley and Bolingbroke, did not "fall readily in with it." Yet during this period Swift repeatedly refers to the general support for his plan, hoping against hope, perhaps, that it will save the ministry: "My Lord Treasurer," Swift writes King again, "hath often promised he will advance my Design of an Academy; so have my Lord Keeper and all the Ministers; but they are now too busy to think of any Thing beside what they have upon the Anvil" (C 1:301).

Swift's political motives, whatever they might be, do not wholly explain the unfocused nature of the *Proposal* or his signature on the document, although it was not one of his better literary efforts. Perhaps the oddness of the *Proposal* can be partially illuminated by looking at events in Swift's life at the time he conceived the idea of the academy, for in many ways it was designed to answer certain implicit and explicit criticisms of his conduct. The rhetoric of the *Proposal* seems to counter accusations that Swift was a low menial in Harley's circle, in general, a follower rather than an initiator; that he was a writer of trifles and propaganda, rather than a serious literary figure; and that he was motivated more by self-interest than idealism. Swift's presentation of himself in a way that modifies these views seems to supersede his concern with the particulars of an academy. The document may have been more important to him as autobiography than as an agent of linguistic reform.

The genre of the *Proposal* and its tone—an epistle to Harley that begins on a note of cozy intimacy—emphasizes Swift's familiarity with the power elite. This approach seems calculated to answer public critics who viewed him merely as a Tory hack and an employee of the state. And the *Proposal* may have been fashioned to quash not just his public critics but his private fears, which were exacerbated by an incident that seems of crucial importance in explaining why Swift proposed the idea of an academy at the time he did. On February 5, 1710 / 11, Swift's putative friend and mentor, Harley, offered him fifty pounds for his work on the *Examiner*. Swift, who cherished the illusion that he was on equal ground with the nation's leaders, was stung by Harley's action, which instantly branded him as "hired help."

How deeply Harley wounded Swift can be seen in the mode of his reaction, his repeated allusions to the event, and the length of time it took his anger to fade. The first notation of the insult appears in the entry for

February 6 in the *Journal to Stella*, when, after describing how Patrick, his servant, had lodged a noisy, dirty bird in their rooms, he tells Stella that he is slow to show annoyance: "I say nothing: I am tame as a clout." Immediately following, however, is the icy statement: "Mr. Harley desired I would dine with him again to-day; but I refused him, for I fell out with him yesterday, and will not see him again till he makes me amends" (*JS* 1:181–82). Significantly, here and throughout the duration of Swift's pique, he was too bruised to name the event directly.

Swift was still furious the next day when writing to Stella: "I was this morning early with Mr. Lewis of the secretary's office, and saw a letter Mr. Harley had sent to him, desiring to be reconciled; but I was deaf to all intreaties. . . . I expect further satisfaction. If we let these great ministers pretend too much, there will be no governing them. He promises to make me easy, if I will but come and see him; but I won't, and he shall do it by message, or I will cast him off" (182). Nine days later, in his February 16 letter to Stella, Swift notes, "We made up our quarrel" (193). On March 7, he writes, "Stella guesses right as she always does. [Harley] gave me"; the rest is a coded message that says "A bankbill for fifty pounds" (208, 208n).

Throughout his life, Swift sought a permanent place in The Great Tradition—he always wanted literary fame—but about the same time as Harley's insult, Swift suffered several other assaults that damaged his concept of himself as a great writer. He was miffed by a review of the *Examiner* in *The Present State of Wit* that implied his hireling status and only tepidly praised his style.[19] In addition, the publication of his *Miscellanies* (1711), which he arranged by stealth, was remarked on by Archbishop King as follows: "You see how malicious some are towards you, in printing a parcel of trifles, falsely, as your works. This makes it necessary that you should shame those varlets, by something that may enlighten the world, which I am sure your genius will reach, if you set yourself to it" (*C* 1:268). A parcel of trifles!

Against this background, Swift started to formulate the idea of a British academy. Perhaps worried about the flukiness of literary fame, he sought to create not a subjective work of art but a permanent cultural edifice, "something," as Archbishop King said, "that will enlighten the world." Charles Kerby-Miller notes that "it does not in any way derogate from Swift's sincerity and high motives in pursuing his plan for an academy to realize that he had a very high personal stake in the matter."[20] This "high personal stake" explains some of the peculiar elements of the *Proposal*. Its pretentious and turgid style can be seen as Swift's self-conscious attempt to counteract the perception that he was a writer of "trifles"; his appeal to Harley in the "Name of all the learned and polite Persons of the Nation" (*PW* 4:6), a stance at which his enemies hooted, was designed to show him as a leader among writers, not as a hack. In the *Proposal*, then, Swift sought to correct, improve, and ascertain his image in his own eyes and in the eyes of others. In this context, he would care little about the actual composition of the academy, only that he be remembered as the promoter of the idea. For that reason he signed his name.[21]

Political and personal concerns, therefore, eclipse Swift's idea of an academy, yet another explanation for his vagueness in the *Proposal* is his fundamental suspicion of institutional solutions. "Methods" come under attack in his writing as do "academies," both of which he associates in other places with enthusiasm and madness. The crazy Lagadans, of course, have a School of Languages in their academy, and in *A Tale of a Tub*, the schools of pederasty, hobbyhorses, looking glasses, salivation, and spelling are components of the academy that the Modern speaker proposes to protect the commonwealth against the "Wits of the present Age" (*PW* 1:24–25).

In the *Proposal* Swift revealingly characterizes himself as a projector, a pejorative term in his vocabulary. At the beginning of the epistle, he calls himself a "visionary Projector . . . [with] his Schemes" (*PW* 4:6) and at the end says, "But I forget my Province: and find my self turning Projector before I am aware" (20). These passages indicate that Swift was uneasy with his *Proposal* because it smacks of the systematization and regimentation that he typically abhorred. Even though the process of creating an academy could involve the country and his party in a useful colloquy that would encourage their unity and at the same time demonstrate his leadership ability, Swift was not wholeheartedly in favor of the institution he was suggesting.

Swift recognizes that he is being vague and offers an overabundance of excuses for it: "Writing by Memory only, as I do at present, I would gladly keep within my Depth; and therefore shall not enter into further Particulars. Neither do I pretend more than to shew the Usefulness of this Design, and to make some general Observations; leaving the rest to that Society." He concludes, furthermore, that any spelling out of details would be unnecessary because "such a Society would be pretty unanimous in the main Points" (16). As to who should constitute it, he tautologically suggest "such Persons, as are generally allowed to be best qualified for such a Work" (13–14). Swift then helpfully notes that these people ought to meet "at some appointed Time and Place," but how they should proceed beyond that, he says, "is not for me to prescribe" (14). Swift says that the English academy should follow the model of the Académie Française "to imitate where [they] have proceeded right, and to avoid their Mistakes" (14), but he does not indicate what these are.

The vagueness of Swift's *Proposal* can be seen when it is contrasted with others of his proposals, such as *A Proposal for Giving Badges to Beggars, Some Reasons against the Bill for Settling the Tyth of Hemp, Flax, & by a Modus*, and the famous *Modest Proposal*. All of these are extremely concrete and detailed. Moreover, Swift's plan seems quite general when compared with a similar proposal for an academy by Daniel Defoe, who itemizes the membership of the proposal academy, saying that there ought to be thirty-six people— twelve nobility, twelve private gentlemen, and "a Class of Twelve to be left open for meer Merit, let it be found in who or what sort it would."[22] In addition, Defoe states who should *not* be members of the academy, except on some "some extraordinary Occasion"—lawyers, clergymen, physicians, or those whose "Business or Trade was Learning"—because they all tend to use one sort of jargon or another. Defoe also points out definite activities the academy might initiate, which include censoring the stage, establishing a program to stop swearing, publishing essays on style, and creating a lecture series on language.[23] In short, Defoe's proposal is more of a blueprint for action than Swift's.

Regardless of his motives, Swift persistently struggled to get the powers-that-be interested in his idea of an academy. He writes Stella on June 22, 1711, that Harley "enters mightily into it, so does the dean of Carlisle; and I design to write a letter to [the] lord treasurer with the proposals of it, and publish it" (*JS* 1:295–96), but Swift's colleagues were too preoccupied to devote much attention to his proposal. When Swift finished the manuscript, he gave it to Harley, who merely passed it along to Prior, who subsequently forgot about it and placed Swift in the embarrassing position of having to retrieve the paper from Prior so that he could give it to the printer.[24]

The *Proposal* finally appeared on May 17, 1712, but no progress on the academy ever resulted. Many years later, when it was republished in 1735 by Faulkner, a headnote (probably written by Swift and certainly approved by him)[25] recounts the reasons Swift's British academy was never established:

> It is well known, that if the Queen had lived a Year or two longer, the following Proposal would in all Probability have taken Effect. For the Lord Treasurer had already nominated several Persons without Distinction of Quality or Party, who were to compose a Society for the Purposes mentioned by the Author; and resolved to use his Credit with Her Majesty, that a Fund should be applyed to support the Expence of a large Room, where the Society should meet, and for other Incidents. But this Scheme fell to the Ground, partly by the Dissentions among the great Men at Court; but chiefly by the lamented Death of that glorious Princess.
>
> (*Textual Notes, PW* 4: 285)

Here Swift mourns what might have been: the continuation of the Tory regime with himself as the English Richelieu—leader of the church, confidant of princes, and founder of the national linguistic academy. Yet one wonders how Swift thought the academy would be realized when his *Proposal* is at once vague and divisive. Throughout, the rhetoric seems at cross-purposes.

Swift felt comfortable about traditional institutions—the Established Church, the common law, and the constitutional monarchy—because they are inextricably intertwined with Britain's history. The order they impose on society gives all men the freedom to develop their talents. A Modern institution, on the other hand, could pose a threat. Unrestrained by traditional ballast, it might disrupt rather than preserve English culture. Swift, of course, does not grant the academy any far-reaching mandate, and particularly not censorship powers such as those possessed by Defoe's proposed academy and the Académie Française. Indeed, the functions of the academy are hardly specified because Swift seems to be avoiding the subject. Instead he praises Harley, recounts the history of the English language, analyzes the causes of linguistic corruption, and argues the importance of a verbal standard. The essay is written in very un-Swiftian prose. The awkward, contradictory, and diffuse style may have been generated by Swift's fundamental uneasiness about what he was saying.

Swift clearly lamented the slow evolution of the language that made Chaucer less accessible than Dryden, yet he might have feared that the academy, isolated in a room in London from the linguistic consensus of the countryside, would change the language more by fiat than linguistic accidents had changed it in three hundred years. In the end, the English academy might become like the Laputan academy in trying to extinguish the discourse "of their Forefathers" (*PW* 11: 185). No doubt Swift feared the elitism that characterized the Académie Française. Paul Pellisson-Fontanier, who wrote its history, characterizes the Académie as follows: "As much as wisdom is above the multitude, the soul above the body, and the desire of knowledge above that of living: so much is the Academy above the Common-wealth."[26] Such a separation of *wisdom* from the *multitude* and the *Academy* from the *Common-wealth* would have been anathema to Swift.[27]

Swift's ambivalence about the academy may have grown out of the fundamental rifts in his personality. But although he had mixed feelings about an institutional effort to improve language, as a moralist he was consistently firm about the individual's responsibility to discourse in the common forms or "Proper Words." Regardless of the linguistic pollution around them, people have the ability to speak clearly and the social duty to do so. This is illustrated by Gulliver in Lilliput. Although the Lilliputian language is circumlocutory and redundant, Gulliver uses it to be brutally blunt about the plight of the Blefescudians: "I plainly protested, that I would never be an Instrument of bringing a free and brave People into Slavery" (*PW* 11: 53). Only by personal acts of will can chaos be abated and society preserved. "Style," or "Putting Proper Words in proper Places," was no minor issue for Swift.

Notes

1. *The Prose Works of Jonathan Swift*, ed. Herbert Davis, 14 vols. (Oxford: Basil Blackwell, 1939–68), 1:65. Further references to this edition will appear in parentheses in the text as *PW* followed by volume and page number. For clarity, a short title of a work will precede *PW* where necessary.

2. "Dedication," *Troilus and Cressida*, in *The Works of John Dryden*, ed. H. T. Swedenberg et al., 20 vols. (Berkeley and Los Angeles: University of California Press, 1956–84), 13:221–22.

3. Paul Pellisson-Fontanier, *The History of the French Academy* (London, 1657), 26. Italics omitted.

4. Jonathan Swift, *Journal to Stella*, ed. Harold Williams, 2 vols. (Oxford: Basil Blackwell, 1948; rpt. 1974), 2: 535. Further references to this edition will appear in parentheses in the text as *JS*.

5. *The Correspondence of Jonathan Swift*, ed. Harold Williams, 5 vols. (Oxford: Clarendon Press, 1963–72), 1:295. Further references to this edition will appear in parentheses in the text as *C*.

6. Thomas Sprat, *History of the Royal Society*, facsim., ed. Jackson I. Cope and Harold W. Jones (St. Louis: Washington University Press, 1958), 66.

7. Murray Cohen, *Linguistic Practices in England, 1640–1785* (Baltimore: Johns Hopkins University Press, 1977), 99.

8. "Dedication," *The Rival Ladies* in *Works of Dryden*, 8:98.

9. Samuel Johnson, "Preface," *A Dictionary of the English Language* (London, 1755), Ar.

10. Ibid., Ar and Av.

11. William Camden, *Remains Concerning Britain*, ed. R. D. Dunn (Toronto: University of Toronto Press, 1984), 32.

12. Ibid., 33.

13. See Susie I. Tucker, *English Examined: Two Centuries of Comment on the Mother-Tongue* (Cambridge: Cambridge University Press, 1961).

14. Charles Butler, *English Grammar*, ed. A. Eichler (1634; rpt. Vienna: Neimeyer, 1910), 9.

15. Murray Cohen, *Sensible Words: Linguistic Practices in England, 1640–1785* (Baltimore: Johns Hopkins University Press, 1977), 48–49.

16. For the debate in the Renaissance, see Jane Donawerth, *Shakespeare and the Sixteenth-Century Study of Language* (Urbana: University of Illinois Press, 1984), 32–33, and in the restoration and eighteenth century, see James Thompson, *Language in Wycherley's Plays: Seventeenth-Century Language Theory and Drama* (University, Ala.: University of Alabama Press, 1984), 31–33.

17. Louis Landa, "Introduction," *Reflections on Dr. Swift's Letter to Harley*, facsim. rpt. in *Poetry and Language*, ed. Landa (Ann Arbor, Mich.: Augustan Reprint Society, 1948), 3.

18. Irvin Ehrenpreis, *Swift: The Man, His Works, and the Age*, 3 vols. (Cambridge, Mass.: Harvard University Press, 1962–83), 2:542–43.

19. [John Gay], *The Present State of Wit* (1711), facsim. rpt. in *Essays on Wit: Number Three* (Ann Arbor, Mich.: Augustan Reprint Society, 1947), 2.

20. Introduction, *The Memoirs . . . of Martinus Scriblerus* (New Haven: Published for Wellesley College by the Yale University Press, 1950), 9. Henry Sams links Swift's *Proposal* to his desire to be Historiographer Royal ("Jonathan Swift's Proposal Concerning the English Language: A Reconsideration," *Studies in Philology* 4 [1967]: 76–87).

21. For a fuller discussion of this issue, see my "Why Did Swift Sign His Name to *A Proposal for Correcting . . . The English Tongue?*" *Neophilologus* 63 (1979): 469–80, where sections of this chapter originally appeared.

22. Daniel Defoe, *An Essay on Projects* (London, 1697), 235–36.

23. Ibid., 234–35.

24. Ehrenpreis, *Swift*, 2:544.

25. Herbert Davis, "The Textual Notes," *PW* 4:285.

26. Pellisson-Fontanier, *History of the French Academy*, 251.

27. Robert Fitzgerald suggests that the Struldbruggs are a satire on the isolation of the French Academicians, who called themselves "Immortals," and that though Swift was enthusiastic about the *Proposal* when it came out, he subsequently had doubts about it. See "The Allegory of Luggnagg and the Struldbruggs in *Gulliver's Travel*," *Studies in Philology* 65 (1968): 657–76.

Swift and the Revolution [of 1688]

F. P. LOCK

The success of the Revolution of 1688, and the permanence of the settlement worked out in 1689, did more than determine the character of English politics and the course of events for the next thirty years or more. It also decisively changed the character of national life. Its repercussions extended well beyond the dynastic change, important as such a change was in the seventeenth century. There were far-reaching constitutional innovations, the result of a shift in the balance of power between the monarch and parliament. Political parties became a permanent fact of national and local political life. The struggle for control of parliament, rather than the pursuit of influence at court (important as that remained) became the primary objective in the business of politics. Hence the new importance of journalism and public opinion. Other changes affected more than the politically active minority. The religious settlement, with its (however limited) recognition of dissent, ended the ideal (not the less cherished for having been long divorced from reality) of a single national church. England's involvement in two long and expensive European wars led to a massive increase in taxation and in the bureaucratic machine needed to organise it and to supervise the expanded government activities that the war began but which tended to become permanent. Both these developments resulted in a weakening of the traditional structures of power and authority. Political power was now increasingly wielded by "new men" whose fortunes derived from government service or funded money rather than from inherited landed estates. In the familiar tory analysis of this movement, it was usually asserted and believed that the wars had been paid for by the landed interest while the profits accrued to the moneyed men. These political and economic changes can be traced back to well before the Revolution; but they were quickened and strengthened by the events of 1688–89, and it became something of a commonplace (for tories) to trace all the national ills back to 1688 and no further, a date that the whigs as naturally tended to treat as a kind of birth-date of liberty.[1]

There are a number of places in Swift's works where, sometimes in a serious and sometimes in a comic context, the Revolution is treated as a

From *Swift's Tory Politics* (Newark: University of Delaware Press, 1983), 105–18. Reprinted with the permission of Associated University Presses.

point from which to measure decay and degeneration. In *Mr Collins's Discourse Put into Plain English* (1713), Swift credits *"Free-thinking* and the *Revolution"* between them with banishing the devil and the fear of him from England.[2] In the introduction to *Polite Conversation* (published in 1738, but begun as early as 1704), Simon Wagstaff (the fictive author) dates the "Refinement" of "abbreviating, or reducing Words of many Syllables into one, by lopping off the rest" as "having begun about the Time of the Revolution" (*PW* 4: 106). We know that Swift seriously regarded this practice as a symptom of linguistic decay (*PW* 2:175–76). In "A History of Poetry" (a Swift-Sheridan exercise in punning) the decline of poetry is dated from the Revolution (*PW* 4:274), while it is the neglect of philology from the same period that is complained of in "A Discourse to Prove the Antiquity of the English Tongue" (*PW* 4:231). These references suggest a habit of mind cognate with that of the Jacobite fox-hunter in the *Freeholder* No. 22 (5 March 1716), whom Addison ridiculed for his belief that "there had been no good Weather since the Revolution." Jacobite satires did not fail to load William with responsibility for the poor weather and harvests of these years.[3] In the light of these jests, the discontents that lie behind them, and of Swift's more serious comments, it is rather surprising that Swift's unequivocal support for the Revolution should usually have been taken, by modern scholars, as axiomatic.[4] For his contemporaries would have marked the author of such remarks as a probable crypto-Jacobite.

It is well known that Swift was hostile to all the developments characteristic of post-Revolution England. From A *Tale of a Tub* (1704) to *The Presbyterians' Plea of Merit* (1733), he fought a strong rearguard action in defence of his ideal of a national church. He attributed the general decline in religion and morality to the weakened position of the anglican church. He would have liked, so far as was possible, to circumscribe the legal toleration (or as he and the tories preferred to call it, "indulgence") allowed to the dissenters. More generally, he was opposed to the various manifestations of the "whig" view of the world, epitomised in the *Spectator* and so congenial to Macaulay: the world of individualism, secularism, commercialism, and imperialism.[5] Swift's attitude to the Revolution was an extremely guarded and qualified approval, arrived at through a balancing of accounts that showed the smallest of surpluses. Revolution he regarded as being justified when "those evils which usually attend and follow a violent change of government" are less than "the grievances we suffer under a present power." He allows this to have been the case in 1688, but adds the rider that the Revolution produced "some very bad effects, which are likely to stick long enough by us" (*PW* 9:31). These "very bad effects" are the subject of frequent comment and extended analysis in Swift's serious political and historical works.

The ideal monarch, in the tory scheme of things, is well represented by David in Dryden's *Absalom and Achitophel* (1681), particularly in David's long speech at the end of the poem where he composes factional strife and restores order. The divine sanction of the monarchy is suggested when God "nodding, gave Consent"; the rule of "Godlike *David* was Restor'd, / And willing Nations knew their Lawfull Lord." Swift draws such a "godlike" monarch in the lofty king of Brobdingnag, whose contempt for the party strife of England expresses the ideal of a "patriot king" in a way that anticipates Bolingbroke's *Idea of a Patriot King* (written about 1738, although not published until 1749). After the Revolution, it was less easy to treat the office of kingship so reverently as Dryden had been able to. The reality of the post-1688 monarchy was unglamorous, neither William nor Queen Anne (nor George I) having any taste for the theatrical pageantry that had contributed so much to the public image of the earlier Stuart courts.[6] Queen Anne resumed a practice disused by William, that of touching for the King's Evil (she touched Samuel Johnson in 1712), and this ceremony was perhaps the last vestige of the formerly magical and even divine nature that the kingship had once possessed. Of much greater practical significance than the essentially symbolic aspects of monarchy was the fact that both William and Anne were forced, though with great reluctance, to take sides in party strife. In his *Examiner* papers Swift makes much of the rudeness and insolence of the way the queen had been treated by her whig ministers (*PW* 3:37, 80, 117). This theme is extended in *The Importance of the Guardian Considered* (1713), where Swift condemns Steele's language in "expecting" the demolition of Dunkirk, comparing it to Bradshaw's at the trial of Charles I (*PW* 8:4). It was always Swift's strategy to identify Queen Anne with the nation as a whole, not just with the tories; in this way she is made to appear above party strife, and her support for the tories looks as disinterested a choice as Swift's own (it should be said that Queen Anne genuinely was a reluctant partisan). Swift's basic charge against George I was that he had allowed himself to become the king not of the nation but of the whigs.[7] This is a view that Swift expresses historically in several pamphlets, allegorically in the "Account of the Court and Empire of Japan" (1728; *PW* 5:99–107), and imaginatively in the character of the Emperor of Lilliput in *Gulliver's Travels*.[8]

One pernicious effect of the rise of party was the way each party sought to force itself on the monarch as a group. This was not especially a whig notion, although naturally it is on the insolence of the whigs that Swift focuses. In the *Examiner* No. 17 (14 December 1710) he attacks the way in which individual whig ministers placed conditions on their willingness to serve the queen. While it was still the theory, and to some extent still the case in practice, that ministers were the personal servants of the crown, it seemed a sinister development that ministers should try to make terms in this way.[9] While individual ministers remained responsible primarily to the crown, there seemed some check against the possibility of an over-mighty group of ministers (such as the whig Junto) seizing control of the government, as Swift thought had happened during the period of whig domination under

Queen Anne. Swift was always distrustful of groups of men, especially of professions or corporations who banded together to practice some fraud on the public (*Corr.* 3:103). Political parties (by which in practice Swift meant the whigs) were formed to do just this. In the *Project for the Advancement of Religion* (1709) he argues that merit and even more morality should be the proper qualifications for public employment (as in the uncorrupted state of Lilliput), and attacks the way men of vicious lives and no obvious qualifications are given jobs because they are reliable party men (*PW* 2:62). Swift was here speaking from personal feeling and experience. The *Project* was published in April 1709. On 8 March 1709 Swift had written to his friend Ford of his disappointed hopes of preferment, attributing his failure to his being "thought to want the Art of being thourow paced in my Party, as all discreet Persons ought to be" (*Corr* 1:125). The systematic use of patronage for political ends was not, of course, a post-Revolution phenomenon. It had been used against the whigs in the tory reaction of 1681–5. But to Swift it seemed one thing to reward the friends of the constitution in church and state (the tories), and quite another to reward a faction that intended the overthrow of both (the whigs). It is true, of course, that in his days of influence under the tory ministry of 1710–14, Swift often tried to help whig friends obtain or retain public employment. To this extent he practiced what he preached about rewarding merit.[10] But the kind of scheme of promotion by piety that he advocates in the *Project for the Advancement of Religion* would have been more partisan than he pretends. It would have ended the use of patronage for party advantage only in the sense of giving it almost exclusively to the tories. When Swift sought to turn the clock back to before the Revolution, it was naturally to the period of tory reaction of 1681–85 that he turned.

The Revolution had inaugurated a period of nearly twenty years of almost continuous war, Britain's part in which had been financed largely by borrowing on the public credit. The result was the creation of a new "moneyed interest" which rivalled and threatened to dominate the traditional power of the landed men. This sinister new factor in politics was the subject of the first *Examiner* paper that Swift wrote (No. 13, 2 November 1710; *PW* 3:5). There were several reasons for regarding the new development as alarming. Landed wealth was thought to be the safest base for political power because it was the most stable form of property and most closely identified its owners' interests with those of the nation at large. A landowner could not take his wealth with him, and would therefore be the less tempted to act or to approve action that was against the national interest. Even the capital of a trading merchant was not so dangerous as money in the stocks, because most of the merchant's time and energy would be taken up with the management of his trade, leaving him little leisure for political activity. Men whose money was in government securities and other funds, however, were not only free to engage full-time in political activity but had the ready cash with which to buy their way into parliament through bribery and corruption. Money in the funds was also untaxed. Worst of all, from the point of view of political stability, apart from being less "real" than land, the value of money in stocks and funds could be manipulated by the owners themselves. It was in the power of the largest stockholders, or of a group of them, to raise or depress the market by large-scale buying or selling. The same people could make it easier, or more difficult, for the government to borrow money. From the conservative viewpoint of Swift and his like, the creation and growth of this "moneyed interest" was probably the single most pernicious result of the Revolution.[11] In 1701–2 Charles Davenant, the tory economist, argued that the recent war (the Nine Years' War) could have been financed from taxes raised within each year, without the need for public borrowing and the creation of a vast national debt. He argued that the policy of deficit financing and public indebtedness had been adopted in order to settle the new government more firmly, since all those who invested any money in the funds would certainly support the Revolution settlement against the threat of a Jacobite restoration, which would inevitably be accompanied by a repudiation of public debts. Further, the debt had grown to such monstrous proportions as a result of corruption on the part of those charged with its management, who had raised vast estates for themselves by robbing the public purse. Davenant made these charges more vivid and effective by dramatising them in a dialogue between "Tom Double" and a subordinate "Mr Whiglove." In Tom Double Davenant drew what he claimed was the type of the modern or "new" whig, a man who had been destitute at the time of the Revolution, but who had subsequently raised himself a fortune of £150,000 through various corrupt dealings with government money. Davenant describes all the government's main expedients for raising funds in terms of how advantageous they proved for men like Tom Double.[12] The result of the war was thus the transfer of vast amounts of wealth away from the rightful, hereditary proprietors to a set of rascally whig upstarts like Tom Double; and with this wealth naturally went political influence. In 1710–11, towards the end of another and even more expensive war, Swift offers exactly the same analysis as Davenant had done ten years earlier. In the *Examiner* and in the *Conduct of the Allies* Swift develops a conspiracy thesis similar to Davenant's yet with even wider ramifications, involving the allies as well as the whigs. Swift adopts Davenant's account of the finances of the 1690s (that the debt was deliberately created to keep people loyal to the government and the Revolution), and extends it to the War of the Spanish Succession. This war, he suggests, has been fought less for the official pretexts given (such as to protect the protestant interest in Europe, to reduce the excessive power of France, to improve the prospects for British trade) than for the private advantage of Marlborough, the Dutch allies, and the rapacious whig financial interest at home. It has been paid for, however, by the now impoverished tory squires.

One of the most pernicious ways, as Swift saw it, in which the "financial revolution" had direct political consequences was in the development of public credit. In particular, with the development of a stock-market trading in government securities as well as in the stocks of private companies, the price of such securities came to be regarded as an index of national well-being. The stocks would naturally rise with "good" news (that is, with news that was welcome to the body of the proprietors of the stocks) and fall with bad. This was a most sinister development. It introduced a new "popular" element into political life, for the rise or fall of share prices involved simple figures easily taken up and spread around, like the simple political slogans ("No Peace without Spain") that proved so effective as political rallying cries. This meant that the unpopularity (with the fund-holders) of government decisions or policies could be readily and instantly publicised in an extra-parliamentary way. Swift was especially annoyed at the way stocks rose and fell with reports of the queen's health in 1713–14. The worse her health, the closer seemed the inevitable Hanoverian accession and the return to power of the whigs. Nothing better symbolised the factiousness and selfishness of the whigs than their rejoicing at the queen's near-fatal illness in December 1713. The deliberate manipulation of the stocks was, of course, practised by the professional stock-jobbers (who in the Queen Anne period were almost universally regarded, by whigs as well as tories, as iniquitous parasites) for purely financial reasons. In the *Examiner* No. 24 (18 January 1711) Swift describes their spreading reports that are calculated to lower prices and therefore allow their friends (who will know that the reports are untrue) to buy at advantageous prices (*PW* 3:67). But the same thing could be done for political purposes. In 1710 the whigs were accused of deliberately trying to lower the public credit in order to increase the difficulties faced by the incoming tory government.[13] In *Gulliver's Travels*, one of the devices of the "profound Politicians" described in the Academy of Lagado, who invent plots in order to exploit them, is to "raise or sink the Opinion of publick Credit, as either shall best answer their private Advantage" (*PW* 11:191). So long as the government needed to borrow money (which in practice it constantly did), it was at the mercy of those who could command large sums of cash; whereas in Swift's view it was the proprietors of the land who should exercise political influence.

Swift thought it a pernicious innovation that "the Wealth of the Nation, that used to be reckoned by the Value of Land, is now computed by the Rise and Fall of Stocks" (*PW* 3:6). This was a typically tory view. A forward-looking whig like Addison had no such reservations about the value and importance of credit. In the *Spectator* No. 3 (3 March 1711) he drew an allegorical representation of "Public Credit" as a main bulwark of the constitution. In this allegory Addison places Magna Carta between the Act of Uniformity on one side and the Toleration Act on the other, giving formal recognition of the dissenters' claim (which Swift could never accept) that the "toleration" was legally and morally the equivalent of the establishment of the church. The main threat to credit (and therefore to national well-being) comes of course from the threat of the Pretender, although Addison makes a show of coupling anarchy with tyranny and bigotry with atheism as equal threats. Credit has a fainting-fit at the threatened approach of the Pretender, to be revived by monarchy in the guise of the Hanoverian successor and by religion in the form of "moderation"; in other words, credit is restored by whig foreign and domestic policies. Swift may have intended a paragraph in the *Examiner* No.37 (19 April 1711) as a response to Addison's vision, for he picks up a phrase which Addison had attributed to "none of her well-wishers," that Credit seemed "troubled with vapours." Swift writes that to hear "some of these worthy Reasoners" talk about credit "you would think they were describing a Lady troubled with Vapours or the Cholick" (*PW* 3:134).[14] He goes on to make a distinction between true national credit and the irrelevant phantom that is the creature of the opinions of a few self-interested stock-jobbers. In the *Conduct of the Allies* he makes a similar distinction when he says that he took it as a "good Omen" when the stocks fell as a result of the ministerial changes in 1710, as though "the young extravagant Heir had got a new Steward . . . which made the Usurers forbear feeding him with Mony, as they used to do" (*PW* 6:56). This analogy between a private and the public estate was a favourite one with Swift. It expresses his commonsensical opposition to the idea that it was a good thing for the public to be in debt. Later he would make the King of Brobdingnag fail to understand "how a Kingdom could run out of its Estate like a private Person. He asked me, who were our Creditors? and, where we found Money to pay them?" (*PW* 11:131). It gives a significant indication of the audience for whom Swift was writing in the *Conduct of the Allies* that he could rather casually propose the expedient of suspending payment on the debts contracted in the previous war as a sensible way of helping to finance the present one (*PW* 6:18). This would have been a most irresponsible financial decision, but one likely to appeal to the heavily taxed tory squires.

In his first *Examiner* paper Swift directed his readers to examine the newest and smartest equipages about town; most would be found to belong to the newly rich military and financial adventurers, many of them men who would formerly have belonged on the outside of such coaches (*PW* 3:5). His objections to such redistribution of wealth are not just financial but social and political: too rapid shifts in wealth cause dislocation and disturb the social hierarchy on which political stability depends. Once it became possible and even easy for a shameless go-getter to rise *"from the dregs of the People"* (*PW* 3:78) to become Lord Chancellor and Lord President of the Council, as Somers had done—or to raise, in Marlborough's case, the largest private fortune in Europe from royal favour and a happy knack of winning battles—more people would become discontented with their appointed places in society and would try to improve their fortunes. This inevitably led to the worst kind of economic and political adventurism, typified by the case of William Wood and his corruptly-obtained patent for coining copper money for Ireland. From the beginning of the first of the *Drapier's Letters*, Swift refers again and again to Wood's humble social origins (*PW* 10:4). Swift expressed his belief in the need for a stable and hierarchical social system through the ideal educational institutions of Lilliput, which perpetuate the existing class-system (*PW* 11:61–63), and more generally still through the caste-divided society of the Houyhnhnms. The Lilliputian politicians who gain advancement by their dexterity in leaping, creeping, and rope dancing perfectly symbolise the new breed of post-Revolution politicians whose special skills (like electoral and financial management) made them necessary in the corrupt world of contemporary politics.[15] Only if politics could be cleaned up would it be possible to dispense with such men and to employ only the men of birth, virtue, and integrity who were the natural leaders of society.

Swift's views on all these post-Revolution developments can be related to the "neo-Harringtonian" political ideas that had been advanced much earlier, by the Earl of Shaftesbury and his followers about 1675, in opposition to the corrupt government of Charles II.[16] These ideas, which derived from the classical-republican tradition of political thought, emphasised the part played by "corruption" in subverting traditional institutions. In 1675 the twin threats of a "standing" parliament (there had been no general election since 1661) and a "standing" army seemed to provide the court with the means to control parliament, with the consequent loss of parliament's ability to act as a check on the executive. In 1675–7 this was "opposition whig" doctrine. After 1688, as the whigs themselves became more closely identified with government rather than opposition, such ideas gradually became the property of the "country tory" backbenchers (although many "old whigs" continued to share them). To such tories, the "Financial Revolution" seemed to have completed the long decline of the ancient and stable "gothic" constitution. The king was now dependent on parliamentary supplies even for the normal business of government. High taxation to pay for the wars meant that the nobility was increasingly attracted to the pursuit of employments in the court and the army in order to supplement their incomes and retain their participation and influence in political life. The independent country gentlemen in the House of Commons were similarly liable to corruption through the distributions of civil and military places and pensions. Thus in both houses of parliament, independence was replaced by subservience, either to the king and the court party (as seemed to be the case in 1675), or (as most commonly after the Revolution) to whatever minister, group, or party was able to control the flow of royal patronage. Further, the membership of both houses was increasingly being filled by men whose qualifications were personal (as proven administrators, financial "experts," useful "managers," or whatever) rather than representative of the traditional hereditary and territorial ruling classes. That this critique of contemporary political developments became, after the Revolution, essentially a tory one, a way of explaining the increasing whig domination of politics despite the fact that the tories regarded themselves as (and almost certainly were) a majority party, is why Swift's highly conservative and authoritarian political thought happens to contain so much that is, in one sense, "whig" and even republican. The attraction of these "republican" ideas and institutions for Swift was that they could provide a strong authoritarian structure within which to contain individualism, as in Lycurgus's Sparta or the Rome of the early republic.

The most important difference between Swift's analysis of the post-1688 political corruptions and Shaftesbury's 1675 critique of the corrupt court of Charles II is in respect of the church. It is this difference that reveals Swift's essential toryism. In 1675 the bishops had been widely regarded as royal stooges, self-interested men who played up to claims of royal absolutism and preached the divine right of monarchy, passive obedience, and such doctrines in exchange for the crown's support of their own extravagant claims for the church's wealth and power.[17] Swift, of course, could never have subscribed to such ideas. In 1675 he would certainly have been a supporter of Danby's government, which was trying to reforge the old cavalier-Clarendonian alliance between church and state. After the Revolution, when the church was very much on the defensive and began to play a somewhat reduced role in national political life (a trend that became much more pronounced after 1714), Swift continued to think of it as a central organisation in the state.

Swift thus regarded every post-Revolution change and development in politics, religion, and society with distrust and hostility. Yet for all his serious reservations, he always accepted the Revolution, if only from greater fear of the more destructive effects of any counter-revolution. To this extent he became a conservative rather than a reactionary. Many of the particular policies that he would have liked to have seen adopted were reactionary ones, but he accepted the broad outlines of the Revolution settlement. He even came to see himself as a moderate, mediating between slavish Jacobitism on the one hand and atheistic whig republicanism on the other. This is his strategy in *A Tale of a Tub* (at least in the religious satire) and in the "Sentiments of a Church-of-England Man." In fact, of course, this grudging, "balance-sheet" approval of the Revolution put Swift firmly on the tory side. Most people, even most tories, accepted the Revolution with less uneasiness than Swift did. He was exceptional in the importance that he attached to the ideal of a truly national church; in his scepticism about the value of Marlborough's victories, and of military conquests and glory generally; and in his indifference to the material prosperity, economic growth, and national prestige that the new order was supposed to bring. In all these respects his backward-looking attitudes contrast with the cultural optimism of whig contemporaries like Addison, Steele, and Defoe. It would have been an easy transition from these views to the kind of backwoods Jacobitism represented after 1714 by William Shippen and Sir William Wyndham. Swift did not follow them because (despite his temperamental bias towards the authoritarian) his dislike of popery and political absolutism was as real as his hatred of whiggism. He could never be a Jacobite any more than he could ever be a whig. He distrusted the individual, whether (to take examples from *A Tale of a Tub*) Louis XIV or Descartes, the Pope or Jack of Leiden. Papal (or royal, or intellectual) infallibility was as obnoxious to him as the pretence of individual inspiration.

Notes

1. For a succinct statement of the tory case, which would later be elaborated by Swift, see Henry St John's letter of 9 July 1709 to the Earl of Orrery, "The letters of Henry St John to the Earl of Orrery, 1709–1711," ed. H. T. Dickinson, *Camden Miscellany* 26 (1975): 146. For the standard modern study, see P. G. M. Dickson, *The Financial Revolution in England: A Study in the Development of Public Credit, 1688–1756* (1967). The *Medley* printed a letter in No. 32 (7 May 1711) which (ironically) traces all current evils back to the Revolution. This parody of a tory complaint is attributed by Oldmixon, *The Life and Posthumous Works of Arthur Maynwaring* (1715), 194, to Anthony Henley, a whig M.P. with whom Swift had been on friendly terms in 1708. (See *The Correspondence of Jonathan Swift*, ed. Harold Williams, 5 vols. [Oxford: Clarendon Press, 1963–72], 1:101–2. Further references to this edition will appear in parentheses in the text, abbreviated *Corr.*; By December 1710 the views parodied were Swift's, so it is not surprising to find him seeking to avoid Henley's company. See Jonathan Swift, *Journal to Stella*, ed. Harold Williams, 2 vols. (Oxford: Basil Blackwell, 1948), 1:115.

2. *The Prose Works of Jonathan Swift*, ed. Herbert Davis, 14 vols. (Oxford: Basil Blackwell, 1939–68), 9:224. Further references to this edition will appear in parentheses in the text as *PW*, followed by volume and page number.

3. Joseph Addison, *The Freeholder*, ed. James Lenehy (Oxford: Oxford University Press, 1979), 131. Bevil Higgons (?) attributes "ten Years of War and dismal Weather" to William's baneful influence in "The Mourners" (1702); see *Poems on Affairs of State*, ed. Frank H. Ellis (New Haven: Yale University Press, 1970–75), 6:362.

4. Among those who have mistaken Swift's politics for a kind of Lockean liberalism are some distinguished scholars: Louis A. Landa, "Introduction to the Sermons," (*PW* 9:224); Ricardo Quintana, *Two Augustans: John Locke, Jonathan Swift* (Madison, 1978), 76. Herbert Davis puts the common view when he says that "Swift never wavered in accepting the Revolution settlement of 1688" (*PW* 2:xvii).

5. For an account of a typical "whig" view of the world see (apart from such primary sources as the *Spectator*) Chapter 3 of Macaulay's *History of England*; and Peter Earle, *The World of Defoe* (1976). In *The Curse of Party: Swift's Relations with Addison and Steele* (Lincoln, Nebr., 1961), Bertrand A. Goldgar discusses some of the reasons for Swift's hostility to the whig world-picture.

6. For Charles I's interest in his "image," and the role of the theatrical at his court, see Peter W. Thomas, "Charles I of England: the tragedy of absolutism," *The Courts of Europe*, ed. A. G. Dickens (1977), 191–211. The character of the post-1688 monarchy is best studied through biographies: Baxter, *William III*; Edward Gregg, *Queen Anne* (1980); and Ragnhild Hatton, *George I: Elector and King* (1978).

7. Hatton, *George I*, 119–28, palliates the extent to which George favoured the whigs on his accession.

8. See F. P. Lock, *Swift's Tory Politics* (Newark: University of Delaware Press, 1983), 170.

9. As late as the 1740s the friction between the theory that ministers were royal servants and the practical importance of their securing parliamentary support could lead to serious political instability; John B. Owen, *The Rise of the Pelhams* (1957).

10. Swift reported to Stella his efforts on behalf of Steele and Philips (*JS* 1:128–29) and of Congreve (*JS* 1:295). In the "Letter to Mr Pope" he claims that he tried to help Addison, Congreve, Rowe, and Steele; this is where he records the ministers teasing him that "I never came to them without a Whig in my sleeve" (*PW* 9:28–30; quotation on 29).

11. There was a bipartisan dislike of the stock-jobber and financial manipulator, and praise from both sides for the genuine merchant; see John Loftis, *Comedy and Society from Congreve to Fielding* (Stanford, 1959), especially 77–100. Hostility to the "moneyed men" was, nevertheless, a distinctively tory theme; see Isaac Kramnick, *Bolingbroke and his Circle* (Cambridge, Mass., 1968), especially 59–60.

12. *The True Picture of a Modern Whig* (1701), especially 32, 34, 51; *Tom Double Returned out of the Country* (1702), especially 32–43. The same characters reappear in *Sir Thomas Double at Court* (1710) and repeat many of Davenant's earlier points. The account of Davenant's ideas in J. G. A. Pocock, *The Machiavellian Moment* (Princeton, 1975), 436–46, suffers (in my view) from purposely disregarding the immediate political context in which Davenant lived and wrote, for which see D. Waddell, "Charles Davenant (1656–1714): a biographical sketch," *Economic History Review* 11 (1958): 279–88.

13. For the problems of credit and finance faced by Harley on taking office, see B. W. Hill, "The change of government and the loss of the city, 1710–11," *Economic History Review* 24 (1971): 395–413.

14. For the iconography of credit, see Paula R. Backscheider, "Defoe's Lady Credit," *Huntington Library Quarterly* 44 (1981): 89–100.

15. See Lock, *Swift's Tory Politics* 177.

16. The important texts are "A Letter from a Person of Quality, to his Friend in the Country"; "The Earl of Shaftesbury's Speech in the House of Lords" on 20 October 1675; and "Two Seasonable Discourses concerning the Present Parliament"; all printed in *State Tracts: Being a Collection of Several Treatises Relating to the Government* (1689), 41–71. Their interpretation is discussed in J. G. A. Pocock, "Machiavelli, Harrington, and English political ideologies in the eighteenth century," in *Politics, Language, and Time* (1972), 104–47.

17. This is a prominent theme in the "Letter from a Person of Quality," and recurs in "The Earl of Shaftesbury's Speech."

Index

◆